Attribute-based Encryption (ABE)

Attribute-based Encryption (ABE)

Foundations and Applications within Blockchain and Cloud Environments

Qi Xia
University of Electronic Science and Technology of China, China

Jianbin Gao
University of Electronic Science and Technology of China, China

Isaac Amankona Obiri
University of Electronic Science and Technology of China, China

Kwame Omono Asamoah
University of Electronic Science and Technology of China, China

Daniel Adu Worae
University of Electronic Science and Technology of China, China

IEEE PRESS
WILEY

Published by John Wiley & Sons, Inc., Hoboken, New Jersey.
Published simultaneously in Canada.

For general information on our other products and services or for technical support, please contact our Customer Care Department within the United States at (800) 762-2974, outside the United States at (317) 572-3993 or fax (317) 572-4002.

Wiley also publishes its books in a variety of electronic formats. Some content that appears in print may not be available in electronic formats. For more information about Wiley products, visit our web site at www.wiley.com.

Library of Congress Cataloging-in-Publication Data

Names: Gao, Jianbin, author.
Title: Attribute-based encryption (ABE) : foundations and applications within blockchain and cloud environments / Jianbin Gao [and four others].
Description: Hoboken, New Jersey : Wiley-IEEE Press, [2024] | Includes index.
Identifiers: LCCN 2023036768 (print) | LCCN 2023036769 (ebook) | ISBN 9781119989356 (cloth) | ISBN 9781119989363 (adobe pdf) | ISBN 9781119989370 (epub)
Subjects: LCSH: Public key cryptography. | Blockchains (Databases)
Classification: LCC TK5102.94 .G365 2024 (print) | LCC TK5102.94 (ebook) | DDC 005.8/24–dc23/eng/20230824
LC record available at https://lccn.loc.gov/2023036768
LC ebook record available at https://lccn.loc.gov/2023036769

Cover design: Wiley
Cover image: © Blackboard/Shutterstock

Set in 9.5/12.5pt STIXTwoText by Straive, Chennai, India
Printed and bound by CPI Group (UK) Ltd, Croydon, CR0 4YY

C9781119989356_260923

Contents

About the Authors

Qi Xia

Orcid id: 0000-0003-2245-2588

Qi Xia received the BSc, MSc, and PhD degrees in computer science from the University Electronic Science and Technology of China (UESTC), Chengdu, China, in 2002, 2006, and 2010, respectively. She is a Professor with the UESTC. She is currently the Deputy Director of the Cyberspace Security Research Centre, the Executive Director of the Blockchain Research Institute, the Executive Director of the Big Data Sharing and Security Engineering Laboratory of Sichuan province, and a Chief Scientist with YoueData Company Limited. She serves as the Principal Investigator of the National Key Research and Development Program of China in Cyber Security and has overseen the completion of more than 30 high-profile projects. She was a Visiting Scholar with the University of Pennsylvania (UPenn), Philadelphia, PA, USA, from 2013 to 2014. She has authored or coauthored more than 40 academic papers. Her research interests include network security technology and its application, big data security, and blockchain technology and its application. Dr. Xia has won the second place at the National Scientific and Technological Progress Awards in 2012. She is a member of the CCF blockchain committee.

Jianbin Gao

Orcid id: 0000-0001-7014-6417

Jianbin Gao received the PhD degree in computer science from the University Electronic Science and Technology of China (UESTC), Chengdu, China, in 2012. He was a Visiting Scholar with the University of Pennsylvania, Philadelphia, PA, USA, from 2009 to 2011. He is currently an Associate Professor with UESTC.

Isaac Amankona Obiri

Orcid id: 0000-0002-1642-0291

Isaac Amankona Obiri received his Master's and PhD in Computer Science and Technology from the University Electronic Science and Technology of China (UESTC), Chengdu, China, in 2022.

Kwame Omono Asamoah

Orcid id: 0000-0001-7361-1986

Kwame Omono Asamoah received a B.Sc. degree in computer science from the Kwame Nkrumah University of Science and Technology, Ghana, in 2014. He continued his academic journey by obtaining his master's degree in computer science and technology from the University of Electronic Science and Technology of China in 2018. Subsequently, he pursued his doctoral degree in computer science and technology from the University of Electronic Science and Technology of China, successfully completing it in 2022. He is currently a postdoctoral fellow at Zhejiang Normal University, where he actively engages in cutting-edge research. His current research interests encompass a wide range of topics, including blockchain technology, big data security, and educational technology.

Daniel Adu Worae

Orcid id: 0000-0002-6774-2725

Daniel Adu Worae received his BSc degree in Computer Engineering from the Kwame Nkrumah University of Science and Technology, Kumasi, Ghana, in 2020. He is currently pursuing his Master's degree in Computer Science and Technology at the University of Electronic Science and Technology of China (UESTC). His research interests include blockchain technology and its application, network and information security, cryptography, and computer networks.

Preface

In the last few decades, information and communication technology (ICT) devices and services have become central to our lives, fundamentally changing areas such as health, communication, travel, business, and recreation. Traditional ICT systems share and store sensitive data in untrusted networks. Thus, these sensitive data must be encrypted before being uploaded to a cloud server and a fine-grained access control must be supported when sharing sensitive data.

Since the emphasis is on multi-user data sharing, and the data encryptor does not know the identities of the data users in advance, symmetric encryption, asymmetric encryption, and identity-based encryption are impractical. The attribute-based encryption (ABE) schemes are excellent for multi-user data-sharing scenarios in which the identity of the data users is unknown in advance. ABE employs an access structure based on attributes in either the ciphertext or the secret key, and it is able to provide fine-grained access control with the guarantee that a user can only decrypt a message if they satisfy the constraints imposed by the access structure.

While blockchain technology has just recently become associated with new means of managing financial assets, its possibilities are practically limitless. Blockchain is a particularly promising and revolutionary technology because it reduces risk, eliminates fraud, and provides scalable transparency for a wide range of applications. Therefore, ABE schemes based on blockchain can achieve immense number of advantages including transparency, accountability, and data immutability.

This book provides guidelines for the current research and future trends in various areas associated with ABE and its integration with blockchain applications in cloud environments so that researchers get ready reference. It is expected that researchers and readers will get adequate information on these subjects, and the book will be helpful in their research endeavors. We'll look at the basic concepts of ABE, from the background knowledge, to specific constructions, theoretic proofs, and applications. Blockchain technology; practical aspects of what makes a blockchain, the inherent vulnerabilities of a decentralized network in the real world, the secret key for encryption and decryption and how to apply blockchain with real-time technologies.

November 2022

Qi Xia, China
Jianbin Gao, China
Isaac Amankona Obiri, Ghana
Daniel Adu Worae, Ghana

Acknowledgments

First, we would like to thank all the contributing authors. Without their work, this book would not have been possible. Namely, our thanks to Juan Wang, Yunbo Ding, Dr. Edson Tavares, and Dr. Christian Cobblah. We also thank them for cross-reading one another's chapters and providing fruitful feedback that has helped improve each chapter, and thus the book as a whole.

This work was supported by the Basic Strengthening Program (2021-JCJQ-JJ-0463), the scientific and technological innovation talents of Sichuan Province (2023JDRC0001), the Fundamental Research Funds for the Central Universities, the National Natural Science Foundation of China (No. U22B2029), and Shenzhen Research Program (No. JSGG20210802153537009).

Part I

Attribute-Based Encryption (ABE)

1

Foundation of Attribute-Based Encryption

1.1 Introduction

What is encryption? Encryption is a key concept in cryptography. To explain the meaning of encryption, let us consider the following scenario without being blown away by the whims of mathematics.

Imagine your friend Bob is organizing a back-alley chess game. Bob does not want anyone to come into his shady gambling den without authorization, so he issues you a pass with the phrase "Knock and wait." When you knock on the right sleazy door, the bouncer asks for the pass in a genre-savvy baritone. You can get in if you say the right phrase. Otherwise, your entry will be denied, and you will stay outside in the metaphorical rain.

To stretch the analogy, Bob can alter the pass each time he hosts a chess game. Knowing the passphrase for the day, you can share it with one of your acquaintances or some of your friends in the criminal investigation bureau. In cryptography, the pass is referred to as a secret key. When plaintext is combined with a secret key, cryptography offers a black box that converts plaintext to ciphertext. The ciphertext is unreadable junk to those without the right secret key. On the other hand, those with a valid secret key can recover the plaintext from a given ciphertext back. The process involved in transforming plaintext into ciphertext is referred to as encryption. Succinctly put, encryption is the cryptographic mechanism of converting information into a secret code that conceals the true meaning of the transformed information (ciphertext). When an unauthorized party intercepts ciphertext, the intruder must determine which algorithm and keys were used to encrypt the message. The computation complexity required in decoding a ciphertext without a valid secret key is what makes encryption a crucial security tool.

Encryption has been a longstanding technique to secure sensitive data. Historically, it was used by governments and militaries. Encryption is used in modern times to secure data stored on computers and storage devices and data in transit across networks. Prior to the advent of public key cryptography, it was widely assumed that for two users to transmit data securely, they would need to establish a mutually held secret key. While this may be acceptable for certain small or close-knit groups, it is infeasible for larger networks, such as the Internet of today, which has billions of users. Diffie and Hellman [1] proposed a novel concept in public key cryptography over thirty years ago, where two parties can securely communicate without sharing a prior mutual secret, dramatically upsetting common knowledge held at the time. Public key encryption is a crucial tool today. It is widely used in developing tools ranging from secure web communication (e.g. secure shell [SSH],

Attribute-based Encryption (ABE): Foundations and Applications within Blockchain and Cloud Environments, First Edition.
Qi Xia, Jianbin Gao, Isaac Amankona Obiri, Kwame Omono Asamoah, and Daniel Adu Worae.
© 2024 The Institute of Electrical and Electronics Engineers, Inc. Published 2024 by John Wiley & Sons, Inc.

secure sockets layer [SSL]) to disk encryption and a secure software patch distribution. Before the introduction of functional encryption, there were widely held views that:

1. Encryption is a method of sending a message or data to a single entity with a secret key.
2. Access to encrypted data is all or nothing – one can either decrypt and read the entire plaintext or learn nothing about the plaintext other than its length.

These views determined the method used for computation of ciphertext and secret key before they were modified by functional encryption. Functional encryption enables a data encryptor to encrypt data with a boolean function, such that only a decryptor with the correct private key can recover the plaintext if the boolean function returns true. Before delving into the details of functional encryption and how it is a superior encryption technique, we will explore the earlier encryption techniques.

1.1.1 Symmetric Encryption

Howbeit, data can be encrypted with symmetric key encryption mechanisms. The symmetric key encryption algorithm uses only one secret key, referred to as a session key, to encipher and decipher information [2]. As seen in Figure 1.1, one secret key is required to cipher and decipher information in symmetric encryption. A key can be a number, a word, or a random sequence of letters. The key is used to scramble the plaintext of a message into unreadable content (ciphertext) and recover the content. Therefore, the session key must be shared in advance between the sender and recipient prior to its usage in the encryption method. Symmetric encryption includes advanced encryption standard (AES), RC4, data encryption standard (DES), RC5, and RC6. Encryption schemes like AES-128, 192, and 256 are the most extensively used symmetric algorithms.

The inherent problem with the symmetric encryption is that a session key must be exchanged between the data owner and data users in advance before a symmetric key encryption algorithm can be used [3]. However, it is impossible to know every potential data user in advance to share data with them in multi-user data sharing systems. Even if the data owner does, it has to encrypt the data repeatedly with each session key shared with the multiple data users in the system. There are as many as $((n-1)n/2)$ key pairs to be managed in an extensive network. Consequently, key management will undoubtedly involve high storage overhead.

1.1.2 Asymmetric Key Encryption

Symmetric encryption has existed for a very long time, whereas asymmetric encryption is very recent. For data encryption and decryption, asymmetric encryption requires two keys, namely

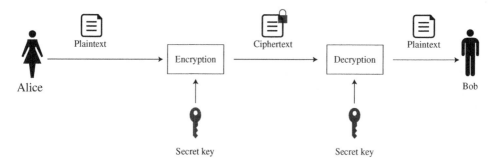

Figure 1.1 Symmetric encryption.

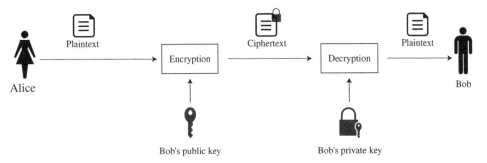

Figure 1.2 Asymmetric encryption.

public and private keys. The public keys are used for data encryption, whereas the private keys are required for data decryption. Asymmetric encryption enables parties to preserve sensitive information in an encrypted format on a public network, such as the Internet, without exchanging a session key in advance. Asymmetric encryption ensures that only the authorized recipient with the proper private key can decipher the encrypted messages. The use of two related keys in asymmetric encryption increases security, as anyone with the secret key can decipher the message. Anyone can send a message to any user using their public key, which is accessible to the public.

As illustrated in Figure 1.2, the public key and private key are utilized to encrypt and decrypt a message, respectively. There is no need to protect the public keys because they are accessible to the whole public. However, the private key must be kept secret such that only the end user knows it; otherwise, any entity with knowledge of the private key can decrypt any communication encrypted with the corresponding public key. Using an asymmetric key for communication is substantially more secure than a symmetric key. Well-known asymmetric key encryption methods include ElGamal and Rivest–Shamir–Adleman (RSA).

To prevent man-in-the-middle attacks, asymmetric encryption relies on the public key infrastructure to associate a user's public key with a certificate. This certificate is "signed" by the Certificate Authority (CA), the digital equivalent of a notary. It is evident that the CA plays a significant role in the public key infrastructure (PKI) model since this approach is founded on the premise that the CA is true, trustworthy, and legitimate. Therefore, a hacker who takes control of a CA can use it to generate fake certificates and impersonate any public key.

Over the years, there have been repeated breaches of CA firms, including DigiNotar, GlobalSign, Comodo, and Digicert Malaysia. These attacks were a direct result of the commoditization of certificates, in which smaller, less qualified businesses have gained a larger proportion of the market for certificate authorities.

Asymmetric key encryption schemes also have some drawbacks similar to symmetric key encryption schemes. For example, the data owner must obtain each data user's public key, encrypt the data multiple times, and store multiple copies of the data in the cloud.

1.1.3 Identity-Based Encryption

Imagine a corporate email system in which the employees send encrypted communications. Alice discovers Bob's public key, writes a message, encrypts it in an email, and sends the email to Bob. However, Bob wrote his private key in his notebook, which he left at an airport. Or maybe Bob's private key was stored on his phone, and one of his children dropped it in the drain. Now that Bob has

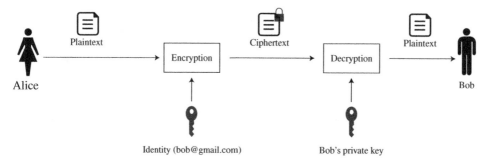

Figure 1.3 Identity-based encryption.

a new phone, he tries to read all of Alice's emails and discovers that he cannot. Without a private key, there are no emails that can be read. However, as is synonymous with key and door systems, when the lone key to a lock is lost, the entire lock must be replaced. Digital cryptosystems are no different; public and private keys are generated as a pair, and it is impossible to generate one from the other, just as it is impossible to construct a key from a lock. Bob must therefore generate a new pair of public and private keys, upload the new public key to the corporate directory, and inform everyone that the previous public key is no longer valid. As shown in Figure 1.3, if Alice does not detect this change, she will continue to send Bob encrypted emails using his previous public key, and Bob will continue to be unable to read them. It turns out that this is a widespread issue in cryptography systems – individuals are lousy at managing keys. In 1984, a cryptographer named Adi Shamir [4] came up with a brilliant concept: what if the firm itself managed the keys? He believed that the entire concept of public keys was excessively onerous and wished that individuals would use something more memorable: their identities (like a name or email). To send an email to Bob, simply use bob@email.com as the recipient's public key. This concept is known as Identity-Based Encryption. In 2001, Dan Boneh and Matt Franklin [5] developed a system that is currently regarded as the most viable implementation of identity-based encryption to date. Identity-based encryption permits anyone within an organization to encrypt text using the identity of another user.

Identity-based encryption (IBE) altered the conventional notion of public-key cryptography by enabling the public-key to be any string, such as the recipient's email address. This means that a sender with access to the system's public parameters can encrypt a message using, for instance, the text-value of the recipient's name or email address as the key. The Private Key Generator provides the decryption key to the recipient (PKG). In order to function, the PKG first publishes a master public key and stores the associated master private key (referred to as the master key). Given the master public key, any party can derive the identity's public key by combining the master public key with the identity value. The person authorized to use the identity ID contacts the PKG to receive their corresponding private key, which is created using the master private key.

Consequently, parties can encrypt messages (or check signatures) without exchanging keys beforehand. This is especially beneficial in situations when pre-distribution of authenticated keys is impractical or impossible owing to technological limitations. However, IBE system has the same drawbacks as symmetric and asymmetric key encryption schemes, which makes it impractical for application in scenarios involving numerous users, particularly when the data owner is aware of the identities of all potential data users in advance. Also, if a Private Key Generator (PKG) is compromised, all communications protected for the lifespan of the public–private key pair utilized by that server are compromised as well. This makes the PKG an extremely desirable target for attackers. To reduce the risk posed by a hacked server, the master private–public key pair could be replaced with a new key pair that is independent. Nonetheless, this creates a key-management issue in which all users must possess the most recent public key for the server.

1.2 Functional Encryption

We will now describe a scenario to vividly highlight the challenges associated with data sharing and the need for functional data encryption. We consider data sharing among multiple entities. The entities in the data scenarios comprise the following:

1. **Data owner**: This entity is the custodian of data that he/she would like to share with other people. He/she might have generated the data him or herself or has acquired the data from data producers such as IoT devices. The data owner can be a single entity, such as a patient, who wants to share their PHRs with a medical doctor for disease diagnosis and treatment, or a large organization, such as a hospital, which intends to share a medical record with a team of doctors in order to find an antidote to a disease outbreak. The data this entity is sharing is sensitive; it is usually encrypted offline before the data is outsourced to the cloud server.
2. **Data users**: The data users' domain is made up of all the authorized recipients of the data as defined by the data owner. The users not only comprise people but devices as well. They access the outsourced data through the cryptographic service provider (CSP).
3. **Cloud service provider**: This entity specializes in data sharing and storage. It stores the owner's encrypted data, which is received through a secure communication connection. It is a semi-trusted entity since it is considered that it will offer its services successfully, but it may attempt to read data.

Here, we consider a hypothetical data sharing between a patient and medical doctors. The patient is the data owner, while the medical doctors are the data users. Let's suppose a patient known as Bob is suffering from a rare disease known as "Achalasia," and he wants to share his Personal Health Records (PHRs) with a specialized doctor in rare disease treatment who can provide medical service to him. In this scenario, Bob does not know beforehand who is actually available to provide the medical care he needs. Since PHRs are sensitive, Bob wants only medical doctors with certain credentials to access his data. So, Bob may encrypt the data over attributes such as ("medical doctor," "rare disease," and "City A"). Attribute-based encryption (ABE) allows only doctors in City A who specialize in rare diseases and are in close proximity to Bob's location to access his PHRs. The scenario of multiple users sharing data is depicted in Figure 1.4.

Traditionally, this kind of expressive access control has been enforced by a trusted server [6]. The server is entrusted with acting as a reference monitor, ensuring that a user has the proper

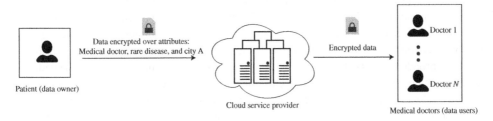

Figure 1.4 Multiple users data sharing scenario.

certification before granting access to records or files. On the other hand, cloud servers are progressively storing data in a distributed manner over multiple cloud partners. Data replication across multiple locations has reliability and performance benefits. However, using multiple cloud data storage services has a high probability of one of the servers being compromised to expose the outsourced data. Hence, we would require the storage of sensitive data in encrypted form, so that the data remains private even if one of the hosting servers is compromised.

The idea of users having access to different segments of a ciphertext depending on the scope of access privileges was not considered in the domain of public key cryptography. However, with the emergence of "cloud" applications due to the improvement of computer networks and computing power, the concepts of public key encryption became wholly insufficient. For example, in many cases, a decryption policy must be specified in the ciphertext, and only those who meet the policy can decrypt. Depending on the decryptor's authority, we might only wish to grant access to a function of the plaintext. Consider a cloud service that stores encrypted photographs as a concrete example. An attacker might try to break into the cloud server to gain access to photographs with a specific face to extort money. As a result, the cloud requires a password-protected secret key that decrypts the target face's photographs but does not divulge any information about other images. More generally, the secret key may only expose a function of the plaintext image, such as a blurred image with the exception of the target face. Such tasks are incompatible with traditional public-key cryptography.

Functional encryption provides a new perspective of public key cryptosystems that offer an excellent balance of flexibility, efficiency, and security. A functional encryption scheme associates ciphertexts with descriptive values x, secret keys with descriptive values y, and a function $f(x, y)$, that defines what a user with a key for value y should learn from a ciphertext with value x. Attribute-based encryption (ABE), first presented by Sahai and Waters in [7], is a well-known form of functional encryption in which the ciphertext and secret key are determined by an access structure specified over attributes and subsets of attributes. A key can decrypt ciphertexts if the associated set of attributes meets the related access policy. ABE schemes are classified into two types: Ciphertext-Policy ABE (CP-ABE), in which access policies are embedded in ciphertexts and keys are associated with sets of attributes, and Key-Policy ABE (KP-ABE), which is the inverse of CP-ABE in which keys are associated with access policies and ciphertexts are associated with sets of attributes.

This section will explain techniques for developing provably secure functional encryption systems. We will concentrate on ABE schemes as an application. We will provide background information on the history of functional encryption and prior work in this field before presenting the summary.

1.2.1 Applications of Attribute-Based Encryption

ABE is beneficial in a range of applications. It can be used to enable fine-grained access control in public cloud computing while sharing encrypted data. Also, it can be used in the encryption of log data. Instead of encrypting each chunk of a log with all of the recipients' keys, the log can be encrypted selectively with attributes that match the recipients' attributes. The ABE primitive can be used for broadcast encryption to reduce the high cost of key management overhead. In vector-driven search engine interfaces, ABE techniques can be utilized. ABE provides a quick and easy technique to do a nearest-neighbor search across an encrypted database. Therefore, it can be used for biometric authentication as well. Because biometrics are inherently noisy, authentication should be effective when the supplied biometric is close to the user's credential in the system. The error-tolerance property of the ABE scheme can enable a private key (computed from a biometric measurement) to decrypt a ciphertext encrypted with a slightly different measurement of the same biometric.

1.2.2 Problems with Attribute-Based Encryption

The following are the key challenges impeding the deployment of the ABE scheme in systems.

- **Central trust**: Attribute-based encryption necessitates reliance on a centralized authority – the Private Key Generator (similar to Identity-Based Encryption). Hence, it is suitable for the business environments. There have been some scholarly studies in the literature on a more distributed version termed "Decentralized Attribute-based Encryption" (DABE); however, these schemes do not completely decentralize ABE. Instead, they expand the number of potential trust roots comparable to the CA architecture used on the web. This approach even makes the ABE scheme less secure.
- **Speed**: For attribute-based encryption, the creation of an access structure is required. The expressiveness of the access structure leads to expensive computation during decryption, which is the worst place to be slow because decryption is usually the most common process we perform against encryption. ABE scheme is roughly 20 times slower than classical symmetric encryption. This is related to ABE's expensive mathematical construct, such as bilinear pairing, exponentiation, and multiplication operations. Furthermore, the ABE scheme gets more computationally expensive as the number of attributes on a given access structure increases.
- **Malicious users revocation**: ABE systems suffer from the non-existence of malicious users revocation mechanisms. Revocation is more challenging in attribute-based systems, given that each attribute possibly belongs to multiple different users. Revoking attributes cannot revoke a specific identified malicious user but automatically revokes all the users in the system who shared the revoked attributes. Thus, revocation on attributes or attribute sets cannot accurately exclude malicious users.

1.2.3 A Brief History of Security Proof of Functional Encryption

Shamir's Identity-Based Encryption (IBE) [4] is credited with the invention of functional encryption. An identity-based encryption method allows any string to serve as a "public key," rather than requiring public keys to be created in tandem with secret keys. For instance, a user can send an encrypted message to a recipient specified by an email address without requiring the recipient to have an established public key. Secret keys are associated with strings (also known as "identities") must be obtained from a central authority who holds the master secret key. Suppose we want to impose a hierarchical structure on keys. In that case, we can generalize identity-based encryption to hierarchical identity-based encryption (HIBE), in which individuals can delegate secret keys to their subordinates.

There are inherent issues in providing security proof for functionality like IBE, which requires generating several secret keys from a single master secret key for different users. It is not enough to prevent one user from maliciously exploiting his own secret key to decrypt a ciphertext meant for another user; a robust security concept must also address collusion attacks, in which a group of users conspire to decipher a ciphertext encrypted to an identity outside of the group. To simulate such attacks, we imagine an adversary that is capable of acquiring a large number of secret keys and selecting the associated identities adaptively. At some stage, the adversary must select one identity to attack (for which no secret key has been collected), and it may then obtain keys for any additional identities. This necessitates security reduction to balance two competing goals: the simulator must be powerful enough to give the attacker as many keys as it adaptively seeks, but it must also be devoid of essential knowledge gained from the attacker's success.

The first security proofs for IBE schemes relied on the random oracle model, a heuristic that treats a fixed function as if it were truly random. The first security proofs presented in the standard model (which did not rely on such a heuristic) reached a weaker notion of security known as selective security. The selective security approach requires the attacker to choose the target of the attack before viewing the system's public settings. Because this is an unrealistic constraint, establishing selective security should be viewed as a step toward achieving comprehensive security rather than as an end in itself.

The concept of selective security makes a lot of sense in the context of the partitioning proof technique used by early research in IBE and HIBE. A partitioning proof splits all possible identities into two categories: those for which the simulator can generate secret keys and those that cannot. This gives the simulator a clear method to balance its competing aims, which include ensuring that all of the adversary's key requests are within the set of keys the simulator may make and that the attacked identity is inside the complement. Because the simulator already knows who is being attacked, the selective model makes the security proof much easier. The selective model enables a simulator to create a perfect partition, with the attacked identity being the only one for which the simulator cannot generate the secret key.

Waters [8] and Boneh and Boyen [9] overcame the requirement for selectivity to obtain an IBE security proof in the standard model. The security proof in [10] instructs the simulator to "guess" a partition and abort if the attacker attempts to exceed its bounds. The rich structure of more advanced schemes like HIBE and ABE, on the other hand, appears to doom using selective security proof owing to exponential security loss, as one must estimate a partition that preserves the partial ordering provided by the powers allocated to the individual keys.

Meanwhile, progress on attributed-based encryption systems slowed to a halt at selective security in the standard model. With the Sahai and Waters introduction of attribute-based systems [7], the subsequent ABE schemes in [11–15] only offered security proofs in the selective model.

Waters developed the dual system encryption approach [10] in response to the relative stagnation in proving methodology for functional encryption systems. Under conventional assumptions, his early work produced fully secure and efficient IBE and HIBE systems. Lewko and waters presented a more elegant implementation of dual system encryption in [16], allowing for even more efficiency gains in the context of HIBE. Lewko et al. [17] expanded the dual system encryption methods to obtain the standard model's first fully secure ABE systems. Okamoto and Takashima [18] used the basic and relatively conventional Decisional Linear Assumption (DLIN) to reach comparable results in a follow-up study. We will continue to explore the dual system encryption methodology in subsequent works [16, 19, 20] to provide a clear insight into a stronger security proof.

1.2.4 Dual System of Encryption

These works investigate the rich structure of composite order bilinear groups, which differs from prime order bilinear groups in several ways, most notably the inclusion of orthogonal subgroups of coprime orders. A composite order bilinear group has the structure of a direct product of prime order subgroups up to isomorphism so that each group member can decompose as the product of components from the individual subgroups. However, computing such a decomposition becomes challenging when the group order is hard to factor. Because of their orthogonality, these sub-groups can serve as independent spaces, allowing a system designer to employ them in various ways without compromising their validity. The idea behind security is that these subgroups are virtually inseparable: given a random group element, determining which subgroups contribute non-trivial components should be difficult.

Although composite order bilinear groups offer appealing properties, it would be preferable to derive the same functionality and strong guarantees from other assumptions, particularly the DLIN in prime order bilinear groups. Working with prime order bilinear groups rather than composite order bilinear groups has various advantages. First, we can achieve security using the more common decisional linear assumption. Second, we can build considerably more efficient systems with the same security standards. This is because the difficulties of factoring the group order are often used to provide security in composite order groups. This requires using large group orders, which in turn slows down pairing computations significantly.

Okamoto and Takashima developed the framework of dual pairing vector spaces in prime order bilinear groups [21, 22]. They observed that dual pairing vector spaces could be used to implement the same proof techniques under the standard Decisional Linear Assumption [18, 23]. Working in prime order groups is advantageous since the group orders can be much smaller, so pairing computations can be much faster. In [24], Lewko further developed the connection between the dual pairing vector space framework based on the prior approach in the composite order setting. Their efforts have yielded a practical understanding of how to move dual system encryption proofs between composite and prime order settings. However, the reliance on q-type assumptions (size assumptions that grow with some parameter q) is a disadvantage of the proving technique provided in [24]. Many q-type assumptions are known to become stronger as q increases [25], and such dynamic and complex assumptions are not well understood in general). Obiri et al. [26] have recently improved the methodologies for establishing adaptive security for attribute-based encryption using static assumptions like the decisional linear assumption and the three-party Diffie–Hellman assumption. The advantage of the scheme in [26] is that it allows arbitrary attribute reuse in the access policy without increasing the size of the ciphertext proportion to the number of times an attribute appears in the access policy. However, because the approach depends on the dual vector subspace assumption, it necessitates large public parameters to achieve full security. Also, the authors in [27, 28] suggested another method for creating security proofs for the dual system of ABE schemes based on the matrix Diffie–Hellman assumption. This technique has proven to be beneficial because it is more efficient and more compact than dual vector space schemes.

This book focuses on using dual systems of encryption proof to construct adaptive, secure attribute-based encryption. This book provides readers with a thorough overview of the components that go into creating a dual ABE system of encryption proofs in:

- Composite bilinear groups
- Dual pairing vector space framework (prime order bilinear group)
- Matrix pairing framework (prime order bilinear group)

After reading the book, the readers will learn which bilinear groups (composite order or prime order) to use in designing a new cryptographic scheme.

1.2.5 Summary

In this chapter, we covered the concepts of encryption and functional encryption and a brief history of functional encryption. This chapter's purpose is to provide a historical development of how the current technique for creating adaptive security of ABE schemes based on a dual system of encryption in the standard model came to be. We also investigated why ABE schemes were required because previous encryption methods could not provide fine-grained access control over encrypted data. Finally, we also investigated the need to construct an adaptive (fully) secure ABE scheme in prime order groups instead of composite order groups.

References

1 Diffie, W. and Hellman, M.E. (1977). Special feature exhaustive cryptanalysis of the NBS data encryption standard. *Computer* 10 (6): 74–84.

2 Simmons, G.J. (1979). Symmetric and asymmetric encryption. *ACM Computing Surveys (CSUR)* 11 (4): 305–330.

3 Boonkrong, S. (2021). Public key infrastructure. In: *Authentication and Access Control*, 31–43. Berkeley, CA: Apress.

4 Shamir, A. (1984). Identity-based cryptosystems and signature schemes. In: *Workshop on the Theory and Application of Cryptographic Techniques*, 47–53. Berlin, Heidelberg: Springer-Verlag.

5 Boneh, D. and Franklin, M. (2001). Identity-based encryption from the Weil pairing. In: *Annual International Cryptology Conference*, 213–229. Berlin, Heidelberg: Springer-Verlag.

6 Sulaiman, O.K. and Saripurna, D. (2021). Network security system analysis using access control list (ACL). *IJISTECH (International Journal of Information System & Technology)* 5 (2): 192–197.

7 Sahai, A. and Waters, B. (2005). Fuzzy identity-based encryption. In: *Annual International Conference on the Theory and Applications of Cryptographic Techniques*, 457–473. Berlin, Heidelberg: Springer-Verlag.

8 Waters, B. (2005). Efficient identity-based encryption without random oracles. In: *Annual International Conference on the Theory and Applications of Cryptographic Techniques*, 114–127. Berlin, Heidelberg: Springer-Verlag.

9 Boneh, D. and Boyen, X. (2004). Secure identity based encryption without random oracles. In: *Annual International Cryptology Conference*, 443–459. Berlin, Heidelberg: Springer-Verlag.

10 Waters, B. (2009). Dual system encryption: realizing fully secure IBE and HIBE under simple assumptions. In: *Annual International Cryptology Conference*, 619–636. Berlin, Heidelberg: Springer-Verlag.

11 Cheung, L. and Newport, C. (2007). Provably secure ciphertext policy ABE. *Proceedings of the 14th ACM Conference on Computer and Communications Security*, 456–465.

12 Goyal, V., Pandey, O., Sahai, A., and Waters, B. (2006). Attribute-based encryption for fine-grained access control of encrypted data. *Proceedings of the 13th ACM Conference on Computer and Communications Security*, 89–98.

13 Goyal, V., Jain, A., Pandey, O., and Sahai, A. (2008). Bounded ciphertext policy attribute based encryption. In: *International Colloquium on Automata, Languages, and Programming*, 579–591. Berlin, Heidelberg: Springer-Verlag.

14 Ostrovsky, R., Sahai, A., and Waters, B. (2007). Attribute-based encryption with non-monotonic access structures. *Proceedings of the 14th ACM Conference on Computer and Communications Security*, 195–203.

15 Waters, B. (2011). Ciphertext-policy attribute-based encryption: an expressive, efficient, and provably secure realization. In: *International Workshop on Public Key Cryptography*, 53–70. Berlin, Heidelberg: Springer-Verlag.

16 Lewko, A. and Waters, B. (2010). New techniques for dual system encryption and fully secure HIBE with short ciphertexts. In: *Theory of Cryptography Conference*, 455–479. Berlin, Heidelberg: Springer-Verlag.

17 Lewko, A., Okamoto, T., Sahai, A. et al. (2010). Fully secure functional encryption: attribute-based encryption and (hierarchical) inner product encryption. In: *Annual International Conference on the Theory and Applications of Cryptographic Techniques*, 62–91. Berlin, Heidelberg: Springer-Verlag.

18 Okamoto, T. and Takashima, K. (2010). Fully secure functional encryption with general relations from the decisional linear assumption. In: *Annual Cryptology Conference*, 191–208. Berlin, Heidelberg: Springer-Verlag.

19 Lewko, A., Rouselakis, Y., and Waters, B. (2011). Achieving leakage resilience through dual system encryption. In: *Theory of Cryptography Conference*, 70–88. Berlin, Heidelberg: Springer-Verlag.

20 Lewko, A. and Waters, B. (2011). Decentralizing attribute-based encryption. In: *Annual International Conference on the Theory and Applications of Cryptographic Techniques*, 568–588. Berlin, Heidelberg: Springer-Verlag.

21 Okamoto, T. and Takashima, K. (2008). Homomorphic encryption and signatures from vector decomposition. In: *International Conference on Pairing-Based Cryptography*, 57–74. Berlin, Heidelberg: Springer-Verlag.

22 Okamoto, T. and Takashima, K. (2009). Hierarchical predicate encryption for inner-products. In: *International Conference on the Theory and Application of Cryptology and Information Security*, 214–231. Berlin, Heidelberg: Springer-Verlag.

23 Okamoto, T. and Takashima, K. (2013). Decentralized attribute-based signatures. In: *International Workshop on Public Key Cryptography*, 125–142. Berlin, Heidelberg: Springer-Verlag.

24 Lewko, A. (2012). Tools for simulating features of composite order bilinear groups in the prime order setting. In: *Annual International Conference on the Theory and Applications of Cryptographic Techniques*, 318–335. Berlin, Heidelberg: Springer-Verlag.

25 Cheon, J.H. (2006). Security analysis of the strong Diffie-Hellman problem. In: *Annual International Conference on the Theory and Applications of Cryptographic Techniques*, 1–11. Berlin, Heidelberg: Springer-Verlag.

26 Obiri, I.A., Xia, Q., Xia, H. et al. (2020). A fully secure KP-ABE scheme on prime-order bilinear groups through selective techniques. *Security and Communication Networks*, 2020: Article ID 8869057.

27 Kowalczyk, L. and Wee, H. (2020). Compact adaptively secure ABE for NC^1 NC1 from k-Lin. *Journal of Cryptology* 33 (3): 954–1002.

28 Tomida, J., Kawahara, Y., and Nishimaki, R. (2021). Fast, compact, and expressive attribute-based encryption. *Designs, Codes and Cryptography* 89 (11): 2577–2626.

2

Mathematical Background

2.1 Group Theory

Groups are one of the fundamental concepts in modern algebra. A group is a set together with an operation that combines two elements to form a third element which contains an identity element and inverse and satisfies certain natural properties such as associativity, cancellation, and solvability properties. In the field of cryptography, group theory is the most practical approach to take when constructing encryption systems. When it comes to cryptographic schemes that are based on integers, group theory is absolutely necessary for selecting prime numbers and the corresponding inverses for the purpose of scheme construction. In particular with the construction of Rivest–Shamir–Adleman (RSA) encryption, the theory is necessary for computing inverses in order to generate users' public and private information. This is because RSA encryption thrives on public and private keys.

2.1.1 Law of Composition

Let G represent a set. A map: $G \times G \to G$ is referred to as a law of composition. For all the elements $x, y \in H$ the image of the pair (x, y) under the law of composition will be represented as $x \cdot y$. If a multiplicative notation is used, we also write xy.

Let G be a set and $\cdot$ denotes the law of composition. The law of composition is called associative if $(w \cdot v) \cdot u = w \cdot (v \cdot u)$ holds for all $u, v, w \in G$. It is called commutative if $w \cdot v = v \cdot w$ holds for all $v, w \in G$.

2.1.2 Groups

Definition 2.1 Let G represents any non-empty set and: $G \times G \to G$ be a law of composition. We say that G forms a **group** in terms of the operation, if all the following conditions are satisfied:

1. **Closure**: For elements $a, b \in G, a \cdot a \in G$.
2. **Existence of identity**: There exists an element $e \in G$ such that for all $a \in G, a \cdot e = e \cdot a = a$.
3. **Associativity**: For all elements $a, b, c \in G$, we have $(a \cdot b) \cdot c = a \cdot (b \cdot c)$.
4. **Existence of inverse**: For an element $a \in G$, there exist $a \in G$ such that $a \cdot b = b \cdot a = e$.
5. **Cancellation**: For all elements $a, b, c \in G$, if $a \cdot b = a \cdot c$ or if $b \cdot a = c \cdot a$, then $b = c$.
6. **Solvability**: For all elements $a, b \in G$, there exists an element $c \in G$ with $a \cdot c = b$, and an element $d \in G$ with $d \cdot a = b$.

Attribute-based Encryption (ABE): Foundations and Applications within Blockchain and Cloud Environments, First Edition. Qi Xia, Jianbin Gao, Isaac Amankona Obiri, Kwame Omono Asamoah, and Daniel Adu Worae. © 2024 The Institute of Electrical and Electronics Engineers, Inc. Published 2024 by John Wiley & Sons, Inc.

Example 2.1

1. $(\mathbb{Z}, +)$ is a group with identity element 0.
2. $(\mathbb{Z}\setminus\{0\}, \cdot)$ is not a group. Only 1 and -1 are invertible.

Definition 2.2   We say a group G is an **Abelian group** if $ab = ba \; \forall \; a, b \in G$; else, the group G is **non-Abelian group**, i.e. $\exists \; a, b \in G$ such that $ab \neq ba$.

Definition 2.3   The **order of group** $g \in G$, represented by $|g|$, is the smallest positive integer (if it exists) n such that $g^n = \underbrace{g \cdot g \cdots g}_{n \text{ times}} = e$ (identity element of G). If such an integer does not exist, the element g is said to have infinite order. To compute the order of an element g in a group G, simply find the sequence $g, g^2, g^3 \ldots$, until the first time the identity e is obtain. If identity e is never obtained, the order of g becomes infinite.

Example 2.2

1. In $(\mathbb{Z}, +)$ the order of 0 is 1 and the order of any non-zero element is ∞. For any non-zero element 'a' (where 'a' is an integer that is not equal to 0), the order is infinite (∞). This is because, in the additive group of integers, there is no positive integer 'n' such that $n + a = 0$, except when 'a' is 0. In other words, no matter how many times you add a non-zero integer 'a' to itself, you will never reach the identity element 0.
2. For $G = (\mathbb{Z}\setminus 6\mathbb{Z}, +)$ and $H = (\mathbb{Z}\setminus 6\mathbb{Z}, \cdot)$ the orders are as follows:

As shown in Table 2.1, the smallest positive integer k with $g^k = 1$ is the order of an element $g \in G$, denoted by $ord_G(g)$. If there is no such k, $ord_G(g)$ is set to ∞. Torsion elements are group elements with a finite order. The cardinality of a group is defined by its order, $ord_{(G)}$. If a group has prime order, the group is cyclic.

2.1.3 Subgroups

Let a group G have the operation $\cdot$ with an identity element e, where the inverse of an element $g \in G$ is denoted g^{-1}. A subgroup H of G is a nonempty subset of G with two properties:

1. if g, h are in H, then $g \cdot h$ is in H; and
2. if g is in H, so is g^{-1}.

Table 2.1 Order of groups.

g	$ord_G(g)$	$ord_G(g)$
0	1	–
1	6	1
2	3	–
3	2	–
4	3	–
5	6	2

Definition 2.4 A subset H of a group G is considered to be a **subgroup** of G if H itself forms a group under the operation of G. If H is a subgroup of G, then it is represented by $H \leq G$. Further to show that H is a proper subgroup of G (proper in the sense of containment), we use $H < G$. The subset e of G is trivially a subgroup of G.

$$H \leq G \Leftrightarrow \text{for any } a, b \in H, ab^{-1} \in H$$

In other words, H is a subset of G, which is closed under multiplication and inverse.

2.1.4 Homomorphisms

Homomorphisms are maps that preserve the structure of two algebraic structures. They allow for the investigation of the interaction between various structures. A homomorphism for a group is defined as follows:

Definition 2.5 A homomorphism between two groups $(G, \cdot), (G', *)$ is a map $f : G \to G'$ with $f(g) \cdot f(h) = f(g * h)$, where $g, h \in G$. If f is bijective, we call f an isomorphism.

A group homomorphism is a map that retains the operation between two groups. This implies that the group homomorphism maps the first group's identity element to the second group's identity element and the inverse of a first-group element to the inverse of its image.

The neutral element, $f(1_G) = 1_{G'}$, is preserved by group homomorphisms. Monomorphism refers to an injective group homomorphism. Epimorphism is when a group homomorphism is subjective. A bijective group homomorphism is an isomorphism. A group homomorphism that maps a group to itself is called endomorphism. Automorphism is an isomorphism that is also an endomorphism. If groups have an isomorphism between two groups, they are called isomorphic group and we write $G \cong G'$.

2.1.5 Cyclic Group

A cyclic group is a collection of elements in which each member is a power of a fixed element. As a result, a cyclic group G can be generated by a fixed element g, with each member in G having the form g^i for some integer i.

Definition 2.6 A group $(G, \cdot)$ is a **cyclic** if

$$G = \langle g \rangle = \{g^i : i \in \mathbb{Z}\} \text{ for some } g \in G.$$

The order of g is the smallest positive integer n such that $g^n = 1$. If there exists no positive integer n such that $g^n = 1$, then g has infinite order. In the case of an abelian group with $+$ operation, 0 is the identity element, the order of the positive integer n has $ng = 0$. For an element $g \in G$, the set of elements generated by g is denoted by $\langle g \rangle$ and comprises all elements of the form g^k for all $k \in \mathbb{Z}$. This set is a subgroup of G.

Example 2.3

1. The group $(\mathbb{Z}, +)$ is cyclic and generated by 1.
2. The group $(\mathbb{Q}, +)$ is not cyclic and is generated by the infinitely large set $\{1 \backslash n! | n \in \mathbb{N}\}$.

Theorem 2.1 *For an element $a \in G$, $\langle a^{-1} \rangle = \langle a \rangle$. If a is a generator of cyclic group (also denoted as $\langle a \rangle$) then $\langle a^{-1} \rangle$ is also a generator of that group.*

Proof: Let $b \in \langle a \rangle$ such that $b = \langle a^k \rangle$ for some $k \in \mathbb{Z}$. Then $b = a^k = (a^{-k})^{-1} = (a^{-1})^{-k} \in \langle a^{-1} \rangle$. Since $b \in \langle a \rangle$ is arbitrary, $\langle a \rangle \subseteq \langle a^{-1} \rangle$. Then, it implies that $\langle a^{-1} \rangle \subseteq \langle (a^{-1})^{-1} \rangle = \langle a \rangle$. Hence, we have $\langle a \rangle = \langle a^{-1} \rangle$. $\qquad\qquad\square$

Example 2.4 A single element generates a cyclic group. Here are two motivating examples:

1. Addition can form a group of numbers generated by 1. By this, we mean that element 1 can be combined with itself to generate the complete set of integers under the group operation and inverses. If n is a positive integer, $\mathbb{Z}_n$ is acyclic group of order n generated by 1. The element 1 generates $\mathbb{Z}_7$, since

$$1 + 1 \mod 7 = 2$$
$$1 + 1 + 1 \mod 7 = 3$$
$$1 + 1 + 1 + 1 \mod 7 = 4$$
$$1 + 1 + 1 + 1 + 1 \mod 7 = 5$$
$$1 + 1 + 1 + 1 + 1 + 1 \mod 7 = 6$$
$$1 + 1 + 1 + 1 + 1 + 1 + 1 \mod 7 = 0$$

In other words, by adding 1 to itself, it will eventually get back to 0. The element 3 also generates $\mathbb{Z}_7$:

$$3 + 3 \mod 7 = 6$$
$$3 + 3 + 3 \mod 7 = 2$$
$$3 + 3 + 3 + 3 \mod 7 = 5$$
$$3 + 3 + 3 + 3 + 3 \mod 7 = 1$$
$$3 + 3 + 3 + 3 + 3 + 3 \mod 7 = 4$$
$$3 + 3 + 3 + 3 + 3 + 3 + 3 \mod 7 = 0$$

2. The "same" group can be represented in multiplicative notation as follows: $\mathbb{Z}_7 = \{1, a, a^2, a^3, a^4, a^5, a^6\}$. In this form, a is a generator of $\mathbb{Z}_7$. It turns out that in $\mathbb{Z}_7 = \{0, 1, 2, 3, 4, 5, 6\}$, 3 and 5 are capable of generating the entire group set as follows:

$$3^1 \mod 7 = 3$$
$$3^2 \mod 7 = 2$$
$$3^3 \mod 7 = 6$$
$$3^4 \mod 7 = 4$$
$$3^5 \mod 7 = 5$$
$$3^6 \mod 7 = 1$$

$$5^1 \mod 7 = 5$$
$$5^2 \mod 7 = 4$$
$$5^3 \mod 7 = 6$$

$$5^4 \mod 7 = 2$$
$$5^5 \mod 7 = 3$$
$$5^6 \mod 7 = 1$$

Lemma 2.1 *Let $G = \langle a \rangle$ denote a finite cyclic group with order n. Then, the powers $\{1, a, \ldots, a^{n-1}\}$ are unique.*

Proof: Since a has order n and the elements $a, a^2, \ldots, a^{n-1}$ are all different from 1, then the powers of $\{1, a, a^2, \ldots, a^{n-1}\}$ are unique. Assume that $a^i = a^j$ where $0 \le j < i < n$, then $0 < j - i < n$ and $a^{i-j} = 1$ which is contrary to the prior observation. Hence, the powers $\{1, a, a^2, \ldots, a^{n-1}\}$ are unique. □

Theorem 2.2 *Consider a as an element of the group G. Then, the cyclic subgroup a has two possibilities:*

Case 2.1 The cyclic subgroup a is finite. In this instance, the smallest positive integer n exists such that $a^n = 1$, and we have:

1. $a^k = 1$ if and only if $n|k$.
2. $a^k = a^m$ if and only *if* $k \equiv m (\mod n)$.
3. $\langle a \rangle = \{1, a, a^2, \ldots, a^{n-1}\}$ and the elements $1, a, a^2, \ldots, a^{n-1}$ are unique.

Case 2.2 The cyclic subgroup $\langle a \rangle$ is infinite. Then

1. $a^k = 1$ if and only if $k = 0$.
2. $a^k = a^m$ if and only if $k = m$.
3. $\langle a \rangle = \{\ldots, a^{-3}, a^{-2}, a^{-1}, 1, a, a^2, a^3, \ldots\}$ and all the exponents of a are unique.

Proof: Case 2.1: Suppose $\langle a \rangle$ is finite and the elements $a, a^2, a^3, \ldots$ are not unique. Let $a^k = a^m$ with $k < m$ and $a^n = 1$, where n is the smallest positive integer.

1. If $n|k$, then for some $q \in n, k = qn$. If $a^k = a^{qn} = (a^n)^q = 1^q = 1$. Conversely, for $a^k = 1$, write $k = qn + r$ with $0 \le r \le n$ using the division algorithm. Then $a^r = a^k(a^n)^{-q} = 1(1)^{-q} = 1$. Since $r < n$, unless $r = 0$, this contradicts minimality of n. Hence, $r = 0$ and $k = a^n, n|k$.
2. $a^k = a^m$, if and only if $a^{k-m} = 1$. Now, use step 1.
3. Obviously, $\{1, a, a^2, \ldots, a^{n-1}\} \subseteq \langle a \rangle$. To prove the other inclusion, let $g \in \langle a \rangle$ with $g = a^k$, where $k \in \mathbb{Z}$. As in step 1, use the division algorithm to write $k = qn + r$, where $0 \le r \le n - 1$. Then

$$g = a^k = a^{qn+r} = (a^n)^q a^r = 1^q a^r = a^r \in \{1, a, a^2, \ldots, a^{n-1}\}$$

which demonstrates that $\langle a \rangle \subseteq \{1, a, a^2, \ldots, a^{n-1}\}$, and hence that

$$\langle a \rangle = \{1, a, a^2, \ldots, a^{n-1}\}.$$

Eventually, assume that $a^k = a^m$, where $0 \le k \le m \le n - 1$. Then $a^{m-k} = 1$ and $0 \le m - k < n$. This shows that $m - k = 0$ because n is the smallest positive exponent of a which is equal to 1. Therefore, all of the elements $1, a, a^2, \ldots, a^{n-1}$ are unique.

Case 2.2 The proof of infinite group is as follows:

1. For $a^k = 1$ if $k = 0$. Also, $a^k = 1$, if $k \ne 0$, then $a^{-k} = (a^k)^{-1} = 1^{-1}$. Hence $a^n = 1$ for some $n > 0$, which shows that $\langle a \rangle$ is finite by the proof of Case 2.1 step 3, contrary to the hypothesis in this case. Thus, $a^k = 1$ implies that $k = 0$.

2. $a^k = a^m$ if and only if $a^{k-m=1}$. Now use step 1.
3. $\langle a \rangle = \{a^k : k \in \mathbb{Z}\}$ by definition of $\langle a \rangle$, so all that remains is to check that these exponents are unique. But this is the content of Lemma 2.1.

$\square$

Note that if a is an element of a group G, then its order is the lowest positive integer n such that $a^n = 1$, which is denoted $o(a) = n$. If no such positive integer exists, we claim that a has infinite order, indicated by $o(g) = \infty$. According to Theorem 2.2, the order of an element a and the order of the cyclic subgroup formed by a are the same.

Theorem 2.3 *A cyclic group has cyclic subgroups. If $G = \langle a \rangle$ is cyclic, then $a^{|G|/d}$ can generate exactly one subgroup of order d for any divisor d of $|G|$.*

Proof: Let $|G| = dn$. Then $1, a^n, a^{2n}, \ldots, a^{(d-1)n}$ are unique and form a cyclic subgroup $\langle a \rangle$ of order d. Therefore, let $H = \{1, a_1, \ldots, a_{d-1}\}$ denote a subgroup of G for some d dividing G. Then for all $i, a_i = a^k$ for some k, and since every element has order dividing $|H|$, $a_i^d = a^{kd} = 1$. Hence $kd = |G|m = ndm$ for some m, and we have $a^i = a^{nm}$ so each a_i is in fact an exponent of a^n. This shows that it must be one of the d subgroups already described.

$\square$

Theorem 2.4 *Every composite order group has its own set of subgroups.*

Proof: Let G has a group of composite order such that $1 \neq a \in G$. If $\langle a \rangle \neq G$, we are done, else the subgroup $\langle a^d \rangle$ for every divisor d of $|G|$.

$\square$

2.2 Ring Theory

A ring is an algebraic structure that generalizes fields in mathematics: multiplication does not have to be commutative, and multiplicative inverses do not have to exist. In other words, a ring is a set of binary operations with properties analogous to integer addition and multiplication. Non-numerical objects such as square matrices, functions, polynomials, and power series can be used as ring elements as well as numbers such as integers or complex numbers. Many of the concepts discussed here are straightforward generalizations of properties found in $\mathbb{Z}$, which is often regarded as the quintessential example of a ring.

Definition 2.7 A set R with two binary operations (multiplication $\cdot$) and (addition $+$) is called a ring if all the three axioms listed below, known as the ring axioms, are satisfied.

1. $(R, +)$ is an abelian group, which means that:
    a. **Associativity**: For all elements $x, y, z \in R$, we have $(x + y) + z = x + (y + z)$.
    b. **Commutativity**: For all elements $x, y \in R$, we have $x + y = y + x$.
    c. **Additive identity**: There exists an element $0 \in R$ such that $x + 0 = x$ for all $x \in R$.
    d. **Additive inverse**: For any element $x \in R$ there exists $-x \in R$ such that $x + (-x) = 0$.
2. $(R, \cdot)$ is a monoid, which means that:
    a. **Associativity**: For all elements $x, y, z \in R$, we have $(x \cdot y) \cdot z = x \cdot (y \cdot z)$.
    b. **Multiplicative identity**: There exists an element $1 \in R$ such that $x \cdot 1 = x$ and $1 \cdot x = x$ for any element $x \in R$.

3. Multiplication is distributive concerning addition, meaning that:
   a. **Left distributivity property**: For all the elements $x, y, z \in R$, we have $x \cdot (y + z) = (x \cdot y) + (x \cdot z)$.
   b. **Right distributivity property**: For all the elements $x, y, z \in R$, we have $(x + y) \cdot z = (x \cdot z) + (y \cdot z)$.

Example 2.5 Let the set $\mathbf{Z}/6\mathbf{Z} = \left\{ \overline{0}, \overline{1}, \dots, \overline{5} \right\}$ with the following operations:

1. The addition $\overline{a} + \overline{b} \in \mathbb{Z}/6\mathbb{Z}$ is the remainder when the integer $a + b$ is divided by 6. For instance, $\overline{5} + \overline{3} = \overline{2}$ and $\overline{5} + \overline{5} = \overline{4}$.
2. The multiplication $\overline{a} \cdot \overline{b} \in \mathbb{Z}/6\mathbb{Z}$ is the remainder when the integer a is divided by 6. For instance, $\overline{5} \cdot \overline{3} = \overline{3}$ and $\overline{5} \cdot \overline{5} = \overline{1}$.

Then $\mathbb{Z}/6\mathbb{Z}$ is a ring: each axiom follows from the associated axiom for $\mathbb{Z}$. If a is an integer, the remainder of a when divided by 6 may be considered as an element of $\mathbb{Z}/6\mathbb{Z}$, and this element is often referred to as "a mod 6" or $\overline{a}$, which is consistent with the notation for $0, 1, 2, 3, 4, 5$. The additive inverse of any $\overline{a} \in \mathbb{Z}/6\mathbb{Z}$ is $=x$. For example, $-\overline{4} = \overline{-4} = \overline{1}$.

$(R, +)$ is called a commutative ring, and $(R, \cdot)$ is also referred to as a commutative ring. The ring is called an **integral domain** if the product of every two non-zero elements in a commutative ring is also non-zero. $R^{\bullet}$ denotes the set of all non-zero members of a ring.

2.2.1 Ideals and Quotient Rings

Ideals are specialized subsets of rings. They generalize the features of specific subsets of integers, such as even numbers.

Definition 2.8 An ideal which is denoted as I is a nonempty subset of R such that if the tuples (x, y) are in I, then $x + y$ is in I, and if x is in I and r is in R, then both xr and rx are in I. An ideal I is said to be closed under addition if $rI \subset I$ and $Ir \subset I$ for all r in R.

Example 2.6

1. Consider x as an element in a commutative ring, R, and let $\langle x \rangle = \{xr : r \in R\}$ be an ideal in R. Obviously, $\langle x \rangle$ is nonempty as $0 = x0$ and $x = x1$ can be found in $\langle x \rangle$. The addition of any two elements in $\langle x \rangle$ is also in $\langle x \rangle$ since $xr + xr' = x(r + r')$. The inverse of xr is $-xr = x(-r) \in \langle x \rangle$. Eventually, if we compute the product of the element $xr \in \langle x \rangle$ with any element, $y \in R$, we can obtain $y(xr) = x(yr)$. Hence, $\langle x \rangle$ satisfies the definition of an ideal.
2. Let R denote a ring such that $r \in R$. The set $rR = \{rx | x \in R\}$ comprises all multiples of r that forms an ideal. An element $x \in R$ is contained in rR if and only if x is divisible by r. If an ideal I can be written as rR for some $r \in R$, then the ideal is referred to as principal. The situation is fairly straightforward in $\mathbb{Z}$, because all of ideals in $\mathbb{Z}$ are principal.

Ideals can be used to make new rings out of the existing ones. Let I denote an ideal of a ring R. Then an equivalence relation $\sim_I$ can be defined as follows: If and only if $a \sim_I b$, and $a - b \in R$. The quotient ring of R modulo I is then set to $R/I = R/\sim_q$.

Example 2.7 Consider the prime number p and the number $\mathbb{Z}$. The quotient ring modulo $p\mathbb{Z}$ can then be constructed. Instead of working with the $\mathbb{Z}/p\mathbb{Z}$ equivalence classes, we can easily express it as the set $\{0, \dots, p - 1\}$ where all operations are performed in modulo p.

2.2.2 Euler's Totient Function

The totient function $\phi(n)$, also known as Euler's totient function, can be referred to as the number of non-negative integers $\leq n$ that are relatively prime to (that is, do not share any factor with) n, where 1 is treated as being relatively prime to all numbers. For example, $\phi(24)$ has eight totatives of $(1, 5, 7, 11, 13, 17, 19,$ and $23)$. The number $n - \phi(n)$ is referred to as the **cototient** of n provided the number of positive integers $\leq n$ have at least one prime factor which is common with n.

Definition 2.9 The map $\phi : \begin{cases} \mathbb{N} \to \mathbb{N} \\ n \mapsto |\mathbb{Z}/n\mathbb{Z}^X| \end{cases}$ is called Euler's totient function. In other words, Euler's totient function counts the number of coprime positive integers $\leq n$. It satisfies $\phi(p^k)$ and $(p^{k-1})(p - 1)$, and coprime $\phi(mn) = \phi(m)\phi(n)$ with $p \in \mathbb{P}$ and $k \in \mathbb{N}$ and coprimes $m, n \in \mathbb{N}$.

2.2.3 Polynomial Rings

From any commutative ring it is feasible to form a canonical ring extension, the polynomial ring.

Definition 2.10 Let R denote a commutative ring. The ring of polynomials in variables $X_1, \ldots, X_n$ over R is as follows:

$$R[X_1, \ldots, X_n] =$$

$$\left\{ \sum_{w_1, \ldots, w_n \in \mathbb{N}_0} a_{w_1}, \ldots, a_{w_n} X_1^{w_1} \ldots X_n^{w_n} | a_{w_1, \ldots, w_n} \in R \, \forall \, w_1, \ldots, w_n \in \mathbb{N}_0 \right\}$$

The multiplication is defined by the standard polynomial multiplication, and the addition is also defined by the component-wise summation. The coefficient ring R is a subring of the polynomial ring $R[X_1, \ldots, X_n]$. The degree of a polynomial $f \in R[X_1, \ldots, X_n]$ is defined as

$$deg(f) = max \left\{ \sum_{j=1}^{n} w_j | a_{w_1}, \ldots, a_{w_n} \neq 0 \right\} .$$

If $f = 0$, we can fix $deg(f) = -\infty$.

2.2.4 Irreducible and Monic Polynomials

Irreducible polynomials are those that cannot be factored into non-constant polynomials, such as $f = gh$ for $g, h \in R[X]$ with either $g \in R$ or $h \in R$. In $\mathbb{Z}$, the concept of irreducibility is analogous to the concept of prime numbers. If the polynomial has the form $f = X^d + \sum_{j=0}^{d-1} a_j X^j$, then it is referred to as monic.

Cyclotomic polynomial
Cyclotomic polynomials are irreducible polynomials with integer coefficients which divide $X^n - 1 \in \mathbb{Z}[X]$ for some $n \in \mathbb{N}$.

Definition 2.11 Let $n \in \mathbb{N}$. An irreducible polynomial $f \in \mathbb{Z}[X]$ is referred to as the n-th cyclotomic polynomial if:

1. $f | X^n - 1$, and
2. $f \nmid X^{k-1}$ for any $k < n$.

The n-th cyclotomic polynomial is distinct and is represented by Φ_n.

Example 2.8   If n is a prime number, then

$$\Phi_n(x) = 1 + x + x^2 + \cdots + x^{n-1} = \sum_{k=0}^{n-1} x^k.$$

If $n = 2p$ where p is an odd prime number, then

$$\Phi_{2p}(x) = 1 - x + x^2 - \cdots + x^{p-1} = \sum_{k=0}^{p-1} (-x)^k.$$

For n up to 10, the cyclotomic polynomials are given as follows:

$$\Phi_1(x) = x - 1$$
$$\Phi_2(x) = x + 1$$
$$\Phi_3(x) = x^2 + x + 1$$
$$\Phi_4(x) = x^2 + 1$$
$$\Phi_5(x) = x^4 + x^3 + x^2 + x + 1$$
$$\Phi_6(x) = x^2 - x + 1$$
$$\Phi_7(x) = x^6 + x^5 + x^4 + x^3 + x^2 + x + 1$$
$$\Phi_8(x) = x^4 + 1$$
$$\Phi_9(x) = x^6 + x^3 + 1$$
$$\Phi_{10}(x) = x^4 - x^3 + x^2 - x + 1$$

2.2.5   Field Theory

Fields are algebraic structures with the ability to add, subtract, multiply, and divide. They are rings with a multiplicative inverse for each non-zero element, allowing division by non-zero elements. Cryptography frequently uses finite fields. Fields are also needed to describe the algebraic geometry concepts.

Definition 2.12   A field is a set F with two composition laws $+$ and $\cdot$ such that

1. $(F, +)$ is a commutative group;
2. $(F^\times, \cdot)$, where $F^\times = F \backslash \{0\}$ is a commutative group;
3. the distributive law holds.

As a result, a field is a nonzero commutative ring with an inverse for each nonzero element. In particular, it is an integral domain. At least two unique elements, 0 and 1, are present in a field. $F_2 = \mathbb{Z} \backslash 2\mathbb{Z} = \{0, 1\}$ is the smallest and one of the essential fields. A subfield, denoted as S, within a field F, can be defined as a subring that remains closed when taking inverses. It inherits the structure of a field from that of F.

2.2.5.1 Quotient Field

Let R denote an integral domain and let Q be the smallest field with R embedded into Q (which can be called quotient field or field of fractions). The construction of this field can be done in the same fashion as $\mathbb{Q}$ can be constructed from $\mathbb{Z}$: for $n \in R, m \in R^{\bullet}$ look at the formal quotient $\frac{n}{m}$. The two quotients $\frac{n}{m}$ and $\frac{n'}{m'}$ are equal when $m'n = n'm$. The addition of $\frac{n}{m} + \frac{n'}{m'}$ is performed as $\frac{nm'+n'm}{mm'}$ while the multiplication $\frac{n}{m} \cdot \frac{n'}{m'}$ is performed as $\frac{nn'}{mm'}$.

Example 2.9 The field of fractions of the ring of integers is the field of rationals: $\mathbb{Q} = \text{Frac}(\mathbb{Z})$.

2.2.6 Field Characteristic

There is a ring homomorphism: $\psi : Z \rightarrow K$ for any field K, with $\psi(1) = 1_K$. K has the characteristic 0 if ψ is injective. On the other hand, if ψ is not injective, there exists a prime $p \in \mathbb{P}$ such that $\psi(p) = 0$, and it is the smallest positive integer that fulfills this property. K is said to have characteristic p in this scenario. The characteristic of a field K is denoted by char (K). Also, if K has the characteristic p, then K contains an isomorphic copy of $\mathbb{F}_p$.

2.2.7 Algebraic Extension Fields

Take two fields, K and L, such that $K \subset L$. If there exists a non-constant polynomial $f \in K[X] \backslash K$ such that $f(\alpha) = 0$, then an element $\alpha \in L$ is considered as algebraic over K. L is also considered as an algebraic extension of K if every element of L is algebraic over K. Else, L is a transcendental extension of K.

K-vector space can also be seen as an extension field L over K. The extension degree of L is denoted as $[L : K]$, and it is the K-vector space dimension of L. The extension degree is finite if the field extension is algebraic.

2.3 Elliptic Curves

The theory of elliptic curves is extensive, diverse, and complex. Our purpose here is not to give a comprehensive overview of the theory, but rather to provide the fundamentals needed to understand the cryptographic application of elliptic curves. We will introduce algebraic geometry concepts like divisors and rational functions along the way, which will come in helpful later when we define bilinear pairings. Finding specific "pairing-friendly" curves will also be discussed in this chapter.

2.3.1 Plane Curve

A plane curve is considered as a curve in a plane, which can be either a Euclidean plane, an affine plane, or a projective plane. An implicit equation of the form $p(x, y) = 0$ for some specific function p can be used to represent a plane curve.

A plane curve X is the set of zeros in the plane F^2 of a bivariate polynomial, $p(x, y)$. We write

$$X = \{(x, y)\} \in F^2 : p(x, y) = 0\}.$$

We can define a plane curve to include points that are appended to the plane but not in it. Points at infinity, often known as basis points, are such points. The letter $\mathcal{O}$ will be used to represent a point at infinity. The plane curve can now be written as

$$X = \{(x,y)\} \in F^2 : p(x,y) = 0\} \cup \{\mathcal{O}\}.$$

We will concentrate on non-singular plane curves, which are plane curves described by non-singular polynomials. To clarify, a singular point of the bivariate polynomial $p(x,y)$, we write a point $P = (x,y)$ such that

$$\frac{\partial p(x,y)}{\partial x} = \frac{\partial p(x,y)}{\partial y} = p(x,y) = 0.$$

If the polynomial $p(x,y)$ contains no singular points in F or any finite extension of F, it is called a nonsingular polynomial. A curve X defined by the zeros of a nonsingular polynomial is called non-singular (projective/smooth) curve. The genus of a plane curve is used to characterize the curve's properties. The genus of a nonsingular curve is given $g = \begin{pmatrix} d - 1 \\ 2 \end{pmatrix}$.

Definition 2.13   An elliptic curve, E, over the field F, is a plane curve with genus 1given by the set of zeros of a nonsingular, smooth, bivariate polynomial of the form

$$p(x,y) = y^2 + a_1 xy + a_3 y - x^3 - a_2 x^2 - a_4 x - a_6$$

in addition to the point at the infinity $\mathcal{O}$, where $a_1, \ldots, a_6 \in F$. The polynomial in the above equation is in the Weierstrauss form.

We can observe that requiring E to be smooth essentially means that the equations:

$$a_1 y = 3x^2 + 2a_2 x + a_4$$
$$2y + a_1 x + a_3 = 0$$

cannot simultaneously satisfy any $(X, Y) \in E(\overline{F})$, where $\overline{F}$ represents the algebraic closure of F. Whenever the field characteristic exceeds three, the appropriate change of variables (particularly $x \to x - \frac{1}{3}$) can express the elliptic curve E as

$$E : y^2 = x^3 + ax + b.$$

The elliptic curve E is represented by the short Weierstrauss form. In this situation, requiring the curve to be smooth basically implies requiring the cubic on the right-hand side not to have multiple roots. This is valid if the discriminant of $x^3 + ax + b$, which is $-(4a^3 + 27b^2)$, nonzero. For cryptography purposes, we are interested in the curve over a prime field. However, if we plot such an elliptic curve over $\mathbb{Z}_p$, we get nothing approximating a curve. However, nothing prohibits us from displaying an elliptic curve equation over the set of real numbers.

Example 2.10   In Figure 2.1 the elliptic curve $y^2 = x^3 - 3x + 3$ is shown over the real numbers.

The figure clearly shows that elliptic curves are not ellipses. They are used to estimate the circumference of ellipses, hence the name. The elliptic curve in figure is symmetric about the x-axis. This is strongly related to the fact that for all x_i values on the elliptic curve, both $y_i = \sqrt{x_i^3 + a \cdot x_i + b}$ and $y_i' = -\sqrt{x_i^3 + a \cdot x_i + b}$ are the solutions. Second, there is one point where the y-axis intersects

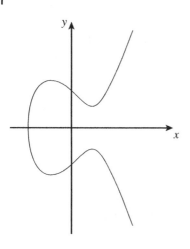

Figure 2.1 $Y^2 = x^3 - 3x + 3$ over $\mathbb{R}$.

the x-axis. This is due to the fact that $y = 0$ is a cubic equation with one real solution (the intersection with the x-axis) and two complex solutions (which do not show up in the plot). There are other elliptic curves that intersect the x-axis three times. We will now revert to our initial goal of identifying a curve with a large cyclic group, which is required for the construction of a discrete logarithm problem.

2.3.2 Group Operations on Elliptic Curves

We can use elliptic curves in cryptography because when the points on the curve are added together, they form a group, denoted as $E(F)$. The operation of point addition on the elliptic curve is represented by the symbol "+." If P and Q are points on the curve E, so is then $P + Q$. The group $E(F)$ identity is the point at infinity, $\mathcal{O}$; thus, $P + \mathcal{O} = P$. The inverse of a point P is indicated as $-P$, so $P + (-P) = \mathcal{O}$. Let $P = (x_1, y_1)$ and $Q = (x_2, y_2)$, we can derive the coordinates of a third point R as

$$P + Q = R$$

$$(x_1, y_1) + (x_2 + y_2) = (x_3 + y_3)$$

2.3.2.1 Point Addition

The summation of two points P and Q on an elliptic curve to obtain another point R on the same elliptic curve is known as point addition. This is shown geometrically in Figure 2.2. The following are the steps in the construction: Draw a line across P and Q to find a third point where the elliptic curve and the line intersect. Then, along the x-axis, mirror this third intersection point. By definition, the mirrored point is the point R. Consider the elliptic curve, E, with the equation $Y^2 = x^3 + ax + b$; this can be calculated as:

$$\lambda = \frac{y_q - y_p}{x_q - x_p}$$
$$x_r = \lambda^2 - x_p - x_q$$
$$y_r = \lambda(x_p - x_r) - y_p$$

These equations are accurate when neither point is the point at infinity, $\mathcal{O}$, and if the points have different x coordinates (they are not mutual inverses).

Figure 2.2 Point addition on an elliptic curve over the real numbers.

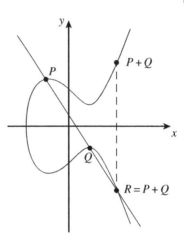

Figure 2.3 Point doubling on an elliptic curve over the real numbers.

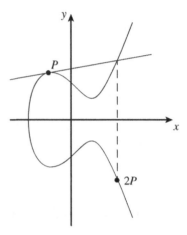

2.3.2.2 Point Doubling

Adding a point P on an elliptic curve to itself to generate another point Q on the same elliptic curve is known as point doubling. For example, consider a point P on an elliptic curve as depicted in Figure 2.3. To double a point P to get Q, find $P = 2Q$. Here, we compute $P + Q$ but $P = Q$. Therefore $R = P + P = 2P$. If the point P's y coordinate is not zero, the tangent line at P will intersect the elliptic curve at exactly one additional point $-Q$. The point Q is the result of doubling the point P by reflecting the point $-Q$ with regard to the x-axis. This mirrored point is the result R of the doubling.

You might be wondering why the group operations have such a haphazard appearance. If two points are already known, the tangent-and-chord approach can be used to generate a third point using only the four standard algebraic operations – add, subtract, multiply, and divide. It turns out that by adding points on the elliptic curve in this way, the set of points meets most of the requirements for a group, including closure, associativity, the existence of an inverse, and the existence of identity element.

One of the intriguing things about the elliptic curve is finding the neutral element or identity element $\mathcal{O}$. The tangent-and-chord method used to construct the third point cannot provide the identity elements. For all of the elliptic curve's points P, there are no points (x, y) that satisfy the requirement $P + \mathcal{O} = P$. So instead, the neutral element $\mathcal{O}$ is defined as an abstract point at infinity.

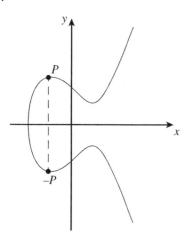

Figure 2.4 The inverse of a point P on an elliptic curve.

This point at infinity can be depicted as a point pointing toward "plus" infinity along the y-axis or pointing toward "minus" infinity along the y-axis. We can now define the inverse P of any group element P using the group definition as:

$$P + (-P) = \mathcal{O}$$

The question is, how do we obtain P? Using the tangent-and-chord method, we can find the inverse of the point $P = (x_p, y_p)$ as $-P = (x_p, -y_p)$, i.e. the point reflected along the x-axis. It is worth noting that finding the inverse of a point $P = (x_p, y_p)$ is now trivial. First, we take the inverse of the y coordinate. In the case of elliptic curves over a prime field $\mathbb{Z}_p$, the inverse is $-y_p = p - y_p \mod p$, resulting in $-P \equiv (x_p, p - y_p)$. Figure 2.4 illustrates the point P together with its inverse.

2.4 Divisors and Bilinear Map

The section provides background studies on divisors and bilinear map which are essential for the construction schemes in attribute-based encryption.

2.4.1 Divisors

In algebraic geometry, divisors have a wide range of definitions, but this book focuses on the aspects that are important for understanding cryptographic pairing calculations [1].

Definition 2.14 A divisor D on curve E is a convenient way to denote a multi-set of points on E [2]

$$D = \sum_{P \in E(\mathbb{F}_q)} n_p(P), \text{ where } n_p \in \mathbb{Z} \tag{2.1}$$

- $Div_{\mathbb{F}_q}(E)$ denotes the set of all divisors on E, which forms a group where divisor addition is natural.
- The zero divisor: the zero divisor $0 \in Div_{\mathbb{F}_q}(E)$ is the divisor with all $n_p = 0$
- If the field $\mathbb{F}_q$ is not specified, it can be omitted and the group of divisors can simply be expressed as $Div(E)$.

A divisor D on curve E specifies the multiplicities of points on E; in other words, it can represent a line–elliptic curve relationship; it is also the foundation of pairing-based algorithms.

2.4.2 The Degree and Support of *D*

1. The degree of a divisor D is $Deg(D) = \sum_{P \in E(\mathbb{F}_q)} n_P$,
2. The support of D, represented by the set $supp(D) = \{P \in E(\mathbb{F}_q) : n_p \neq 0\}$.

For example, let $P, Q, R, S \in E(\mathbb{F}_q)$. Let $D_1 = 3(P) - 4(Q)$, and $D_2 = 4(Q) + (R) - 2(S)$, therefore the $Deg(D_1) = 3 - 4 = -1$, and $Deg(D_2) = 4 + 1 - 2 = 3$. The summation of $D_1 + D_2 = 3(P) + (R) - 2(S)$, and naturally $Deg(D_1 + D_2) = Deg(D_1) + Deg(D_2) = 2$. The supports are $supp(D_1) = \{P, Q\}, supp(D_2) = \{Q, R, S\}$, and $supp(D1 + D2) = \{P, R, S\}$.

2.4.3 The Divisor of a Function *f* on *E*

1. The divisor of a function f on E is used to indicate the intersection points (and their respective multiplicities) of f and E.
   - Let $ord_P(f)$ denote the multiplicity of f at P, which is positive if f has a zero at P, and negative if f has a pole at P. The divisor of a function f is defined as

$$(f) = \sum_{P \in E(\mathbb{F}_q)} ord_P(f)(P) \tag{2.2}$$

   - Observe that in all instances, $Deg(\ell) = 0$. This holds true for any function f on E.
2. The relationship of a function f and a divisor D: A divisor $D = \sum_P n_P(P)$ is denoted as a divisor function if and only if $\sum_p n_p = 0$ and $\sum_p [n_p]P = \mathcal{O}$ on E. For instance, given f as a line which intersects E at P and Q, the divisor $(f) = (\ell_{P,Q}) = (P) + (Q) + ([-1](P + Q)) - 3(\mathcal{O})$, since

$$\sum_P n_P = n_P + n_Q + n_{n[-1](P+Q)+n_\mathcal{O}} = 1 + 1 + 1 - 3 = 0.$$

$$\sum_P [n_p]P = P + Q + ([-1](P + Q)) = \mathcal{O} \text{ (Elliptic Curve Points Operation)}.$$

3. There are three instances where the straight line f intersects curve E:
   - As illustrated in Figure 2.5, the chord line $\ell_{P,Q}$ intersects E in P, Q, and $[-1](P + Q)$, all with multiplicity 1, and $\ell_{P,Q}$ also intersects E with multiplicity -3 at O, namely, $\ell_{P,Q}$ has a pole of order 3 at $\mathcal{O}$. Thus, $\ell_{P,Q}$ has divisor

$$(\ell_{P,Q}) = (P) + (Q) + ([-1](P + Q)) - 3(\mathcal{O}).$$

Figure 2.5 The function $(\ell_{P,Q})$.

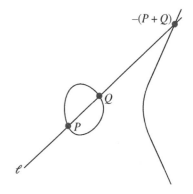

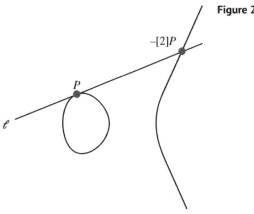

Figure 2.6 The function $(\ell_{P,P})$.

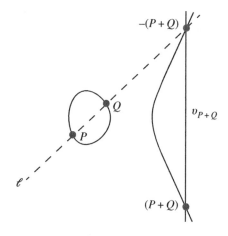

Figure 2.7 The function (v_{P+Q}).

- As illustrated in Figure 2.6, the tangent line $\ell_{P,P}$ intersects E with multiplicity 2 at P, with multiplicity 1 at $[-2]P$, and again with multiplicity -3 at $\mathcal{O}$, so in this

$$(\ell_{P,P}) = 2(P) + ([-2](P)) - 3(\mathcal{O}).$$

- As illustrated in Figure 2.7, the vertical line v_{P+Q} intersects E in $(P+Q)$ and $[-1](P+Q)$ with multiplicity 1.

$$(v_{P+Q}) = ((P+Q)) + ([-1](P+Q)) - 2(\mathcal{O}).$$

4. Properties of divisors of the functions:
   - $(fg) = (f) + (g)$
   - $(f/g) = (f) - (g)$
   - $(f) = 0$ if and only if f is constant.
   - If $(f) = (g)$, then $(f/g) = 0$, so f is a constant multiple of g.

2.4.4 Equivalence of Divisors

The divisors D_1 and D_2 can be called equivalent, written as $D_1 \sim D_2$, $D_1 = D_2 + (f)$ for some function f. The notion of equivalence allows us to reduce divisors of any size D into much smaller divisors. For instance,

- Let $R = P + Q$ on E, so the line (ℓ) joining P and Q have divisor $(\ell) = (P) + (Q) + (-R) - 3(\mathcal{O})$, while the vertical line $v = x - x_R$ has divisor $(v) = (-R) + (R) - 2(\mathcal{O})$. In addition, the quotient ℓ/v has divisor $(\ell/v) = (P) + (Q) - (R) - (\mathcal{O})$. Thus, the equation $R = P + Q$ on E is the same as the divisor equality $(R) - (\mathcal{O}) = (P) - (\mathcal{O}) + (Q) - (\mathcal{O}) - (\ell/v)$. It reduces $(P) + (Q) - 2(\mathcal{O})$ to $(R) - (\mathcal{O})$.

- Similarly, in order to obtain $([2]Q) - (Q) = (Q) - (\mathcal{O})$, there exists a $(f) = 2(Q) - ([2]Q) - (\mathcal{O})$. This equivalence is used to substitute $D_Q = (Q) - (\mathcal{O})$ with $D_Q = ([2]Q) - (Q)$, such that it is convenient to compute D_Q using $[2]Q$ and Q, rather than Q and $\mathcal{O}$ [3, 4].

2.4.5 Bilinear Map

In definite terms, a bilinear pairing is the mapping of elements from two cyclic groups (say additive groups) $\mathbb{G}_1$ and $\mathbb{G}_2$ to a third group (say multiplicative group) G_T of some prime order. When the first two groups are the same (as in $\mathbb{G}_1 = \mathbb{G}_2$), the pairing is referred to as symmetric, with a mapping known to be from two elements in one group to another element from the target group. Otherwise, the pairing is referred to as asymmetric. Bilinear pairings are formally defined as follows:

Definition 2.15 (Bilinear Maps) Let $\mathbb{G}$ and $\mathbb{G}_T$ be two multiplicative cyclic groups of prime order p. Let P be a generator of $\mathbb{G}$ and e be a bilinear map,

$$e : \mathbb{G} \times \mathbb{G} \rightarrow \mathbb{G}_T.$$

Usually, bilinear map defines the groups $\mathbb{G}_1$ in $E(\mathbb{F}_q)$, $\mathbb{G}_2$ in $E(\mathbb{F}_{q^k})/E(\mathbb{F}_q)$, as well as the target group G_T in the multiplicative group $\mathbb{F}_{q^k}^*$, so it can be called $\mathbb{G}_1$ and $\mathbb{G}_2$ are additive, while $\mathbb{G}_T$ is multiplicative [5]. If points P and Q are the elements of $\mathbb{G}_1$ and $\mathbb{G}_2$, respectively, then bilinear map can be rewritten as

$$e(P, Q) : \mathbb{G}_1 \times \mathbb{G}_2 \rightarrow \mathbb{G}_T$$

where $P \in \mathbb{G}_1 = E(\mathbb{F}_q)$, $Q \in \mathbb{G}_2 = E(\mathbb{F}_{q^k})/E(\mathbb{F}_q)$, and $e(P, Q) \in \mathbb{G}_T = \mathbb{F}_{q^k}^*$. The bilinear map e has the following properties:

- **Bilinearity**: For all $P, Q \in \mathbb{G}$ and $y, z \in \mathbb{Z}_p$, we have $e(P^y, Q^z) = e(P, Q)^{yz}$.
- **Non-degeneracy**: $e(P, Q) \neq 1$.
- **Computability**: There is an efficient algorithm to compute $e(P, Q)$ for all $P, Q \in \mathbb{G}$.

Note that the map e is symmetric if $e(P^y, Q^z) = e(P, Q)^{yz} = e(P^z, Q^y)$. The permissible map e is usually obtained from Tate or modified Weil pairings.

2.4.6 Weil Pairing

Several standard definitions from curve theory are required to provide the definition for Weil pairing (see [6] or [7] for details). Let $P, Q \in E(\mathbb{F}_{q^k})[r]$ and let D_P and D_Q be degree zero divisors with disjoint supports such that $D_P \sim (P) - (\mathcal{O})$ and $D_Q \sim (Q) - (\mathcal{O})$. There exist functions f and g such that $(f) = rD_P$ and $(g) = rD_Q$. w_r is a map:

$$w_r : E(\mathbb{F}_{q^k})[r] \times E(\mathbb{F}_{qk})[r] \mapsto \mathbb{F}_{qk}[r] \tag{2.3}$$

such that

$$w_r e(P, Q) = \frac{f(D_Q)}{g(D_P)}$$

- Observe that r is the largest prime factor of $\#E(\mathbb{F}_q)$.
- For a given point $P \in E(\mathbb{F}_{q^k})[r]$, the function $f = f_{r,P}$, with divisor $r(P) - r(\mathcal{O})$ plays an important role in Weil pairing definition.
- Likewise, for a given point $Q \in E(\mathbb{F}_{q^k})[r]$, the function $g = g_{r,Q}$ has the divisor $r(Q) - r(\mathcal{O})$.
- Based on Eq. (2.3), $w_r(P, Q)$ equals to $f(D_Q)$ divides $g(D_P)$. Also, $f(D_Q)$ and $g(D_P)$ can be computed with Miller's Algorithm, respectively.

2.4.7 Miller's Algorithm

In this section, you must recall your prior knowledge of divisors and the function f. A number of significant equations will be deduced.

1. For any $m \in \mathbb{Z}$ and $P \in E$, it follows that there exists a function $f_{m,P}$ with the divisor

$$(f_{m,P}) = m(P) - ([m]P) - (m-1)(\mathcal{O}) \tag{2.4}$$

- where it is noted that for $m = 0$, it can take $f_{0,P} = 1$ with $f_{0,P}$ being the zero divisor.

$$(f_{0,P}) = 0(P) - ([0]P) - (0-1)(\mathcal{O}) = 0 \tag{2.5}$$

- where it is noted that for $m = 1$, it can take $f_{1,P} = 1$ with $f_{1,P}$ being the zero divisor.

$$(f_{1,P}) = 1(P) - ([1]P) - (1-1)(\mathcal{O}) = 0 \tag{2.6}$$

- **Note**: $(f_{0,P}) = (f_{1,P}) =$ zero divisor, according to "properties of divisors of functions: $(f) = 0$ if and only if f is constant," so it is convenient to take $f_{0,P} = f_{1,P} = 1$ for setting the initial value.
2. from $f_{n,P} \to f_{n+1,P}$:
- When $\P \in E[r]$, means r is the order of P, then following Eq. (2.4), $f_{r,P}$ has divisor

$$(f_{r,P}) = r(P) - r(\mathcal{O}) \tag{2.7}$$

furthermore,

$$(f_{m+1,P}) = (m+1)(P) - ([m+1]P) - (m)(\mathcal{O}) \tag{2.8}$$

Observe that, Eq. (2.7) subtracts Eq. (2.8), then acquires

$$(f_{m+1,P}) - (f_{m,P}) = (P) + ([m]P) - ([m+1]P) - (\mathcal{O}) \tag{2.9}$$

- In Figure 4.1, according to the functions of chord line and vertical line, it is obtained

$$(\ell_{[m]P,P}) = (P) + ([m]P) + (-[m+1]P) - 3(\mathcal{O}) \tag{2.10}$$

$$(v_{[m+1]P}) = (-[m+1]P) + ([m+1]P) - 2(\mathcal{O}) \tag{2.11}$$

thus,

$$\left(\frac{\ell_{[m]P,P}}{v[m+1]P}\right) = (\ell_{[m]P,P}) - (v_{[m+1]P}) = (P) + ([m]P) - ([m+1]P) - (\mathcal{O}) \tag{2.12}$$

where $\ell_{[m]P,P}$ and $v_{[m+1]P}$ are the chord and vertical lines used in the chord-and-tangent addition of the point $[m]P$ and P (Figure 2.8). From Eqs. (2.8) and (2.10) it can be seen that $(f_{m+1,P}) - (f_{m,P})$ is exactly the divisor of the function $\ell_{[m]P,P}/v_{[m+1]P}$, which means $f_{m+1,P}$ can be built from $f_{m,P}$ via

$$f_{m+1,P} = f_{m,P} \times \frac{\ell_{[m]P,P}}{v_{[m+1]P}} \tag{2.13}$$

Figure 2.8 The function $\left(\frac{\ell_{[m]P,P}}{v_{[m+1]P}} \right)$.

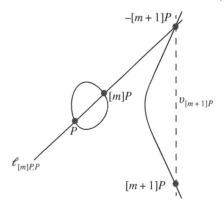

3. From $f_{m,P}$ to $f_{m,P}^2$:
   - In addition, according to Properties "$(fg) = (f) + (g)$":

$$(f_{m,P}^2) = (f_{m,P} \times f_{m,P}) = (f_{m,P}) + (f_{m,P}) = 2(f_{m,P}) \tag{2.14}$$

   Hence, following Eq. (2.7)

$$(f_{m,P}^2) = 2(f_{m,P}) = 2m(P) - 2([m]P) - 2(m-1)(\mathcal{O}) \tag{2.15}$$

   Moreover, also following Eq. (2.7)

$$(f_{2m,P}) = 2m(P) - ([2m]P) - (2m-1)(\mathcal{O}) \tag{2.16}$$

   Observe that,

$$(f_{2m,P}) - (f_{m,P}^2) = 2([m]P) - ([2m]P) - (\mathcal{O}) \tag{2.17}$$

4. Now, the functions of chord line and vertical line can be rewritten as:

$$(\ell_{[m]P,[m]P}) = ([m]P) + ([m]P) + (-[2m]P) - 3(\mathcal{O}) \tag{2.18}$$

$$(v_{[2m]P}) = (-[2m]P) + ([2m]P) - 2(\mathcal{O}) \tag{2.19}$$

   Similarly, according to Eq. (2.12), it is obtained

$$\left(\frac{\ell_{P[m]P,[m]P}}{v_{[2m]P}} \right) = (\ell_{[m]P,[m]P}) - (v_{[2m]P}) = 2([m]P) - ([2m]P) - (\mathcal{O}) \tag{2.20}$$

   Therefore,

$$(f_{2m,P}) - (f_{m,P}^2) = 2([m]P) - ([2m]P) - (\mathcal{O}) = \left(\frac{\ell_{[m]P,[m]P}}{v_{[2m]P}} \right) \tag{2.21}$$

   At last,

$$f_{2m,P} = f_{m,P}^2 \times \frac{\ell_{[m]P,[m]P}}{v_{[2m]P}} \tag{2.22}$$

5. Based on Eq. (2.22), one can straightaway jump from $f_{m,P}$ to $f_{2m,P}$, in comparison with the naive method of progressing one-by-one in Figure 2.9:

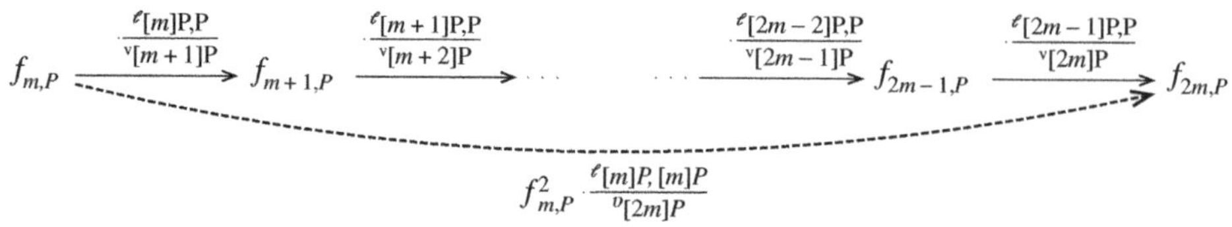

Figure 2.9 Jump from $f_{m,P}$ to $f_{2m,P}$. Source: Adapted from [2].

So far, for any m, either $f_{m+1,P}$, or $f_{2m,P}$ can be obtained quickly, and Miller observed that it then gives rise to a double-and-add style algorithm.

Algorithm 2.1 Miller's Algorithm [8]

Data: $P \in E(\mathbb{F}_{q^k})[r], D_Q \sim (Q) \sim (\mathcal{O})$ with support disjoint from $(f_{r,P})$, and $r = (r_{n-1} \dots r_1 r_0)_2$ with $r_{n-1} = 1$.

Result: $f_{r,P}(D_Q) \leftarrow f$

1 $R \leftarrow P, f \leftarrow 1$

2 **for** $i = n - 2$ *down to* 0 **do**

3 $\quad$ Compute the line function $\ell_{R,R}$

4 $\quad$ $R \leftarrow [2]R$

5 $\quad$ Compute the line function v_R

6 $\quad$ $f \leftarrow f^2 \times \frac{\ell_{R,R}}{v_R}(D_Q)$

7 $\quad$ **if** $r_i = 1$ **then**

8 $\quad\quad$ computer the line function $\ell_{R,P}$

9 $\quad\quad$ $R \leftarrow R + P$

10 $\quad\quad$ compute the line function v_R

11 $\quad\quad$ $f \leftarrow f^2 \times \frac{\ell_{R,P}}{v_R}(D_Q)$

12 **return** f

- Steps 3 through 6 in Algorithm 2.1 can be referred to as a doubling stage, which is distinct from the doubling of elliptic curve points.
- Lines 7–12 of Algorithm 2.1 can be referred to as an addition stage, which is distinct from the addition operation performed on the points of an elliptic curve.
- Algorithm 2.1 computes from the most significant digit to the least significant digit (where r is a binary number of length n), i.e. from left to right.

2.4.8 The Tate Pairing

Let E be an elliptic curve with n points over a field $\mathbb{F}_q$. Let $\mathbb{G}$ be a cyclic subgroup of $E(\mathbb{F}_q)$ with order r and coprime r and q. Let k be the smallest positive integer for which $r | q^k - 1$. For succinctness, put $K = \mathbb{F}_{q^k}$. $K = \mathbb{F}_{q^k}$ is the smallest extension of $\mathbb{F}_q$ that contains the rth roots of unity, which is an equivalent description. Tate (or Tate–Lichtenbaum) pair is represented as:

$$e : E[r] \cap E(K) \times E(K)/rE(K) \to K^*/K^{*r} \qquad (2.23)$$

let f_P represent a rational function with divisor $(f_P) = (P)^r$. Choose an $R \in E(K)$ such that $R \neq P, P - Q, \mathcal{O}, -Q$. Then define

$$f(P, Q) = f_P(Q + R)/f_P(R) \qquad (2.24)$$

It can be shown that the above value is independent of the choice of R, and:

1. $f(aP, bQ) = e(P, Q)^{ab}$ for all P, Q, a, b.
2. $f(P, Q) = 1$ for all P if and only if $Q = \mathcal{O}$.
3. $f(P, Q) = 1$ for all Q if and only if $P = \mathcal{O}$.
4. $f(\Phi(P), \Phi(Q)) = f(P, Q)^q$ for all $P, Q \in E[r]$, where Φ denotes the Frobenius map.

The output of this pairing is some $x \in K^*$ that represents the coset xK^{*r}. To standardize the coset representative, we exponentiate the output of the Tate pairing by $(qk - 1)/r$, which can take a substantial amount of time. On the positive side, the second input to the Tate pairing is also a coset representative. This means it can be any point of $E(K)$ and may be of any order. (For example, if the order of a point Q is not a multiple of r then Q represents the coset $\mathcal{O} + rE(K)$. Otherwise Q represents some nonidentity element.) In contrast, the Weil pairing requires that the second input Q satisfy $rQ = \mathcal{O}$.

Algorithm 2.2 Miller's algorithm for Tate pairing $x = f_P(Q)$

Data:

Result:

1   $x \leftarrow 1$

2   $Z \leftarrow P$

3   **for** $i \leftarrow t - 1$ *down to* 0 **do**

4   Compute the line function $\ell_{R,R}$

5      $x \leftarrow x^2 \cdot T_Z(Q)/V_{2Z}(Q)$

6      $Z \leftarrow 2Z$ **if** $r_i = 1$ **then**

7         $x \leftarrow x \cdot LZ, P(Q)/V_{Z+P}(Q)$

8         $Z \leftarrow Z + P$

Algorithm 2.2 is used to compute $f_P(Q)$ where f_P has divisor $(P)^r$. We can view our current situation as a special case of the above with $R = O$. Thus define the intermediate functions f_k by

$$(f_k) = (P)^k/(kP) \qquad (2.25)$$

We have $(f_r) = (f_P)$. The following identities can be obtained simplifying earlier formulas using $R = \mathcal{O}$, but it is easy enough to check them directly. For example, we can show

$$(f_k) = \left(\prod_{i=1}^{k-1} \frac{L_{iP}}{V_{(i+1)P}} \right) \qquad (2.26)$$

via

$$(f_k) = \frac{(P)(P)}{(2P)} \cdot \frac{(P)(2P)}{(3P)} \cdots \frac{(P)(k-1)P)}{(kP)} \tag{2.27}$$

We could compute $f_r(Q)$ using this formula, but this is clearly impractical for large r. We find

$$(f_{2k}) = (f_k^2 T_{kP}/V_{2kP}) \tag{2.28}$$

which can be shown with direct calculation:

$$\frac{(P)^{2k}}{(2kP)} = \frac{(P)^{2k}}{(kP)^2} \cdot \frac{(kP)^2(-2KP)}{(2kP)(-2kP)} \tag{2.29}$$

and similarly we can show

$$(f_{k+1}) = (f_k L_{kP,P})/V_{(k+1)P} \tag{2.30}$$

leading to the following algorithm that computes $f_P(Q)$ given points P, Q (where P has order r). Let the binary representation of r be $r_t \cdots r_0$. When the algorithm finishes we have $x = f_r(Q)$ (and $Z = r_P = \mathcal{O}$).

2.5 Summary

This section includes preliminary results on group theory, ring theory, elliptic curves, divisors, and bilinear mappings. The theories described in this chapter are fundamental for understanding the creation of attribute-based encryption. To create an attribute-based encryption method, bilinear pairing is necessary. The cryptographic assumptions based on bilinear pairing will be exploited in Chapter 4, which will form the basic component of attribute-based encryption.

References

1 Galbraith, S.D., Paterson, K.G., and Smart, N.P. (2008). Pairings for cryptographers. *Discrete Applied Mathematics*, 156 (16), 3113–3121.

2 Koblitz, N. (1994). *A Course in Number Theory and Cryptography*, vol. 114. Springer Science & Business Media.

3 Yan, S.Y. (2013). *Computational Number Theory and Modern Cryptography*. Wiley.

4 Scheidler, R. (1993). Applications of algebraic number theory to cryptography. A Thesis Degree of Doctor of Philosophy. University of Manitoba.

5 Hoffstein, J., Pipher, J., Silverman, J.H., and Silverman, J.H. (2008). *An Introduction to Mathematical Cryptography*, vol. 1. New York: Springer.

6 (a) Demailly, J.P. (2012). *Analytic Methods in Algebraic Geometry*, vol. 1. Somerville, MA: International Press; (b) Shafarevich, I.R. and Reid, M. (1994). *Basic Algebraic Geometry*, vol. 2. Berlin: Springer-Verlag.

7 Cohen, H., Frey, G., Avanzi, R. et al. (Eds.). (2005). *Handbook of Elliptic and Hyperelliptic Curve Cryptography*. CRC Press.

8 Kraft, J.S. and Washington, L.C. (2018). *An Introduction to Number Theory with Cryptography*. Chapman and Hall/CRC.

3

Attribute-Based Encryption

3.1 Introduction

Public-key cryptography is one of the technologies that can be used to guarantee the privacy of data. Nonetheless, the majority of public-key cryptosystems, such as Rivest–Shamir–Adleman (RSA) [1] and ElGamal [2], have issues with the dissemination of keys, as they must be validated prior to use. There are numerous proposed solutions for this issue, such as the usage of certificate authorities (CA), which enable a user to produce a key-pair and then receive a certificate from a CA that certifies the possession of that key (see Figure 3.1 for a schematic overview of this particular setup). Identity-based encryption (IBE) [3] enables us to associate identities with a key-pair in a manner that makes authentication of keys straightforward. One key-pair is generated by a trusted third party, and all subsequent key-pairs are derived from it using the identities of the users. The identification could be anything, including a name, a social security number, or any combination of identifying characteristics that the individual desires to employ. The primary difference between IBE and traditional public-key cryptography is the encryption step: instead of looking up a public key that matches to an identity, which is then used to encrypt a message, we can utilize the identity to encrypt the message instantly. In other words, there is no need for a trusted third party during the encryption process. Instead, the trusted third party is transferred to the key distribution phase (see Figure 3.2 for a schematic overview of IBE). Now, this system is totally based on the concept of identification and provides us with a new means to send messages to other users. However, we can also envision a scenario in which we do not wish to send messages to specific users, but rather to people who possess specific traits. For instance, we may want to send a message to everyone who lives on the same street, or to all computer science students, or to anyone else with a more specific interest. One approach to accomplish this would be to "simply" search up the identities of all of these users and then send each one a message encrypted with their corresponding public key. However, this presents a number of difficulties, such as locating all of these identities.

In 2005, Sahai and Waters [2] developed the first attribute-based encryption (ABE) concept, Fuzzy IBE, which was a revolutionary variation of the ABE approach. In an IBE system, each ciphertext and secret key is associated with only one attribute (identity). In contrast, in an ABE system, each ciphertext and secret key is connected with a collection of descriptive attributes. The fuzzy IBE is generally referred to as the basic ABE scheme because of its fundamental and descriptive algorithms. The basic ABE allows a user to encrypt data by specifying a set of attributes S, with the guarantee that the ciphertext can be decrypted by users whose secret keys share the constraints $|S \cup S'| \geq d$, where d is a threshold value set by a trusted key authority during the system setup phase and S' is a set of attributes a user required to decrypt a ciphertext.

Attribute-based Encryption (ABE): Foundations and Applications within Blockchain and Cloud Environments, First Edition.
Qi Xia, Jianbin Gao, Isaac Amankona Obiri, Kwame Omono Asamoah, and Daniel Adu Worae.

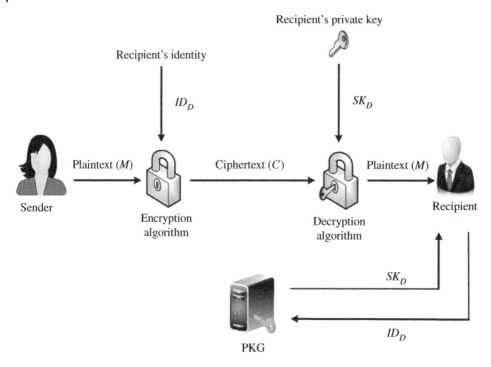

Figure 3.1 Identity-based cryptography.

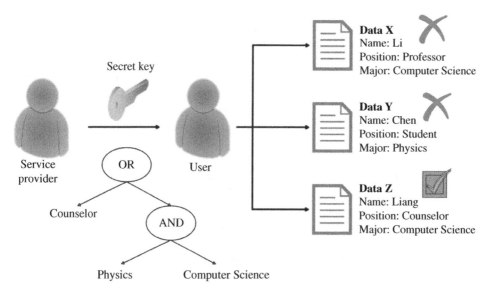

Figure 3.2 Key policy attribute-based encryption scheme.

ABE is a type of public-key encryption in which both the ciphertext and the user's secret key are created from attributes (e.g. the school a student attends, or the department a student is affiliated with). In such a system, ciphertext can only be decrypted if the qualities of the user key match those of the ciphertext [1]. The concept behind ABE is that we can specify access controls for attributes using Boolean expressions. Thus, if we wish to enforce the following policy: the user must be a nurse or doctor student from Africa, we may express this with the following Boolean expression: Student

AND Africa AND Nurse OR Doctor (nurse OR doctor). Note that this is not an exclusive representation, since it may also be expressed as (Student AND Africa AND nurse) OR (Student AND Africa AND Doctor) or any other representation that can be rewritten as the same formula. The question at hand is how to integrate the policy. First, the access policy (which is represented by a Boolean formula) is converted to an appropriate representation of an access structure. Then, the access structure can be incorporated into the encryption system by imposing it either on the secret keys or on the ciphertexts. In the first scenario, the access structure is incorporated into the key generation process, but in the second case, it is incorporated into the encryption algorithm. Because in the first case, the policy is imposed on the secret keys by the key issuer, this type of ABE is also known as key-policy attribute-based encryption (KP-ABE) (see Figure 3.9), while the second type of ABE imposes the policies on the ciphertexts by the encryptor and is therefore known as ciphertext-policy attribute-based encryption (CP-ABE) (see Figure 3.10). Before providing the formal definitions of the ABE scheme: KP-ABE and CP-ABE, we will describe the fundamental components of ABE.

3.2 Basic Components of ABE Construction

This section provides the components such as secret-sharing schemes and access structures needed for the construction of ABE schemes.

3.2.1 Secret-Sharing Schemes

Secret sharing (alternatively referred to as "secret splitting") is a term that refers to techniques for dividing a secret among a group of individuals, each of whom is assigned a share of the secret. The secret can be recovered only if a sufficient number of shares of various types are merged; individual shares are useless on their own. Adi Shamir and George Blakley separately devised secret sharing in 1979 [4–7]. Figure 3.3 illustrates an access structure that employs secret sharing and access policies to regulate access among three entities: Li, Chen, and Liang. The embedded policy in the ABE scheme is represented by the logical expression "(counselor or (physics and computer science))". This policy explicitly outlines the conditions for granting legitimate access to decrypt the plaintext. To successfully decrypt the ciphertext and access the plaintext, a user must possess either the "counselor" attribute or both the "physics" and "computer science" attributes. Now, let us consider the scenario where Liang seeks to access the encrypted data. Liang has the necessary

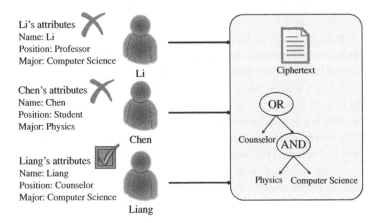

Figure 3.3 Ciphertext policy attribute-based encryption scheme.

attribute set, possessing the "counselor" attribute. Consequently, he fulfills the access structure specified in the embedded policy. As a result, Liang can employ his secret shares to successfully decrypt the ciphertext and gain access to the plaintext.

In the context of secret-sharing arrangements, the ABE scheme involves a dealer and n players. The dealer distributes a portion/shadow/share of the secret to each player, but the players cannot reconstruct the secret from their shares unless certain criteria are met. The dealer does this by allocating shares to each player in such a way that any group of t or more players can reconstruct the secret collectively, but no group of less than t players can. This type of system is referred to as a (t, n)-threshold scheme (sometimes written as a (n, t)-threshold scheme).

The secret-sharing scheme (SSS) is a concept that makes it easier for multiple participants to take authorized actions. Consider the following problem: 11 scientists are working on a secret project and want to lock the records in a cabinet so that only 6 or more scientists can open them. How many locks are needed, and how many keys does each scientist need to carry?

The solution is 462 locks and 252 keys per scientist. Clearly, this is not feasible. Consider this more plausible scenario: Software developers typically sign their software with an RSA secret key to verify its legitimacy. However, this can be inconvenient if there are multiple senior developers who need to be able to sign releases. One solution is to give each senior developer a copy of the key, but this can be easily abused. Another solution is to create multiple keys and require all of them to be used to sign each release. This ensures the software's legitimacy, but it is still inconvenient. A better solution is to use a secret sharing scheme (SSS). SSS allows a secret key to be divided into multiple shares, such that any k out of n shares can be used to reconstruct the secret key. This means that the secret key can be distributed to n senior developers, and any k of them can sign releases. This eliminates the inconvenience of having to give each senior developer a copy of the key, and it also makes it more difficult for the key to be abused. Additionally, SSS allows for dropouts. If a senior developer leaves the company, their share of the secret key can be destroyed, and the remaining shares can still be used to sign releases. This ensures that the software's legitimacy is not compromised even if a senior developer leaves.

Secret-sharing methods are perfect for keeping highly sensitive and critical information secret. Examples include encryption keys, missile launch codes, and bank account numbers. Each of these bits of information must be kept extremely confidential, as their disclosure might be catastrophic; nonetheless, they must not be lost. Traditional encryption techniques are unsuitable for providing both high degrees of confidentiality and reliability. This is because, when storing the encryption key, one must decide whether to store a single copy in a single location for maximum secrecy or numerous copies in separate locations for increased reliability. Increasing the key's dependability by storing numerous copies compromises confidentiality by introducing extra attack vectors; there are more chances for a copy to slip into the wrong hands. A secret-sharing method solves this problem because it allows for high level of confidentiality and reliability to be achieved.

Secret sharing allows someone who has less than the required number of shares to possess as much knowledge as someone who has no shares. The practice of secret sharing is considered to have been invented independently by both Shamir and Blackley in 1979. Secret sharing is also able to increase the redundancy of keys. If a key is lost, secret sharing allows all participants in a party to come together to reconstruct the secret, or in this case, the key. Secret sharing is considered information sharing that is theoretically secure. This means that it is as secure as the information.

Numerous secret-sharing schemes are assumed to be information-theoretically secure, while others trade up unconditional security for increased efficiency by maintaining a level of security comparable to that of other common cryptographic primitives. For example, using 128-bit entropy in secret share construction, each share would be considered sufficient to defeat any conceivable attacker in the contemporary period with a brute force attack with an average size of 2^{127}. All approaches for unconditionally secure secret sharing have limitations:

1. Each component of the secret must be at least equal in value to the secret's entire value. This result is based on information theory but is understandable intuitively. No information regarding the secret can be determined based on the t-1 shares. As a result, the final share must have exactly the same information as the secret. At times, this restriction can be overcome by compressing the secret prior to its release. This is not always achievable, as many secrets (for example, keys) appear to be high-quality random data and are therefore difficult to compress.

2. All techniques for secret information exchange rely on random bits. $t-1$ random bits are required to distribute a one-bit secret to t individuals. To disperse a secret of any length b bits, it is necessary to have $(t-1) \times b$ bits of entropy.

Definition 3.1 (*Secret-sharing scheme*). The algorithms of secret-sharing scheme are as follows:

1. **Share**: a randomized algorithm that accepts a message $m \in M$ as input and returns a sequence of shares $s = (s_1, \ldots, s_n)$.

2. **Reconstruct**: a deterministic algorithm that accepts an input collection of t or more shares and returns the message m.

M denotes the scheme's message space, while t denotes the threshold. The distribution of a secret m among n parties as s_i, with the ability of t parties to pool their shares together to reconstruct the secret, is depicted in Figure 3.4

3.2.2 Polynomial Interpolation

You are probably aware of the fact that a line is formed by the intersection of two points (in Euclidean geometry). In addition, it is true that three points determine a parabola, and so on and so forth. The next Shamir secret-sharing scheme we will explore is based on the following principle: $t+1$ points determine a unique degree-t polynomial.

A word on terminology: A degree-t polynomial is one that may be expressed as $f(x) = \sum_{i=0}^{t} f_i X^i$. Because we allow the leading coefficient f_t to be zero, it would be more technically correct to say that the degree of f is at most t. For the sake of simplicity, we will refer to "degree-t" as "degree at most t."

3.2.2.1 Polynomials Over the Reals

Let $(x_1, y_1), \ldots, (x_t + 1, y_t + 1) \subseteq \mathbb{R}^2$ denote a set of points with distinct x_i values. Then, for all i, there is a unique degree-t polynomial f with real coefficients that satisfies $y_i = f(x_i)$.

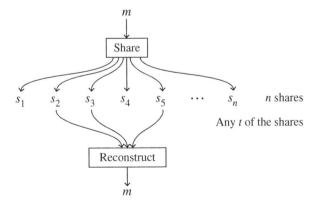

Figure 3.4 Secrets sharing of a secret m among n parties.

To start, consider the following polynomial:

$$\ell_1(x) = \frac{(\mathbf{x} - x_2)(\mathbf{x} - x_3)\dots(\mathbf{x} - x_{t+1})}{(x_1 - x_2)(x_1 - x_3)\dots(x_1 - x_{t+1})} \tag{3.1}$$

The notation has the potential to be confusing. ℓ_1 is a polynomial containing the formal variable $\mathbf{x}$ as one of its variables (written in bold). The x_i values that are not bold are merely simple numbers (scalars). As a result, ℓ_1 numerator is a degree-t polynomial in $\mathbf{x}$. We are not dividing by zero because the denominator is merely a scalar, and all of the x_i's are distinct. In general, ℓ_1 is a degree-t polynomial.

What happens when we evaluate ℓ_1 at one of the special x_i values? When $\ell_1(x_1)$ is evaluated, the numerator and denominator are equal, and thus $\ell_1(x_1) = 1$. Evaluating' $\ell_1(x_i)$ for $i \neq 1$ results in a numerator term $(x_i - x_i)$ and thus $\ell_1(x_i) = 0$.

Naturally, ℓ_1 can be evaluated at any point (not just the special points $x_1, \dots, x_{t+1}$), but we are unconcerned with what occurs in those instances. Other polynomials ℓ_j can be defined similarly.

$$\ell_j(x) = \frac{(\mathbf{x} - x_2)(\mathbf{x} - x_3)\dots(\mathbf{x} - x_{t+1})}{(x_j - x_2)(x_j - x_3)\dots(x_j - x_{t+1})} \tag{3.2}$$

The pattern is that the numerator lacks the term $(\mathbf{x} - x_j)$ and the denominator lacks the term $(x_j - x_j)$, as we do not want a zero in the denominator. LaGrange polynomials are polynomials of this type. They are all polynomials of degree-t and possess the property:

$$\ell_j(x_i) = \begin{cases} 1 \text{ if } i = j, \\ 0 \text{ if } i \neq j \end{cases}$$

To illustrate this point, take the following polynomial:

$$f(\mathbf{x}) = y_1\ell_1(\mathbf{x}) + y_2\ell_2(\mathbf{x}) + \dots + y_{t+1}\ell_{t+1}(\mathbf{x})$$

The f is a degree-t polynomial as it is the sum of degree-t polynomials (again, the y_i values are just scalars). What happens when f is evaluated on one of the special x_i values? Since $\ell_j(x_i) = 0$ for $j \neq i$, we get:

$$\begin{aligned} f(x_i) &= y_1\ell_1(x_i) + y_2\ell_2(x_i) + \dots + y_{t+1}\ell_{t+1}(x_i) \\ &= y_1 \cdot 0 + \dots + y_i \cdot 1 + \dots + y_{t+1} \dots 0 \\ &= y_i \end{aligned}$$

Therefore, $f(x_i) = y_i$ for every x_i as wanted. This demonstrates that there is some degree-t polynomial with this property. Now let's argue that this f is unique. Suppose there are two degree-t polynomials f and f_0 such that $f(x_i) = f_0(x_i) = y_i$ for $i \in \{1, \dots, t+1\}$. Then the polynomial $g(x) = f(x) - f_0(x)$ also is degree-t, and it satisfies $g(x_i) = 0$ for all i. In other words, each x_i is a root of g, so g has at least $t + 1$ roots. But the only degree-t polynomial with $t + 1$ roots is the identically zero polynomial $g(x) = 0$. If $g(x) = 0$ then $f = f0$. In other words, any degree-d polynomial f_0 that satisfies $f_0(x_i) = y_i$ must be equal to f. So f is the unique polynomial with this property.

Example 3.1 Determine the degree-3 polynomial that passes through the points (2,5)(4,12) (6,8)(7,15):

i	1	2	3	4
x_i	2	4	6	7
y_i	5	12	8	15

To begin, let us construct the LaGrange polynomials:

$$\ell_1(x) = \frac{(x - x_2)(x - x_3)(x - x_4)}{(x_1 - x_2)(x_1 - x_3)(x_1 - x_4)} = \frac{(x - 4)(x - 6)(x - 7)}{(2 - 4)(2 - 6)(2 - 7)} = \frac{x^3 - 17x^2 + 94x - 168}{-40}$$

$$\ell_2(x) = \frac{(x - x_1)(x - x_3)(x - x_4)}{(x_2 - x_1)(x_2 - x_3)(x_2 - x_4)} = \frac{(x - 2)(x - 6)(x - 7)}{(4 - 2)(4 - 6)(4 - 7)} = \frac{x^3 - 15x^2 + 68x - 84}{12}$$

$$\ell_3(x) = \frac{(x - x_1)(x - x_2)(x - x_4)}{(x_3 - x_1)(x_3 - x_2)(x_3 - x_4)} = \frac{(x - 2)(x - 4)(x - 7)}{(6 - 2)(6 - 4)(6 - 7)} = \frac{x^3 - 13x^2 + 50x - 56}{-8}$$

$$\ell_4(x) = \frac{(x - x_1)(x - x_2)(x - x_3)}{(x_4 - x_1)(x_4 - x_2)(x_4 - x_3)} = \frac{(x - 2)(x - 4)(x - 6)}{(7 - 2)(7 - 4)(7 - 6)} = \frac{x^3 - 12x^2 + 44x - 48}{15}$$

Take note of the following as a sanity check:

$$\ell_1(2) = \frac{2^3 - 17 \cdot 2^2 + 94 \cdot 2 - 168}{-40} = \frac{-40}{-40} = 1$$

$$\ell_1(4) = \frac{4^3 - 17 \cdot 4^2 + 94 \cdot 4 - 168}{-40} = \frac{0}{-40} = 1$$

Our desired polynomial is

$$f(x) = y_1 \cdot \ell_1(x) + y_2 \cdot \ell_2(x) + y_3 \cdot \ell_3(x) + y_4 \cdot \ell_4(x)$$
$$= 5 \cdot \ell_1(x) + 12 \cdot \ell_2(x) + 8 \cdot \ell_3(x) + 15 \cdot \ell_4(x)$$
$$= 0.875 \cdot x^3 - 11.875 \cdot x^2 + 50.25 \cdot x - 55$$

Using the function f, it is possible to derive the correct values of y, as illustrated in Figure 3.5. The values can be derived as follows:

$$f(x_1) = f(2) = 0.875 \cdot 2^3 - 11.875 \cdot 2^2 + 50.25 \cdot 2 - 55 = 5$$

$$f(x_2) = f(4) = 0.875 \cdot 4^3 - 11.875 \cdot 4^2 + 50.25 \cdot 4 - 55 = 12$$

$$f(x_3) = f(6) = 0.875 \cdot 6^3 - 11.875 \cdot 6^2 + 50.25 \cdot 6 - 55 = 8$$

$$f(x_4) = f(7) = 0.875 \cdot 7^3 - 11.875 \cdot 7^2 + 50.25 \cdot 7 - 55 = 15$$

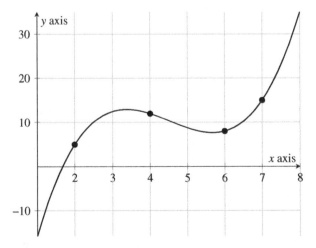

Figure 3.5 Graph showing equation $f(x) = 0.875 \cdot x^3 - 11.875 \cdot x^2 + 50.25 \cdot x - 55$.

3.2.2.2 Polynomials Modulus *P*

We employed a polynomial-based secret-sharing method in which the share algorithm must find a polynomial with uniformly random coefficients. Due to the impossibility of obtaining a uniform distribution over the real numbers, we must consider polynomials with coefficients in $\mathbb{Z}_p$ instead. When working modulo p, the $t + 1$ points define a distinct degree-t polynomial. We can generalize the observation that $t + 1$ points define a degree-t polynomial in a unique way. It turns out that for every k points, there are exactly p^{t+1-k} polynomials of degree-t that hit those points in mod p. Take note that for $k = t + 1$, there is only a single polynomial that hits the points.

Theorem 3.1 *Let* $\mathcal{P} = \{(x_1, y_1), \ldots, (x_{t+1}, y_{t+1})\} \subseteq (\mathbb{Z}_p)^2$ *be a set of points whose* x_i *values are distinct. Let t satisfy* $k \leq t + 1$ *and* $p > t$. *Then the number of degree-t polynomials f with coefficients in* $\mathbb{Z}_p$ *that satisfy the condition* $y_i \approx_p f(x_i)$ *for all i is exactly p.*

Proof: The proof is based on induction with respect to the value $t + 1 - k$. When $t + 1 - k = 0$, the base case is true. Then $k = t + 1$ distinct points exist. Due to the fact that $p^{t+1-k} = p^0$, and $p^0 = 1$, the base case is true. In the inductive case, $\mathcal{P}$ contains $k \leq t$ points. Assume that $x \in \mathbb{Z}_p$ is not one of the x_i's. When evaluated at x^*, every polynomial must produce some value. Therefore,

[# of degree-t polynomials passing through points in $\mathcal{P}$]

$$= \sum_{y^* \in \mathbb{Z}_p} [\text{\# of degree-}t \text{ polynomials passing through points in } \mathcal{P} \cup \{(x^*, y^*)\}]$$

$$\overset{(*)}{=} \sum_{y^* \in \mathbb{Z}_p} p^{t+1-(k+1)}$$

$$= p \cdot (p^{t+1-(k+1)}) = p^{t+1-k}$$

The equality denoted by (*) derives from the inductive hypothesis, as each term consists of a polynomial passing through a given set of $k + 1$ points with distinct x-coordinates. □

What does a "polynomial mod p" look like? Consider the previous equation $f(\mathbf{x}) = 0.875 \cdot \mathbf{x}^3 - 11.875 \cdot \mathbf{x}^2 + 50.25 \cdot \mathbf{x} - 55$ in mod 17 as $f(\mathbf{x}) = 3 \cdot \mathbf{x}^3 + 3 \cdot \mathbf{x}^2 + 12 \cdot \mathbf{x} + 13$. Hence, we have

$$f(x_1) = f(2) = 3 \cdot 2^3 + 3 \cdot 2^2 + 12 \cdot 2 + 13 \mod 17 = 5$$
$$f(x_2) = f(4) = 3 \cdot 4^3 + 3 \cdot 4^2 + 12 \cdot 4 + 13 \mod 17 = 12$$
$$f(x_3) = f(6) = 3 \cdot 6^3 + 3 \cdot 6^2 + 12 \cdot 6 + 13 \mod 17 = 8$$
$$f(x_4) = f(7) = 3 \cdot 7^3 + 3 \cdot 7^2 + 12 \cdot 7 + 13 \mod 17 = 15$$

When plot the equation $f(\mathbf{x}) = 0.875 \cdot \mathbf{x}^3 - 11.875 \cdot \mathbf{x}^2 + 50.25 \cdot \mathbf{x} - 55$ over the real number (see Figure 3.5), we get a familiar parabola. However, when the equivalent equation in mod 17 in Figure 3.6, there is a "wrap around" each time the polynomial crosses over a multiple of 17 along the y-axis.

Geometrically, an attacker might leverage knowledge of the polynomial's order over real numbers to get insight into the paths it may follow between known points. This significantly decreases the number of possible values for unknown points, as they must lie on a smooth curve. The problem is addressed using finite field arithmetic. A field of size p is used. The graph in Figure 3.6 depicts a polynomial curve over a finite field 17, in contrast to the usual smooth curve it appears very disorganized and disjointed.

Since everyone who receives a point also has to know the value of p, it may be considered to be publicly known. Therefore, one should select a value for p that is not too low.

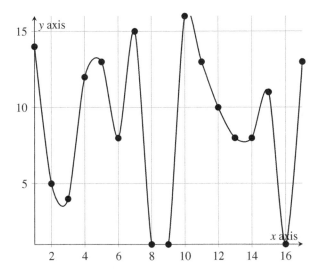

Figure 3.6 Graph showing equation $f(\mathbf{x}) = 3 \cdot \mathbf{x}^3 + 3 \cdot \mathbf{x}^2 + 12 \cdot \mathbf{x} + 13 \mod 17$.

3.2.3 Shamir Secret Sharing

One of the difficulties in constructing a secret-sharing scheme is ensuring that the secret can be recovered by any authorized group of users. As demonstrated previously, any $t + 1$ points on a degree-t polynomial are sufficient to uniquely reconstruct it. Thus, an obvious way to implement secret sharing is to make each user's share a point on a polynomial. Formally, Shamir's secret-sharing scheme is defined as follows:

Definition 3.2 **(Shamir's t, n)-secret-sharing scheme [8]).** Consider that D and $P_1, \dots, P_n$ represent a dealer and participants, respectively. Assume that $t \in [1, n]$ is the threshold, indicating that at least t participants is required to recover the secret s. The secret s is an element in Z_p^*, where p is a prime greater than n, such that each participant can be uniquely represented in $\mathbb{Z}_p$. Then s is shared as follows:

1. **Share**: Dealer D chooses a random polynomial of degree t_1 over $\mathbb{Z}_p$ with coefficients in $\mathbb{Z}_p$, i.e. $f(\mathbf{x}) = \sum_{j=1}^{t-1} x_0 + y_j \mathbf{x}^j$, where $x_0 = s$ and $x_i \in_R \mathbb{Z}_p$. Each participant P_i is allotted an individual share $(i, f(i))$.
2. **Reconstruct**: Using Lagrange interpolation, any group of t participants $Q \subseteq [1, n]$ can reconstruct the secret s by Lagrange interpolation, i.e.

$$s = \sum_{i \in Q} \ell_i y_i \text{ such that } \ell_i = \prod_{j \in Q/\{i\}} \frac{j}{j - i} \tag{3.3}$$

Notably, this method of secret sharing is perfect because any set of participants $Q \in [1, n]$ such that $|Q| < t$ attempts to retrieve the secret would fail and, more importantly, they would be unable to learn anything about the secret.

Example 3.2 Here is a toy example of 3-out-of-5 Shamir secret sharing over $\mathbb{Z}_{11}$. Consider the secret being shared is $x_0 = 7 \in \mathbb{Z}_{11}$. The share algorithm selects a random degree polynomial with constant coefficient 7. Suppose the rest of the two coefficients are selected as $f_1 = 4$ and $f_2 = 1$, the resultant polynomial is:

$$f(\mathbf{x}) = x^2 + 4x + 7 \qquad (3.4)$$

The polynomial of Eq. (3.4) is illustrated in Figure 3.7. For each user $i \in \{1, \dots, 5\}$, the distribution of the share is $(i, f(i)) \mod 11$. The share is as follows (Table 3.1): With the given three points: (1,1)(2,8)(3,6), the secret is reconstructed as:

$$7 = f(0) = f(1) \cdot \ell_1 + f(2) \cdot \ell_2 + f(3) \cdot \ell_3 = 3 + 8 \cdot 8 + 6$$

where $\ell_1 = \frac{2 \cdot 3}{(1-2)(1-3)} = 3, \ell_2 = \frac{1 \cdot 3}{(2-1)(2-3)} = 8$ and $\ell_2 = \frac{2 \cdot 1}{(3-1)(3-2)} = 1$.

Definition 3.3 Linear Secret-Sharing Schemes (LSSS) [9]) A secret-sharing scheme over a set of participants P is called linear (over $\mathbb{Z}_p$)

1. The shares for each participant form a vector over $\mathbb{Z}_p$.
2. There exists an $n_1 \times n_2$ matrix $\mathbf{M}$ called the share-generating matrix. For all $i \in [1, n_1]$, the i-th row of $\mathbf{M}$ is denoted by $\mathbf{M}_i$, and we define ρ to be the function that maps rows to a subset of participants P. Let $v = (s, v_2, \dots, v_{n_2})$ be a column vector, where $s \in \mathbb{Z}_p$ represents the secret to

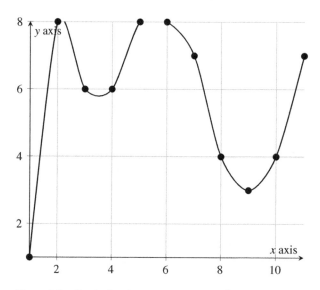

Figure 3.7 Graph showing equation $f(\mathbf{x}) = x^2 + 4x + 7 \mod 11$.

Table 3.1 Secret sharing.

User(i)	f_i	Share $(i, f_i \mod 11)$
1	$f(1) = 12$	(1,1)
2	$f(2) = 19$	(2,8)
3	$f(3) = 28$	(3,6)
4	$f(4) = 39$	(4,6)
5	$f(5) = 52$	(5,8)

be shared, and $v_2, \ldots, v_{n_2} \in_R \mathbb{Z}_p$ are chosen uniformly at random, then $\mathbf{M}v$ is the vector of n_1 shares of the secret s. The i-th element of $\mathbf{M}v$, denoted as $(\mathbf{M}v)_i$, is the share that is assigned to participant $\rho(i)$.

Remark 3.1 Take into account that n_1 denotes the number of individuals who participate in the sharing, and that there is no requirement for a threshold of participants in Shamir's SSS. As a result, we can express each linear threshold secret-sharing scheme (for example, the SSS proposed by Shamir) in terms of a share-generating matrix, but not every linear threshold secret-sharing scheme that can be represented as a share-generating matrix is a threshold scheme. Section 2.6 will introduce the concept of access structures, which will be used to describe this in greater detail.

3.2.4 Verifiable Secret Sharing (VSS)

Despite the fact that secret-sharing schemes are a useful tool, they do rely on the honesty of those who participate in the protocol to some degree. An unapproved set of participants cannot extract the secret, as demonstrated above, and this is a security feature that we would like to implement. On the other hand, we might want the protocol's participants to be honest in the sense that the share they use to obtain the secret is the same share they received during distribution, not a modified version.

VSS is characterized by the dealer providing some additional information about a participant's share in the open, so that other participants can verify during the reconstruction step whether the share that a participant provides is actually identical to the share that was received during the distribution. It is also known as the verification key because it contains additional information.

Using verification keys, Feldman [10] improves on Shamir's secret-sharing scheme, allowing the shares provided by participants during the reconstruction process to be independently verified by the system. Consider the following definition of the scheme.

We will talk about attribute-based encryption soon. Secret sharing is an interesting cryptographic primitive on its own, but it also serves as the foundation for other cryptographic primitives.

Definition 3.4 *(Access structure) [9].* Let $P = \{\rho_1, \rho_2, \ldots, \rho_n\}$ be a set of parties. A collection $\mathbb{A} \subseteq 2^P$ is monotone if $B \in \mathbb{A}$ and $B \subseteq C$ imply that $C \in \mathbb{A}$. An access structure (monotone access structure, respectively) is a collection of non-empty subsets of P. The sets in $\mathbb{A}$ are authorized sets, and the sets not in $\mathbb{A}$ are non-authorized sets.

Definition 3.5 *(Linear Secret-Sharing Scheme (LSSS)).* A linear secret-sharing scheme is made of two algorithms, thus share and reconstruct. To distribute a secret $s \in \mathbb{Z}_p$ among n parties, the share algorithm sets $r_1 = s$, randomly selects $(r_1, r_2, \ldots, r_t) \in \mathbb{Z}_p^t$ and computes $p(i) = \sum_{k=1}^t r_k i^k$ for all $1 \leq i \geq n$. The shadows or shares $p(i) = \lambda_i$ are distributed to the n distinct parties. Since the secret is the constant term $s = r_1 = p(1)$, the reconstruct algorithm recovers the secret from any t shares λ_i, for an access set $S \in \mathbb{A}$ and $I = \{i \mid p(i) \in S\}$, by computing a linear function of the shares as, $\sum_{i \in I} \omega_i \lambda_i = s$, where each constant $\omega_i = \prod_{j \in I, j \neq i} \dfrac{i}{j - i}$ can be obtained efficiently in the polynomial time [9].

3.2.4.1 Algorithm for Converting Access Structure Into LSSS Matrix
An access tree with AND, OR gates as interior nodes and attributes as leaf nodes could be used to represent a monotone access structure. Algorithm 3.1 shows how the Lewko–Waters conversion works.

Algorithm 3.1 The Lewko-Waters algorithm

Data: An access tree $T, c = 1$

Result: The associated LSSS matrix

1 **foreach** *each level of the tree T* **do**
2   **foreach** *node i in T* **do**
3   **if** *the parent node is an OR gate labeled by the vector v* **then**
4   Label the right child of i by vector $\leftarrow v$
5   Label the left child of i with vector $\leftarrow v$
6   **else**
7   Pad i's vector with 0 at the end (if required) to make it of length c Label the left child by vector $\leftarrow v||1$
8   Label the right child by vector $\leftarrow (0, \ldots, 0)|| - 1$, where $(0, \ldots, 0)$ denotes vector 0 of length c
9          $c \leftarrow c + 1$

3.2.4.2 Access Structure Example

In this example, we demonstrate how to convert a Boolean formula to an access tree and then from an access tree to an access structure expressed by an LSSS matrix.

Denote attributes by A_1, A_2, A_3, A_4, and A_5. The example Boolean formula is as follows $A_5 \wedge ((A_1 \wedge A_2) \vee (A_3 \wedge A_4))$. The access tree with "AND" and "OR" gate is shown in Figure 3.8. Each subset of the rows of matrix M includes $(1, 0, 0)$ in its span, if and only if the associated attributes satisfy the Boolean formula $A_5 \wedge ((A_1 \wedge A_2) \vee (A_3 \wedge A_4))$. The corresponding rows of the matrix will be $(1, 1, 0), (0, 1, 1)$, and $(0, 0, 1)$, respectively, if a user has attributes A_1, A_2, and A_5. When we combine these three vectors, we get $(1, 0, 0)$. These are the most important properties of an attribute-based encryption scheme, which means that only authorized users can recover the vector $(1, 0, 0)$. The recovered vector is created by a random vector $v = (s, r_1, r_2)$ that changes M to $M = M_v(s, 0, 0)$. The value s is used in the encryption scheme to hide the message.

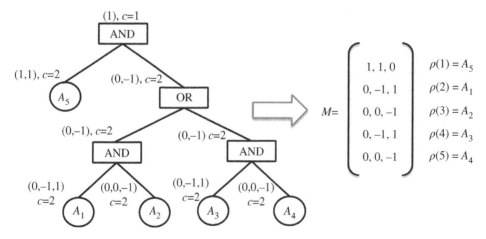

Figure 3.8 Access tree and LSSS matrix.

Definition 3.6 *(Monotone Span Programs (MSP))*. A MSP is a linear algebraic model for computing monotone functions. Let $\mathbb{F}$ be a finite field and $\{w_1, \ldots, w_n\}$ be a variables. A *MSP* is a tuple $\Delta = (M, \rho)$ where, $M \in F^{t \times n}$ is a matrix and $\rho : \{1, 2, \ldots, \rho_t\} = \{w_1, \ldots, w_n\}$ is labeling function. The MSP Δ actualizes the monotone access structure $\mathbb{A} \subset 2^P$ when $B \in \mathbb{A}$ if and only if n is spanned by the rows of the matrix M whose labels belong to B. The size of Δ is t, the number of rows in M. With regard to secret sharing, the size of the *MSP* is the total number of shares that were given to all parties in P [11].

3.2.4.3 Algorithms in Attribute-Based Encryption

Here, we consider the two main variants of ABE and demonstrate how they are used in encryption [12–14].

1. **Key-policy attribute-based encryption**: In a KP-ABE scheme, ciphertexts are labeled with a set of attributes, and a user's private key is associated to an access policy that determines which ciphertexts this user is allowed to decrypt [15].

   Definition 3.7 *(KP-ABE definition)*. Under standard definition, a key-policy attribute-based encryption scheme is a quintuple algorithm (**setup, Enc, KeyGen, Dec**):
   - **Setup** $(1^\lambda) \to (msk, pp)$: It takes a security parameter 1^λ and returns a master secret key *msk* and public parameters *pp*
   - **Enc** $(m, pp, S\}) \to ct$: It takes message *m*, public parameters *pp*, and set of attributes *S*. It outputs the ciphertext *ct*
   - **KeyGen** $(pp, msk, \mathbb{A}) \to sk_{\mathbb{A}}$: It takes public parameters *pp*, master secret key *msk*, and an access structure $\mathbb{A}$. It output a secret key $sk_{\mathbb{A}}$.
   - **Dec** (pp, ct, sk): It takes public parameters *pp*, ciphertext *ct*, and secret key *sk* and returns a message *m* or $\perp$

   Correctness: KP-ABE construction is correct if it meets the following requirements. With a given ciphertext and a secret key, if the ciphertext attributes set match the key's access structure, then for any $m \in m$, we have:

   $$\left[m = m^* \left| \begin{array}{l} pp, msk \leftarrow \textbf{Setup}(1^\lambda, \mathcal{U}) \\ ct \leftarrow \textbf{Enc}(pp, m, S) \\ sk \leftarrow \textbf{KeyGen}(pp, msk, \mathbb{A}) \\ m^* \leftarrow \textbf{Dec}(pp, ct, sk) \end{array} \right. \right]$$

   In the KP-ABE cryptographic system, as shown in Figure 3.9, if Alice wants to send a message to Bob, she must encrypt the data with Bob's attributes. Because Bob's secret key is linked to the access structure, if the set of attributes embedded in the ciphertext matches the access structure associated with Bob's secret key, Bob will be able to decrypt the message successfully.

2. **Ciphertext policy attribute-based encryption**: In a CP-ABE scheme, a user's secret key is labeled with a set of attributes, and a ciphertext is associated to an access policy that determines which user is allowed to decrypt [8].

   Definition 3.8 *(CP-ABE definition)*. Under standard definition, a CP-ABE scheme is a quintuple algorithm (**setup, Enc, KeyGen, Dec**):
   - **Setup** $(1^\lambda) \to (msk, pp)$: It takes a security parameter 1^λ and returns a master secret key *msk* and public parameters *pp*

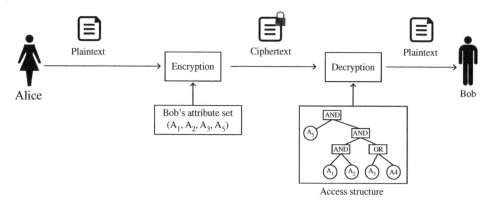

Figure 3.9 KP-ABE cryptographic system.

- **Enc** $(m, pp, \mathbb{A}\}) \rightarrow ct$: It takes message m, public parameters pp, and an access structure $\mathbb{A}$. It outputs the ciphertext ct
- **KeyGen** $(pp, msk, S) \rightarrow sk_{\mathbb{A}}$: It takes public parameters pp, master secret key msk, and a set of attributes S. It output a secret key sk_S.
- **Dec** (pp, ct, sk): It takes public parameters pp, ciphertext ct, and secret key sk and returns a message m or $\perp$

Correctness: CP-ABE construction is correct if it meets the following requirements. With a given ciphertext and a secret key, if the ciphertext attributes set match the key's access structure, then for any $m \in$ m, we have:

$$
\begin{bmatrix}
 & & pp, msk \leftarrow \textbf{Setup}(1^{\lambda}) \\
 & & ct \leftarrow \textbf{Enc}(pp, m, \mathbb{A}) \\
m = m^* & sk \leftarrow \textbf{KeyGen}(pp, msk, S) \\
 & & m^* \leftarrow \textbf{Dec}(pp, ct, sk)
\end{bmatrix}
$$

In the CP-ABE cryptographic system, as shown in Figure 3.10, if Alice wants to send a message to Bob, she must encrypt the data with the access structure. Bob's secret key is linked to a set of attributes, so if the access structure embedded in the ciphertext satisfies the attributes in Bob's secret key, Bob will be able to decrypt the message successfully.

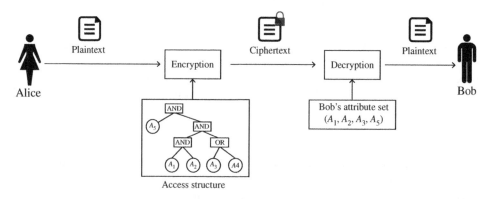

Figure 3.10 CP-ABE cryptographic system.

3.2.5 Properties of Attribute-Based Encryption

The following are some of the properties of an ABE scheme as illustrated by Shamir [3] and Qiao et al. [16]:

1. **Data confidentiality**: After data has been encrypted using an ABE scheme, only authorized parties can obtain access to or learn anything from it.
2. **Fine-grained access control**: When various private keys are provided for users, the system authority can restrict users' access privileges to specific data.
3. **User revocation**: Users' access to the data can be revoked at any moment. The user should not access the encrypted data once their key has been revoked.
4. **Resistance to collusion**: Colluded users cannot combine their secret keys to create a new set of secret keys with higher access permissions. When a group of malicious individuals pool their private keys to decrypt ciphertext that none of them has the authority to decrypt, the ABE scheme should protect the ciphertext.
5. **Scalability**: The system can continue to function effectively as the number of authorized users grows.
6. **Accountability**: This feature ensures that legitimate users' private keys are not shared with unauthorized users [17].

3.2.6 Prime Order Group

Definition 3.9 *(Bilinear Groups).* A generator $\mathcal{G}$ takes a secret parameter λ and returns a description of a group $\mathbb{G} \to (p, G_R, G_2, G_T, g_1, g_2, e)$, where p is a prime number, G_R, G_2, and G_T are cyclic groups of order p, $g_1 \in G_R$ and $g_2 \in G_2$ are the respective generators, and a bilinear map $e : G_R \times G_2 \to GT$, which has two properties.

- **(Bilinearity)**: $\forall g_1 \in G_R, g_2 \in G_2, z, y \in \mathbb{Z}_p, e(g_1^z, g_2^y) = e(g_1, g_2)^{zy}$
- **(Non-degeneracy)**: For generators g_1 and g_2, $e(g_1, g_2) \neq 1$

Notice that the map e is asymmetric since $e(g_1^z, g_2^y) \neq e(g_1^y, g_2^z)$. Thus, there is no existence of efficient isomorphisms between the groups G_R and G_2. We give the definition of the matrix Diffie–Hellman (MDDH) assumption on G_R as it has been specified in [18].

3.3 Cryptographic Hard Assumptions

Computational cryptography assumptions claim that a problem does not have an efficient solution. In this case, efficient refers to polynomial time. Until now, there has been no known method for essentially proving the unconditional hardness of any problem. Alternatively, cryptographers use reductions to relate the intractability of a complex problem to a computational hardness assumption in a formal way. Provably secure schemes are deduced using a number of computational assumptions. The following computational assumptions are used for the concrete construction of the schemes in this dissertation unless otherwise specified.

Definition 3.10 *(ECDL Assumption).* Let P and Q be a set of points on an elliptic curve (say E) over a finite field (say $\mathbb{F}_p$). An elliptic curve discrete logarithm (ECDL) problem is to find the value a given (P, aP), where $Q = aP \in \mathbb{G}_1$ and $a \in \mathbb{Z}_q^*$.

Definition 3.11 An elliptic curve computational Diffie–Hellman (ECDH) problem in $\mathbb{G}_1$ is to find abP given (P, aP, bP) where $a, b \in \mathbb{Z}_q^*$.

Definition 3.12 Given a random instance $(P, aP, bP, T) \in G_1$ for unknown $a, b \in \mathbb{Z}_q^*$, the decisional Diffie–Hellman (DDH) problem is to decide whether or not $T = abP \in G_1$. If $T = abP \in G_1$, then DDH oracle outputs **TRUE**, else the oracle outputs **FALSE**.

Definition 3.13 Computation Diffie–Hellman Assumption: Given the tripple (g, g^a, g^b), where a and b are random elements in $\in \mathbb{Z}_q^*$ and $g \in \mathbb{G}$, the hard assumption is to compute g^{ab}

Definition 3.14 *(q-bilinear Diffie–Hellman exponent (DHE) Assumption).* We say the (t, ϵ) q-DHE assumption holds in a group $\mathbb{G}$, if there is no probabilistic polynomial time (PPT) adversary who is able to compute $g^{\alpha^{q+1}}$ just given $(g, h, g^\alpha, g^{\alpha^2}, \dots, g^{\alpha^q}, g^{\alpha^{q+2}}, \dots, g^{\alpha^{2q}}) \in \mathbb{G}^{2q+1}$ running in time at most t with probability at least ϵ, where $\alpha \in \mathbb{Z}_p^*$ and $g \in \mathbb{G}$ are chosen independently and uniformly.

Definition 3.15 *(q-DBDHE Assumption).* Let $\mathbb{G}$ be a bilinear group of order p and e be a bilinear map such that $e : \mathbb{G} \times \mathbb{G} \to \mathbb{G}_T$. The q-DBDHE problem in $\mathbb{G}_T$ is stated as follows: Given the element $\overrightarrow{Y} = (g, h, g^\alpha, g^{\alpha^2}, \dots, g^{\alpha^q}, g^{\alpha^{q+2}}, \dots, g^{\alpha^{2q}}) \in \mathbb{G}^{2q+1}$ as input, where α is selected at random from $\mathbb{Z}_p^*$, it is difficult for a PPT algorithm $\mathcal{A}$ to distinguish $e(g, h)^{\alpha^{q+1}} \in \mathbb{G}_T$ from the random element $Z \in \mathbb{G}_T$. The Algorithm $\mathcal{A}$ can solve the q-DBDHE problem with the advantage ϵ if

$$|Pr[\mathcal{A}(\overrightarrow{Y}, T = e(g, h)^{\alpha^{q+1}}) = 0] - Pr[\mathcal{A}(\overrightarrow{Y}, T = Z) = 0]| \geq \epsilon.$$

We say that the q-DBDHE assumption holds if no PPT algorithm $\mathcal{A}$ has a non-negligible advantage in solving the q-DBDHE problem.

Definition 3.16 *(The Decisional Linear (DLIN) Assumption)* With a given group-generating algorithm $\mathcal{G}$, we define the following distribution:

$$\mathbb{G} := (G, p, G_T, e) \xleftarrow{R} \mathcal{G},$$

$$g, b, d \xleftarrow{R} G, a_1, a_2 \xleftarrow{R} \mathbb{Z}_p,$$

$$D := (\mathbb{G}, g, b, d, b^{a_1}, d^{a_2}),$$

$$T_0 = g^{a_1 + a_2}, T_1 \xleftarrow{R} G.$$

The advantage an algorithm $\mathcal{A}$ has in breaking this assumption is:

$$Adv_{\mathcal{G},\mathcal{A}}^{dL}(\lambda) := |P[\mathcal{A}(D, T_0) = 1] - P[\mathcal{A}(D, T_1) = 1]| \tag{3.5}$$

We declare that DLIN assumption is satisfied by $\mathcal{G}$, if for any probabilistic polynomial time (PPT) algorithm $\mathcal{A}$, $Adv_{\mathcal{G},\mathcal{A}}^{dL}(\lambda)$ is negligible.

Definition 3.17 *(The Three Party Diffie–Hellman (TPDH) Assumption).* With a given group-generating algorithm $\mathcal{G}$, we define the following distribution:

$$\mathbb{G} := (G, p, G_T, e) \xleftarrow{R} \mathcal{G},$$

$$g \xleftarrow{R} G, x, y, z, R \xleftarrow{R} \mathbb{Z}_p,$$

$$D := (\mathbb{G}, g, g^x, g^y, g^z),$$

$$T_0 = g^{xyz}, T_1 \xleftarrow{R} G.$$

The advantage an algorithm A has in breaking this assumption is:

$$Adv_{G,A}^{3DH}(\lambda) := |Pr[\mathcal{A}(D, T_0) = 1] - Pr[\mathcal{A}(D, T_1) = 1]| \tag{3.6}$$

We declare that TPDH assumption is satisfied by $\mathcal{G}$, if for any probabilistic polynomial time (PPT) algorithm $\mathcal{A}$, $Adv_{G,A}^{3DH}(\lambda)$ is negligible.

Definition 3.18 *(Dual Pairing Vector Spaces).* We follow the definition of double vector pairing spaces in [19, 20]. The individual elements of G will be considered as "vectors" of group elements. For $\mathbf{u} = (u_1, \dots, u_n) \in \mathbb{Z}_p^n$ and $g \in G$, we write $g^{\mathbf{u}}$ to represent the n-tuple of elements of G:

$$g^{\mathbf{u}} := (g^{\mathbf{u}_1}, \dots, g^{\mathbf{u}_n})$$

We can execute scalar product and exponentiation in the exponent. For any $a \in \mathbb{Z}_p$ and $\mathbf{u}, \mathbf{v} \in \mathbb{Z}_p$, we have:

$$g^{a\mathbf{u}} := (g^{au_1}, \dots, g^{au_n})$$
$$g^{\mathbf{u}+\mathbf{v}} := (g^{u_1+v_1}, \dots, g^{u_n+v_n})$$

We define a bilinear map *en* to represent the product of the component wise pairings:

$$en(g^{\mathbf{u}}, g^{\mathbf{v}}) := \prod_{i=1}^{n} e(g^{u_i}, g^{v_i}) = e(g, g)^{\mathbf{u}.\mathbf{v}}$$

Here, the dot product is executed using modulo p. We select two random sets of vectors: $\mathbb{B} := \{\mathbf{b}_1, \mathbf{b}_2, \dots, \mathbf{b}_n\}$ and $\mathbb{B}^* := \{\mathbf{b}_1^*, \mathbf{b}_2^*, \dots \mathbf{b}_n^*\}$ of $\mathbb{Z}_p^n$ subject to the following constraints:

1. The basis $\mathbb{B}$ with the family $\mathbf{b}_i$ and dual basis $\mathbb{B}^*$ with the family $\mathbf{b}_i^*$ are dual orthonormal when $\mathbf{b}_i.\mathbf{b}_j^* = 0 \mod p$, for $i = 1, \dots, n$, whenever $i \neq j$. Therefore the two vectors are perpendicular to each other. As a consequence, their dot product yields zero.
2. Conversely, $\mathbf{b}_i$ is orthonormal to $\mathbf{b}_j^*$ when they have the same index, i.e. $\mathbf{b}_i.\mathbf{b}_j^* = \delta$, for $i = 1, \dots, n$, whenever $i = j$, where δ denotes non-zero element of $\mathbb{Z}_p$. Here, it can be seen that we have abused the terminology "orthonormal," since δ is not constrained to 1.

Note that the random selection of sets $(\mathbb{B}, \mathbb{B}^*)$ from sets that satisfy requirements of dual orthonormality can be done via selecting a set of n vectors $\mathbb{B}$ at uniformly random from $\mathbb{Z}_p^n$ such that under high probability they are linearly independent, then determine each vector $\mathbb{B}^*$ from its orthonormality constraints. The randomly selection of dual orthonormal sets will be denoted as: $(\mathbb{B}, \mathbb{B}^*) \xleftarrow{R} Dual(\mathbb{Z}_p^n, \delta)$.

Definition 3.19 *(The Subspace Assumption)* With a given group-generating algorithm $\mathcal{G}$, we define the subspace assumption as:

$$\mathbb{G} := (G, p, G_T, e) \xleftarrow{R} \mathcal{G}, g \xleftarrow{R} G, \delta, \eta, \beta, \tau_1, \tau_2, \tau_3, \mu_1, \mu_2, \mu_3 \xleftarrow{R} \mathbb{Z}_p,$$

$$(\mathbb{B}_1, \mathbb{B}_1^*) \xleftarrow{R} Dual(\mathbb{Z}_p^{n_1}, \delta), \dots, (\mathbb{B}_m, \mathbb{B}_m^*) \xleftarrow{R} Dual(\mathbb{Z}_p^{nm}, \delta),$$

$$U_{1,i} := g^{\mu_1 \Upsilon_1 \mathbf{b}_{1,i} + \mu_2 \Upsilon_2 \mathbf{b}_{k_i+1,i} + \mu_3 \mathbf{b}_{2k_i+1,i}}, U_{2,i} := g^{\mu_1 \Upsilon_1 \mathbf{b}_{2,i} + \mu_2 \Upsilon_2 \mathbf{b}_{k_i+2,i} + \mu_3 \mathbf{b}_{2k_i+2,i}},$$

$$, \dots, U_{k_i,i} := g^{\mu_1 \Upsilon_1 \mathbf{b}_{k_i,i} + \mu_2 \Upsilon_2 \mathbf{b}_{2k_i,i} + \mu_3 \mathbf{b}_{3k_i,i}} \; \forall i \in [m],$$

$$V_{1,i} := g^{\tau_1 \Upsilon_1^* \eta \mathbf{b}_{1,i}^* + \tau_2 \Upsilon_2^* \beta \mathbf{b}_{k_i+1,i}^*}, V_{2,i} := g^{\tau_1 \Upsilon_1^* \eta \mathbf{b}_{2,i}^* + \tau_2 \Upsilon_2^* \beta \mathbf{b}_{k_i+2,i}^*}, \dots,$$

$$V_{k_i,i} := g^{\tau_1 \Upsilon_1^* \eta \mathbf{b}_{k_i,i}^* + \tau_2 \Upsilon_2^* \beta \mathbf{b}_{2k_i,i}^*} \ \forall i \in [m],$$

$$W_{1,i} := g^{\tau_1 \Upsilon_1^* \eta \mathbf{b}_{1,i}^* + \tau_2 \Upsilon_2^* \beta \mathbf{b}_{k_i+1,i}^* + \tau_3 \mathbf{b}_{2k_i+1,i}^*}, \ W_{2,i} := g^{\tau_1 \Upsilon_1^* \eta \mathbf{b}_{2,i}^* + \tau_2 \Upsilon_2^* \beta \mathbf{b}_{k_i+2,i}^* + \tau_3 \mathbf{b}_{2k_i+2,i}^*},$$

$$\ldots, W_{k_i,i} := g^{\tau_1 \Upsilon_1^* \eta \mathbf{b}_{k_i,i}^* + \tau_2 \Upsilon_2^* \beta \mathbf{b}_{2k_i,i}^* + \tau_3 \mathbf{b}_{3k_i,i}^*} \ \forall i \in [m],$$

$$D := (\mathbb{G}, g, \{g^{\mathbf{b}_{1,i}}, g^{\mathbf{b}_{2,i}}, \ldots, g^{\mathbf{b}_{2k_i,i}}, g^{\mathbf{b}_{3k_i+1,i}}, \ldots, g^{\mathbf{b}_{n_i,i}}, g^{\eta \mathbf{b}_{1,i}^*}, \ldots, g^{\eta \mathbf{b}_{k_i,i}^*}, g^{\beta \mathbf{b}_{k_i+1,i}^*}, \ldots,$$

$$g^{\beta \mathbf{b}_{2k_i,i}^*}, g^{\mathbf{b}_{2k_i+1,i}^*}, \ldots, g^{\mathbf{b}_{n_i,i}^*}, U_{1,i}, U_{2,i}, \ldots, U_{k_i,i}\}_{i=1}^m, \mu_3).$$

We assert that for any PPT algorithm $\mathcal{A}$ which return a value in $\{0,1\}$, is negligible in the security parameter λ according to Eq. (3.7).

$$Adv_{\mathcal{G},\mathcal{A}} := |Pr[\mathcal{A}(D, \{V_{1,i}, \ldots, V_{k_i,i}\}_{i=1}^m) = 1] - \quad Pr[\mathcal{A}(D, \{W_{1,i}, \ldots, W_{k_i,i}\}_{i=1}^m) = 1]| \quad (3.7)$$

The Subspace Assumption is the application of the DLIN Assumption with vectors. The proof of this assumption can be found in pages 37–38 [21].

Definition 3.20 *(MDDH$_{j,k}^\ell$ Assumption).* Let $k > j \geq 1$ and $\ell \geq 1$. We assert that the MDDH$_{j,k}^\ell$ assumption holds if for all probabilistic polynomial time (PPT) adversaries $\mathcal{A}$ has negligible *negl*(λ) advantage over the following distribution.

$$Adv_{\mathcal{A}}^{MDDH_{j,k}^\ell}(\lambda) := |Pr[\mathcal{A}(\mathbb{G}, [M]_1, [MS]_1) = 1] - Pr[\mathcal{A}(\mathbb{G}, [M]_1, [V]_1) = 1]| \quad (3.8)$$

where $M \xleftarrow{R} \mathbb{Z}_p^{k \times j}$, $S \xleftarrow{R} \mathbb{Z}_p^{j \times \ell}$ and $V = \xleftarrow{R} \mathbb{Z}_p^{k \times \ell}$.

The distribution of the MDDH assumption on G_2 can be defined in an analogous way. Escala et al. [23] demonstrated that

$$k - Lin \implies MDDH_{j,j+1}^1 \implies MDDH_{j,k}^\ell \ \forall \ell > j, m \geq 1 \quad (3.9)$$

with a tight security reduction (that is, $Adv_{\mathcal{A}}^{MDDH_{j,k}^\ell}(\lambda) = Adv_{\mathcal{A}}^{k-Lin}(\lambda)$). Succinctly, the MDDH assumption is a generalization of the k-Lin assumption, such that the k-Lin assumption is analogous to the MDDH$_{j,j+1}^1$ Assumption as shown in equation 3.9.

Definition 3.21 *(k-Lin assumption).* Let $k \geq 1$. We assert that the k-Lin assumption holds if for all PPT adversaries $\mathcal{A}$, has negligible *negl*(λ) advantage over the following distribution.

$$adv_{\mathcal{A}}^{k-Lin}(\lambda) := Adv_{\mathcal{A}}^{MDDH_{j,j+1}^1}(\lambda) \quad (3.10)$$

From now on, we will use MDDH$_j$ to represent MDDH$_{j,j+1}^1$. Finally, we indicate that the k-Lin assumption itself is a generalization, where putting $k = 1$ yields the Symmetric External Diffie–Hellman Assumption (SXDH), and putting $k = 2$ yields the standard Decisional Linear Assumption (DLIN).

3.3.1 Composite Order Bilinear Groups

Our scheme is based on composite order bilinear groups [21]. Let $\mathcal{G}$ be an algorithm that takes security parameter λ as input and returns a collection of output of bilinear group G such as $(p_1, p_2, p_3, G, G_T, e)$ where $p_1 p_2 p_3$ are distinct prime numbers, G and G_T are cyclic group of order $N = p_1 p_2 p_3$, and $e: G \times G \to G_T$ is a bilinear map such that:

1. **Bilinearity**: $\forall g, h \in G$ and $a, b \in \mathbb{Z}_N$, we have $e(g^a, h^b) = e(g, h)^{ab}$.
2. **Non-degenerate**: $e(g, h) \neq 1$.

Assume that the group operations in G and G_T as well as the bilinear map e can be computed in polynomial time. Composite order bilinear groups have a useful feature of orthogonality between two elements from different subgroups. Let G_{p_1}, G_{p_2}, and G_{p_3} denote the subgroup of order p_1, p_2, p_3 in G, respectively. When $h_i \in G_{p_i}$ and $h_j \in G_{p_j}$ for $i \neq j$, $e(h_i, h_j)$ is the identity element in G_T. Consider $h_1 \in G_{p_1}$ and $h_2 \in G_{p_2}$, g is a generator of G. Then, $g^{p_3 p_2}$ generates G_{p_1}, $g^{p_1 p_3}$ generates G_{p_2} and $g^{p_1 p_2}$ generates G_{p_3}, for some α_1, α_2, $h_1 = g^{(p2p3)\alpha_1}$ and $h_2 = g^{(p2p3)\alpha_2}$. Then under the bilinear map e yields $e(h_1, h_2) = e(g^{p2p3\alpha_1}, g^{p2p3\alpha_2}) = e(g^{\alpha_1}, g^{p3\alpha_2})^{p_1 p_2 p_3} = 1$.

Forward secrecy ensures that malicious users with inadequate attributes should not be able to combine their keys to decrypt a ciphertext that none of them are individually authorized to decrypt. To ensure that, we associate each attribute with a unique element in $\mathbb{Z}_N^*$. (This could be accomplished by means of a collision-resistant hash function $H : \{0,1\}^* \to \mathbb{Z}_N^*$).

3.3.2 Complexity Assumptions

Assumption 1 Given a group generator $\mathcal{G}$, we define the following distribution:

$$\Gamma = (N = p_1 p_2 p_3, G, G_T, e) \xleftarrow{R} \mathcal{G}$$

$$g_1 \xleftarrow{R} G_{p_1}$$

$$D = (\Gamma, g_1)$$

$$T_1 = G_{p_1 p_2}, T_2 = G_{p_1}$$

We define the advantage of an algorithm $\mathcal{A}$ in breaking Assumption 1 to be:

$$Adv1_{\mathcal{G},\mathcal{A}}(\lambda) := |Pr[\mathcal{A}(D, T_1) = 1] - Pr[\mathcal{A}(D, T_2) = 1]| \tag{3.11}$$

We say that $\mathcal{G}$ satisfies Assumption 1 if for any *PPT* algorithm $\mathcal{A}$, $Adv1_{\mathcal{G},\mathcal{A}}$ is negligible.

Assumption 2 Given a group generator $\mathcal{G}$, we define the following distribution:

$$\Gamma = (N = p_1 p_2 p_3, G, G_T, e) \xleftarrow{R} \mathcal{G}$$

$$X_1, Y_1 \xleftarrow{R} G_{p_1}$$

$$X_2, Y_2 \xleftarrow{R} G_{p_2}$$

$$X_3, Y_3 \xleftarrow{R} G_{p_3}$$

$$D = (\Gamma, X_1, Y_1, X_2, Y_3)$$

$$T_1 = G_{p_1 p_2 p_3}, T_2 = G_{p_1 p_3}$$

We define the advantage of an algorithm $\mathcal{A}$ in breaking Assumption 2 to be:

$$Adv2_{\mathcal{G},\mathcal{A}}(\lambda) := |Pr[\mathcal{A}(D, T_1) = 1] - Pr[\mathcal{A}(D, T_2) = 1]| \tag{3.12}$$

We say that $\mathcal{G}$ satisfies Assumption 2 if for any PPT algorithm $\mathcal{A}$, $Adv2_{\mathcal{G},\mathcal{A}}$ is negligible.

Assumption 3 Given a group generator $\mathcal{G}$, we define the following distribution:

$$\Gamma = (N = p_1 p_2 p_3, G, G_T, e) \xleftarrow{R} \mathcal{G}$$

$$g_1 = G_{p_1}, g_2, X_2, Y_2 \xleftarrow{R} G_{p_2}, g_3 \xleftarrow{R} G_{p_3}$$

$$\alpha, s \xleftarrow{R} \mathbb{Z}_N$$

$$D = (\Gamma, g_1, g_2, g_3, g_1^{\alpha} X_2, g_1^s Y_2)$$

$$T_1 = e(g_1, g_2)^{\alpha s}, T_2 \xleftarrow{R} G_T$$

We define the advantage of an algorithm $\mathcal{A}$ in breaking Assumption 3 to be:

$$Adv3_{\mathcal{G}, \mathcal{A}}(\lambda) := |Pr[\mathcal{A}(D, T_1) = 1] - Pr[\mathcal{A}(D, T_2) = 1]| \qquad (3.13)$$

We say that $\mathcal{G}$ satisfies Assumption 3 if for any PPT algorithm $\mathcal{A}$, $Adv3_{\mathcal{G}, \mathcal{A}}$ is negligible.

3.4 Provable Security

Traditionally, provable security has been asymptotic: it uses polynomial-time reducibility to classify the hardness of computational problems. As a result, any computationally bounded adversary has a negligible advantage in breaking the hard assumptions in the secured schemes. For example, consider the ECDL problem, find a, when given $(Q = aP)$, which is well known to be intractable by any probabilistic polynomial-time algorithm. Then, we provide a polynomial reduction to the problem Q of breaking the cryptographic scheme constructed from this mathematical problem. Finally, we show that if an algorithm $\mathcal{A}$ exists that breaks the scheme in polynomial time, we could build a probabilistic polynomial-time algorithm $\mathcal{A}$ that obtains a contradiction by using $\mathcal{A}$ as a subroutine. Therefore, we declare that the scheme is computationally secure [23].

Because such security proofs in the standard model are inefficient, only a few practical public key schemes can be proven secure in the standard model to date. But, under standard intractability assumptions, Cramer and Shoup [22] proposed a practical and provably secure scheme against adaptive chosen-ciphertext attacks. Researchers attempted to provide security proofs of public key encryption schemes in an efficient manner due to the inefficiency of proving security in the standard model.

Bellare and Rogaway [20] made the first attempt. As an alternative to the standard version, they proposed the random oracle model (ROM). Hash functions are thought to behave like truly random functions in this model. As a result, it is reasonable to model a secure hash function as a completely random function in security analysis. This significantly reduces the time it takes to prove the security of a cryptographic scheme. By doing so, we can be sure that the hash function's output is completely random and generated independently on different inputs. As a result, even though the adversary knows the hash values for several different inputs, they do not have advantage over the outputs for any other inputs. Furthermore, the ROM allows the scheme's designer to construct responses to the outputs in order to demonstrate the scheme's security, i.e. we can control the attacker's behavior, which is impossible in the real world.

When the hash function is fixed, the schemes with security proofs in the random oracle model may not be necessarily secure. Canetti et al. [19] demonstrated that in the ROM, it is possible to construct an encryption scheme that is provably secure but insecure when the random oracle is instantiated with any hash function. In this regard, our proposed schemes are constructed on the standard model.

3.5   Security Notions

Formal definition or features of any secure cryptographic system should encompass the concrete construction of the scheme, threat model, and relatively quantify a certain attacker's success (often defined in threat model) to solve a predefined underlying hard problem probably. Therefore, security notions showcase security goals and possible attack scenarios [20]. From the perspective of public key authenticated encryption (PKAE) schemes, we define the frequently used terminologies in security notions. The definitions will pertain to secure public key encryption. In specific, public key encryption ensures confidentiality.

Encryption schemes used to encrypt a message in a cryptosystem must generate ciphertext that does not leak information about any bit strings that make up a message or plaintext. The mere disclosure of any sensitive information to an attacker/adversary negates the entire point of confidentiality. Cryptosystems have several security goals, including one wayness (*OW*), indistinguishability of encryption (*IND*), and non-malleability (*NM*), which are listed in order of strength [20]. The adversary cannot extract the message from a given ciphertext for *OW* goals. Likewise, when the plaintext and a given ciphertext are meaningfully related in *NM* goal systems, the adversary should not generate another ciphertext. However, the emphasis of security notions in this thesis is on the*IND* schemes. This means that the adversary cannot distinguish which message a particular ciphertext encrypts.

Any cryptographic system usually has three attack models: Chosen Plaintext Attack (*CPA*), Non-adaptive Chosen Ciphertext Attack (*CCA-1*), and Adaptive Chosen Ciphertext Attack (*CCA-2*). The adversary can encrypt the plaintext of his choice in a CPA model. In addition, the adversary has the right to decrypt a ciphertext in CCA-1 models, but only before the challenge ciphertext is given to him. The attacker can then use a decryption oracle at any time in a CCA-2 model, with the caveat that he cannot ask the oracle to decrypt the challenge ciphertext. As a result, a security notion is defined as a goal attack tuple, with goal $\in \{OW, IND, NM\}$ and attack $\in \{CPA, CCA-1, CCA-2\}$ [20].

The difference between the attack models is that the changes of the adversary's decryption oracle. The adversary can query the decryption oracle on any ciphertext CT, except the challenge ciphertext CT^*, which presents decryption on CT with the secret target key.

3.5.1   Summary

This chapter has attribute-based encryption scheme and its components, such as secret-sharing schemes, access structure constructions, properties, bilinear pairing, cryptographic assumptions, and security concepts. A great deal of focus is placed on the design of polynomial-based secret sharing. The two fundamental types of attribute-based encryption, thus, key policy attribute-based encryption and ciphertext attribute-based encryption are also discussed in this chapter. In addition, this chapter evaluates identity-based encryption primitives to illustrate the superiority of attribute-based encryption over identity-based encryption in terms of maintaining fine-grained access control when data is shared among numerous data users. This chapter outlined the prerequisites necessary for the development of attribute-based encryption in Chapters 5 and 6.

References

1 Bellare, M. and Rogaway, P. (1996). The exact security of digital signatures-How to sign with RSA and Rabin. In: *International Conference on the Theory and Applications of Cryptographic Techniques*, 399–416. Berlin, Heidelberg: Springer-Verlag.

2 Sahai, A. and Waters, B. (2005). Fuzzy identity-based encryption. *Advances in Cryptology-EUROCRYPT 2005: 24th Annual International Conference on the Theory and Applications of Cryptographic Techniques*, Aarhus, Denmark (22–26 May 2005). Proceedings 24, 457–473. Berlin, Heidelberg: Springer-Verlag.

3 Shamir, A. (1984). Identity-based cryptosystems and signature schemes. In: *Workshop on the Theory and Application of Cryptographic Techniques*, 47–53. Berlin, Heidelberg: Springer-Verlag.

4 Blakley, G.R. and Kabatianskii, G.A. (1993). Linear algebra approach to secret sharing schemes. In: *Workshop on Information Protection*, 33–40. Berlin, Heidelberg: Springer-Verlag.

5 Yan, S.Y. (2013). *Computational Number Theory and Modern Cryptography*. Wiley.

6 Brickell, E.F. (1989). Some ideal secret sharing schemes. In: *Workshop on the Theory and Application of of Cryptographic Techniques*, 468–475. Berlin, Heidelberg: Springer-Verlag.

7 Weisstein, E.W. (2004). Lagrange interpolating polynomial. https://mathworld.wolfram.com/ (accessed 20 April 2023).

8 Shamir, A. (1979). How to share a secret. *Communications of the ACM* 22 (11): 612–613.

9 Beimel, A. (1996). Secure schemes for secret sharing and key distribution. The degree is Doctor of Science. Israel Institute of Technology.

10 Feldman, P. (1987). A practical scheme for non-interactive verifiable secret sharing. *28th Annual Symposium on Foundations of Computer Science (SFCS 1987)*, pp. 427–438. IEEE.

11 Karchmer, M. and Wigderson, A. (1993). On span programs. *Proceedings of the 8th Annual Structure in Complexity Theory Conference*, 102–111. IEEE.

12 Waters, B. (2011). Ciphertext-policy attribute-based encryption: an expressive, efficient, and provably secure realization. In: *International Workshop on Public Key Cryptography*, 53–70. Berlin, Heidelberg: Springer-Verlag.

13 Lee, C.C., Chung, P.S., and Hwang, M.S. (2013). A survey on attribute-based encryption schemes of access control in cloud environments. *International Journal of Network Security* 15 (4): 231–240.

14 Lewko, A. and Waters, B. (2012). New proof methods for attribute-based encryption: achieving full security through selective techniques. In: *Annual Cryptology Conference*, 180–198. Berlin, Heidelberg: Springer-Verlag.

15 Han, F., Qin, J., Zhao, H., and Hu, J. (2014). A general transformation from KP-ABE to searchable encryption. *Future Generation Computer Systems* 30: 107–115.

16 Qiao, Z., Liang, S., Davis, S., and Jiang, H. (2014). Survey of attribute based encryption. *15th IEEE/ACIS International Conference on Software Engineering, Artificial Intelligence, Networking and Parallel/Distributed Computing (SNPD)*, 1–6. IEEE.

17 Li, J., Ren, K., Zhu, B., and Wan, Z. (2009). Privacy-aware attribute-based encryption with user accountability. In: *International Conference on Information Security*, 347–362. Berlin, Heidelberg: Springer-Verlag.

18 Morillo, P., Ràfols, C., and Villar, J.L. (2016). The Kernel Matrix Diffie-Hellman assumption. *Advances in CryptologyASIACRYPT 2016: 22nd International Conference on the Theory and Application of Cryptology and Information Security*, Hanoi, Vietnam (4–8 December 2016), Proceedings, Part I, 729–758. Berlin, Heidelberg: Springer-Verlag.

19 Canetti, R., Goldreich, O., and Halevi, S. (2004). The random oracle methodology, revisited. *Journal of the ACM (JACM)* 51 (4): 557–594.

20 Bellare, M. and Rogaway, P. (1993). Random oracles are practical: a paradigm for designing efficient protocols. *Proceedings of the 1st ACM Conference on Computer and Communications Security*, 62–73.

21 Lewko, A. and Waters, B. (2012). New proof methods for attribute-based encryption: Achieving full security through selective techniques. Advances in CryptologyCRYPTO 2012: 32nd Annual Cryptology Conference, Santa Barbara, CA, USA (19–23 August 2012). Proceedings,180–198. Berlin, Heidelberg: Springer-Verlag.

22 Cramer, R. and Shoup, V. (1998). A practical public key cryptosystem provably secure against adaptive chosen ciphertext attack. In: *Annual International Cryptology Conference*, 13–25. Berlin, Heidelberg: Springer-Verlag.

23 Escala, A., Herold, G., Kiltz, E. et al. (2013). An algebraic *framework* for Diffie-Hellman assumptions. In: *CRYPTO 2013. LNCS* (eds. R. Canetti and J.A. Garay), vol. 8043, pp. 129–147. Springer, Heidelberg. doi: 10.1007/978-3-642-40084-1_8.

4

Data Access Control

4.1 Introduction

From Samarati and Vimercati [1], "Access control is the process of mediating every request to resources and data maintained by a system and determining whether the request should be granted or denied." Access control is crucial for data security because it determines who has access to and uses information and resources. Access control verifies various login credentials, such as usernames and passwords, PINs, biometric scans, and security tokens, to identify users. Multifactor authentication, for example, is a type of access control system in which a user's identity is verified using multiple authentication methods. Access control authorizes the appropriate access level and allows actions associated with a user's credentials after that user has been authenticated. Figure 4.1 depicts a basic access control system. A user requests access to a particular resource. A reference monitor, also known as an access enforcer, is responsible for verifying whether or not a user has the privilege to access the resource center. The access control system has three primary security components [2]:

- **Authentication**: This process involves verifying the authenticity of a person's identity, ensuring that they are indeed who they claim to be. During verification, the provided credentials are meticulously cross-referenced against the information stored in a secure database. The process is completed and the user is granted access if the credentials match. The approved account's privileges and preferences are determined by the user's permissions, which are either saved locally or on the authentication server. An administrator controls the settings. Multi-factor authentication, which uses a card and a keypad, has become popular in higher-security situations for system logins and transactions.
- **Integrity**: This ensures that digital information is uncorrupted and that only those who are permitted can access or modify it. Data must not be changed in transit to retain integrity. Consequently, precautions must be taken to ensure that data cannot be manipulated by an unauthorized person or program. Backups or redundancies must be available in the event that data becomes corrupted, allowing the impacted data to be restored to its original state. Because environmental dangers such as heat, dust, or electrical difficulties might jeopardize data consistency, correctness, and trustworthiness, steps must be taken to control the physical environment of networked terminals and servers. Hardware and storage media should be protected from power surges, electrostatic discharges, and magnets, as well as transmission medium (such as cables and connections) to guarantee that they cannot be tapped.
- **Non-repudiation**: This states that a user cannot dispute the legitimacy of their signature on a document or the transmission of a message that they sent. A digital signature employs a powerful mathematical technique to validate the authenticity and integrity of digital messages, software,

Attribute-based Encryption (ABE): Foundations and Applications within Blockchain and Cloud Environments, First Edition.
Qi Xia, Jianbin Gao, Isaac Amankona Obiri, Kwame Omono Asamoah, and Daniel Adu Worae.

Access request   Access request

User   Access enforcer   Database

Figure 4.1 Basic access control system.

or documents. This sophisticated method serves a dual purpose: firstly, it guarantees that the content has been electronically signed by the claimed sender, and secondly, it prevents any possibility of denial from the sender's end. The uniqueness of a digital signature lies in its exclusivity, as it can only be generated by a single individual. This ensures utmost trust and accountability in digital communications, bolstering the confidence of both senders and recipients.

The four basic types of access control mechanisms are listed below:

1. **Discretionary access control**: In this system, the owner of the protected resource determines who has access to the resource.
2. **Mandatory access control**: Users are granted access to this system based on their information clearance. A central authority manages access rights based on different security levels.
3. **Role-based access control**: As the name implies, access is granted based on predefined functions rather than on the identities of users. This method gives users access to only the data required for their job within an organization. A complex combination of role assignments, authorizations, and permissions is commonly used in the role-based access control.
4. **Attribute-based access control**: Access is granted based on a set of attributes and environmental conditions in this dynamic method. This could include the time of day and the location of both users and resources. Identity-based access control is a variant of attribute-based access control methods.

In general, access control can be classified as:

1. Coarse-grained
2. Fine-grained

4.1.1 Coarse-Grained

Coarse-grained access control can involve discretionary, mandatory, and role-based access controls. With the coarse-grained access control, the capacity to allow or restrict access to resources is based on a single factor, such as role or entitlement. Consider the following scenario involving coarse-grained access control list based on roles:

- Role A
  - Includes Employees X, Y, and Z.
  - Has access to Folders 3, 4, and 5.
- Role B
  - Includes Employees A, B, and C.
  - Has access to Folders 3, 4, and 5.

As demonstrated by the preceding access control list, coarse-grained access control can grow highly complex and difficult to administer. Consequently, coarse-grained access control is not optimal for data-sharing scenarios involving several users and partial access to a data file based on varying scopes of access privileges. The management of access control lists becomes somewhat muddled if the access privileges granted to system users are dynamic and the roles allocated to users are constantly changing. Therefore, coarse-grained access control is required when access control parameters are not dynamic, complex, or overlapping. In situations when access control rights are static and limited, coarse-grained access control can be implemented without causing significant management concerns. Coarse-grained access control may function in situations where data types are kept independently and access to certain data types is simply assigned depending on storage location (e.g. Tim has access to X folder, Natalie has access to Y folder, and so on), such as on-premises environments. However, storing data in the cloud simultaneously necessitates the implementation of fine-grained access control, as it plays a crucial role in allowing data with diverse access requirements to seamlessly coexist within the same storage area without compromising security or compliance.

4.1.2 Fine-Grained Access Control

Fine-grained access control is a more robust, elegant, and granular approach of controlling data and resource access. Attribute-based access control is a sort of fine-grained access control where users are granted access privileges based on their attributes. The usage of attributes in an access control list allows the scope of access privileges to be defined down to the individual bits of data that a user has access to. As a result, data owners can declare the finest degree of access privileges authorized to access a specific dataset utilizing fine-grained access control approaches.

In contrast to "coarse-grained" access control, the term "fine-grained" refers to the precision and specificity with which access control mechanisms operate. As the name implies, fine-grained access is substantially more discriminating in terms of who has access to certain data and employs more nuanced and variable techniques for allowing data access. Fine-grained access control is frequently used in cloud computing, where a large number of data sources are stored in the same space. It assigns each piece of data its own unique access policy. These criteria can be customized to a variety of unique conditions, such as the individual requesting access's role and intended use of the data. For instance, one individual may have the ability to edit and modify a piece of data, while another just has the ability to read it.

The capacity to store vast volumes of data in a centralized location provides a significant competitive advantage in cloud computing. However, outsourced data might differ in terms of nature, source, and level of protection – notably when considering compliance with data security rules and regulations governing consumer data or financial information.

The cloud allows for the storage of vast amounts of data of many types in a centralized location. Data owners cannot simply provide roles broad access to these storage segments – specific data types may be accessible to a particular role but not to others. Therefore, fine-grained access control is critical, as it establishes access parameters for distinct data types, even when they are stored together. One of the most notable advantages of fine-grained access control is that it enables various degrees of access dependent on the individual, their position, or the organization to which they belong, rather than a pass/fail approach. In coarse-grained systems, data is simply classified as authorized or banned, depending on who is attempting to access it. However, with fine-grained access control, additional nuance and variation are possible.

Consider three employees who each have a distinct position and access level. You might provide settings for a particular piece of data, allowing one of the employees to read, modify, and even relocate the file. The second employee may be permitted to view and move the file but not to modify it. Permission may be granted to the third employee to merely read the file. Access Control Elements with a Fine-Grained Approach Access control systems are often classified into three broad categories:

1. Access control on a role-based basis
2. Access control using attributes
3. Access restriction on a policy basis

Role-based systems are called coarse-grained because they categorize people into "roles" and grant or restrict access rights only on the basis of these roles, ignoring any other variables. As a result, they may be too wide or restrictive, and hence incapable of scaling effectively. When it comes to fine-grained access control, two basic techniques are attribute-based and purpose-based.

- **Access control using attributes**: Attribute-based access control associates individual users and data with "attributes," and then determines access based on those associations. These attributes may include the user's position or role, but also their location, the time of day, and other circumstances. The type of data, its creation date, and its storage location are all examples of data properties.
- **Access control on a purpose-basis**: Purpose-based access control is the most adaptable type of authorization since it integrates a variety of roles and features through adaptable and growing logical linkages. It is referred to be a fine-grained access control solution due to the fact that it makes use of various attributes to determine whether data can be accessed or not and to what extent.

4.1.3 Importance of Fine-Grained Access Control

As data has grown in importance and become a critical component of modern businesses, the ability to apply fine-grained access control has become critical. Here are a few reasons why this component is so critical:

1. **Confidentiality**: If storing sensitive data, such as personal information about your clients, you must adhere to a variety of legislation and compliance standards. Additionally, we've seen a noticeable increase in societal pressure in this space as a result of data exposure and data leak situations. Regulators are working nonstop to hold businesses accountable for their effective handling of sensitive personal data. Fine-grained access control arms you with the tools necessary to comply with applicable regulations and maintain the maximum confidentiality of any personal information you hold. Only authorized people have access to such data, and you may rest assured that your risk has been considerably decreased.
2. **Centralized data storage**: Data Storage on a centralized Scale Businesses that are data-driven realize the numerous benefits (economic and administrative) associated with keeping data in a centralized data storage, such as a data warehouse or a data lake. You can have a single storage mechanism but an endless number of alternative access control choices for splicing and parsing data for daily use while still benefiting from economies of scale. This is accomplished by fine-grained access control, which prevents internal data from being exposed to the entire organization. You may eliminate redundant data repositories and enforce security and privacy on your primary data warehouse by implementing fine-grained access control.
3. **Precision**: By implementing a fine-grained access control system, you get far greater control over who has access to your internal data. Enabling this type of access provides a level of flexibility that no other technique does. Rather than relying on lengthy categorizations, you can

provide each piece of data with its own access control policy. As a result, if you have specific pieces of data that require special handling, you may do so swiftly and efficiently without affecting other aspects of the process. You avoid unnecessarily creating bottlenecks, which adds value to the firm as a whole.

4. **Significantly enhanced security**: Implementing a fine-grained access control mechanism increases your chances of mitigating security and compliance issues significantly. When access control is granular but unambiguous, security concerns such as data exposure can be mitigated or reduced. Your potential damage may also be greatly reduced in the event of a data breach or exposure.

5. **Efficient non-employee authorizations**: In certain circumstances, a business may wish to disclose specific data to non-internal stakeholders. These could be partners, vendors, or customers, to name a few. Such data sharing can introduce significant security risks, but fine-grained access control enables you to limit the scope of data shared with third parties to just what you wish to share, thereby mitigating risks. Additionally, when the access is no longer required, it can be revoked.

These are the primary reasons why fine-grained access control is critical for your company, as well as the benefits associated with its implementation. For any organization that stores and utilizes a variety of different types of data, it makes a lot of sense to maintain total control over access rights and to tailor them to specific use cases.

4.2 Concerns About Cloud-Based Access Control that Are Trustworthy

Historically, data owners relied on third-party cloud servers to act as the omniscient enforcer of access control lists, denying or allowing users access to outsourced data depending on their allowed credentials. The rationale for this is that the cloud server will be active 24 hours a day to perform the role of access enforcer. However, the solution comes with the caveat that the cloud server may be hacked, either through financial incentives or through an attacker getting into the cloud servers and allowing access to users who should not have access to the outsourced data.

The alternative that was deemed acceptable to data users was for the data owner to employ encryption to regulate who has access to cloud resources, rather than depending on a cloud server to implement access control that required unconditional trust. Fortunately, the access control list can be integrated directly into the ciphertext to enable access control to be applied. Thus, the data owner exerts direct control over access control via encryption, with the data decrypted by a user who possesses the associated private key.

The advantage of encryption access control is that even if the cloud server hosting the data is successfully hacked, the hackers will not be able to obtain the plaintext of the message because decryption requires private keys that the hackers do not possess.

4.2.1 Encryption Access Control

Data encryption is the most effective method for ensuring client-side access control. A number is encrypted with an algorithm and a key, resulting in ciphertext that can only be decrypted with the correct key to reveal its original form. There are two types of encryption methods available today: symmetric (private) and asymmetric (public) [3].

Most cryptographic methods encrypt data transmissions with symmetric encryption but encrypt and exchange the secret key via asymmetric encryption. In symmetric encryption, also known as private key encryption, the same private key is used for both encryption and decryption. The danger here is that if any party loses or has the key intercepted, the system would be disrupted and messages would no longer be safe.

Asymmetric cryptography, often known as public key cryptography (PKC), utilizes two distinct but mathematically related keys: a private key and a public key. These keys serve different purposes, with either key being used for encryption or decryption based on the intended action. When one key is used for encryption, the associated key is used for decryption. The public key can be freely shared with other users as it enables encryption of messages sent to the owner of the corresponding private key. However, the private key, which is necessary for decrypting the encrypted messages and reading communications, is kept exclusively by the receiving party.

Access cards can be authenticated to readers and the back-end system using one or both of the following cryptographic methods: symmetric and asymmetric encryption. Many current cards offer symmetric cryptography options like 3DES or the advanced encryption standard (AES), which the government uses to safeguard classified information. Alternatively, some cards implement TEA (tiny encryption algorithm), which is known for its high transaction speed. For higher-grade cards, asymmetric encryption, such as Rivest–Shamir–Adleman (RSA), is also supported. By using asymmetric encryption, valuable master keys no longer need to be stored in the door controller, which streamlines system design and facilitates keeping it up to date. The underlying difficulty is that before a symmetric key encryption scheme can be utilized, a session key must be exchanged between the data owner and data users in advance [4]. However, in multiuser data sharing systems, it is hard to know every potential data user ahead of time in order to share data with them. Even if the data owner does, it must encrypt the data many times with each session key shared across the system's multiple data users. In a large network, there may be as many as $((n-1)n/2)$ key pairs to maintain. As a result, key management will almost certainly require a lot of storage. The disadvantages of the asymmetric key encryption technique are comparable to those of the symmetric key encryption system. The data owner must obtain the public keys of each data user, encrypt the data numerous times, and store multiple copies of the same data in the cloud.

Furthermore, identity-based encryption (IBE), also known as identification (ID)-based encryption, is a type of public-key encryption (PKE) that uses an identifier as the encryption mechanism's foundation. In IBE, parties can encrypt messages without the need for prior key distribution, making it particularly useful when key distribution is infeasible, technically challenging, or impractical. The master public key, generated from a Private Key Generator, along with the identity ID (e.g., an email address) are used to calculate a public key unique to the identity. This computed public key enables the transmission of encrypted messages to the person or entity associated with the identity ID. One of the key advantages of ID-based encryption techniques is that if the number of users is finite, the third party's secret can be securely destroyed after all users have been issued keys. This is possible because one of the system's assumptions is that keys remain valid once provided. Such a finite property is not present in systems with key revocation processes.

IBE, on the other hand, faces the similar difficulties, as it requires the data encrypter to know every potential data user ahead of time in order to encrypt a message with their identity. This may not be appropriate for the data sharing scenario we're examining, in which the data owner has no prior knowledge of the potential data users and encryption cannot be accomplished using an identity or public key.

This book focuses mostly on attribute-based encryption (ABE) schemes because they offer fine-grained access control of data without requiring the data encryptor to define the identity or audience of data users. As a result, ABE schemes do not necessitate the specificity of data users necessary to decrypt a ciphertext, as it thrives primarily on attribute. ABE grants the data encryptor the ability to encrypt messages without prior knowledge of the identity of potential data users, with the assurance that the data user can decrypt the ciphertext only if the attributes of the user satisfy the constrained (access structure in the case of CP-ABE and attributes in the case of KP-ABE) embedded into the ciphertext. As a result, ABE schemes make it easier to share sensitive data among multiple data consumers.

4.2.2 Requirements for Encryption-Based Access Control

While encryption is the most viable way for supporting secure access control, the following conditions must be satisfied in order for encryption-based access control systems to be deployed securely and efficiently.

1. **Indistinguishability**: The encrypted data must not expose any information about the encryption key or the decryption key that is required.
2. **Privacy constraint**: Encrypted data should adhere to the requirement of exclusively utilizing a designated set of private and public keys for decrypting the ciphertext. Before a private key is generated and assigned to an entity, the entity that is to be the holder of the private key must meet the requirements. Unauthorized users cannot combine parts of their private key to wrongly decrypt a ciphertext that none of the malicious parties has the private key to decrypt. Hence, the private key must have coalition resistance. The private keys must be embedded with a unique random number that assures that only the authorized user can use them and that their components cannot be shared. To make key management simple, we need a framework that allows for fine-grained access constraints.
3. **Granularity awareness**: To make key management easier, the decryption key for coarse-grained data should be derived from the key for fine-grained information.
4. **Asymmetry**: Service-independent access rights imply that the same information will be decryptable with the same decryption key if various services supply it. As a result, with a symmetric cryptosystem, a service that encrypts data can access the same data as another service. By employing a public key cryptosystem with fine-grained property, we may circumvent this issue. Because encryption based on fine-grained access control is client-independent by design and does not require personalization.

4.3 Summary

This chapter covers access control, which is a critical component of data sharing since it ensures that only authorized users have access to data. While access control was traditionally enforced by in-house servers, which served as omniscient enforcers to ensure that only authorized users could access data resources, the use of cloud computing has presented a challenge that cloud servers cannot be trusted with plaintext to enforce access control. Even if the cloud server does not become malicious to use the outsourced data for its own gain, an attacker can exploit it. As a result, establishing access control from the data owner's perspective appears suitable. However, in situations where multiple users with dynamic access privileges are required, encryption techniques based on symmetric, traditional public key encryption and identity-based encryption have coarse-grained access control mechanisms and may result in high key management and ciphertext overhead. Finally, we arrive at a fine-grained access control mechanism, where we discover that attribute-based encryption can provide a many-to-many encryption approach, which may be practical for a dynamic users control system with a wide range of access rights.

References

1 Samarati, P. and Vimercati, S.C.D. (2000). Access control: policies, models, and mechanisms. In: *International School on Foundations of Security Analysis and Design. FOSAD 2000, Lecture Notes in Computer Science*, vol. 2171 (ed. R. Focardi and R. Gorrieri), 137–196. Berlin, Heidelberg: Springer-Verlag.

2 Yu, S., Wang, C., Ren, K., and Lou, W. (2010). Achieving secure, scalable, and fine-grained data access control in cloud computing. *2010 Proceedings IEEE INFOCOM*, March 2010, pp. 1–9. IEEE.

3 Lee, C.C., Chung, P.S., and Hwang, M.S. (2013). A survey on attribute-based encryption schemes of access control in cloud environments. *International Journal of Network Security* 15 (4): 231–240.

4 Delfs, H., Knebl, H., Delfs, H., and Knebl, H. (2007). Symmetric-key encryption. *Introduction to Cryptography: Principles and Applications*, 11–31.

5

Selective Secure ABE Schemes Based on Prime Order Group

5.1 Introduction

The attribute-based encryption (ABE) scheme provides adequate expressive access controls over a large range of attributes. To attain the requisite flexibility, current access structures in the ABE construction utilize boolean formulas or linear secret sharing systems as access policies. Due to the great degree of flexibility in ABE, keys and ciphertexts have a complicated structure of vast universe of possible access policies and attribute sets. This makes defining a security model more difficult since a secure notion in the ABE context must impose collusion resistance, which implies that several users should be unable to decrypt a message that none of them is individually authorized to access. Consequently, a security proof must account for an attacker who may collect a huge number of different keys, but only one of them is allowed to decrypt the ciphertext.

This needs security reductions in order to strike a balance between two competing goals: the simulator must be robust enough to adaptively provide the attacker with the multiple keys demanded, but it must also be empty of crucial knowledge gathered from the attacker's success. The earliest security proofs in the standard model for ABE systems (e.g. [1]) employed a very natural paradigm termed partitioning to balance these two aims. This proof method had already been used to identity-based encryption [2]. The simulator configures the system in a partitioning proof so that the space of all possible secret keys is divided into two sections: keys that the simulator can produce and keys that the simulator cannot generate. Previous works [3–5] relied on a weaker security model called as selective security to verify that all keys requested by the attacker fall within the set of keys that the simulator may create and that any key capable of decrypting the challenge ciphertext falls within the opposite set. Before obtaining the public parameters, the attacker must first reveal the challenge ciphertext, according to the selective security paradigm.

Consider the case below: A challenger and adversary compete in a series of close games in which the adversary is tasked with attacking and stealing valuable gems in a living room with eight tightly shut doors. With selective security, the adversary must notify the challenger of the particular door from which it intends to attack so that the challenger can install a security lock to prevent the attack. The purpose of selective security is to determine how long a lock installed at the challenge door can withstand an attack; in computer words, this is routinely performed with an adversarial algorithm running in polynomial probabilistic time (PPT). The security locks set on the door are ineffective if the adversary can break the challenged door to gain access to the living room and take the gems. Similarly, breaking the security doors could be construed as compromising a scheme's security. Alternative means for the adversary to gain access to the room and take the jewels, such as loose windows, are ignored by selective security. Thus, the purpose of ABE selective security is to test if the adversary can win the security game using the adversary's challenge attribute sets before

Attribute-based Encryption (ABE): Foundations and Applications within Blockchain and Cloud Environments, First Edition. Qi Xia, Jianbin Gao, Isaac Amankona Obiri, Kwame Omono Asamoah, and Daniel Adu Worae.

generating the public parameters. Selective security, on the other hand, does not represent the way people think about security in the actual world. The selective security approach, on the other hand, establishes that a target attribute set used in message encryption is secure against adversarial attack based on hard security problems such as Bilinear Diffie–Hellman Decision (BDDH) problem. The adversary cannot access the plaintext based on the challenged attribute sets without the associated secret.

The selective security concept aided the development of attribute-based encryption schemes in their early stages. The security of ABE would not have been conceivable in the standard model without the selective security concept. The selected security model laid the stage for additional advancements in the ABE construction security model.

5.1.1 Selective Security Model for KP-ABE

The following is selective-Set security model for ABE:

- **Init**: The adversary defines the set of attributes S^* that it wants to be challenged upon.
- **Setup**: The challenger runs the Setup algorithm and outputs the public parameters to the adversary.
- **Phase 1**: The adversary is allowed to issue queries for private keys on a series of access structures $\mathbb{A}_j$, where $j = 1, \ldots, n$ with condition that $S^* \notin \mathbb{A}_j$ for all j. With every query the challenger runs the KeyGen algorithm and outputs the private key for $\mathbb{A}_j$ to the adversary.
- **Challenge**: The adversary outputs two messages m_0 and m_1 of the same length. The challenger tosses a binary coin b, and encrypts m_b with S^*. The challenged ciphertext is given to the adversary.
- **Phase 2**: Phase 1 is repeated.
- **Guess**: The adversary outputs a guess b' of b. In this game, the advantage of the adversary is defined as $Pr[b' = b] - \frac{1}{2}$. We note that by enabling decryption queries in Phase 1 and Phase 2, the model can be modified to handle chosen-ciphertext attacks.

Definition 5.1 A KP-ABE scheme is secure in the selective security model under an IND–Chosen Plaintext Attack (IND–CPA), if all PPT adversaries have at most a negligible advantage in winning the above security game.

5.1.2 Selective Security Model for CP-ABE

The following is selective-Set security model for ABE:

- **Init**: The adversary defines the access structure $\mathbb{A}^*$ that it wants to be challenged upon.
- **Setup**: The challenger runs the Setup algorithm and outputs the public parameters to the adversary.
- **Phase 1**: The adversary queries the challenger for private keys for sets of attributes $S_1, \ldots, S_n$ with the condition that $S_j \notin \mathbb{A}^*$, where $j = 1, \ldots, n$. With every query the challenger runs the KeyGen algorithm and outputs the private key for S_j to the adversary.
- **Challenge**: The adversary outputs two messages m_0 and m_1 of the same length. The challenger tosses a binary coin b and encrypts m_b with $\mathbb{A}$. The challenged ciphertext is given to the adversary.
- **Phase 2**: Phase 1 is repeated.
- **Guess**: The adversary outputs a guess b' of b. In this game, the advantage of the adversary is defined as $Pr[b' = b] - \frac{1}{2}$. We note that by enabling decryption queries in Phases 1 and 2, the model can be modified to handle chosen-ciphertext attacks.

Table 5.1 Notation.

Symbols	Meanings
$\mathbb{U}$	Attribute universe
MSK	Master secret key
PP	Public parameters
g	The generator of the bilinear group $\mathbb{G}_1$
S_U	A set of attributes assigned to U
SK_U	Secret key of user U
E_m	Encrypted m
CT_m	Ciphertext of message m
DK_m	Data decryption key for m
DA	A universe of data attributes
ADK_m^i	Attribute decryption key for attribute $i \in (W, \rho)$
S_m	A set of attributes assigned to m
APK^i	Attribute public key for attribute $i \in UA$
DEK	Data encryption key
KGK	Key generation key

Definition 5.2 A CP-ABE scheme is secure in the selective security model under an IND–CPA, if all PPT adversaries have at most a negligible advantage in winning the above security game.

5.1.3 ABE Schemes

This section provides two ABE schemes: KP-ABE and CP-ABE. The KP-ABE scheme was proposed by Goyal et al. [6], whereas the CP-ABE scheme was proposed by Waters [7]. The KP-ABE and CP-ABE schemes are proven secure under bilinear Diffie-Hellman (BDH) and bilinear Diffie-Hellman exponent (BDHE) security assumptions, respectively. Table 5.1 provides the main notions used in our description.

5.2 The KP-ABE Scheme

KP-ABE scheme of [1] is described in detail in this section. Both the description of the cryptographic design and security proof of the scheme will be presented.

5.2.1 Concrete Scheme Construction

The KP-ABE scheme comprises four algorithms: Setup, KeyGen, Encrypt, and Decrypt. These algorithms are described as follows:

- **Setup**(DA, λ) $\rightarrow$ (PP, MSK): The Setup algorithm is used to generate a public parameter and master secret key for the system. It usually takes the input of security parameter λ and Universal attribute set DA, where the attributes are expressed as integers $1, \dots, |DA|$. It selects a bilinear group $\mathbb{G}_1$ with a prime order p and generator $g \in \mathbb{G}_1$, where the size of the group is determined by λ, i.e. $p \geq 2^\lambda, \lambda \geq 160$. Eventually, the algorithm returns the public parameters PP and the master secret key MSK. The structure of these keys is provided as follows:

$$PP = (g, DEK, \{APK^i\}_{i \in \mathbb{U}}),$$

where the PP comprises the following:
1. The data encryption key $DEK = e(g,g)^\alpha$, where e is a bilinear map such that $e : \mathbb{G}_1 \times \mathbb{G}_1 \rightarrow \mathbb{G}_2$. This Encrypt algorithm uses this key together with a random number to perform data encryption.
2. The attributes i's public key is provided as $\{APK^i\} = g^{z_i}$, where $z_i \in \mathbb{Z}_p$. The Encrypt algorithm uses this key to generate attribute decryption keys.

$$MSK = (\alpha, \{Z_i\}_{i \in \mathbb{U}}),$$

where the random values $\alpha \in \mathbb{Z}_p$ and the random value z_i for each attribute $i \in DA$. The MSK values are kept secret while the PP values are published to the public.

- **KeyGen(MSK, S_U) $\rightarrow$ (SK_U):** The KeyGen algorithm is used to generate a secret key for user U. It takes master secret key MSK and monotone span program (MSP) $\delta = (W, \rho)$ (which is equivalent to linear secret sharing scheme (LSSS) access structure [1]),where the function ρ is associated with the rows (i.e. attributes) of matrix W. The algorithm selects W of $\ell \times n$ matrix and sets a random vector $\mathbf{v} \in \mathbb{Z}_p^n$ such that $\mathbf{1} \cdot \mathbf{v}^T = \alpha$. Thus, $\mathbf{v} = (\alpha, v_2, \ldots v_n)$. For $i = 1, \ldots, \ell$, the algorithm set $\Lambda_i = v_i \cdot W_i$, where W_i is the vector associated with the ith row of W. Furthermore, the algorithm generates attribute decryption key ADK_U^i for attribute i as $ADK_U^i = g^{\frac{\Lambda_i}{z_i}}$. The structure of U's key is provided as follows:

$$SK_U = ((W, \rho), \{ADK_U^i\}_{i \in \rho(i)})$$

The SK_U comprises the following:
1. User U decryption keys $UDK_{1,U} = g^{r_1}$ and $UDK_{2,U} = g^{\alpha + r_1 \cdot \alpha}$, where $r_1 \in \mathbb{Z}_p$.
2. The attribute i's decryption key $ADK_U^i = g^{r_1 \cdot z_i}$ is assigned to U for each $i \in S_U$.

- **Encrypt(PP, m, S_m) $\rightarrow$ (CT_m):** The Encrypt algorithm encrypts a message and outputs a ciphertext. It takes PP, a message m, and attribute set S_m. The algorithm selects $s \in \mathbb{Z}_p$. For each attribute $i = 1 \rightarrow |S_m|$, the algorithm computes $ADK_m^i = g^{s \cdot z_i}$ and encrypts the message m as $E_m = m \cdot DEK^s$. Eventually, the ciphertext CT_m is returned by the algorithm. The structure of the ciphertext is provided as follows:

$$CT_m = (E_m, S_m, \{ADK_m^i\}_{i \in S_m})$$

- **Decrypt(CT_m, SK_U) $\rightarrow$ (m):** The Decrypt algorithm takes the ciphertext CT_m with the attribute set S_m and the private key SK_U for access structure (W, ρ), where W is $\ell \times n$ matrix. The algorithm lets $I \subseteq \{1, 2, \ldots, \ell\}$ be defined as $I = \{i : \rho(i) \in S_m\}$. Next, the algorithm selects $\omega_i \in \mathbb{Z}_p$ as a set of constants. If $\{\Lambda_i\}$ are valid shares of any secret α, according to W, then $\sum_{i \in I} \omega_i \Lambda_i = \alpha$. The decryption algorithm performs the following computations:

$$C = \prod_{i=1}^{I} e(ADK_m^i, ADK_U^i)^{\omega_i} = e(g,g)^{s \cdot \alpha}.$$

The algorithm then utilizes the value C to output the message as $m = E_m / C$.

5.2.2 Security Proof

This section summarizes the security analysis of the KP-ABE scheme adopted in [1]. The security proof is carried out in accordance with the Decisional BDH assumption outlined in Chapter 3. The proof is performed by comparing the KP-ABE construction presented in Section 3.12 to the selective chosen-plaintext attack security game (detailed in Section 5.1.1). The proof is undertaken in the following manner. Assume an adversary with a non-negligible advantage initiates the security game outlined in this section against the CP-ABE construction.

- **Init**: Adversary $\mathcal{A}$ selects a challenge attribute S^* upon which it would like to be challenged.
- **Setup**: C produces PP by firstly, setting $DEK = e(A, B) = e(g, g)^{ab}$. For each $i \in \mathbb{U} \wedge i \in S^*$, it sets $APK^i = g^{r_i}$ (which implicitly defines ($z_i = r_i \in \mathbb{Z}_p$); else if $i \in \mathbb{U} \wedge i \notin S^*$, it selects random r_i and sets $APK^i = B^{r_i} = g^{br_i}$ (which implicitly defines ($z_i = br_i \in \mathbb{Z}_p$). Eventually, C outputs the following components $DEK, \{APK^i\}_{i \in \mathbb{U}}$ to $\mathcal{A}$.
- **Phase 1**: $\mathcal{A}$ queries for a secret key SK_U for user U whose access structure in the form (W, ρ) does not satisfy the challenged attribute set S^*. Then, C creates secret key SK_U as follows:
  1. Sets the dimension of W to be $d \times \ell$ and denotes the submatrix of W as W_{S^*} comprising the row labels in S^*.
  2. Selects a random $\mathbf{w} = (w_1, \dots w_\ell) \in \mathbb{Z}^\ell$ with $\mathbf{w} \cdot \mathbf{1} = ab$, where $w_i = b\Lambda_i$. Here, we consider a theorem to demonstrate why it is intractable to compute the secret value α without enough share of the secret Λ_i.

Theorem 5.1 *[1] A vector $\boldsymbol{\pi}$ is independent of set of vectors denoted by matrix N if and only if there exist a vector $\boldsymbol{\omega}$ such that $N\boldsymbol{\omega} = \mathbf{0}$ while $\boldsymbol{\pi} \cdot \boldsymbol{\omega} \neq 0$.*

Since $\mathbf{1}$ is independent of W_{S^*}, there exists a vector $\boldsymbol{\omega}$ with $W_{S^*} \cdot \boldsymbol{\omega} = \mathbf{0}$ and $\mathbf{1} \cdot \boldsymbol{\omega} \neq 0$. From [1], these vectors can be efficiently calculated. Therefore $\boldsymbol{\omega} = \{\omega_1, \omega_2, \dots, \omega_\ell\}$ and it can finally define the vector $\mathbf{u}$ as: $\mathbf{u} = \mathbf{v} + \psi\boldsymbol{\omega}$ such that $\psi = \frac{ab - b\sum_{k=1}^{\ell} \lambda_k}{h}$. Note that $u_i = v_i + \psi\omega_i = b\lambda_i + \frac{ab - b\sum_{k=1}^{\ell} \lambda_k}{h}\omega_i$. Here, $W_j = (x_{1j}, x_{2j}, \dots, x_{\ell j})$ and the private key for the row W_j is provided as follows:
if $\rho(j) \in S^*$, the

$$ADK_U^j = B^{\phi_1}, \text{where } \phi_1 = \frac{\sum_{i=1}^{\ell} x_{i,j}\lambda_j}{r_j}$$

From [1], the proof of the secret key's correctness is provided as follows:

$$\frac{W_j \cdot \mathbf{u}}{z_j} = \frac{W_j \cdot (\mathbf{u} + \phi\boldsymbol{\omega})}{z_j}$$

$$= \frac{W_j \mathbf{v} + \psi(W_j\boldsymbol{\omega})}{z_j} = \frac{W_j \mathbf{v} + \psi(0)}{z_j} = b \cdot \frac{\sum_{i=1}^{\ell} x_{i,j}\lambda_j}{r_j}$$

$$= b\phi_1$$

If $\rho(j)\cancel{\in}S^*$, then $ADK_U^j = A^{\phi_2} \cdot g^{\phi_3}$, where $\phi_2 = \frac{\sum_{k=1}^{\ell} x_{i,j}}{h \cdot r_j}$ and $\phi_3 = \frac{\sum_{i=1}^{\ell} x_{i,j}(h\lambda_i - \sum_{k=1}^{\ell} \lambda_k)}{h \cdot r_j}$. The proof of the legitimacy of the private key is provided as follows:

$$\frac{W_j \cdot \mathbf{u}}{b \cdot r_j} = \frac{b \sum_{k=1}^{\ell} x_{i,j} \left(\lambda_i + \dfrac{a - \sum_{k=1}^{\ell} \lambda_k}{h} \right)}{b \cdot r_j}$$

$$\times \frac{\sum_{i=1}^{\ell} x_{i,j} \left(\lambda_i + \dfrac{a = \sum_{k=1}^{\ell} \lambda_k}{h} \right)}{r_j}$$

$$= a \cdot \frac{sum_{k=1}^{\ell} x_{i,j}}{h \cdot r_j} + \frac{sum_{i=1}^{\ell} x_{i,j} (h\lambda_i - \sum_{k=1}^{\ell} \lambda_k)}{h \cdot r_j} = a\phi_2 + \phi_3$$

- **Challenge**: $\mathcal{A}$ outputs two challenge messages m_0 and m_1 of the same size to the challenger. The challenger tosses a fair binary coin n and chooses m_b. The C then creates $E_{m_b} = m_b \cdot Z$. The C outputs the ciphertext as:

$$CT = (S_{m_b}, E_{m_b}, \{ADK^i_{m_b} = g^{CT_i}\}_{i \in S^*})$$

  If $u = 0$, $Z = e(g,g)^{abc}$ and let $s = c$. Then we have $DEK = e(g,g)^{abc}$; thus, the ciphertext in a valid random encryption message m_b. If $u = 1$, $Z = e(g,g)^z$, then we have $E_{m_b} = m_b \cdot e(g,g)^z$; thus, the ciphertext in a random encryption of $\mathbb{G}_2$ from the adversary.

- **Phase 2**: Same as Phase 1.

- **Guess**: $\mathcal{A}$ submits a guess b' of b. If $b' = b$, the challenger returns $\mu' = 0$ to indicate that it was given a valid BDHE-tuple (i.e. $T = e(g,g)^{abc}$); else, it returns $\mu' = 1$ to indicate that it was given a random number (i.e. $T = e(g,g)^z$).

  If $\mu = 1$ the adversary gains no information about m_b. Since the challenger guesses $\mu' = 1$ whenever $b' \neq b$, we have $Pr[\mu' = \mu | \mu = 1] = \frac{1}{2}$. Else if $\mu = 0$, then we have $Pr[b = b' | \mu = 0] = \frac{1}{2} + \epsilon$ and the adversary see an encryption of m_b. The advantage of the adversary in this situation is ϵ by the definition. Since the challenger guesses $\mu' = 0$ whenever $b' = b$, we have $Pr[\mu' = \mu | \mu = 0] = \frac{1}{2} + \epsilon$. Therefore, the overall advantage of the challenger correctly answers the BDHE challenge is $\frac{1}{2}Pr[\mu' = \mu | \mu = 0] + \frac{1}{2}Pr[\mu' = \mu | \mu = 1] - \frac{1}{2} = \frac{1}{2}(\frac{1}{2} + \epsilon) + \frac{1}{2}\frac{1}{2} - \frac{1}{2} = \frac{1}{2} + \epsilon$.

5.3 The CP-ABE Scheme

CP-ABE scheme of [7] is described in detail in this section. Both the description of the cryptographic design of the system and security proof of the scheme will be presented.

5.3.1 Concrete Scheme Construction

The KP-ABE scheme comprises four algorithms: Setup, KeyGen, Encrypt, and Decrypt. These algorithms are described as follows:

- **Setup(DA, λ)** $\rightarrow$ **(PP, MSK)**: The Setup algorithm is used to generate a public parameter and master secret key for the system. It usually takes the input of security parameter λ and Universal attribute set DA, where the attributes are expressed as integers $1, \ldots, |DA|$. It selects a bilinear group $\mathbb{G}_1$ with a prime order p and generator $g \in \mathbb{G}_1$, where the size of the group is determined by λ, i.e. $p \geq 2^{\lambda}$, $\lambda \geq 160$. Eventually, the algorithm returns the public parameters PP and the master secret key MSK. The structure of these keys is provided as follows:

$$PP = (g, KGK, DEK, \{APK^i\}_{i \in \mathbb{U}}),$$

  where the PP comprises the following:

1. The data encryption key $DEK = e(g,g)^\alpha$, where e is a bilinear map such that $e : \mathbb{G}_1 \times \mathbb{G}_1 \rightarrow \mathbb{G}_2$. This Encrypt algorithm uses this key together with a random number to perform data encryption.
2. The key generation key $KGK = g^a$, where $a \in \mathbb{Z}_p$. The KeyGen algorithm used this key in creating attribute decryption key.
3. The attributes i's public key is provided as $\{APK^i\} = g^{z_i}$, where $z_i \in \mathbb{Z}_p$. The Encrypt algorithm uses this key to generate attribute decryption keys.

$$MSK = (\alpha, a, \{Z_i\}_{i \in \mathbb{U}}),$$

where the random values $\alpha, a \in \mathbb{Z}_p$ and the random value z_i for each attribute $i \in DA$. The MSK values are kept secret, while the PP values are published to the public.

- **KeyGen**$(MSK, S_U) \rightarrow (SK_U)$: The KeyGen algorithm is used to generate a secret key for user U. It takes master secret key MSK and a set of attributes $S_U \subseteq \mathbb{U}$ as input and returns the secret key SK_U. The structure of the key is provided as follows:

$$SK_U = (S_U, UDK_{1,U}, UDK_{2,U}, \{ADK_U^i\}_{i \in S_U})$$

The SK_U comprises the following:
1. User U decryption keys $UDK_{1,U} = g^{r_1}$ and $UDK_{2,U} = g^{a+r_1 \cdot \alpha}$, where $r_1 \in \mathbb{Z}_p$.
2. The attribute i's decryption key $ADK_U^i = g^{r_i \cdot z_i}$ is assigned to U for each $i \in S_U$.

The Decrypt algorithm makes use of both the user decryption keys and the attribute decryption keys to recover the encrypted message.

- **Encrypt**$(PP, m, (W, \rho)) \rightarrow (CT_m)$: The Encrypt algorithm encrypts a message and outputs a ciphertext. It takes PP, a message m, and LSSS access structure (W, ρ), where ρ is a function that associates rows of the matrix W with attributes. The algorithm selects W with $\ell \times n$ matrix and a sets of random vector $\mathbf{v} = (s, y_2, \ldots, y_n) \in \mathbb{Z}_p^n$. The values in vector $\mathbf{v}$ are used to share the master secret s. For $i = 1 \rightarrow \ell$, the algorithm computes $\Lambda_i = \mathbf{v} \cdot W_i$ and returns the ciphertext CT_m. The structure of the ciphertext is provided as follows:

$$CT_m = (E_m, (W, \rho), DK_m, \{ADK_m^i\}_{i \in \rho(i)})$$

The CT_m comprises the following components:
1. The encrypted message $E_m = m \cdot DEK^s$.
2. The data decryption key $DK_m = g^s$.
3. Attribute i's decryption key $ADK_m^i = (APK^i)^{-s} \cdot (KGK)^{\Lambda_i}$ for each $i \in \rho(i)$.

- **Decrypt**$(CT_m, SK_U) \rightarrow (m)$: The Decrypt Algorithm takes the ciphertext CT_m with the access structure (W, ρ) and the private key SK_U for attribute set S_U, and returns the plaintext message m if and only if $S_U \in \mathbb{A} = (W, \rho)$. The algorithm selects ℓ number of rows in W and lets $I \subseteq \{1, 2, \ldots, \ell\}$ be defined as $I = \{i : \rho(i) \in S_U\}$. Next, the algorithm selects $\omega_i \in \mathbb{Z}_p$ as a set of constants. If $\{\Lambda_i\}$ are valid shares of any secret s, according to W, then $\sum_{i \in I} \omega_i \Lambda_i = s$. The decryption algorithm performs the following computations:

$$C = \frac{e(DK_m, UDK_{2,U})}{\prod_{i=1}^i e(ADK_m^i, UDK_{1,U})^{\omega_i} \cdot \prod_{i=1}^i e(DK_m^i, ADK_U^i)^{\omega_i}} = e(g,g)^{s \cdot \alpha}$$

The algorithm then utilizes the value C to output the message as $m = E_m / C$. As stated in [6], the ω_i value will be either 0 or 1 if the access structure is a Boolean formula.

5.3.2 Security Proof

This section summarizes the security analysis of the CP-ABE system adopted in [7].

The security proof is carried out in accordance with the Decisional q-BDHE assumption outlined in Chapter 3 (see Section 3.15). The proof is performed by comparing the CP-ABE construction presented in this section to the selective chosen-plaintext attack security game (detailed in Section 5.1.2). The proof is undertaken in the following manner. Assume an adversary with a non-negligible advantage initiates the security game outlined in Section 3.15 against the CP-ABE construction. A simulator is utilized to model the Decisional q-BDHE problem using the following parameters.

- **Init**: Adversary $\mathcal{A}$ selects a challenge matrix W^* with a maximum dimension of q columns. The challenger $\mathcal{C}$ is then provided with the challenge access structure (W^*, ρ^*), where W^* contains $n^* \leq q$ column.
- **Setup**: $\mathcal{C}$ produces PP by firstly, selecting a random $\alpha' \in \mathbb{Z}_p$ and sets $e(g,g)^\alpha = DEK = e(g,g)^{\alpha'} \cdot e(g^a, g^{a^q})$ which implicitly defines $(\alpha' + a^{q+1})$. Then, $\mathcal{C}$ sets $KGK = g^a$ from the Decisional q-BDHE assumptions. Eventually, $\mathcal{C}$ returns APK^x by selecting random $z_1, \ldots, z_{|U|} \in \mathbb{Z}_p$ for $x \in [1|U]$ and makes:

$$APK^x := \begin{cases} g^{z_x} \text{ if } \rho^*(i) \neq x, \\ g^{z_x} \cdot g^{a w_{i,1}^*} \cdot g^{a^2 w_{i,2}^*} \ldots g^{a^{n^*} w_{i,n^*}^*} \text{ if } \rho^*(i) = x \end{cases}$$

Now, $\mathcal{C}$ sets $PP = (DEK, KGK, APK^x_{x \in [1|U]})$.

- **Phase 1**: $\mathcal{A}$ queries for a secret key SK_U for user U whose attribute set does not satisfy W^*. Then, $\mathcal{C}$ creates the $UDK_{1,U}$ and $UDK_{2,U}$ components of the secret key SK_U as follows:
  1. Sets vector $\mathbf{w} = (w_1, \ldots w_{n^*}) \in \mathbb{Z}^{n^*}$ with $w_1 = -1$ and restriction that for all i where $\rho^*(i) \in S_u$, $\mathbf{w} \cdot W_i^* = 0$.
  2. Selects a random $t \in \mathbb{Z}_p$ and implicitly defines r_1 as $t + w_1 \cdot a^q + w_2 \cdot a^{q-1} + \cdots + w_{n^*} \cdot a^{q-n^*+1}$.
  3. Computes user U's decryption key as $UDK_{1,U} = g^t \prod_{i=1}^{n^*} (g^{a^{q+1-i}})^{\omega_i} = g^{r_1}$.
  4. Computes user U's decryption key $UDK_{2,U}$ as $UDK_{2,U} = (g^{\alpha' + a^{q+1}}) \cdot (KGK)^{r_1} = g^{\alpha'} g^{at} \prod_{i=2}^{n^*} (g^{a^{q+2-i}})^{\omega_i}$.

Note that with the $UDK_{2,U}$ definition, the term $(KGK)^{r_1}$ has the component $g^{-a^{q+1}}$, which has been cancelled out by the unknown term in g^α. Next, $\mathcal{C}$ creates the ADK^x_U components of the secret key SK_U for each attribute $x \in S_U$ as follows:

  1. For each $x \in S_U$, if there is no i such that $\rho^*(i) = x$, defines the attribute decryption key as $ADK^x_U = (UDK_{1,U})^{z_x}$.
  2. For each $x \in S_U$, if there is i such that $\rho^*(i) = x$, defines the attribute decryption key as

$$ADK^x_U = (UDK_{1,U})^{z_x} \cdot \prod_{j=1,\ldots,n^*} \left(g^{t \cdot a^j} \prod_{k=1,\ldots,n^*, k \neq j} (g^{a^{q+1+j-k}})^{w_k} \right)^{W_{i,j}^*}$$

Eventually, $\mathcal{C}$ outputs users U's secret key as

$$(S_U, UDK_{1,U}, UDK_{2,U}, \{ADK^i_U\}_{i \in |S_U|})$$

- **Challenge**: $\mathcal{A}$ outputs two challenge messages m_0 and m_1 of the same size to the challenger. The challenger tosses a fair binary coin n and chooses m_b. First, $\mathcal{C}$ selects a random $s \in \mathbb{Z}_p$ and creates $E_{m_b} = m_b \cdot m_b e(g^s, g^{\alpha'})$ and $DK_{m_b} = g^s$. Secondly, $\mathcal{C}$ selects $y'_2, y'_3, \ldots, y'_{n^*}$ and set the secret s in the vector $\mathbf{v}$ as $\mathbf{v} = (s, sa + y'_2, \alpha^2 + y'_3, \ldots, \alpha^{n^*} + y'_{n^*}) \in \mathbb{Z}_p^{n^*}$. For $i = 1, 2, \ldots, n^*$ computes the attribute decryption key $ADK^i_{m_b}$ as $ADK^i_{m_b} = (\prod_{j=1,\ldots,n^*} (g^a)^{W_{i,j}^* \cdot y'_j})(g^s)^{-z_{\rho^*(i)}}$.
- **Phase 2**: Same as Phase 1.

- **Guess**: $\mathcal{A}$ submits a guess b' of b. If $b' = b$, the challenger returns $\mu' = 0$ to indicate that it was given a valid Decisional q-BDHE-tuple (i.e. $T = e(g, g)^{\alpha^{q+1}s}$); else, it returns $\mu' = 1$ to indicate that it was given a random number (i.e. $T \xleftarrow{\text{random}} \mathbb{G}_1$).

As shown in the construction the challengers' generation of the public parameters and secret keys are identical that of the actual scheme.

If T is random element in $\mathbb{G}_1$, we have $Pr[C(\mathbf{y}, T \xleftarrow{\text{random}} \mathbb{G}_1) = 1] = \frac{1}{2}$ and adversary gain no information about b. Since the challenger guesses $\mu' = 1$ whenever $b' \neq b$, we have $Pr[\mu' = \mu \mid \mu = 1] = \frac{1}{2}$. Else if T is valid, then we have $Pr[C(\mathbf{y}, T = e(g, g)^{\alpha^{q+1}s}) = 0] = \frac{1}{2} + \epsilon$ and the adversary sees an encryption of m_b. The advantage of the adversary in this situation is ϵ by the definition. Since the challenger guesses $\mu' = 0$ whenever $b' = b$, we have $Pr[\mu' = \mu \mid \mu = 0] = \frac{1}{2} + \epsilon$. Therefore, the overall advantage of the challenger correctly answers the Decisional q-BDHE challenge is $\frac{1}{2}Pr[\mu' = \mu \mid \mu = 0] + \frac{1}{2}Pr[\mu' = \mu \mid \mu = 1] - \frac{1}{2} = \frac{1}{2}(\frac{1}{2} + \epsilon) + \frac{1}{2}\frac{1}{2} - \frac{1}{2} = \frac{1}{2} + \epsilon$.

5.4 Summary

This chapter has described two ABE schemes, the CP-ABE and KP-ABE schemes. The schemes were proven in the selective security model. With the selective security model, the adversary $\mathcal{A}$ has to announce the challenged attributes (in the case of KP-ABE) or the challenged access structure (in the case of CP-ABE) before the security game commences. However, the selective security game model seems unnatural when the concepts are applied in a real-world scenario. As there is no adversary who will give the system/user clues about the specific attributes or access policy it would like to attack. In Chapter 6, we will explore ABE schemes whose security is based on semi-adaptive security.

References

1 Verma, A. and Kaushal, S. (2011). Cloud computing security issues and challenges: a survey. *Communications in Computer and Information Science*.

2 Ananda, A. and Poo, G. (1995). Distributed systems: Concepts and design: By George Coulouris, Jean Dollimore and Tim Kindberg, Addison-Wesley, 2nd Ed, 1994, 644 pp, ISBN 0201624338. *Computer Communications* 18 (7): 521–522. https://doi.org/10.1016/0140-3664 (95)90005-5.

3 Goyal, V., Pandey, O., Sahai, A., and Waters, B. (2006). Attribute based encryption for fine-grained access control of encrypted data. *Proceedings of the ACM Conference on Computer and Communications Security*, 89–98. Alexandria, VI, USA, October 2006.

4 Waters, B. (2011). Ciphertext-policy attribute-based encryption: an expressive, efficient, and provably secure realization. *Proceedings of the Public Key Cryptography-PKC*, 53–70. Taormina, Italy, March 2011.

5 Sahai, A. and Waters, B. (2005). Fuzzy identity-based encryption. *Proceedings of the EUROCRYPT*, 457–473. Aarhus, Denmark, May 2005.

6 Goyal, V., Pandey, O., Sahai, A., and Waters, B. (2006). Attribute based encryption for fine-grained access control of encrypted data. *ACM Conference on Computer and Communications Security (ACM CCS)*.

7 Waters, B. (2011). Ciphertext-policy attribute-based encryption: an expressive, efficient, and provably secure realization. In: *International Workshop on Public Key Cryptography*, 53–70. Berlin, Heidelberg: Springer-Verlag.

6

Fully Secure ABE Schemes Based on Composite and Prime Order Groups

6.1 Introduction

In recent years, there has been a growing interest in expanding the expressiveness of encryption systems so that ciphertexts can be targeted at certain user groups. Attribute-Based Encryption (ABE) is among the crypto primitive which is able to provide flexible access control with less key overhead when compared with the traditional public key encryption systems. Obtaining systems that were provably secure under robust security specifications was a challenge early in ABE research. As the number of attributes employed in constructing ABE ciphertexts increased, the security of early versions of ABE schemes [1, 2] experienced a decline. As a result, Canetti et al. [3] devised the selective model to do the first (standard model) security proofs. In this weaker approach, an attacker disclosed the challenge identity he was targeting (artificially) before discovering the system's public parameters. The adversary's capabilities is constrained in the selective security paradigm, as it must declare the target ciphertext prior to seeing any system parameters. This makes partitioning more appropriate, as the simulator may separate the target keys prior to responding to any query for the other keys. Additionally, a model of semi-adaptive security is considered [4, 5]. The adversary declares the target after seeing public keys but before querying any private key in a semi-adaptive model.

Although those security models are useful for proving the basic minimum security of schemes, the adaptive security model for ABE is preferable. When a target ciphertext is set, the adversary gathers a large number of secret keys before and after setting the target ciphertext it desires to decrypt, and then colludes those keys to break the ciphertext, much like an adversary would in the real world. Traditional techniques require a separation between keys that are secure from the adversary and other keys that are compromised by the adversary, which is difficult in this case. Responding to this adaptive adversary, on the other hand, is difficult, especially if the simulator does not know the target before the adversary declares it. The challenge occurs due to the fact that the traditional techniques require a distinction between keys that are secure from the opponent and other keys that have been compromised by the adversary. While the partitioning technique is still useful for proving adaptive security of simple functional encryptions like identity-based encryption [6–8] and hierarchical identity-based encryption [9], it becomes significantly difficult to prove adaptive security of more complicated functional primitives such as attribute-based encryption.

Dual system groups, a notion developed from dual system encryption, was introduced by Chen and Wee [10]. Six algorithms are specified over the groups in such a way that certain properties are maintained, and these algorithms are defined over the triple of groups. It will then be possible to employ these groups and algorithms to create generic encryption systems. Coupled with

Attribute-based Encryption (ABE): Foundations and Applications within Blockchain and Cloud Environments, First Edition.
Qi Xia, Jianbin Gao, Isaac Amankona Obiri, Kwame Omono Asamoah, and Daniel Adu Worae.
© 2024 The Institute of Electrical and Electronics Engineers, Inc. Published 2024 by John Wiley & Sons, Inc.

encryption, Attrapadung gives another generic framework for evaluating the security of encryption schemes, this time concentrating on the exponents of group elements and their relationships. Consequently, as proved by Agrawal and Chase [11], any definition of dual system groups that fits particular criteria, as well as any pair encoding approach that has been demonstrated to be secure, can be used to produce secure encryption schemes in general.

To provide adaptive security of ABE scheme, the earlier ABE were constructed in composite order groups. However, composite order groups require a large parameters which yield in higher efficiency loss compared to other encryption scheme which is constructed in prime order group. Guillevic [12] specifies 256 and 2,644 bits for prime and composite order bilinear groups, respectively, at a 128 bit security level. Composite order bilinear groups are also 254 times slower than prime order bilinear groups. Constructing adaptively secure ABE schemes in prime order groups is critical to practical adoption.

Dual Pairing Vector Spaces (DPVS) have properties that can be used to translate composite order groups into prime order groups. DPVS uses orthogonal vectors made up of prime order group members to create composite order group elements. In [13], Lewko and Waters provide a general technique to convert composite order groups into prime order groups using DPVS. However, the size of vectors causes a decrease in efficiency. For example, in [13], the vector size increases linearly with the predicate size. This implies a large efficiency loss. Sparse DPVS [14, 15] uses vectors with numerous zeros as elements to mitigate the DPVS disadvantage. However, how sparse DPVS may be used for generic conversions for ABE is unclear. Many strategies [16–18] have been proposed to transform composite order groups to prime order groups. However, the techniques in [16–18] do not apply to dual system encryption since they do not mask the values of parameters employed in semi-functional spaces. Because those techniques use dual system encryption, they cannot be applied to encoding frameworks.

Chen et al. [19] presented a modular framework for the design of efficient dual system ABE schemes for a large class of predicates under the standard k-Lin assumption in prime-order groups; this is the first uniform treatment of dual system ABE across different predicates and across both composite and prime-order groups. Via this framework, they obtained concrete efficiency improvements for several ABE schemes. Based on k-Lin and matrix Diffie–Hellman assumption, the authors in [20] expanded the predicates encoding to provide efficient ABE scheme. This approach of simulate all of the structure in composite-order groups (e.g. orthogonality) based on matrix appears to be efficient than that of DPVS as it has less structure (associativity). Thus, the framework simulates composite-order groups by imposing more structure to the encodings, which we can achieve without increasing the size of the encodings.

Note that the whole security proof will not be presented in this chapter since proving the adaptive security of the ABE scheme is a difficult task that requires a considerable number of pages. As a result, this chapter will not cover the full security proof. Nevertheless, the reasoning behind the methodologies used to prove adaptive security ABE schemes will be presented in this chapter. It is necessary to play several security games to demonstrate the ABE scheme's adaptive security. The way the security games are chosen at each stage of the security proof may appear just as intriguing. The primary purpose of this chapter is to present a general overview of the process of establishing the adaptive security of the ABE scheme and an intuition for how the security games are played. Precisely, we will consider that accord which enables the challenger and attacker to play the tight adaptive security of the ABE scheme in such a way that eventually, the underlying hard cryptographic assumption prevents the adversary (challenger) from being able to break the security of the scheme. In other words, we will consider the accord that enables the challenger and attacker to play the tight adaptive security of the ABE scheme.

In this chapter, we shall explore the dual system of encryption-based scheme on from Lewko and Waters [21], Obiri et al. [22], and Tomida et al. [20] that thrives on composite order, Dual Pairing Vector Spaces, and matrix, respectively.

6.2 A Fully Secure CP-ABE from Composite Order Group

This section provides a fully secure CP-ABE scheme from Lewko and Waters [21]. Dual system encryption is accomplished by generating a "semi-functional space" in which semi-functional keys and ciphertexts behave like a parallel clone of the system's normal components, minus the public parameters. This creates a mechanism in the semi-functional space that permits delayed parameters, allowing relevant variables to be created later in the simulation as opposed to being determined during the setup phase. As part of the hybrid structure of a dual system encryption argument, a key isolation mechanism is supplied, indicating that some or all of the semi-functional parameters are only relevant to the distribution of a single semi-functional key at a time. Together, these two procedures provide the semi-functional space with its own set of fresh parameters, which the simulator can choose on the fly as they become relevant. These parameters are only relevant for the semi-functional ciphertext and a single semi-functional key.

Previous dual system encryption arguments used the isolated usage of these delayed semi-functional parameters as a source of entropy from the attacker's perspective to construct an information-theoretic argument. We find that these methods can also be used to build previous tactics for selective security proofs without requiring the attacker to apply the selective restriction. To elaborate, we examine the crucial step of the hybrid security proof when a particular key becomes semi-functional. The undisclosed semi-functional parameters are defined belatedly, according to our approach, when the simulator first issues either the questionable key or the semi-functional ciphertext. We shall illustrate with a CP-ABE system. If the ciphertext is transmitted first, the simulator learns the challenge policy prior to creating the delayed semi-functional parameters, similar to how a CP-ABE system configures selective security. If the key is issued first, the simulator learns the required set of attributes prior to establishing the delayed semi-functional parameters, similar to how a KP-ABE system configures selective security. This affords us the opportunity to combine the approaches used to demonstrate selective security for both CP-ABE and KP-ABE systems with the dual system encryption methodology to produce a new demonstration of full security that maintains the efficiency of selectively secure systems.

Definition 6.1 *(CP-ABE full (adaptive) security definition).* We now formalize the IND-CPA (indistinguishability under Chosen Plaintext Attack) definition of CP-ABE scheme in the fully secure model. This is a game denoted by Game_{real} between a challenger $\mathbb{C}$ and an adversary $\mathcal{A}$. The security game between the challenger $\mathbb{C}$ and adversary $\mathcal{A}$ proceeds as follows:

1. **Setup**: The challenger $\mathbb{C}$ executes Setup $(1^{\lambda}) \rightarrow (pp, msk)$, and submits pp to adversary $\mathcal{A}$.
2. **Phase 1**: $\mathcal{A}$ adaptively queries the $\mathbb{C}$ for the secret keys corresponding to a set of attributes $\{S_1, \dots, S_{Q_1}\}$. For each time, it obtains $sk \leftarrow \text{KeyGen}(pp, msk, \mathbb{A}_k)$ from $\mathbb{C}$.
3. **Challenge**: $\mathcal{A}$ sends two messages $\{msg_0^*, msg_1^*\}$ of equal size together with an access structure $\mathbb{A}$ to $\mathbb{C}$. Then $\mathbb{C}$ tosses a binary coin b and executes $ct^* \leftarrow \text{Enc}(pp, msg_b^*, S^*)$ and gives ct^* to $\mathcal{A}$ on a condition that $\mathbb{A}$ does not satisfy any of the attribute sets queried in Phase 1.
4. **Phase 2**: $\mathcal{A}$ adaptively queries the $\mathbb{C}$ for the secret keys corresponding to a set of attributes $\{S_{Q+1}, \dots, S_Q\}$ with the condition that none of these satisfy $\mathbb{A}^*$. For each k key query, it obtains $sk_k \leftarrow \text{KeyGen}(pp, msk, S_k)$ from $\mathbb{C}$.
5. At the end, $\mathcal{A}$ returns b^* as a guess for b, the adversary $\mathcal{A}$ is a winner if $b = b^*$.

The advantage of $\mathcal{A}$ for this indistinguishable game is defined as:

$$Adv^{\mathcal{A}}_{\text{Game}_{real}}(\lambda) = |Pr[b = b^*] - 1/2| \tag{6.1}$$

Definition 6.2 A KP-ABE scheme is IND-CPA if for all probabilistic polynomial time (PPT) adversary $\mathcal{A}$, the advantage $Adv^{\mathcal{A}}_{\text{Game}_{real}}(\lambda)$ is a negligible function of λ in the above security game.

6.2.1 CP-ABE Construction

1. **Setup**: The setup algorithm chooses a bilinear group of order $N = p_1 p_2 p_3$. G_{p_i} represents the subgroup of order p_i in G. The setup algorithm Setup(λ) runs $(N = p_1 p_2 p_3, G, G_T, e) \leftarrow \mathcal{G}$. Next, it chooses randomly $\{\alpha, a, \kappa\}$ $R \leftarrow Z_N$ and a random group element $g \in G_{p_1}$. For every attribute $i\mathcal{U}$, it selects a random element $h_i \in Z_N$. Finally, the setup algorithm returns the public parameters pp as:

$$pp = \{N, g, g^a, g^{\kappa}, \ldots, e(g,g)^{\alpha}, H_i = g^{h_i} \forall i\} \tag{6.2}$$

The secret master key MSK is:

$$MSK = \{g^{\alpha}, g_3\} \tag{6.3}$$

Note: g_3 is a generator of G_{p_3}.

2. **KeyGen(PP, MSK, S)**: The algorithm computes a secret key associated with attribute set S that enables the user to decrypt encrypted message only if the key satisfy the access structure $\mathbb{A}$. The algorithm selects random elements $t, u, \in Z_N$ and $R, R', R'', \{R_i\}_{iS} \in G_{p3}$. The secret key SK_S is returned as:

$$SK_S = \begin{cases} k = g^{\alpha} g^{at} g^{\kappa u} R, \\ k' = g^u R', \\ k'' = g^t R'', K_i = H_i^t R_i \forall_i \in S. \end{cases} \tag{6.4}$$

3. **Enc($(A, \rho), PP, M$)**: To encrypt a message $m \in G_T$ under access structure A an $\ell \times n$ matrix and ρ a map from each row A_j of A to an attribute $\rho(j)$, the encryption algorithm selects a random vector $v \in Z_N^n$, denoted $v = (s, v_2, \ldots, v_n)$. For every row A_j of A, it selects a random $r_j \in Z_N$. The ciphertext is (we also include (A, ρ)) in the ciphertext, here it is omitted) as:

$$C_T = \begin{cases} C_0 = me(g,g)^{\alpha s}, \\ C = g^s, \\ C' = (g^{\kappa})^{\kappa}, \\ C_j = (g^a)^{A_j \cdot v} H_{\rho(j)}^{-r_j}, \\ D_j = g^{r_j} \forall_j \in [\ell] \end{cases} \tag{6.5}$$

(The notation $[\ell]$ denotes the set $\{1, \ldots, \ell\}$.)

4. **Dec(PP, C_T, SK_S)**: Given a ciphertext C_T and decryption key SK_S, first the key holder checks if $S \in (A, \rho)$. If not the output is empty. If $S \in (A, \rho)$, then the key holder computes constants $\omega_j \in Z_N$ with $\sum_{\rho(j) \in S} \omega_j A_j = (1, 0, \ldots, 0)$. It the computes

$$e(C, K)e(C', K')^{-1} / \prod_{\rho(j) \in S} \left(e(C_j, K'')e(D_j, K_{\rho(j)})_j^{\omega} = e(g,g)^{\alpha s} \right) \tag{6.6}$$

Eventually, the message M is retrieved as $C_0/e(g,g)^{\alpha,s}$.

Correctness: We observe that $e(C,K)e(C',K')^{-1} = e(g,g)^{\alpha,s}e(g,g)^{sat}$. For every $j, e(C_j,K'')$ $e(D_j,K_{\rho(j)}) = e(g,g)^{atA_j\cdot v}$, So we have:

$$\prod_{\rho(j)\in S}\left(e(C_j,K'')e(D_j,K_{\rho(j)})_j^\omega\right) = e(g,g)^{at\sum\limits_{\rho(j)\in S}\omega_j A_j\cdot v} = e(g,g)^{sat} \tag{6.7}$$

6.2.2 Adaptive Security Proof

6.2.2.1 Description of Hybrids

To describe the hybrid distributions, it would be helpful to first give names to the various forms of ciphertext and keys that will be used. For the sake of simplicity, the term Semi-functional will be denoted as SF hereafter.

- **SF Keys**: To produce a SF key for an attribute set S, one first calls the normal key generation algorithm to produce a normal key consisting of $K, K', K'', Kii \in S$. One then chooses a random element $W \in G_{p_2}$ and forms the SF key as:

  $$KW, K', K'', \{K_i\}_{i\in S}$$

  In other words, all of the elements remain unchanged except for K, which is multiplied by a random element of G_{p_2}.

- **SF ciphertexts**: To produce a SF ciphertext for an LSSS matrix (A, ϕ), one first calls the normal encryption algorithm to produce a normal ciphertext consisting of $C0, C, C', C_j, D_j$. One then chooses random exponent $a', \kappa', s' \in Z_N$ a random vector $\omega \in Z_N$ with s' as its first entry, a random exponent $\eta_i \in Z_N$ for each attribute i, and a random exponent $\Gamma_j \in Z_N$ for each $j \in [\ell]$. The SF ciphertext is formed as:

  $$C_0, Cg_2^{s'}, C'g_2^{s'k'}, \{C_j, g_2^{a'A_j\cdot\omega}g_2^{-\eta_{\rho(j)}\gamma_j}, D_j g_2^{\gamma_j}\}$$

  We observe that the structure of the elements in G_{p_2} here is similar to the structure in G_{p_1}, but is unrelated to the public parameters. More specifically, s' plays the role of s, w plays the role of v, a plays the role of a, κ plays the role of $\kappa', \eta\rho(j)$ plays the role of $h_\rho(j)$, and γj plays the role of rj. While the values of a', κ', and the values $h\rho(j)$ are determined modulo p_1 by the public parameters, the values of $a', \kappa', \eta\rho(j)$ are freshly random modulo p_2. These values $a', \kappa', \eta i$ are chosen randomly once and then fixed – these same values will also be involved in additional types of SF keys which we will define below.

- **Nominal SF keys**: These keys will share the values a', κ', η_i modulo p_2 with the SF ciphertext. To produce a nominal SF key for an attribute set S, one first calls the normal key generation algorithm to produce a normal key consisting of $K, K', K'', \{K_i\}i \in S$. One then chooses random exponents $t', \mu' \in Z_N$ and forms the nominal SF key as:

  $$Kg_2^{a't'+\kappa'\mu'}, K'g_2^{\mu'}, K''g_2^{t'}, K_ig_2^{t'\eta_i}\forall i \in S$$

- **Temporary SF keys**: These keys will still share the values η_i modulo p_2 with the SF ciphertext, but the G_{p_2} component attached to K will now be randomized. More formally, to produce a temporary SF key for an attribute set S, one first calls the normal key generation algorithm to produce a normal key consisting of $K, K', K'', \{K_i\}i \in S$. One then chooses a random $W \in G_{p_2}$ and random exponents $t', \mu' \in Z_N$. The temporary SF key is formed as:

  $$KW, K'g_2^{\mu'}, K''g_2^{t'}, K_ig_2^{t'\eta_i}\forall i \in S$$

6.2.3 Security Proof

Theorem 6.1 *Under the general subgroup decision assumption, the three party Diffie–Hellman assumption in a subgroup, and the source group q-parallel BDHE assumption in a subgroup defined in Section 2.2, our CP-ABE scheme defined in Section 3 is fully secure (in the sense of Definition 3*

The security proof is provided in a hybrid argument over a sequence of games. Let $Game_{real}$ represent the real security game as defined in Section 2.3.2. To describe the rest of the games, we must first define SF keys and ciphertexts. We let g_2 denote a fixed generator of the subgroup G_{p_2}.

Proof sketch: This theorem is proven in [13] based on dual system of encryption. We provide Table 2.2 to summarize the dual system encryption with Lewko and Waters' doubly selective security proving sequences. Two other types of private keys are included in the table. Waters' dual system encryption (Table 2.1) uses only regular or SF private keys. In doubly selective security, two more types of private keys are defined: supposedly SF keys and temporarily SF keys. A presumably SF key contains SF components, but these components are associated with the challenge ciphertext's SF components. As a result, they are capable of decrypting SF ciphertexts. This is conceivable because in dual system encryption, the SF sections of keys and ciphertexts are projected from their normal components. Temporary SF keys operate in the same manner as SF keys in the original dual system encryption. They preserve some correlation as supposedly SF keys, but the SF parts also contain random elements. As a result, they are unable to decrypt partially functioning ciphertexts.

The fundamental premise of doubly selective security is that the invariance between a nominally SF key and a temporarily SF key may be computationally established using two selective security proofs. They give CP-ABE for attribute multi-use as an implementation of their technique. The invariance between a supposedly SF key and a temporarily SF key was established in their work utilizing the selective KP-ABE proof when the simulator's type key is requested prior to the challenge ciphertext (i.e. co-selective security). Additionally, if the key was queried after the challenge ciphertext (i.e. selective security), the selective CP-ABE demonstration demonstrated the invariance of those two types of keys. They demonstrate that it is possible to demonstrate the co-selective security of CP-ABE by utilizing selectively secure KP-ABE, because the order in which information is given from the attacker to the simulator is similar in those schemes. In detail, a set of attributes for a private key is provided to the simulator prior to an access structure for the challenge ciphertext in the co-selective proof of CP-ABE. This is the exact same order as KP-ABE.

6.3 A Fully Secure KP-ABE Scheme Based on Dual Vector Space

This section provides a fully secure ABE scheme from Obiri et al. [22]. Our dual encryption system is constructed over SF and normal space. The SF components of ciphertext and keys are much like the normal component of the actual system except that they are decoupled from the public parameters. This gives us the chance to obtain belated parameters in the semi-function space to create relevant variables during the course of simulation rather than to have all the parameters fixed up in the setup phase. The SF space can supply fresh parameters to the simulator for key isolation mechanism; this implies that every SF key should have unique distribution through the use of fresh parameters in the SF space. When the simulator first issues a secret key, then the challenge access policy is known before the SF parameters are defined. Based on the known access policy, the simulator can embed a difficulty in the secret key from the SF space and later annul this difficulty in the ciphertext. On the other hand, if a ciphertext is first issued, then the attributes set of the challenge ciphertext is known before semi-function parameters are specified. Based on the known attributes, the simulator can also embed a difficulty in the ciphertext from the SF space and later annul this difficulty in the key. The difficulty is random variables chosen in the SF space with their attachment to either the secret key or the ciphertext renders invalid decryption unless those variables are cancelled out. The difficulty which is embedded in either the key or ciphertext requires a complete set of key's component to cancel them out. However, based on the restriction that the adversary cannot obtain a complete components of a secret key, computationally this difficulty is unknown to him. Therefore, the two selective ways of embedding difficulties to prevent correctly decryption of ciphertext can be combined to attain full security in the standard model.

Definition 6.3 *(KP-ABE full (adaptive) security definition).* We now formalize the IND-CPA (indistinguishability under Chosen Plaintext Attack) definition of KP-ABE scheme in the fully secure model. This is a game denoted by Game_{real} between a challenger $\mathbb{C}$ and an adversary $\mathcal{A}$. The security game between the challenger $\mathbb{C}$ and adversary $\mathcal{A}$ proceeds as follows:

1. **Setup**: The challenger $\mathbb{C}$ executes Setup $(1^\lambda) \rightarrow (pp, msk)$, and submits pp to adversary $\mathcal{A}$.
2. **Phase 1**: $\mathcal{A}$ adaptively queries the $\mathbb{C}$ for the secret keys corresponding to a set of access structures $\{\mathbb{A}_1, \dots, \mathbb{A}_{Q1}\}$. For each time, it obtains $sk \leftarrow \text{KeyGen}(pp, msk, \mathbb{A}_k)$ from $\mathbb{C}$.
3. **Challenge**: $\mathcal{A}$ sends two messages $\{msg_0^*, msg_1^*\}$ of equal size together with a set of attributes S^* to $\mathbb{C}$. Then $\mathbb{C}$ tosses a binary coin b and executes $ct^* \leftarrow \text{Enc}(pp, msg_b^*, S^*)$ and gives ct^* to $\mathcal{A}$ on a condition that S^* does not satisfy any of the access structures queried in Phase 1.
4. **Phase 2**: $\mathcal{A}$ adaptively queries the $\mathbb{C}$ for the secret keys corresponding to a set of access structures $\{\mathbb{A}_{Q+1}, \dots, \mathbb{A}_Q\}$ with the condition that none of these satisfy S^*. For each time, it obtains $sk \leftarrow \text{KeyGen}(pp, msk, \mathbb{A}_k)$ from $\mathbb{C}$.
5. At the end, $\mathcal{A}$ returns b^* as a guess for b, the adversary $\mathcal{A}$ is a winner if $b = b^*$.

The advantage of $\mathcal{A}$ for this indistinguishable game is defined as:

$$Adv_{\text{Game}_{real}}^{\mathcal{A}}(\lambda) = |Pr[b = b^*] - 1/2| \tag{6.8}$$

Definition 6.4 A KP-ABE scheme is IND-CPA if for all PPT adversary $\mathcal{A}$, the advantage $Adv_{\text{Game}_{real}}^{\mathcal{A}}(\lambda)$ is a negligible function of λ in the above security game.

6.3.1 KP-ABE Construction

We use the dual framework of data encryption proof technique in prime-order settings, where orthogonal sub-spaces within the exponents perform the role of both normal and SF components. Since SF vectors are never published, they can serve as "hidden parameters" which create new randomness even with a fixed size of public parameters. We provide fresh pair of vectors for each attribute to produce enough randomness to ensure an information-theoretic transition from a nominal SF key (one with SF components but still capable of correctly decrypting SF ciphertext) to a real SF one (a key which is incapable of decrypting SF ciphertext). Again, we denote the attribute universe $[\mathcal{U}] = \{1, 2, \dots, \mathcal{U}\}$ as the complete number of attributes within the system. This construction is shown below.

Setup $(1^\lambda, \mathcal{U}) \rightarrow pp, msk$. The private key generator (PKG) runs the Setup algorithm by selecting a bilinear group G of prime order p and a generator g. It picks at random two pairs of dual orthonormal bases $(\mathbb{B}, \mathbb{B}^*)$, $(\mathbb{B}_0, \mathbb{B}_0^*)$ of dimension 3 and $\mathcal{U}$ pairs of dual orthonormal bases $(\mathbb{B}_1, \mathbb{B}_1^*)$, ..., $(\mathbb{B}_{\mathcal{U}}, \mathbb{B}_{\mathcal{U}}^*)$ of dimension 6, bound to the restriction that they all hold the same value δ. We let $\mathbf{b}_i$, $\mathbf{b}_i^*$ denote the family vectors of $(\mathbb{B}, \mathbb{B}^*)$, and $\mathbf{b}_{i,j}$, $\mathbf{b}_{i,j}^*$ are the basis vectors of $(\mathbb{B}_j, \mathbb{B}_j^*)$ for each j from 0 to $\mathcal{U}$. The setup algorithm also picks a quadruple of random exponents $\{\alpha_1, \alpha_2, r_1, r_2\} \xleftarrow{R} \mathbb{Z}_p$ and another quadruple of random exponents $\{y_1, y_2\} \xleftarrow{R} \mathbb{Z}_p$, $\{y_1^*, y_2^*\} \xleftarrow{R} \mathbb{Z}$ with the restriction that for all $i = j\ y_i.y_j^* = 1$. The public parameters comprise:

$$pp := \{G, p, g^{y_1 \mathbf{b}_{1,i}}, g^{r_1 \mathbf{b}_{1,i}}, g^{y_2 \mathbf{b}_{2,i}}, g^{r_2 \mathbf{b}_{2,i}}, g^{r_1 \mathbf{b}_3}, g^{r_2 \mathbf{b}_4}, g^{\mathbf{b}_{5,i}}, g^{\mathbf{b}_6}\ \forall i \in [\mathcal{U}],$$
$$e(g,g)^{\alpha_1 \delta}, e(g,g)^{\alpha_2 \delta}\}.$$

Additionally, the master secret key *msk* is:

$$msk := \{\alpha_1, \alpha_2, g^{y_1^* \mathbf{b}_{1,i}^*}, g^{r_1 \mathbf{b}_{1,i}^*}, g^{y_2^* \mathbf{b}_{2,i}^*}, g^{r_2 \mathbf{b}_{2,i}^*}, g^{r_1 \mathbf{b}_3^*}, g^{r_2 \mathbf{b}_4^*}\ \forall i \in [\mathcal{U}]\}$$

The PKG publishes the public parameters *pp* and keeps the master secret *msk* private. **KeyGen** $(pp, msk, \mathbb{A} = (M, \rho)) \to sk_{\mathbb{A}}$. The PKG runs the KeyGen algorithm by getting the public key *pp*, a master key *msk*, and access structure $\mathbb{A} = (M, \rho)$, the algorithm picks randomly $\{z_0, z_1, \ldots, z_t, r_0, r_1, \ldots, r_t\} \in \mathbb{Z}_p$. Then, set $z_0 = \alpha_1$, $r_0 = \alpha_2$, and computes the shares $\lambda_i = \sum_{k=0}^{t} z_k i^k$ and $\omega_i = \sum_{k=0}^{t} r_k i^k$ for all $\leq i \geq n$, where $(i^1, i^2, \ldots, i^t)$ is the vector of $M_i \in M$ which correspond to the i-th row of M. It, then picks randomly $a_1, a_2 \in \mathbb{Z}_p$ and outputs

$$sk_{\mathbb{A}} = \{K_{1,i} = g^{\lambda_i y_1^* \mathbf{b}_{1,i}^* + a_1 r_1 y_1^* \mathbf{b}_{1,i}^*} . g^{\omega_i y_2^* \mathbf{b}_{2,i}^* + a_2 r_2 y_2^* \mathbf{b}_{2,i}^*}, K_2 = g^{a_1 r_1 \mathbf{b}_3^* + a_2 r_2 \mathbf{b}_4^*}\}\ i \in \rho(i) \tag{6.9}$$

Enc$(msg, S, pp) \to ct$. A data owner runs this algorithm getting the message *msg*, attribute sets S, public parameter *pp* and picks randomly $s_1, s_2 \leftarrow \mathbb{Z}_p$ and outputs

$$ct = \{C_0 = msg.e(g,g)^{\alpha_1 s_1 \delta + \alpha_2 s_2 \delta}, C_{1,i} = g^{s_1 y_1 \mathbf{b}_{1,i} + s_2 y_2 \mathbf{b}_{2,i}}, C_2 = g^{s_1 \mathbf{b}_3 + s_2 \mathbf{b}_4}\}\ i \in \rho(i) \tag{6.10}$$

Dec$(ct, sk_{\mathbb{A}}, pp) \to msg$. A system user runs this algorithm with its secret key $sk_{\mathbb{A}}$, ciphertext ct and the public parameters *pp*. Let S^* correspond to the set of attributes associated to ciphertext ct, and M be the policy matrix. If S^* satisfies $\mathbb{A}$, the decryption algorithm computes $\alpha_1 = \sum_{i \in S^*} \lambda_i.\sigma_i$ and $\alpha_2 = \sum_{i \in S^*} \omega_i.\sigma_i$, where each constant $\sigma_i = \prod_{j \in S^*, i \neq j} \frac{i}{j-i}$ can be obtained efficiently in the polynomial time. It, then computes:

$$\Omega = \prod_{i \in S^*} \left(\frac{en(K_{1,i}, C_{1,i})}{en(K_2, C_2)} \right)^{\sigma_i}$$

$$= \prod_{i \in S^*} \left(\frac{en(g^{\lambda_i y_1^* \mathbf{b}_{1,i}^* + a_1 r_1 y_1^* \mathbf{b}_{1,i}^*} . g^{\omega_i y_2^* \mathbf{b}_{2,i}^* + a_2 r_2 y_2^* \mathbf{b}_{2,i}^*}, g^{s_1 y_1 \mathbf{b}_{1,i} + s_2 y_2 \mathbf{b}_{2,i}})}{en(g^{a_1 r_1 \mathbf{b}_3^* + a_2 r_2 \mathbf{b}_4^*}, g^{s_1 \mathbf{b}_3 + s_2 \mathbf{b}_4})} \right)^{\sigma_i}$$

$$= \prod_{i \in S^*} \left(\frac{en(g^{\lambda_i y_1^* \mathbf{b}_{1,i}^* + a_1 r_1 y_1^* \mathbf{b}_{1,i}^*}, g^{s_1 y_1 \mathbf{b}_{1,i} + s_2 y_2 \mathbf{b}_{2,i}}).en(g^{\omega_i y_2^* \mathbf{b}_{2,i}^* + a_2 r_2 y_2^* \mathbf{b}_{2,i}^*}, g^{s_1 y_1 \mathbf{b}_{1,i} + s_2 y_2 \mathbf{b}_{2,i}})}{en(g^{a_1 r_1 \mathbf{b}_3^* + a_2 r_2 \mathbf{b}_4^*}, g^{s_1 \mathbf{b}_3 + s_2 \mathbf{b}_4})} \right)^{\sigma_i}$$

$$= \prod_{i \in S^*} \left(\frac{en(g,g)^{(\lambda_i y_1^* \mathbf{b}_{1,i}^* + a_1 r_1 y_1^* \mathbf{b}_{1,i}^*) + (s_1 y_1 \mathbf{b}_{1,i} + s_2 y_2 \mathbf{b}_{2,i})} .en(g,g)^{(\omega_i y_2^* \mathbf{b}_{2,i}^* + a_2 r_2 y_2^* \mathbf{b}_{2,i}^*) + (s_1 y_1 \mathbf{b}_{1,i} + s_2 y_2 \mathbf{b}_{2,i})}}{en(g,g)^{(a_1 r_1 \mathbf{b}_3^* + a_2 r_2 \mathbf{b}_4^*) + (s_1 \mathbf{b}_3 + s_2 \mathbf{b}_4)}} \right)^{\sigma_i}$$

$$= \prod_{i \in S^*} \left(\frac{en(g,g)^{(\lambda_i s_1 y_1^* y_1 \mathbf{b}_{1,i} \mathbf{b}_{1,i}^*) + (a_1 r_1 s_1 y_1^* y_1 \mathbf{b}_{1,i} \mathbf{b}_{1,i}^*)} .en(g,g)^{(\omega_i s_2 y_2^* y_2 \mathbf{b}_{2,i}^* \mathbf{b}_{2,i}) + (a_2 r_2 s_2 y_2^* y_2 \mathbf{b}_{2,i}^* \mathbf{b}_{2,i})}}{en(g,g)^{(s_1 a_1 r_1 \mathbf{b}_3^* \mathbf{b}_3) + (s_2 a_2 r_2 \mathbf{b}_4^* \mathbf{b}_4)}} \right)^{\sigma_i}$$

$$= \prod_{i \in S^*} \left(\frac{e(g,g)^{(\lambda_i s_1)} .e(g,g)^{(\omega_i s_2) + (a_1 r_1 s_1) + (a_2 r_2 s_2)}}{e(g,g)^{(s_1 a_1 r_1) + (s_2 a_2 r_2)}} \right)^{\sigma_i}$$

$$= e(g,g)^{\sum\limits_{i \in S^*} \lambda_i.\sigma_i s_1 \delta}.e(g,g)^{\sum\limits_{i \in S^*} \omega_i.\sigma_i s_2 \delta}$$

$$= e(g,g)^{\alpha_1 s_1 \delta + \alpha_1 s_1 \delta}$$

Then, the message is retrieved as:

$$msg = \frac{C_0}{\Omega} = \frac{msg.e(g,g)^{\alpha_1 s_1 \delta + \alpha_2 s_2 \delta}}{e(g,g)^{\alpha_1 s_1 \delta + \alpha_1 s_1 \delta}}$$

6.3.2 Adaptive Security

Under the decision linear (DLIN) assumption and two-Party Diffie-Hellman (TPDH) assumption defined in Section 3.19, our KP-ABE construction is fully secure (i.e. see Definition 6.4).

The security proof for our construction depends on a hybrid argument over series of games. We will define the set of keys and ciphertext that will be used in the games.

- **SF ciphertext**: To create this ciphertext for a set of attributes S, firstly, we execute the normal encryption algorithm in Eq. (6.10). The ciphertext is made up of the following components $C_0, C_{1,i}, \{C_2\}$ $i \in \rho(i)$. Then, we pick a random value $s_3 \in \mathbb{Z}_p$ and multiply $C_{1,i}$ by $g^{s_3 \mathbf{b}_{5,i}}$. Also, we multiply C_2 by $g^{s_3 \mathbf{b}_6}$. The other component of the ciphertext stay unaltered as shown in Eq. (6.3.2).

$$C_{1,i} = g^{s_1 y_1 \mathbf{b}_{1,i} + s_2 y_2 \mathbf{b}_{2,i} + s_3 \mathbf{b}_{5,i}},$$
$$C_2 = g^{s_1 \mathbf{b}_3 + s_2 \mathbf{b}_4 + s_3 \mathbf{b}_6}\} \; i \in \rho(i)$$

- **SF keys**: To generate these keys for a monotone span program (MSP) (M, ρ), we first execute the normal key generation algorithm in Eq. (6.9) to get a normal key made up of the following components of $\{K_{1,i}\} \in \rho(i), K_2$. We then pick random secret values $a_3, \alpha_3 \in \mathbb{Z}_p$ and a random vector $v = (r_0, r_1, \dots, r_t) \in \mathbb{Z}_p^t$ and set the index $r_0 = \alpha_3$. We produce shares for the secret as $\Phi_i = M_i.v^T$, where M_i is the row vector in M with the label $\rho(i)$. The SF key is output as:

$$sk_{\mathbb{A}} = \{K_{1,i} = g^{\lambda_i y_1^* \mathbf{b}_{1,i}^* + a_1 r_1 y_1^* \mathbf{b}_{1,i}^*}.g^{\omega_i y_2^* \mathbf{b}_{2,i}^* + a_2 r_2 y_2^* \mathbf{b}_{2,i}^*}.$$
$$g^{\Phi_i \mathbf{b}_{5,i}^* + a_3 \mathbf{b}_{5,i}^*}, K_2 = g^{a_1 r_1 \mathbf{b}_3^*}.g^{a_2 r_2 \mathbf{b}_4^*}.g^{a_3 \mathbf{b}_6^*}\} \; i \in \rho(i)$$

- **Nominal SF keys**: To create these keys for a MSP (M, ρ), we first execute the normal key generation algorithm in Eq. (6.9) to get a normal key made up of the following components of $\{K_{1,i}\} \in \rho(i), K_2$. We then pick random secret values $a_3, \alpha_3 \in \mathbb{Z}_p$ and a random vector $v = (r_0, r_1, \dots, r_t) \in \mathbb{Z}_p^t$ with the first index having the value of zero. We set the index $r_0 = \alpha_3$. We produce shares for the secret as $\Phi_i = M_i.v^T$, where M_i is the row vector in M with the label $\rho(i)$. The SF key is output as:

$$sk_{\mathbb{A}} = \{K_{1,i} = g^{\lambda_i y_1^* \mathbf{b}_{1,i}^* + a_1 r_1 y_1^* \mathbf{b}_{1,i}^*}.g^{\omega_i y_2^* \mathbf{b}_{2,i}^* + a_2 r_2 y_2^* \mathbf{b}_{2,i}^*}.$$
$$g^{\Phi_i \mathbf{b}_{5,i}^* + a_3 \mathbf{b}_{5,i}^*}, K_2 = g^{a_1 r_1 \mathbf{b}_3^*}.g^{a_2 r_2 \mathbf{b}_4^*}.g^{a_3 \mathbf{b}_6^*}\} \; i \in \rho(i)$$

Recall that we do not put a partition on a simulator with a nominal SF key. Therefore, the nominal SF key correlates correctly with the SF ciphertext to allow decryption, regardless of the presence or absence of SF components. This happens because the share of the secret α_3 in the SF space is zero.

- **Ephemeral SF keys**: These keys are indistinguishable to nominal keys, with the exception that SF components attach to either $K_{1,i}$ or K_2 is now being randomized (which prevent accurate SF ciphertext decryption). Concretely, to create an ephemeral SF key for the access matrix M, we first execute the normal key generation algorithm in Eq. (6.9) to get a normal key made up of the following components: $\{K_{1,i}\} \in \rho(i)$ and K_2. We then pick random secret values $a_3, a_4, a_5, \alpha_3 \in \mathbb{Z}_p$ and a random vector $v = (r_0, r_1, \ldots, r_t) \in \mathbb{Z}_p^t$ and set the index $r_0 = \alpha_3$. Note that value of the secret α_3 in the SF space is zero. We produce shares for the secret as $\Phi_i = M_i.v^T$, where M_i is the row vector in M with the label $p(i)$. The SF key is output as:

$$sk_{\mathbb{A}} = \{K_{1,i} = g^{\lambda y_1^* \mathbf{b}_{1,i}^* + a_1 r_1 y_1^* \mathbf{b}_{1,i}^*} . g^{\omega y_2^* \mathbf{b}_{2,i}^* + a_2 r_2 y_2^* \mathbf{b}_{2,i}^*}.$$
$$g^{a_4 \Phi_i \mathbf{b}_{5,i}^* + a_3 \mathbf{b}_{5,i}^*}, K_2 = g^{a_1 r_1 \mathbf{b}_3^*} . g^{a_2 r_2 \mathbf{b}_4^*} . g^{a_3 a_5 \mathbf{b}_6^*}\} \; i \in \rho(i)$$

Lemma 6.1 *Under the subspace assumption, no PPT adversary can achieve a non-negligible advantage in distinguishing Game$_{real}$ and Game$_0$.*

6.3.3 Security Proof

Our hybrid proof is executed over a series of games as shown in Table 6.1. Denoting Q as the total number of key requested by adversary, we define the series of games as follows:

Table 6.1 Security proof structure.

Security games	Private keys	Ciphertext	Description
Game$_{real}$	Normal	Normal	Equivalent to Adaptive Security Model
$\approx$ Game$_0$	Normal	Semi-functional	Semi-functional Ciphertext Invariance
$\vdots$	$\vdots$	$\vdots$	Semi-functional Key Invariance (Co-selective Security)
$\approx$ Game$_k^N$	Semi-functional $(< k)$ Nominally Semi-functional $(= k)$ Normal $(> k)$	Semi-functional	
$\approx$ Game$_k^T$	Semi-functional $(< k)$ Temporary Semi-functional $(= k)$ Normal $(> k)$	Semi-functional	
$\approx$ Game$_k$	Semi-functional $(\leq k)$ Normal $(> Q_1)$	Semi-functional	
$\vdots$	$\vdots$	$\vdots$	
$\approx$ Game$_{Q_1}$	(if $\leq Q_1$) Semi-functional (if $> Q_1$) Normal	Semi-functional	
$\approx$ Game$_{Q_1+1}$	(if $\leq Q_1 + 1$) Semi-functional (if $> Q_1 + 1$) Normal	Semi-functional	Semi-functional Key Invariance (Selective Security)
$\vdots$	$\vdots$	$\vdots$	
$\approx$ Game$_Q$	Semi-functional	Semi-functional	
$\approx$ Game$_{final}$	Semi-functional	Semi-functional + random message	Semi-functional security

$Game_{real}$ is a real security game as in Section 6.3 (see Definition 6.3). In $Game_k$, the ciphertext submitted to the adversary is SF, as are the first k keys. The rest of the keys are normal. $Game_k^N$ is similar to $Game_k$, besides that the k-th key delivered to the adversary is a nominal SF key. The first $k - 1$ keys are SF, whereas the rest of the keys are normal. $Game_k^T$ is similar to $Game_k$, besides that the k-th keys delivered to the adversary is an ephemeral SF. The first $k - 1$ keys are SF, whereas the rest of the keys are normal. $Game_{final}$ is analogous to $Game_Q$, besides that the SF ciphertext delivered to the adversary is encryption of random message.

The layout of our hybrid argument will be as follows. Firstly, we move from $Game_{real}$ to $Game_0$, then to $Game_1$, next to $Game_2$, and so on. Eventually, we get to $Game_Q$, where all of the keys and the ciphertext delivered to the adversary are SF. Then, we move to $Game_{final}$ and this completes our security proof since any adversary in this final game has negligible advantage.

The transitions from $Game_{real}$ to $Game_0$ and from $Game_Q$ to $Game_{final}$ are not complicated and can be done with the help of the computational assumptions. However, the transition from $Game_{k-1}$ to $Game_k$ is a bit complicated and requires other steps. For these steps, we will consider making transition between two phases. phase 1, is when the adversary requests a challenge ciphertext after obtaining the secret key. In phase 2, the adversary requests a secret key after obtaining the challenge ciphertext. Therefore, in order to get from $Game_{k-1}$ to $Game_k$, we will transition first from $Game_{k-1}$ to $Game_N^k$, then to $Game_T^k$, and finally to $Game_k$. We let Q_1 represents the number of queries in Phase 1, and we will tackle this transition independently for $k \le Q_1$ and $k \ge Q_1$. The security proof for phase 1 queries and phase 2 is similar to the selective security proof in the KP-ABE settings and CP-ABE settings, respectively.

6.4 KP-ABE Scheme Based on Matrix

Here we take a brief look at Kowalczyk and Wee's piecewise guessing framework [24], which is based on Jafargholi et al.'s framework [23]. The framework enables us to prove adaptive security of cryptographic construction that are selectively secure. The proof is through a sequence of hybrids in which the valid secret share associated with various gates are gradually replaced with fake random values. Once the output gate is fake, it decouples the secret shares from the secret that proves security. The gates that we can substitute with fake values are the gates in which the adversary cannot determine the secret. Thus, the adversary does not have enough valid share to reconstruct the secret. Since the adversary controls an unqualified set there must be a sequence that ultimately results in replacing the secret associated with the root gate. The number of hybrids in the access structure is at most the number of gates since we handle one gate in each hybrid and never consider it again.

The hybrid argument enables us to prove that two games G_L and G_R are computationally indistinguishable by constructing a sequence of hybrid games $G_L := H^{h_0}, H^{h_1}, \ldots, H^{h_\ell} := G_R$ and showing that each pair of neighboring hybrids H^{h_i} and $H^{h_{i+1}}$ are indistinguishable.

In this section, we present our compact KP-ABE for NC1 that is adaptively secure under the $MDDH^k$ assumption in asymmetric prime-order bilinear groups [20].

6.4.1 The Scheme

The KP-ABE scheme is defined as follows:

1. **Setup($1^\lambda, 1^n$):** Run $\mathbb{G} = (p, G_1, G_2, G_T, e) \leftarrow \mathcal{G}(1^\lambda)$. Sample $\mathbf{A} \leftarrow \mathbb{Z}_p^{k \times (k+1)}$, $\mathbf{W}_i \leftarrow \mathbb{Z}_p^{(k+1) \times k} \forall i \in [n], \mathbf{v} \leftarrow \mathbb{Z}_p^{k+1}$ and output:

$$msk := (\mathbf{v}, \mathbf{W}_1, \ldots, \mathbf{W}_n)$$

$$mpk := ([\mathbf{A}]_1, [\mathbf{AW}_1]_1, \ldots, [\mathbf{AW}_n]_1, e([\mathbf{A}]_1, [\mathbf{v}]_2))$$

2. **Enc(mpk, x, M)**: Sample $s \leftarrow \mathbb{Z}_p^k$. Output:

$$ct_x = (ct_1, \{ct_{2,i}, ct_3\}_{x_i=1})$$
$$:= \left([\mathbf{s}^T\mathbf{A}]_1, \{[\mathbf{s}^T\mathbf{AW}_i]_1\}_{x_i=1}, e([\mathbf{s}^T\mathbf{A}]_1, [\mathbf{v}]_2) \cdot M \right)$$

3. **KeyGen(msk, mpk, f)**: Sample $(\{\mathbf{v}_j, \rho\}) \leftarrow \mathbf{share}(f, v), r_j \leftarrow \mathbb{Z}_p^k$. Output:

$$\mathbf{sk}_f = (\{sk_{1,j}, sk_{2,j}\})$$
$$:= (\{[\mathbf{v}_j + \mathbf{W}_{\rho(j)}\mathbf{r}_j]_2, [\mathbf{r}_j]_2\})$$

where $\mathbf{W}_0 = 0$.

4. **Dec(ct_x, sk_f, mpk)**: compute ω such that $\mathbf{v} = \sum_{\rho(i)=0 \vee x_{\rho(j)}=1}$. Output: $ct_3 \cdot \displaystyle\prod_{\rho(i)=0 \vee x_{\rho(j)}=1}$

$$\left(\frac{e(ct_{2,\rho(j)}, sk_{2,j})}{e(ct_1, sk_{1,j})} \right)^{\omega_j}$$

Correctness: The correctness relies on the fact that for all j, we have $\dfrac{e(ct_1, sk_{1,j})}{e(ct_{2,\rho(j)}, sk_{2,j})} = [\mathbf{s}^T\mathbf{Av}_j]_T$ which follows from the fact that

$$\mathbf{s}^T\mathbf{Av}_j = \underbrace{\mathbf{s}^T\mathbf{A}}_{ct_1} \cdot \underbrace{(\mathbf{v}_j + \mathbf{W}_{\rho(j)}\mathbf{r}_j)}_{sk_{1,j}} - \underbrace{\mathbf{s}^T\mathbf{AW}_{\rho(j)}}_{ct_{2,\rho(j)}} \cdot \underbrace{\mathbf{r}_j}_{sk_{2,j}}$$

Therefore, for all f, x such that $f(x) = 1$, we have

$$ct_3 \cdot \prod_{\rho(j)=0 \vee x_{\rho(j)}=1} \left(\frac{e(ct_{2,\rho(j)}, sk_{2,j})}{e(ct_1, sk_{1,j})} \right)^{\omega_j} = M \cdot [\mathbf{s}^T\mathbf{Av}]_T \cdot \prod_{\rho(j)=0 \vee x_{\rho(j)}=1} [\mathbf{s}^T\mathbf{AV}_j]_T^{\omega_j}$$
$$= M \cdot [\mathbf{s}^T\mathbf{Av}]_T \cdot [-\mathbf{s}^T\mathbf{A} \sum_{\rho(j)=0 \vee x_{\rho(j)}=1} \omega_j\mathbf{v}_j]_T$$
$$= M \cdot [\mathbf{s}^T\mathbf{Av}]_T \cdot [-\mathbf{s}^T\mathbf{Av}]_T$$
$$= M$$

6.4.2 Adaptive Security

Description of hybrids To describe the hybrid distributions, it would be helpful to first give names to the various forms of ciphertext and keys that will be used. A ciphertext can be in one of the following forms:

- **Normal**: generated as in the scheme.
- **SF**: same as a Normal key, except $\mathbf{s}^T\mathbf{A}$ replaced with $\mathbf{c}^T \leftarrow \mathbb{Z}_p^{k+1}$, that is

$$ct_x := ([\mathbf{c}^T]_1, \{[\mathbf{c}^T\mathbf{W}_i]_1\}_{x_i=1}, e([\mathbf{c}^T]_1, [\mathbf{v}]_2 \cdot M))$$

where $(\{\mathbf{v}_j, \rho\}) \leftarrow \mathbf{share}(f, \mathbf{v} + \delta\mathbf{a}^\perp), \mathbf{r}_j \leftarrow \mathbb{Z}_p^k$.

A secret key can be in one of the following forms:

- **Normal**: generated as in the scheme.
- **SF**: same as a Normal key, except $\mathbf{v}$ replaced with $v + \delta a^{\perp}$, where a fresh $\delta \leftarrow \mathbb{Z}_p$ is chosen per SF key and $a^{\perp}$ is any fixed $a^{\perp} \in \mathbb{Z}_p^{k+1}/\{\mathbf{0}\}$ such that $\mathbf{A}a^{\perp} = 0$ that is

$$sk_f := (\{[\mathbf{v}_j + \mathbf{W}_{\rho(j)\mathbf{r}_j}]_2, [r_j]_2\})$$

where $(\{\mathbf{v}_j, \rho\}) \leftarrow \mathbf{share}(f, \mathbf{v} + \delta \mathbf{a}^{\perp}), \mathbf{r}_j \leftarrow \mathbb{Z}_p^k$.

Hybrid sequence. Suppose the adversary A makes at most Q secret key queries. The hybrid sequence is as follows:

- H_0: real game
- H_1: same as H_0, except we use a SF ciphertext.
- $H_{2,\ell}, \ell = 0, \ldots, Q$: same as H_1, except the first ℓ keys are SF and the remaining $Q = \ell$ keys are Normal.
- H_3: replace M with random $\tilde{M}$.

6.4.3 Security Proof

- We have $H_0 \approx_c H_1 = H_{2,0}$ through k-Lin, which indicates that $([\mathbf{A}]_1, [\mathbf{s}^T\mathbf{A}]_1) \approx_c ([A]_1, [c^T]_1)$. Here, the security reduction has to select $\mathbf{W}_1, \ldots, \mathbf{W}_n$ and $\mathbf{v}$ such that it can simulate the mpk, the ciphertext and the secret keys.
- We have $H_{2,\ell} \approx_c H_{2,\ell}$ for all $\ell \in [Q]$. The difference between the two is that we switch the ℓth sk_f from Normal to SF using the adaptive security of our core 1-ABE component in G^{1-abe} from Section 5. The idea is to sample

$$\mathbf{v} = \tilde{\mathbf{v}} + \mu\mathbf{a}^{\perp}, \mathbf{W}_i = \tilde{\mathbf{W}}_i + \mathbf{a}^{\perp}\mathbf{w}_i^T$$

so that mpk can be computed using $\tilde{\mathbf{v}}, \tilde{\mathbf{W}}_i$ and perfectly hide $\mu, \mathbf{w}_1, \ldots, \mathbf{w}_n$. Therefore, the reduction performs

- uses $\mathcal{O}X(x)$ in G^{1-abe} to simulate the challenge ciphertext
- uses $\mathcal{O}F(f)$ in G^{1-abe} to simulate ℓth secret key
- uses $\mu^{(0)}$ from G^{1-abe} together with $\mathcal{O}E(i, \cdot) = Enc(\omega_i, \cdot)$ to simulate the remaining $Q - \ell$ secret keys.

- We have $H_{2,Q} \equiv H_3$. In $H_{2,Q}$, the secret keys leak $\mathbf{v} + \delta_1 \mathbf{a}^{\perp}, \ldots, \mathbf{v} + \delta_Q \mathbf{a}^{\perp}$. This means that $\mathbf{c}^T\mathbf{v}$ is statistically random (as long as $\mathbf{c}^T\mathbf{a}^{\perp} \neq 0$).

6.5 Summary

This chapter provides the usage of composite groups, vectors, and matrices in prime order groups to construct fully secure attribute-based encryption using dual system of encryption. As composite order groups are not efficient in constructing ABE, it becomes necessary to explore approach that can be used to simulate the features of composite order group using predicate encoding techniques based on vectors and matrices. Vectors and matrices thrive on predicate encoding techniques and dual system groups to construct ABE schemes in prime order groups that are more efficient than composite order groups.

References

1 Sahai, A. and Waters, B. (2005). Fuzzy identity-based encryption. In: *Annual International Conference on the Theory and Applications of Cryptographic Techniques*, 457–473. Springer-Verlag.

2 Goyal, V., Pandey, O., Sahai, A., and Waters, B. (2006). Attribute based encryption for fine-grained access control of encrypted data. *ACM Conference on Computer and Communications Security (ACM CCS)*.

3 Canetti, R., Halevi, S., and Katz, J. (2003). A forward-secure public-key encryption scheme. In: *International Conference on the Theory and Applications of Cryptographic Techniques*, 255–271. Springer-Verlag.

4 Chen, J. and Wee, H. (2014). Semi-adaptive attribute-based encryption and improved delegation for boolean formula. In: *International Conference on Security and Cryptography for Networks*, 277–297. Cham: Springer.

5 Takashima, K. (2014). Expressive attribute-based encryption with constant-size ciphertexts from the decisional linear assumption. In: *International Conference on Security and Cryptography for Networks*, 298–317. Cham: Springer.

6 Boneh, D. and Boyen, X. (2004). Secure identity based encryption without random oracles. In: *Advances in Cryptology - CRYPTO 2004, 24th Annual International Cryptology Conference*, Santa Barbara, CA, USA (15–19 August 2004), Proceedings, vol. 3152, *Lecture Notes in Computer Science* (ed. M.K. Franklin), 443–459. Springer-Verlag.

7 Waters, B. (2005). Efficient identity-based encryption without random oracles. In: *Annual International Conference on the Theory and Applications of Cryptographic Techniques*, 114–127. Berlin, Heidelberg: Springer-Verlag.

8 Gentry, C. (2006). Practical identity-based encryption without random oracles. In: *Advances in Cryptology - EUROCRYPT 2006, 25th Annual International Conference on the Theory and Applications of Cryptographic Techniques*, St. Petersburg, Russia (May 28 -June 1 2006), Proceedings, vol. 4004 *Lecture Notes in Computer Science* (ed. S. Vaudenay), 445–464. Springer-Verlag.

9 Gentry, C. and Halevi, S. (2009). Hierarchical identity based encryption with polynomially many levels. In: *Theory of Cryptography. TCC 2009, Lecture Notes in Computer Science*, vol. 5444 (ed. O. Reingold), 437–456. Berlin, Heidelberg: Springer.

10 Chen, J. and Wee, H. (2014). Doubly spatial encryption from DBDH. *Theoretical Computer Science* 543: 79–89.

11 Agrawal, S. and Chase, M. (2016). A study of pair encodings: predicate encryption in prime order groups. In: *Theory of Cryptography Conference*, 259–288. Springer-Verlag.

12 Guillevic, A. (2013). Comparing the pairing efficiency over composite-order and prime-order elliptic curves. In: *Applied Cryptography and Network Security. ACNS 2013, Lecture Notes in Computer Science*, vol. 7954 (ed. M.J. Jacobson Jr., M.E. Locasto, P. Mohassel, and R. Safavi-Naini), 357–372. Springer-Verlag.

13 Lewko, A.B. (2012). Tools for simulating features of composite order bilinear groups in the prime order setting. In: *Advances in Cryptology - EUROCRYPT 2012. EUROCRYPT 2012, Lecture Notes in Computer Science*, vol. 7237, (ed. D. Pointcheval and T. Johansson), 318–335. Springer-Verlag.

14 Okamoto, T. and Takashima, K. (2015). Achieving short ciphertexts or short secret-keys for adaptively secure general inner-product encryption. *Designs, Codes and Cryptography* 77 (2–3): 725–771.

15 Okamoto, T. and Takashima, K. (2011). Achieving short ciphertexts or short secret-keys for adaptively secure general inner-product encryption. In: *Cryptology and Network Security - 10th International Conference, CANS 2011*, Sanya, China (10–12 December 2011). Proceedings, vol. 7092, *Lecture Notes in Computer Science* (ed. D. Lin, G. Tsudik, and X. Wang), 138–159. Springer-Verlag.

16 Freeman, D.M. (2010). Converting pairing-based cryptosystems from composite-order groups to prime-order groups. In: *Advances in Cryptology - EUROCRYPT 2010. EUROCRYPT 2010. Lecture Notes in Computer Science*, vol. 6110 (ed. H. Gilbert), 44–61. Berlin, Heidelberg: Springer-Verlag.

17 Herold, G., Hesse, J., Hofheinz, D. et al. (2014). Polynomial spaces: a new framework for composite-to-prime-order transformations. In: *Annual Cryptology Conference*, 261–279. Berlin, Heidelberg: Springer-Verlag.

18 Seo, J.H. (2012). On the (IM) possibility of projecting property in prime-order setting. In: *International Conference on the Theory and Application of Cryptology and Information Security*, 61–79. Berlin, Heidelberg: Springer-Verlag.

19 Chen, J., Gay, R., and Wee, H. (2015). Improved dual system ABE in prime-order groups via predicate encodings. In: *Annual International Conference on the Theory and Applications of Cryptographic Techniques*, 595–624. Berlin, Heidelberg: Springer-Verlag.

20 Tomida, J., Kawahara, Y., and Nishimaki, R. (2021). Fast, compact, and expressive attribute-based encryption. *Designs, Codes and Cryptography* 89 (11): 2577–2626.

21 Lewko, A. and Waters, B. (2012). New proof methods for attribute-based encryption: achieving full security through selective techniques. In: *Annual Cryptology Conference*, 180–198. Berlin, Heidelberg: Springer-Verlag.

22 Obiri, I.A., Xia, Q., Xia, H. et al. (2020). A fully secure KP-ABE scheme on prime-order bilinear groups through selective techniques. *Security and Communication Networks* 2020: Article ID 8869057.

23 Jafargholi, Z., Kamath, C., Klein, K. et al. (2017). Be adaptive, avoid overcommitting. In: *Annual International Cryptology Conference*, 133–163. Cham: Springer.

24 Kowalczyk, L. and Wee, H. (2020). Compact adaptively secure ABE for NC 1 from k-Lin. *Journal of Cryptology* 33 (3): 954–1002.

Part II

Concepts of Blockchain Technology

7

Blockchain Technology

7.1 Introduction

Blockchain is a distributed, unchangeable ledger that makes recording transactions and managing assets in a corporate network much easier. An asset could be tangible or intangible. A tangible asset (example a house, car, cash, or land) and intangible asset (example intellectual property, patents, copyrights, branding). On a blockchain network, virtually anything of value may be monitored and traded. Information is the lifeblood of business. The faster and more accurate it is received, the better. Blockchain excels at delivering immediate, shareable, and completely transparent information, securely stored on an immutable ledger accessible only to authorized network users. With a blockchain network, various aspects such as orders, payments, accounts, production, and more can be efficiently tracked. The transparency and shared view of the truth among network members enable a comprehensive end-to-end view of each transaction. This not only enhances users confidence but also leads to increased efficiencies and opens up new opportunities for optimization. While blockchain technology has just recently become associated with new means of managing financial assets, its possibilities are practically limitless. However, spreading information accountability in this new democracy creates new issues and practicalities, particularly for security-conscious citizens. We'll look at the basic concepts of blockchain technology, practical aspects of what makes a blockchain, and the inherent vulnerabilities of a decentralized network in the real world in this chapter. A Google Doc is a good analogy for understanding blockchain technology. When we produce a document and share it with a group of individuals, instead of being duplicated or transferred, the document is disseminated. This provides a decentralized distribution chain in which everyone has simultaneous access to the document. No one is locked out while waiting for another party to make changes, and all changes to the document are logged in real time, making them entirely transparent. Blockchain is a particularly promising and revolutionary technology because it reduces risk, eliminates fraud, and provides scalable transparency for a wide range of applications.

7.1.1 History

Cryptographer David Chaum introduced a blockchain-like architecture in his 1982 dissertation titled "Computer Systems Established, Maintained, and Trusted by Mutually Suspicious Groups." In 1991, two other people named Stuart Haber and W. Scott Stornetta published more work on a cryptographically secured chain of blocks. They sought to create a system that would prevent tampering with document timestamps. Later in 1992, two more people named Haber, Stornetta, and Dave Bayer added Merkle trees to the design, enhancing its capabilities by allowing diverse

Attribute-based Encryption (ABE): Foundations and Applications within Blockchain and Cloud Environments, First Edition. Qi Xia, Jianbin Gao, Isaac Amankona Obiri, Kwame Omono Asamoah, and Daniel Adu Worae.

document certificates to be combined into a single block. Consequently, their document certificate hashes have been consistently published every week in The New York Times under their firm Surety since 1995. Satoshi Nakamoto, a group of people (or a single person), created the first decentralized blockchain in 2008. By employing a Hashcash-like approach to timestamp blocks without requiring them to be signed by a trusted party and presenting a hard parameter to balance the rate at which blocks are added to the chain, Nakamoto significantly improved the concept. The next year, Nakamoto included the design as a core component of the cryptocurrency bitcoin. It functioned as the network's public ledger for all transactions. In August 2014, the bitcoin blockchain file size, which contains the records of all network transactions, surpassed 20 gigabyte (GB). In January 2015, the size had increased to over 30 GB, and within a year, from January 2016 to January 2017, the bitcoin blockchain had grown from 50 to 100 GB. By early 2020, the ledger had grown above 200 GB. The terms "block" and "chain" were used individually in Satoshi Nakamoto's initial paper; however in 2016, they then became synonymous as "blockchain." According to an application of the diffusion of innovations theory, blockchains achieved a 13.5 percent adoption rate within financial services in 2016, putting them in the early adopter's phase, according to Accenture (an Irish multinational professional services firm). In 2016, the Chamber of Digital Commerce envisioned the Global Blockchain Forum. This forum was formed thanks to the participation of industry trade organizations. Only 1% of CIOs (chief information officer (CIO)), chief digital information officer (CDIO), or information technology (IT) director) indicated any kind of blockchain adoption within their organizations in May 2018, according to Gartner, and only 8% of CIOs were "planning active experimentation with blockchain" in the short term. According to Gartner, 5% of CIOs believe blockchain technology will be a "game-changer" for their organization in 2019 and beyond [1].

7.1.2 Preliminary Concepts of Blockchain Technology

1. **Peer-to-peer (P2P) network**: A peer-to-peer (P2P) network is a distributed network design that allows participants to share resources. Participants make their resources (processing power, link capacity, printers, and storage capacity, among other things) accessible for other participants to use. In such a network, each participating node (peer) performs both responsibilities (client and server). At any given time, peer A (as a client) can request services and/or material directly from peer B (as a server) on the network, bypassing any intermediary entities. Peer A may later function as a server in response to a content or service request from peer B, who is operating as a client [1].
2. **Cryptography**: Cryptography is the mathematical art of making communication secure. Most current security protocols make use of it [2]. A mathematical value known as a "key" plays a crucial function in cryptography. Cryptography is the art of science encompassing the principles and methods of transforming an intelligent message into one that is unintelligible, and then retransforming that message back to its original form. Cryptography is divided into two types, namely symmetric cryptography and asymmetric cryptography.

    In symmetric cryptography also known as private key cryptography, a single shared key is used to encrypt and decrypt data between two parties. The security of symmetric cryptography relies on the key exchange protocol that is going to be used by the system.

    Asymmetric cryptography also known as public key cryptography makes use of a pair of related keys (one public key and one private key) to encrypt and decrypt data. In this cryptography, communications are encrypted with the public key of the receiver and decrypted with the receiver's private key. Asymmetric cryptography is slower than the symmetric cryptography due to the two keys (private and public keys) generation which consume a lot of computational power. Symmetric cryptography is very fast due to the fact that it makes use of only one shared secret key, and the keys used are shorter than those in asymmetric cryptography.

3. **Hash function**: Hash function is a one-way mathematical function that ensures data integrity. For each variable or arbitrary input, it calculates a fixed-sized unique value called a "hash value." Because the hash function is one-way, the original data cannot be deduced from the unique output. Its security strength is based on the one-way characteristic, which is utilized to safeguard data integrity. A hash function must be collision-resistant in order to be considered secure; this means that finding two inputs that produce the same hash output is exceedingly difficult (almost impossible). This necessitates the following characteristics:
   - There are no flaws in the hash function.
   - There are a lot of options for outputs.
   - A one-way hash function (in which the input cannot be deduced from the output).
   - The results of same inputs are vastly diverse.

   A hash function can be used in blockchain if it fits these characteristics. However, if any of these rules are broken, the blockchain's security is jeopardized. To ensure that transactions cannot be edited after being stored in the ledger, blockchain mainly relies on cryptographic hash algorithms.

4. **Hash chain**: By repeatedly applying the hash function to a piece of data, a hash chain is created. A hash value h_1 is formed, for example, by applying the hash function $f(x)$ to data x. The first hash value, h_1, is passed to the second hash function, $f(h_1)$, which calculates the second hash value, h_2, and so on. A chain of hashes of length n is formed by these calculated hash values $h_1, h_2, \ldots, h_n$. Because hash functions are irreversible, h_1 cannot be computed from h_2, and vice versa [3]. Hash chains have a wide range of applications for data integrity security and play an important part in Blockchain.

5. **Merkle tree**: By arranging data and related hash values in the shape of a tree, Merkle trees, also known as hash trees, allow efficient and safe data verification. Bobry leaf node in the tree structure has the hash value of some data, and every non-leaf node has the hash value of its offspring nodes. Figure 7.1 depicts an example of a Merkle tree in which data blocks D1 and D2 are supplied to the Merkle Tree's leaf nodes (hashes of D1 and D2). Another hash is computed from the hashes h_1 and h_2 and added as the parent node of child nodes [4].

6. **Digital signatures and timestamp**: Along with the contents, digital signatures are employed as proof of authorship. Signatures are commonly implemented via public key cryptography, in which a signer signs a document with his or her private key and the recipient verifies the signatures with the signer's public key. Digital signatures are trusted because they are unforgeable, reusable, and irreversible. It means that a digital signature cannot be used for any other document or content, and that no one other than the original signer can claim the signature, and that the original signer cannot dispute it [5, 6]. Signing and verification phases are the two phases entangled with typical digital signature. For example, a user with the name Bob wants to send a message to another user by name Bob, In the Signing phase, Bob with her private key, encrypts all her data and then forwards them to Bob including the original data. In the verification phase, Bob could tell easily if the data has been tampered with or no by validating the value with Bob's public key. A typical digital signature algorithm is elliptic curve digital signature algorithm (ECDSA), that is Elliptic curve digital signature algorithm A timestamp is the time at which a computer records the occurrence of an event, rather than the time of the event itself. It usually captures the date and time of the incident, and is accurate to a fraction of a second. The data from this timestamp is recoded in a consistent manner alongside the original data to allow for easy comparison of two different records to measure progress over time [7].

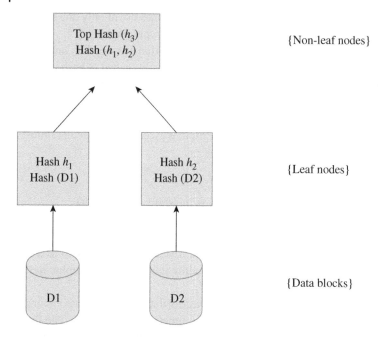

Figure 7.1 An example of Merkle Tree (binary hash tree).

7.1.3   Characteristics of Blockchain

This section compiles a list of significant Blockchain properties based on research. As a result, the study shows differences in terminology for some of these qualities, which is to be expected for a technology in its early stages. The goal of this section is to standardize terminology for distinct qualities. Each characteristic's benefits and any potential concerns are also mentioned. Furthermore, existing concerns with Blockchain technology are identified, as well as major research challenges. Below are some key characteristics of blockchain:

1. **Decentralization**: With traditional centralized transaction systems, each transaction must be certified by a central trusted agency, such as a central bank, resulting in cost and performance limitations at the central servers. In contrast to this centralized paradigm, consensus algorithms are utilized in blockchains to preserve data integrity in dispersed networks, eliminating the requirement for a third party. Perhaps the most important feature of the Blockchain is its decentralization. The Blockchain ledger is distributed across numerous computers known as nodes. These nodes create a Blockchain network, with multiple of them working in a peer-to-peer (P2P) fashion to validate information access without the need for a centralized authority [8–10]. For recording, storing, updating, transmission, verification, maintenance, and a variety of other functions linked to the information in the Blockchain network, the Blockchain system employs a distributed system structure [11, 12].

   This feature of decentralization reduces the need for powerful central authorities and instead passes control to the individual user, making the system fairer and safer. To ensure that information is consistent and incorruptible, the Blockchain nodes use a set of rules and algorithms called consensus protocols to record information and validate transactions. When a large number of devices agree on what should be recorded on a Blockchain, consensus is reached. Chain nodes can create trust among themselves using a pure mathematical mechanism (asymmetric cryptography) without the need for a central authority or regulatory agency to change data unilaterally. Each distributed node in this network is largely self-contained, has equal rights and obligations, and does not affect the entire network if a node-level corruption occurs, ensuring the Blockchain system's improved dependability and robustness [12]. It is possible to be confident that the information is legitimate due to the sophisticated consensus method necessary to update or manipulate multiple copies of information recorded on the Blockchain.

The Blockchain's multiple copies of distributed information also eliminate the risk of data loss or destruction due to reliance on a centralized place. Furthermore, removing a centralized entity that collects, records, maintains, and, in general, has unfettered access to information increases user privacy and reduces data misuse. Finally, not relying on a centralized body for transaction execution and validation can drastically save intermediary costs and improve performance bottlenecks at central servers [12].

2. **Transparency**: Blockchain-based transactions are entirely transparent, and anybody can view the details and history of each transaction on the blockchain network. It is only through Blockchain technology that this level of transparency is possible, and it ensures a high level of accountability and integrity to the information, ensuring that nothing is unfairly altered, fraudulently added, or withdrawn. This tremendous amount of transparency, particularly for huge financial systems, is unprecedented in history. This level of transparency is achieved as a result of the fact that a Blockchain network has several validating peer nodes without the need for a centralized authority [13], as well as the fact that the holdings and transactions of each public address are accessible and open to viewing by anyone, resulting in transaction records that can be traced back to their source.

Occasionally, the term "openness" is used to refer to the same concept [12]. Because the technical underpinning of Blockchain is open source [12], any node can develop appropriate applications to query Blockchain data via an open interface, the data content and operating rules of the entire system are extremely public and transparent, with no deception between nodes. The same requirements about transparency apply to any revisions to any data on the Blockchain.

The phrase auditability refers to the same notion, which facilitates transaction visibility, tracking, and verification. Apart from its critical role in the financial auditability of large organizations, another critical area where transparency has found application is in healthcare and clinical trial data transparency. Individual patients can utilize Blockchain technology in healthcare to readily examine their claims, medical history, transactions, and past-due payments. Historically, clinical trial data have been withheld from researchers, physicians, and patients, resulting in a lack of trust and credibility in the findings. Methods based on blockchain technology have been proposed for tracing the existence of clinical trial papers containing pre-specified end points. Additionally, the use of smart contracts to function as a trusted administrator was recommended to address data manipulation difficulties that are widespread in clinical trials. Malpractices in supply chain management and the obscurity of product history are also demonstrated to benefit from Blockchain's transparency [14]. Transparency is also considered to benefit non-fraudulent public elections and enhancing voters' faith in the political process [15].

3. **Autonomy**: Generally, all transactions are built on trust, which ensures that the parties involved can rely on one another to keep their obligations. The blockchain technology enables the creation of a system in which trust is no longer an issue. This "trustless" system enables the Blockchain to operate in a peer-to-peer fashion without the need for a trusted third party to ensure trust. Blockchain technology utilizes cryptography to totally eliminate the need for a third party to act as the governor of trust. The Blockchain system protects the contents

of messages and confirms the sender's identity by utilizing the privacy and unforgeability of asymmetric cryptography. This ensures the Blockchain system's transactions are reliable. Complex distributed consensus algorithms are used by participating nodes on the Blockchain network to unanimously and securely add or update data to the Blockchain's distributed ledger, while also resolving the issue of ownership confirmation during the transaction process and maintaining the system's integrity [12]. Due to the implementation of failsafe consensus mechanisms, these Blockchain transactions are completed without the intervention of a third party to ensure confidence [11]. By eliminating these "middlemen" and so ensuring trust, the overall cost of transactions is reduced.

4. **Security**: Blockchain systems are intrinsically secure because they make use of asymmetrical cryptography, which consists of a set of public keys that are visible to everyone and a set of private keys that are only visible to the owner. These keys are used to confirm that a transaction is owned by the rightful owner and that the transaction cannot be tampered with [12, 16]. The integrity, secrecy, and authorization of transactions are all important aspects of the Blockchain system's overall security. Unlike data that is centrally held and hence considerably more vulnerable to being compromised, the distributed structure of Blockchain systems necessitates the use of P2P consensus mechanisms, which eliminates the possibility of a single point of failure.

5. **Immutability**: It is also known as un-tamperability [12], persistency, and unforgeability, and immutability in the context of blockchain technology [16] means that once data is uploaded to a Blockchain, it cannot be altered or tampered with. The data blocks in a Blockchain structure are time stamped, and each block is encrypted with a hash algorithm, which makes the input of data permanent and tamper-proof unless a majority of the nodes in the entire system agrees to change it. Regardless of when they are viewed, once they have been confirmed and uploaded to the Blockchain, they are irreversible and unchangeable. Any alteration, no matter how insignificant, will result in a new hash, which can be identified immediately, rendering the shared ledger immutable and unchangeable. This feature is extremely beneficial for financial transactions and financial audits because it confirms that the data has not been altered, regardless of whether you are the source or the recipient of the data. This trait also contributes to the development of confidence in the Blockchain system. However, immutability for Blockchain has its own set of concerns and obstacles, and some have begun to cast doubt on immutability's merits [17].

6. **Traceability**: Data traceability is the process of determining the origin, destination, and sequence of various modifications that data undergoes across nodes. While data traceability is required for data integrity and increased levels of trust in information, it also offers various other benefits, including improved data governance, regulatory compliance, understanding the impact of change, and data quality enhancement. Due to the fact that information uploaded or updated in a Blockchain system is time stamped, it enables data traceability. Each data block is given a time dimension using time stamp technology, and the hash values contained in each block correctly identify the current and parent blocks [12]. Financial transactions, clinical trials, and supply chain management [18] all benefit significantly from data traceability.

7. **Anonymity**: With the anonymity provided by Blockchain, users may maintain their privacy, which is defined as being shielded from illegal access or observation. Anonymity is achieved by the authentication of transactions, which does not require the disclosure of any personal information about the parties to the transaction. As long as the information transmitted between nodes is done using a predetermined mechanism that establishes confidence, there is no need

to divulge or verify the information of the nodes, and the information transfer can be done anonymously. Users in a Blockchain system can interact with Blockchain addresses that have been generated in order to keep their true identities hidden. However, due to the inherent nature of a distributed and public environment, Blockchain cannot guarantee perfect privacy. As a result, some researchers have coined the term pseudonymity [9] to describe the characteristic of the Blockchain where anyone can create a Blockchain address and it is not possible to connect that address to a person without additional information from other sources; this characteristic of the Blockchain has been called into question.

8. **Democratized**: P2P decision-making is used in a blockchain system [9], where choices are made democratically by all nodes. In order to allow specific nodes to add new blocks to an existing blockchain, consensus algorithms must be used by all decentralized nodes. Additionally, consensus algorithms must ensure that the block is appropriately appended to the shared ledger and that its copies across the blockchain nodes are properly synchronized. All nodes involved in this decision-making process are generally autonomous, have equal rights and obligations, share data, and collaborate to keep information in the blockchain up to date, resulting in lower maintenance and operating costs. A node's voting power is determined by its processing capacity, with legitimate blocks being accepted by working on them and invalid blocks being rejected by refusing to work on them [19].

9. **Integrity**: By definition, blockchain systems are resistant to data modifications. The term "data integrity" refers to the assurance that the data in the blockchain is correct and consistent throughout its existence. This capability is enabled by the Blockchain network's decentralized and virtually immutable shared ledgers, which means that once a data block is agreed upon for inclusion in a blockchain, its transaction record cannot be changed or updated. This data is permanently stored in the blockchain system and replicated in different nodes throughout the blockchain network, effectively ensuring the data's trustworthiness and integrity [12].

10. **Fault tolerance**: By design, blockchain is inefficient and redundant in order to achieve high degrees of immutability and fault tolerance, which are critical aspects of blockchain. Due to the P2P architecture of the Blockchain network, each node is regarded equal to every other node, and each node can act as both a client and a server, giving the network an exceptionally large margin of error for nodes going offline, network transit issues, and so on. Blockchains are supposed to be Byzantine Fault Tolerant, which means they will reach consensus even if some nodes are unavailable or performing improperly. A consensus protocol is said to be fault tolerant if it is capable of recovering from the failure of a consensus node [20]. The Blockchain system's fault tolerance can recover from either fail-stop faults, in which certain nodes stop participating in the consensus process owing to software or hardware issues, or Byzantine faults, in which nodes begin misbehaving due to software vulnerabilities or malicious attacks [20].

11. **Automatic**: Smart contracts on the Blockchain are capable of doing transaction generation, decision-making, and data storage [9] entirely on their own initiative. All nodes in the system are capable of autonomously transacting and verifying data through the use of consensus protocols that are specific to the system. The Blockchain is automatically maintained and validated through the use of a protocol, requiring no manual interaction. Smart contracts, like any other computer program, can, however, develop faults and errors, and there is currently no straightforward means to amend or update these contracts. As with any other software application, smart contracts are susceptible to hacking attacks, same as any other software application.

7.1.4 Evolution and Types of Blockchain

In Section The Blockchain 1.0 categorizes the evolution of Blockchain technology into three stages.

7.1.4.1 The Blockchain 1.0

The Blockchain 1.0 technology, which is part of Bitcoin, is affiliated with an anonymous corporation identified by the tag "Satoshi Nakamoto" since 2008 [2]. As explained below, Bitcoin uses Blockchain 1.0 to solve the long-standing problems of double spending of digital cash and transaction processing without the need for any trusted third party.

1. **Transaction processing**: For a long period of time, financial institutions relied on reputable third parties to execute electronic payments. These third parties assist merchants and customers in resolving conflicts. These third parties invest effort in providing more information to customers and, if necessary, reversing transactions. It may increase the cost per transaction and restrict the number of transactions processed for a merchant within a specified time period, but there is no other mechanism for making payments through a communication channel without involving a trusted third party. The blockchain enables consenting parties to conduct transactions directly with one another without relying on an existing trusted third party. The money of stakeholders is safeguarded through the use of cryptographic proofs rather than any pre-existing trustworthy entity [2].
2. **Double spending**: Online payment systems have existed for a long period of time, but they have always had the inherent problem of double spending. The double spending problem is a potential weakness in online payment systems, where the same digital money might be spent on several transactions. This is done by taking advantage of implementation details that save money in the form of duplicated files or by giving out false information [21], which is how this is done.

    The blockchain technology used in cryptocurrencies serves as a public ledger, storing all of the transactions that take place. Blocks are a type of data structure used in Blockchain technology to store transactions. As transactions take place, new blocks are constantly being added to the blockchain, which allows it to grow indefinitely.

    Cryptocurrencies are widely regarded as the first blockchain-based application, and they have already been shown to be effective as a digital payment system on the Internet. Due to the ability to program bitcoin as a network for the decentralized trade of all resources, Blockchain 2.0 has already been developed to take advantage of the more powerful functionality offered by digital money.

7.1.4.2 Blockchain 2.0

Blockchain 2.0, also known as "Smart Contracts," was the next significant step in the evolution of the Blockchain industry. It is a concept for market decentralization in general, as well as support for the transfer of a wide variety of assets, such as stocks, bonds, loans, mortgages, and smart properties, beyond digital currency [21]. It was created to automate the enforcement of rules agreed upon by interested parties, just like traditional corporate contracts do. With advancements in technology, it has become clear that Blockchain technology has the potential to change all industries, not only markets, payments, financial services, and economies. This resulted in the birth of Blockchain 3.0, also known as Blockchain Applications, which spans sectors such as government, health, literature, and culture [21].

7.1.4.3 Blockchain 3.0

Blockchain 3.0 is a framework for developing distributed and secure applications for areas other than financial markets. It facilitates a universal and worldwide scope and size through interconnection with web technology. It is seen as a way to help build a "Smart World," especially when it comes to how resources are used for both physical and human assets [22].

7.1.5 Permissionless vs Permissioned Blockchains

Permissionless, permissioned, or both are terms that can be applied to all sorts of blockchains. Permissionless blockchains allow any user to join the blockchain network pseudo-anonymously (that is, to become "nodes" of the network) and do not limit the privileges of the network's nodes. Permissioned blockchains, on the other hand, limit access to the network and may also limit the rights of those nodes on the network. The identity of a permissioned blockchain's users is known to the other permissioned blockchain's users. Because there are numerous nodes to validate transactions, permissionless blockchains are more secure than permissioned blockchains. It would be impossible for bad actors to collaborate on the network. Due to the vast number of nodes and the large number of transactions, permissionless blockchains have long transaction processing times. Permissioned blockchains, on the other hand, are more efficient. Because network access is limited, there are fewer nodes on the blockchain, resulting in faster transaction processing. The centralization of permissioned blockchains to some central authority (be it a government, a company, a trade group, or some other entity or group that is granting the permission to nodes and creating the blockchain's restrictions) makes it a less secure system that is more prone to traditional hacking vulnerabilities. Because it is easier for bad actors to collude when there are fewer nodes on a blockchain, private blockchain administrators must ensure that nodes adding and validating blocks are highly trustworthy.

7.1.6 Types of Blockchain

There are four different types of blockchain structures to choose from:

1. **Public blockchains**: Public blockchains are permissionless and entirely decentralized, allowing anybody to participate. All nodes of the blockchain have equal rights to access the network, create new blocks of data, and validate blocks of data in public blockchains. Currently, public blockchains are mostly used for bitcoin exchange and mining. Popular public blockchains like Bitcoin, Ethereum, and Litecoin may be familiar to you. On these public blockchains, nodes "mine" for cryptocurrency by solving cryptographic equations to create blocks for the transactions requested on the network. The miner nodes are compensated for their efforts with a tiny amount of bitcoin. The miners are essentially modern-day bank tellers who formulate transactions and are compensated (or "mined") for their labor.

2. **Private blockchains**: Private blockchains, also known as managed blockchains, are permissioned blockchains that are administered by a single entity. The central authority in a private blockchain decides who can be a node. In addition, the central authority does not always grant each node identical rights to execute functions. Because public access to private blockchains is restricted, they are only partially decentralized. Ripple, a business-to-business virtual currency exchange network, and Hyperledger, an umbrella project for open-source blockchain applications, are two instances of private blockchains. Both private and public blockchains have disadvantages: public blockchains take longer to validate new data than private blockchains, and private blockchains are more susceptible to fraud and bad actors. Consortium and hybrid blockchains were created to overcome these flaws.

3. **Consortium blockchains**: Consortium blockchains, unlike private blockchains, are permissioned blockchains administered by a consortium of organizations rather than a single institution. As a result, consortium blockchains have more decentralization than private blockchains, resulting in increased security. However, forming consortiums can be a difficult process because it necessitates collaboration among a number of firms, which poses logistical obstacles as well as the risk of antitrust violations (which we will examine in an upcoming article). The corporate software developer R3 has developed a popular set of consortia blockchain solutions for the financial services industry and beyond. CargoSmart has created the Global Shipping Business Network Collaboration, a non-profit blockchain consortium aimed at digitizing the shipping industry and allowing maritime industry operators to collaborate more effectively.
4. **Hybrid blockchains**: Hybrid blockchains are those that are managed by a single entity but have some oversight from the public blockchain, which is necessary to conduct certain transaction validations. IBM Food Trust is an example of a hybrid blockchain, which was created to improve efficiency across the whole food supply chain. In a subsequent piece in this series, we'll go through IBM Food Trust in further depth.

7.2 Architecture of Blockchain

7.2.1 Architecture of Blockchain 1.0 (Cryptocurrencies)

Blockchain 1.0 is a distributed ledger technology that enables the effective storage of digital monetary transactions between two parties. The transactions are maintained in the form of an ever-growing list of data dubbed "Blocks." These blocks are impervious to modification and are permanently verifiable. Typically, a group of users connected via a P2P network oversees the ledger record verification. To make any modifications within a block, a consensus between more than half of the network's users is required. This section delves into the specifics of the design, operation, and open research issues of various Blockchain components, which include blocks, networks, and consensus.

7.2.2 Block

A block is the data structure used to hold transaction information in Blockchain 1.0. As illustrated in Figure 7.2, it is separated into two sections. (i) Block header and (ii) Block body. The block header has the following fields:

- **Block version**: defines the rules for validating blocks.
- **Merkle Tree Root Hash**: It maintains the hash value of all transactions contained within the block.
- **Time stamp**: Since January 1, 1970, this stamps the current time in seconds according to universal time.
- **nBits**: The criterion for a valid block hash.
- **Nonce**: A mathematical value that begins with 0 and increases with each hash computation or calculation.
- **Parent block hash**: a hash value of 256 bits that points to the previous block. A transaction counter and transactions make up the block body. The maximum number of transactions that a block can hold is determined by the size of the block and the size of each transaction. Blockchain employs an asymmetric cryptography technique to validate transaction authentication. In an untrustworthy environment, a digital signature based on asymmetric cryptography is used.

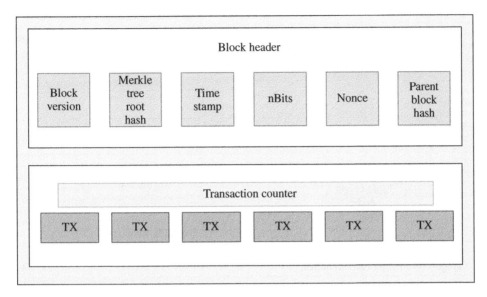

Figure 7.2 Block structure.

7.2.3 Node

Decentralization is one of the most essential concepts in blockchain technology. A single computer or entity cannot own the chain. Instead, the nodes connecting to the chain form a distributed ledger. Any type of electronic equipment that saves copies of the blockchain and keeps the network running is referred to as a node. Each node has its own copy of the blockchain, and in order for the chain to be updated, trusted, and confirmed, the network must algorithmically approve any newly mined block. Every action in the ledger can be easily reviewed and examined since blockchains are transparent. A unique alphanumeric identification number is assigned to each participant, which is used to track his or her transactions. Combining public information with a system of checks-and-balances helps the blockchain maintain integrity and creates trust among users. Essentially, blockchains can be thought of as the scalability of trust via technology.

7.2.4 Types of Blockchain Nodes

In general, there are two types of nodes in a Blockchain network:

1. Full node
2. Lightweight node, i.e. a node that has limited functionalities. However, as demonstrated in Figure 7.3, the authors in [2] have classified these nodes further according to their capabilities.

1. **Full node**: The term "full node" refers to a fully functional node in the Blockchain network that serves as the server. The full node is capable of storing a copy of all the blockchain nodes' data and the blockchain's history. When a transaction occurs on a blockchain network, the full node is responsible for establishing consensus among the other nodes through the use of a consensus algorithm and for verifying the transaction. Additionally, it is involved in future policy and decision-making.
2. **Pruned node**: In comparison to the archival node, this is a decreased function node. It becomes clearer when considering the blocks in the blockchain architecture [23]. The blockchain's

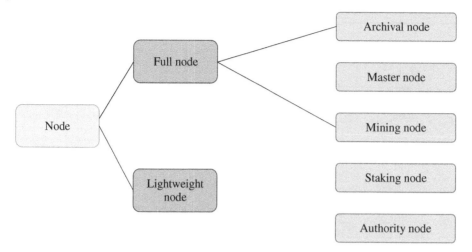

Figure 7.3 Categorization of blockchain nodes.

pruned nodes have a predefined block storage limit. These nodes preserve the block information from the beginning, but once they reach the specified limit, they retain only the block header and chain placement.

3. **Archival node**: In terms of space utilization, it is a fully capable node. They can be seen as full servers capable of hosting any blockchain. These nodes are capable of adding blocks to the blockchain, validating existing blocks, and enforcing the necessary consensus for a blockchain transaction.

4. **Miner nodes**: Every chain is made up of several blocks, each of which has three main functions. Mining is the process by which miners add new blocks to the chain. Every block in a blockchain has its own unique nonce and hash, but it also refers to the hash of the previous block in the chain, making mining a block difficult, particularly on big chains. Miners utilize specialized software to solve the exceedingly difficult math issue of generating an acceptable hash using a nonce. Because the nonce is only 32 bits long and the hash is 256 bits long, there are around four billion nonce–hash combinations to mine before finding the proper one. Miners are considered to have discovered the "golden nonce" when this happens, and their block is added to the chain. Making a change to any block earlier in the chain necessitates re-mining not only the affected block, but all subsequent blocks as well. This is why manipulating blockchain technology is so tough. Consider it "safety in math," because identifying golden nonces takes a long time and a lot of computational resources. When a block is successfully mined, all nodes in the network acknowledge the change, and the miner is compensated financially. Figure 7.4 shows a blockchain-based network made up of numerous computers (known as miners) collaborating as peers so that the data in the blocks can only be modified by using the blockchain protocol (or blockchain consensus). Furthermore, each block in this network has two hash values: one that defines the block's identity and another that identifies the block's unique parent (i.e. the previous block). The genesis block is the first block in the blockchain, and it has no parents. If all other nodes agree, miner nodes [24] undertake the appropriate operations to add a block to the network. The transaction is kept in a decentralized node after this consensus. Validating transactions on a public blockchain earns these nodes money.

5. **Staking node**: The concept of a staking node exists in the cryptocurrency blockchain. This node chooses which node will build the next block in the blockchain in order to get a reward

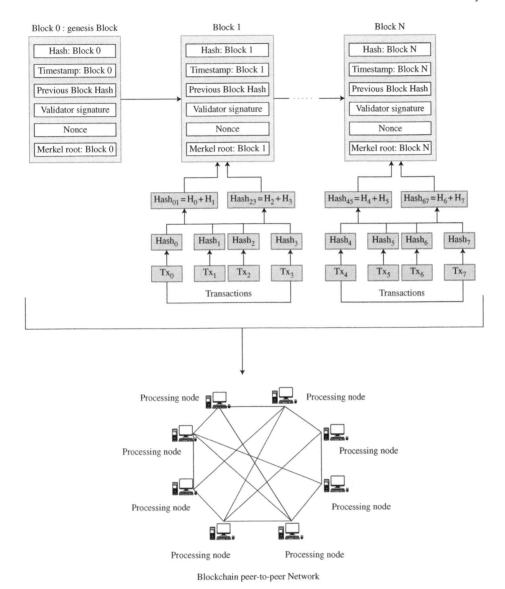

Figure 7.4 Blockchain peer-to-peer network.

based on rules and chance (proof of luck [25]). Which node is rewarded is determined by the proof-of-work algorithm. Additionally, cryptocurrency nodes such as the Raspberry Pi cryptocurrency node [26] might be regarded as examples of this type of node.

6. **Authority node**: The nodes in the Blockchain network that implement the consensus process or Proof-of-Authority are commonly referred to as authority nodes [27].
7. **Master node**: In a Blockchain network, the master node maintains a complete record of all transactions and validates them. Master nodes are also referred to as the network's back-end nodes, as they offer proof-of-stake for the cryptocurrency network [28]. Master nodes can also be thought of as a distributed wallet that runs on millions of computers, enabling the Blockchain to operate in real time.

8. **Lightweight node**: A lightweight node is often referred to as a node for simple payment verification [27]. According to the authors in [29], because lightweight nodes consume fewer resources, they are becoming more practical for blockchain implementation. The authors of [29] emphasize the issue of lightweight nodes receiving a reward while full nodes serving lightweight clients receive no incentive. The authors argue that smart contracts can facilitate a more equitable deployment environment. A payment system is part of the SmartLight unifying mechanism, which they say could help make the Blockchain network more efficient. Full nodes should be compensated for supporting lightweight clients in the network.

7.2.5 Consensus

Consensus is essential for transaction validation and ledger updates. Proof-of-Work was the first consensus algorithm utilized in Blockchain 1.0.

1. **proof-of-work (pow)**: PoW is regarded as Bitcoin's primary success in achieving consensus on a distributed decentralized Blockchain network that might have 1000 nodes [30]. The consensus algorithm governs how Blockchain nodes agree to append a new block to the chain and the verification process. To add a block and receive a reward in the PoW process, the initiator node uses a cryptographic procedure to produce a winning value that is smaller than the network's established value [30]. When more than one node produces value, the situation is handled by assessing the largest value of PoW, which reflects the greater amount of work done by the node. This node is then allowed to add a block and earn a reward. This strategy is better suited for a scalable Blockchain network. However, it has a few limitations, such as the high cost of mining equipment for nodes, a low transaction rate, and vulnerability to attack. More consensus algorithms are explained in depth later in this book.

7.3 Architecture of Blockchain 2.0 (Smart Contracts)

7.3.1 Introduction to Smart Contracts

Smart contract platforms make use of the underlying blockchain technology but modify it to allow third-party programs to run on top of it. Instead of actual financial transactions, transactions include computer instructions that the blockchain's virtual machine can execute. Simple "if/when…then…" lines are written into code on a blockchain to make smart contracts work. When preset circumstances are satisfied and validated, the activities are carried out by a network of computers. These activities could include transferring payments to the proper parties, registering a vehicle, providing alerts, or issuing a ticket. When the transaction is complete, the blockchain is updated. That means the transaction can't be modified, and the results are only visible to those who have been granted access. There can be as many specifications as needed in a smart contract to convince the participants that the task will be executed correctly. Participants must agree on how transactions and associated data are represented on the blockchain, agree on the "if/when…then…" rules that govern those transactions, investigate all conceivable exceptions, and design a framework for resolving disputes in order to set the terms. There is no central computer platform that runs the code and maintains the state-of-the-smart contract platform because the blockchain network is dispersed and decentralized. Instead, each node in the network runs its own virtual computer, which executes the code included in each block of the blockchain's transactions. The network can stay synchronized at all times because code is designed to be predictable and grouped into blocks before execution.

7.3.2 How Smart Contracts Work

As a means of transferring assets or currency within a software, smart contracts are used. The program runs the code according to the circumstances set forth in it. It does it automatically and checks the validity of a transaction using the data it receives. When the requirement is met, the smart contract is activated. If the condition is not met, the smart contract will be executed depending on the specified condition. A decentralized ledger creates copies of the smart contract or document in order to ensure immutability and security.

7.3.3 Example of Smart Contract

Blockchain is being used in the real estate industry. You can see smart contracts in action if you decide to buy real estate in the future utilizing a blockchain-powered platform. So, you came across a property and decided to purchase it. During a real-estate transaction, there are numerous factors to consider. You'll need to set loan amounts, instalment times, and other special circumstances, for example. To activate the smart contract, you must first sign it and set it in motion. For example, suppose you agreed to pay 20% of the property's value up front. Following that, you decided to pay the remainder of the real-estate worth in instalments, as well as any other terms you may have. Based on the agreed conditions, the seller builds a smart contract. Once both of you agree that everything is properly documented, the smart contract is activated. You will pay the instalments over time, and the smart contract will keep track of it. Once the seller has received all of the payments, the property ownership is transferred to you. Everything is carried out without the involvement of any intermediaries or third parties. In comparison to a traditional real-estate transaction, you will be able to save time and work in completing the transaction. Because there are no middlemen, both the buyer and the vendor save money. In addition, if an event occurs in the smart contract, the smart contract will alert all related parties, including banks, buyers, sellers, and the insurer.

7.3.4 Uses of Smart Contracts

Smart contracts can be applied in a wide range of industries, including healthcare, supply chain management, and financial services. The following are some examples:

1. **Government voting system**: Smart contracts create a safe environment for voting, making it less vulnerable to tampering. Smart contract votes would be ledger-protected, making them very difficult to interpret. Furthermore, smart contracts have the potential to raise voter turnout, which has historically been low due to an inefficient system that requires voters to queue, show identification, and fill out paperwork. Voting can expand the number of participants in a voting system when it is transferred online using smart contracts.
2. **Healthcare**: With a private key, blockchain can store patients' encoded health records. Due to privacy considerations, only particular individuals would have access to the records. Similarly, smart contracts can be used to conduct research in a private and secure manner. All patient hospital receipts can be kept on the blockchain and shared with insurance providers automatically as proof of service. Furthermore, the ledger can be used for a variety of tasks, including supply management, drug supervision, and regulatory compliance.
3. **Supply chain**: Paper-based systems, in which forms are routed through many channels for approval, have historically harmed supply chains. The time-consuming procedure raises the danger of fraud and loss. By providing parties involved in the chain with an accessible and secure digital version, blockchain can eliminate such concerns. Smart contracts can be used for inventory management as well as payment and task automation.

4. **Financial services**: In a variety of ways, smart contracts assist in the transformation of traditional financial services. When it comes to insurance claims, they verify for errors, route them, and then send funds to the user if everything checks up. Smart contracts include essential book-keeping capabilities and eliminate the chance of accounting records being tampered with. They also allow shareholders to participate in transparent decision-making. They also assist in trade clearing, which is the process of transferring payments after the amounts of trade settlements have been computed.

7.3.5   Advantages of Smart Contracts

You should have a strong grasp on smart contracts and how they work by now. In this section, we'll look at the advantages of smart contracts and what they have to offer as a whole.

1. **Secure**: Smart contracts provide a safe environment for contract execution. This prevents the contract details and other sensitive data from being leaked. Furthermore, no third-party or human intervention affects the execution of smart contracts, making them hacker-proof. To ensure security, cryptography is used to encrypt all sensitive data.
2. **Autonomous**: Smart contracts are self-contained, which raises their utility to unprecedented heights. After smart contracts have been launched, they can execute and complete themselves without the need for human intervention.
3. **Interruption-free**: If the smart contract was not supposed to be interrupted in the first place, it cannot be disrupted by a third party.
4. **Trustless**: Smart contracts create a trustless environment in which all parties' interests are safeguarded.
5. **Cost effective**: Smart contracts are cost-effective since they are self-contained and do not require the use of a middleman.
6. **Fast performance**: Smart contracts move quickly. When compared to real-world document-based contracts, a contract can be executed in minutes rather than hours.

7.3.6   Limitations of Smart Contracts

1. **Difficult to change**: It's nearly impossible to change smart contract operations, and any programming fault can be time-consuming and costly to fix.
2. **Possibility of loopholes**: Parties will deal fairly and not benefit unethically from a contract, according to the principle of good faith. Smart contracts, on the other hand, make it difficult to ensure that the provisions are followed exactly as promised.
3. **Third party**: Despite the fact that smart contracts aim to eliminate third-party involvement, it is impossible to do so. Third parties have a different role in conventional contracts than they do in traditional contracts. Lawyers, for example, will not be required to prepare individual contracts; but developers will require their assistance in understanding the provisions in order to generate smart contract software.
4. **Vague terms**: Smart contracts aren't always able to handle ambiguous terms and conditions since contracts involve terminology that aren't always understood. Smart contracts, in the context of Blockchain, automatically enforce agreements between two or more parties without the need for a trusted intermediary. Smart contracts are embedded as computer programs in Blockchain software such as Ethereum and Hyperledger. Depending on the type of Blockchain, participants can join the network and request the execution of a specific contract

for a transaction in the Blockchain P2P network. Similar to digital currencies, the history of these transactions is stored in Blockchain. The sequence of transactions on the Blockchain determines the state of the contract and the assets of participants [31].

Similar to cryptocurrencies, smart contracts do not rely on a trusted third party to execute correctly. Consensus Protocols are in place to address any conflicts between contractual parties. There are a variety of available consensus techniques for resolving conflicts, depending on the platform [31].

7.4 Architecture of Blockchain 3.0 (Blockchain Applications)

Apart from the financial sector, Blockchain technology has been adopted in a variety of industries for the development of distributed applications, including games, user-generated content networks, the internet of things (IoT), smart hardware, supply chain management, source tracing, and credit sharing in the economy. These distributed applications benefit from a variety of features enabled by blockchain technology, including improved performance in terms of low latency and high through-put, simplified identity management, the ability to conduct transactions offline, and flexible main-tainability for system upgrades and easy bug recovery [32]. There are several unique applications of blockchain technology, which are briefly discussed below. For example, the authors in [33] assert that integrating blockchain technology into currently deployed cloud solutions can significantly improve the performance and security of cloud data centers. The authors of [34] recently proposed using Blockchain to address the difficulties of identity authentication in the smart grid using a safe and mutual authentication protocol. Similarly, the authors of [35] first discuss the security risks associated with smart grid infrastructure before proposing a blockchain-based lightweight authen-tication system for the smart grid. The authors of [36] suggest an effective approach for storing and exchanging medical data using a double blockchain. They use the term "dual blockchain" to refer to two blockchains: one for data storage and another for data sharing among hospitals and health-care institutions. Blockchain applications are used for a variety of purposes, including validating identities and tracking manufactured goods via a chain of objects.

As seen in Figure 7.5, a general Blockchain architecture is provided in the literature as a layered architecture for developing distributed applications [9].

- Business apps built on blockchain technology serve as the application layer.
- The contact layer demonstrates possible Blockchain programming approaches.
- Nodes involved in application management receive incentives based on the mechanisms detailed in the incentive layer.
- For Blockchain applications, the consensus layer offers a variety of consensus algorithms avail-able.
- Data propagation and data verification techniques, as well as distributed networking mecha-nisms, make up the network layer.
- The data layer includes timestamped data blocks. The security of these blocks is managed via a chain structure, a Merkle tree, cryptography, and hash functions.

7.4.1 Consensus Mechanism

The consensus mechanism is used to validate the transaction and come to a consensus in the event of updating a ledger with a transaction. Various consensus models have been presented in the litera-ture and are implemented by various blockchain systems. According to the authors in [37], Quorum

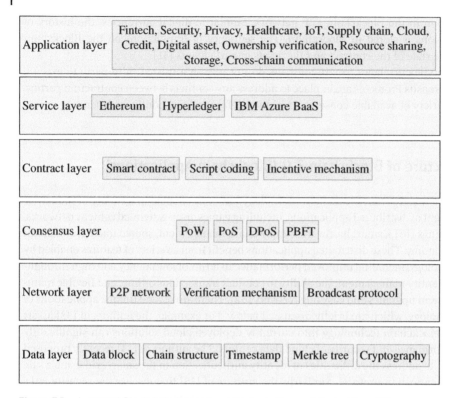

Figure 7.5 A general Blockchain layered architecture. *Source:* Adapted from [8].

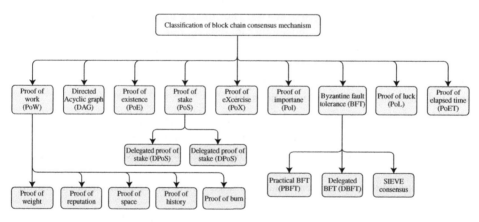

Figure 7.6 classifications of blockchain consensus mechanisms.

is the first blockchain platform to use a different consensus approach. In this section, we examine, analyze, and compare various consensus algorithms used and proposed for blockchain technology. According to our analysis of the literature, Figure 7.6 illustrates our classification of blockchain consensus models. As shown in Figure 7.6, consensus models are broken down into eight broad groups, with some of them broken down even more into smaller groups based on how they work.

- **Proof of work (PoW)**: Proof of work is the original consensus algorithm, and it entails making people perform work, as the name implies. Miners are the ones who try to make a new block in Proof of Work. The block creator is chosen by holding a race in which the winner is the one who produces the block (and earns the associated rewards). This race entails constructing a legitimate block, with the requirement that the block's header hashes to a value smaller than a specified threshold. Random guessing is the easiest technique to accomplish this due to the nature of hash functions. As a result, the network's miners test a variety of hashes until one finds a nonce that produces the desired hash output. The first miner to find a legitimate block sends it to the rest of the network, which uses it to produce the next block. The major problem with Proof of Work is that the capacity to construct a valid block is the only criterion for block creation. There's nothing stopping two miners from discovering different versions of the block at the same moment. If this happens, various areas of the network may grow on top of different blocks, resulting in a diverging blockchain. The longest block rule, which states that if two versions of the blockchain conflict, the longer one shall be accepted, is how blockchain resolves this. Using the concept of difficulty, Proof of Work also seeks to reduce the likelihood of divergent blockchains. The hash of a valid block header must be smaller than a threshold value that can be changed in a distributed manner. The difficulty is changed at regular intervals to ensure that blocks are created at the required block rate (based on the current processing power of the blockchain network). The research community has presented various variations of PoW algorithms, which are noted in Figure 7.6 in our classification.

1. **Proof of weight**: The Proof of Weight consensus model [38] is based on the Algorand consensus that incorporates the concept of "weight" into the core concept of PoW. These weights are proportional to the values that nodes generate to indicate their contribution to the network. The primary objective is to avoid "double spending" forking by incorporating the relative weight feature.

2. **Proof of reputation**: A consensus mechanism known as "proof of reputation" [39] establishes a node's reputation based on its involvement, transactions, and assets. The node with the highest reputation value creates a new block, which is then approved by the blockchain network through voting. This technique provides for the degrading of nodes' reputations in the event of prior wrongdoing and also contributes to the blockchain's security.

3. **Proof of space**: Proof of space [40] is a variant of PoW in which a node requesting service is required to allocate an inordinate amount of disk space in comparison to performing the computation in PoW. Information is sent to the verifier node to show that enough space has been set aside for a service request. This is a technique for demonstrating a legitimate interest in a service by allocating a non-trivial amount of memory or disk space to answer a challenge posed by the service provider.

4. **Proof of history**: The Proof of history consensus mechanism necessitates node to produce a proof of History [40]. It generates a historical record in order to offer proof that an event occurred at a specific period. This gives an alternative to relying on the transaction's timestamp.

5. **Proof of burn**: The proof of burn [41] consensus mechanism is built on the idea of burning coins in order to compete for the privilege of mining the next block in the Blockchain. Burning coins in this context refers to sending the digital currency to an address from which it cannot be retrieved. The nodes raise their coin burn rate in order to increase their chances of being selected in the lottery.

In comparison to PoW, the Directed Acyclic Graph (DAG) [42] has been presented as a viable Blockchain consensus mechanism for the IoT Blockchain framework. Scalability is a key element of DAG, as blocks are created in parallel to the Blockchain in DAG. It enables them to immediately add a block to the ledger as they process previous transactions. Additionally, DAG addresses the issue of "double spending" by the use of effective algorithms.

- **Proof of stake (PoS)**: PoS (Proof of Stake) is a more energy-efficient version of PoW. Miners in PoS are required to demonstrate possession of a specified amount of currency. It is expected that those who possess a greater number of currencies will be less likely to attack the network. Selection based on account balance is highly unjust, as the network's richest individual is inevitably dominant. As a result, numerous strategies are offered, using the stake size to choose which one should forge the next block. Blackcoin [43], in particular, takes advantage of randomization to forecast the next generation. It employs a formula that seeks the lowest hash value possible given the stake size. Peercoin [44] prefers to select coins depending on their age. In Peercoin, currencies that are older and larger have a greater chance of mining the next block. In comparison to PoW, PoS consumes less energy and is more efficient. Unfortunately, because mining is essentially free, attacks may occur as a result. Numerous blockchains begin with PoW and gradually transition to PoS. For example, ethereum is planning to transition from Ethash (a form of PoW) [45] to Casper (a form of PoS) [46]. The primary advantage of Proof-of-Stake is that it eliminates the need for expensive mining equipment on the node. In PoS, a node can mine or validate a block based on the proof of its stake, which is the number of coins. PoS recommends acquiring cryptocurrency and utilizes it to purchase block creation chances [43].
    1. **Delegated proof of stake (DPoS)**: Delegated Proof-of-Stake is a version of the PoS algorithm proposed in [47]. It is suggested that stakeholders vote to nominate the witness node, which will generate a block in the chain. The witness node is compensated for block creation, but if the chosen witness node is unable to create a block, it will be barred from participating in future voting processes.
- **Proof of existence (PoE)**: PoE is proposed as a system for establishing the presence of particular documents at a specific time based on the transaction's timestamp. It could be used to offer information about data ownership without releasing the data itself. This PoE approach is advantageous for establishing the existence of copyright documents, such as a patent.
- **Proof of exercise (PoX)**: Proof of eXercise (PoX) is a public distributed ledger mechanism that utilizes the system's computing resources (or hashrate) and is a conceptual consensus protocol that requires focused study to implement in practice. It is an attempt to repurpose the PoW hash-based puzzle mining technique in order to provide valuable output and reduce resource loss. The annual electricity usage required to mine Bitcoin was similar to that of Ireland in 2014, rendering it unsustainable in the future. It presents a variation of PoW that uses matrices to tackle real-world scientific computation issues as an eXercise. There are numerous real-world applications of scientific problems based on matrices, including image processing, DNA and RNA matching and sequencing, and data mining.
- **Byzantine fault tolerance**: Byzantine Fault Tolerance (BFT) is a property of distributed networks that enables them to achieve consensus (agreement on the same value) even when some nodes in the network fail to respond or respond with inaccurate information. The purpose of a BFT mechanism is to protect against system failures through the use of collective decision making (both correct and faulty nodes) with the goal of reducing the influence of faulty nodes. The Byzantine Generals' Problem inspired the BFT. Consensus is required in the event of system failure or failure due to a Byzantine fault in Blockchain. Bobn if some nodes fail to respond, the network's nodes should reach consensus and ensure the consistency of this information in the Blockchain network. Considering the distributing system, it is a hurdle.
    1. **Practical byzantine fault tolerance (PBFT)**: As detailed in [48], the Practical Byzantine Fault Tolerance (PBFT) algorithm requires numerous rounds of voting by all nodes in the network to commit state changes. The PBFT method makes global voting more practicable by utilizing an efficient, encrypted message exchange. This algorithm requires $n \leq 3f + 1$ nodes

to tolerate *f* failing nodes in order to solve the Byzantine Generals problem via several rounds of voting. One node is designated as the "leader" in PBFT consensus, who compiles a collection of sequential transactions into a block and broadcasts it to the network. The network's validating peers generate a hash of the block and broadcast it. Validating peers keep an eye on the hashes received from the rest of the network, which can be thought of as "votes" across several rounds. If two-thirds of peers vote in favor of a candidate block, it is added to their copy of the blockchain. While PBFT consensus delivers high throughput and low latency when validating transactions, the overhead associated with broadcasting blocks and votes limits its scalability to networks with tens of validators.

In [49], the authors propose "Practical Byzantine Fault Tolerance," a technique for dealing with Byzantine faults. The authors of [49] present the first state-machine replication algorithm for efficiently surviving Byzantine failures in asynchronous networks. They take distributed file systems into account and employ Byzantine fault tolerance.

2. **Delegated byzantine fault tolerance**: The next evolution of onchain (NEO) whitepaper discusses delegated Byzantine Fault Tolerance, a variant of standard Byzantine Fault Tolerance [42]. Currently, the NEO Blockchain core library makes use of it. They propose it as a novel mathematical model that use a discrete model to test consensus behavior. This algorithm is more capable of dealing with untrustworthy participants than other algorithms.

3. **Sieve consensus**: Sieve [50] is a sort of Practical Byzantine Fault Tolerance (PBFT) consensus algorithm that is used to deal with non-deterministic chain code execution. Diverse outputs might be generated when replicas execute non-deterministic chain code. Sieve can evaluate the output in case a minor divergence in a limited number of replicates is observed.

- **Proof of luck (PoL)**: The authors of [51] considered the limits of PoW and suggested a new consensus model dubbed Proof-of-Luck in order to lower the processing power required for a transaction while increasing its throughput. This algorithm is based on TEE (trusted execution environment). It is composed primarily of the functions PollRound and PollMine. Each block that is mined is assigned a luck value, a random number between 0 and 1. A cumulative luck value is computed by adding the luck values within each block of the chain. The chain with the highest luck value is the one a Miner would want to add their block to.

- **Proof of importance**: New economy movement (NEM) (XEM) makes use of this algorithm [52]. This cryptocurrency introduces a process similar to mining called harvesting. This technique employs network theory to assign a rating to each account based primarily on vested and unvested coins. PoI estimates a node's "importance" based on the number of days' coins in its account. Each day, 10% of the existing unvested amount vests. Additionally, it is calculated depending on the account's rank within the network, taking into consideration the number of vested coins possessed.

- **Proof of elapsed time (PoET)**: This consensus mode employs a lottery-based election approach to choose a new leader for the purpose of adding a block to the blockchain [30]. The Trusted Execution Environment (TEE) is employed to ensure the security of this election process. The following are the important steps in the process of electing a leader:

1. The Validator and miner nodes run TEE by Intel software guard extensions (SGX).
2. Each validator node makes a request for a wait time.
3. The node with the least wait time wins the election and becomes the leader node.
4. The primary disadvantage of using this consensus technique is that it is hardware-dependent [53].

Table 7.1 compares consensus algorithms on the basis of essential parameters such as the consensus model's salient feature, its fault tolerance, and scalability.

Table 7.1 Comparison of consensus algorithms.

Consensus algorithm	Main feature	Fault tolerance	Power consumption	Scalability
Proof-of-Work (PoW)	Computational (Processing) Power	Low	High	High
Proof-of-Stake	Stake	< 51% stake [54]	low	High
Delegated Proof-of-Stake (DPoS)	Voting to elect witness node	< 51% validators	low	High
Proof-of-Elapsed Time (PoET)	Fair lottery-based election	Yes	High	High
Byzantine Fault Tolerance (BFT)	Consensus can be reached even if some nodes do not respond	33% nodes being faulty	low	low
Delegated Byzantine Fault Tolerance (DBFT)	Consensus formation with untrustworthy participants	<33% replicas [54]	Medium	low
Proof-of-Importance (PoI)	PoI estimates a node's "importance" based on the number of days' coins in its account	Unknown	Energy savings are minimal	Fair
Proof-of-Luck	Cumulative luck value	Not applicable	Reduce the computational capacity	Scalability is poor
Proof-of-eXercise (PoX)	Miner will address matrix-related issues or problems	Not applicable	Energy conservation on a limited scale	Unknown
Proof-of-Existence (PoE)	Utilize the transaction's timestamp to verify the document's existence	Not applicable	Unknown	Unknown
Directed Acyclic Graph (DAG)	Consensus for the Internet of Things (IoT) blockchain	Not applicable	High	Very high

7.5 Blockchain 4.0

The third generation of Blockchains is still growing and establishing itself in the industry. Is it too early to talk about Blockchain 4.0? It's not because Blockchain is presently advancing at a rapid pace. Blockchain technology has progressed from the stage of discovery and experimentation to the stage of implementation and extension. While Blockchain 3.0 was primarily concerned with resolving difficulties with second-generation blockchains, Blockchain 4.0 is concerned with using blockchain to innovate. As firms from many industries adopt blockchain at a quicker rate, we should expect tremendous improvements in the blockchain space.

Blockchain 4.0 aims to make Blockchain a more business-friendly environment for developing and deploying more advanced and mainstream decentralized applications. The major focus areas for Blockchain 4.0 will be speed, user experience, and usage by a bigger and more common mass.

7.5.1 Blockchain 4.0 Applications

We may divide blockchain 4.0 applications into the Web 3.0, Metaverse, and Industry 4.0.

Web 3.0 We are on the cusp of the third generation of internet services, which will be propelled by technical advancements such as IoT, Blockchain, and Artificial Intelligence. Blockchain plays a crucial part in Web 3.0's growth, as decentralization is key to its design.

Web 2.0 has been revolutionary in terms of providing new opportunities for social participation. However, in order to take advantage of these prospects, we, as consumers, have centralized all of our data, sacrificing our privacy and exposing ourselves to the normal cyber hazards. Web 2.0 platforms are administered by centralized authorities that prescribe transactional rules and own user information. The global financial crisis of 2008 revealed the flaws of centralized governance, paving the path for decentralization. The world needs Web 3.0, a platform with user sovereignty.

Web 3.0, which promises to establish an independent, open, and smart internet, will rely on Blockchain's decentralized protocols. Some third-generation blockchains are already set up to work with web 3.0, but as Blockchain 4.0 becomes more popular, we can expect to see more web 3.0-focused chains with features like interoperability, automation through smart contracts, seamless integration, and storage of P2P data files that can't be deleted.

7.5.2 Metaverse

The dream projects of tech titans such as Facebook, Nvidia, and many more, will be the next big thing in the coming years on Metaverses. We are connected to virtual worlds through a variety of touchpoints, including social interaction, gaming, working, and networking. Metaverse will enhance the realism and vividness of these encounters. Advanced AI, IoT, augmented reality (AR) & VR, Cloud computing, and Blockchain technologies will be utilized to construct the virtual-reality spaces of the Metaverse, in which users will interact with a computer-generated world and other users via realistic experiences. The more we examine Metaverse, the more astounding it will look, especially when we consider it in terms of games, major art exhibitions, concerts, virtual workplace board rooms, etc. But first, let's examine how blockchain technology might aid in the building of the Metaverse. More intensive user interactions, deeper usage of internet services, and more disclosure of user personal information necessitate more intensive user interactions. All of these factors virtually certainly increase the risk of cybercrime. Giving centralized authorities the power to govern, control, and share user data is not a good way for the Metaverse to develop in the future. Consequently, a great deal of attention has been placed on the development of decentralized metaverse systems that offer user autonomy. All of Decentraland, Axie Infinity, and Starl are all blockchain-powered decentralized metaverses: Moreover, the enhanced solutions of Blockchain 4.0 can assist Metaverse users in regulating their security and trust requirements. Consider the Metaverse gaming platform, where players may purchase, possess, and exchange in-game things with huge potential worth. To stop people from making fake copies of these assets, proof of ownership will have to be an non-fungible token (NFT) that can't be changed. Blockchain technologies, especially those that are expected in Blockchain 4.0, can help regulate the following Metaverse development needs:

- Interoperability
- Decentralization
- Digital collectability of assets (such as NFTs)
- Security
- Transfer of value through crypto

- Decentralized data management
- Digital Proof of ownership
- Governance

7.5.3   Industrial Revolution 4.0

We may consider Blockchain 4.0 to be a concept that drives all development activities targeted at making Blockchain viable in Industry 4.0. Industrial revolutions have always been needed to shake up clichés and inject some originality into the world. Blockchain is fueling the fourth industrial revolution's upheavals in the same way that the steam engine and the Internet sparked earlier industrial revolutions. Blockchain is the fourth industrial revolution's cornerstone, according to World Bank analysts, since the technology has the ability to minimize corruption by boosting transparency in business operations, government procedures, and supplier networks.

The World Bank is also working to guarantee that emerging economies can benefit from blockchain technology in order to reduce extreme poverty and create shared prosperity. The World Bank has created Bond-i, a new debt instrument based on Blockchain technology. Throughout the instrument's life cycle, blockchain is utilized to manufacture, allocate, and maintain the instrument.

7.5.4   Blockchain 4.0 for Businesses

We all have a pretty good idea of how businesses work or try to work in an Industry 4.0 setting. Industry 4.0 companies work in fields like healthcare, manufacturing, finance, logistics, education, and government. They have smart factories, smart supply chains, digitized service offerings, new business models made possible by digital technology, and customer transparency.

Now, if we look at the Blockchain maturity and adoption graph in Industry 4.0, we can see that the wave of awareness happened from 2011 to 2016. From 2016 to 2018, a lot of testing was done on Blockchain to make it more useful for business use cases like R3 in banking and B3i in insurance. The blockchain transformation phase started in 2018, when new frontends and APIs were built to help with corporate integration and a whole new way of managing data.

Blockchain 4.0 will add to this wave of change by making it possible to combine the real and virtual worlds into smart cyber-physical systems that are decentralized, open, verifiable, impossible to change, and automated. Blockchain works with other Industry 4.0 technologies like IoT, AI, AR, and VR to make smart solutions, smart supply chains, smart factories, and smart products.

References

1 Kumar, R.R., Mohamed, S.M.S.U., and Babu, H.M.R. (2020). Introductory of blockchain technology and application for education. *International Journal of Engineering Applied Sciences and Technology* 5 (2): 543–548.

2 Schollmeier, R. (2001). A definition of peer-to-peer networking for the classification of peer-to-peer architectures and applications. *Proceedings of the 1st International Conference on Peer-to-Peer Computing*, pp. 101–102.

3 Anderson, J.R. (2008). *Security Engineering: A Guide to Building Dependable Distributed Systems.* Indianapolis, IN: Wiley.

4 Lamport, L. (1981). Password authentication with insecure communication. *Communications of the ACM* 24 (11): 770–772.

5 Bernstein, A.P. and Newcomer, E. (2009). *Principles of Transaction Processing*. Burlington, VT: Morgan Kaufmann.

6 Schneier, B. (1996). *Applied Cryptography Protocols Algorithms and Source Code in C*. Hoboken, NJ: Wiley.

7 Merkle, R.C. (1982). Method of providing digital signatures. US Patent 4, 309, 569. Leland Stanford Junior University.

8 Esposito, C., De Santis, A., Tortora, G. et al. (2018). Blockchain: a panacea for healthcare cloud-based data security and privacy? *IEEE Cloud Computing* 5 (1): 31–37.

9 Lu, Y. (2018). Blockchain: a survey on functions applications and open issues. *Journal of Industrial Integration and Management* 3 (4): 1850015.

10 Xie, J., Tang, H., Huang, T. et al. (2019). A survey of blockchain technology applied to smart cities: research issues and challenges. *IEEE Communications Surveys & Tutorials* 21 (3): 2794–2830.

11 Lin, I.-C. and Liao, T.-C. (2017). A survey of blockchain security issues and challenges. *International Journal of Network Security* 19 (5): 653–659.

12 Xinyi, Y., Yi, Z., and He, Y. (2018). Technical characteristics and model of blockchain. Proceedings of the 10th APCA International Conference on Control and Soft Computing (CONTROLO), June 2018, pp. 562–566.

13 Yang, R., Yu, F.R., Si, P. et al. (2019). Integrated blockchain and edge computing systems: a survey some research issues and challenges. *IEEE Communications Surveys & Tutorials* 21 (2): 1508–1532.

14 Chang, S.E. and Chen, Y. (2020). When blockchain meets supply chain: a systematic literature review on current development and potential applications. *IEEE Access* 8: 62478–62494.

15 Moura, T. and Gomes, A. (2017). Blockchain voting and its effects on election transparency and voter confidence. *Proceedings of the 18th Annual International Conference on Digital Government Research*, June 2017, pp. 574–575.

16 Ferrag, M.A., Derdour, M., Mukherjee, M. et al. (2019). Blockchain technologies for the Internet of Things: research issues and challenges. *IEEE Internet of Things Journal* 6 (2): 2188–2204.

17 Dunjic, M. (2018). Blockchain immutability. Blessing or curse? https://www.finextra.com/blogposting/15419/Blockchain-immutability-blessing-or-curse (accessed 6 April 2023).

18 Tian, F. (2017). A supply chain traceability system for food safety based on HACCP blockchain & Internet of Things. Proceedings of the International Conference on Service Systems and Service Management (ICSSSM), Jun. 2017, pp. 1–6.

19 Zheng, Z., Xie, S., Dai, H. et al. (2017). An overview of blockchain technology: architecture consensus and future trends. Proceedings of the IEEE 6th International Conference on Big Data Analytics (ICBDA), June 2017, pp. 557–564.

20 Baliga, A. (2017). Understanding blockchain consensus models. *Persistent* 2017 (4): 1–14. https://ieeexplore.ieee.org/ielx7/6287639/6514899/09184895.pdf.

21 Swan, M. (2015). *Blockchain Blueprint for a New Economy*. Sebastopol, CA: O'Reilly Media.

22 Ali, M.S., Vecchio, M., Pincheira, M. et al. (2019). Applications of blockchains in the Internet of Things: a comprehensive survey. *IEEE Communications Surveys & Tutorials* 21 (2): 1676–1717.

23 Pluralsight (2019). Blockchain architecture. http://Pluralsight.com (accessed 6 April 2023).

24 Kroll, E.J.A. (2013). The economics of Bitcoin mining or Bitcoin in the presence of adversaries. *Proceedings of the 12th Workshop on the Economics of Information Security (WEIS)*, p. 11.

25 Milutinovic, M. (2016). Proof of luck: an efficient blockchain consensus protocol. *Proceedings of the 1st Workshop on System Software for Trusted Execution*, December 2016.

26 Raspnode (2015). DIY Raspberry Pi Cryptocurrency Node, June 2015. http://raspnode.com/ (accessed 6 April 2023).

27 Evans, J. (2019). Blockchain nodes: an in-depth guide, January 2019. http://Nodes.com (accessed 6 April 2023).

28 Mazlan, A.A., Daud, S.M., Sam, S.M. et al. (2020). Scalability challenges in healthcare blockchain system-a systematic review. *IEEE Access* 8: 23663–23673.

29 Hertig, L. (2018). Hidden blockchain opportunities (2): masternodes & enterprise blockchain hosting. http://Plesk.com (accessed 6 April 2023).

30 Atzei, N., Bartoletti, M., Cimoli, T. et al. (2018). SoK: unraveling Bitcoin smart contracts. *Proceedings of the International Conference on Principles of Security and Trust*, pp. 217–242.

31 Gruber, D., Li, W., and Karame, G. (2018). Unifying lightweight blockchain client implementations. *Proceedings of the Workshop Decentralized IoT Security and Standards (DISS)*.

32 Bhutta, M.N.M., Khwaja, A.A., Nadeem, A. et al. (2021). A survey of blockchain technology: evolution, architecture and security. *IEEE Access, Special Section on Intelligent Big Data Analytics for IoT, Services and People* 9: 61048–61073.

33 Cai, W., Wang, Z., Ernst, J.B. et al. (2018). Decentralized applications: the blockchain-empowered software system. *IEEE Access* 6: 53019–53033.

34 Gai, K., Guo, J., Zhu, L., and Yu, S. (2020). Blockchain meets cloud computing: a survey. *IEEE Communications Surveys & Tutorials* 22 (3): 2009–2030.

35 Wang, W., Huang, H., Zhang, L., and Su, C. (2020). Secure and efficient mutual authentication protocol for smart grid under blockchain. *Peer-to-Peer Networking and Applications* 13 (6): 1–3.

36 Wang, W., Huang, H., Zhang, L. et al. (2021). BlockSLAP: blockchain-based secure and lightweight authentication protocol for smart grid. *Proceedings of the IEEE 19th International Conference on Trust, Security and Privacy in Computing and Communications (TrustCom)*, pp. 1332–1338, January 2021.

37 Sankar, L.S., Sindhu, M., and Sethumadhavan, M. (2017). Survey of consensus protocols on blockchain applications. *Proceedings of the 4th International Conference on Advanced Computing and Communication Systems (ICACCS)*, January 2017.

38 Lejun, Z., Minghui, P., Weizheng, W. et al. (2020). Secure and efficient medical data storage and sharing scheme based on double blockchain. *Computers, Materials and Continua* 66 (1): 499–515.

39 Compare, P. (2019). What is proof of weight a web article published by coincodex. https://coincodex.com/article/2617/what-is-proof-of-weight/ (accessed 6 April 2023).

40 Zhuang, Q., Liu, Y., Chen, L., and Ai, Z. (2019). Proof of reputation: a reputation-based consensus protocol for blockchain based systems. Proceedings of the International Electronics Communication Conference (ACM IECC), July 2019, pp. 131–138.

41 Dziembowski, S., Faust, S., Kolmogorov, V., and Pietrzak, K. (2015). Proofs of space. *Proceedings of the 35th Annual Cryptology Conference (CRYPTO)*, August 2015, pp. 585–605.

42 Castro, M. and Liskov, B. (1999). Practical Byzantine fault tolerance. In: *Proceedings. of the 3rd Symposium. on Operating System.s Design and Implement OSDI*, Volume 99, pp. 173–186.

43 Li, Y., Cao, B., Peng, M. et al. (2019). Direct acyclic graph based blockchain for Internet of Things: performance and security analysis. *arXiv:1905.10925*. https://arxiv.org/abs/1905.10925.

44 Vasin, P. (2014). Blackcoins proof-of-stake protocol V2. https://blackcoin.co/blackcoin-pos-protocol-v2-whitepaper.pdf (accessed 6 April 2023).

45 King, S. and Nadal, S. (2012). Ppcoin: peer-to-peer crypto-currency with proof-of-stake. Self-Published Paper, Volume 19.

46 Wood, G. (2014). Ethereum: a secure generalized transaction ledger. Ethereum Project Yellow Paper.

47 Zamfir, V. (2015). Introducing Casper the friendly ghost. Ethereum Blog. https://blog. ethereum. org/2015/08/01/introducing-casper friendly-ghost (accessed 6 April 2023).

48 Smith, R. (2019). Proof of Burn—Consensus Through Coin Destruction Article Published by Coin Central. https://coincentral.com/proof-of-burn/ (accessed 6 April 2023).

49 Androulaki, E., Cachin, C., Ferris, C. et al. (2018). Hyperledger fabric: a distributed operating system for permissioned blockchains. *arXiv:1801.10228*. https://arxiv.org/pdf/1801.10228.pdf.

50 Larimer, D. (2018). DPOS consensus algorithm-the missing white paper. New York, NY, USA.

51 Baliga, A. (2017). Understanding blockchain consensus models. *Persistent* 2017 (4): 114.

52 Coelho, I.M., Coelho, V.N., Lin, P., and Zhang, E. (2019). Delegated Byzantine fault tolerance: technical details challenges and perspectives. https://neoresearch.io/assets/yellowpaper/yellow_ paper.pdf (accessed 6 April 2023).

53 nem (2018). Investor harvesting: proof-of-importance. https://nem.io/xem/harvesting-and-poi/ (accessed 6 April 2023).

54 Chen, L., Xu, L., Shah, N. et al. (2017). On security analysis of proof-of-elapsed-time (POET). *Proceedings of the International Symposium on Stabilization, Safety, and Security of Distributed Systems.*

8

Scaling-Out Blockchains with Sharding

8.1 Introduction

Over the past decade, Bitcoin and blockchain technology have experienced an unprecedented surge in popularity, captivating the world's attention. For a long time, the majority of public blockchains were focused on financial applications such as decentralized cryptocurrencies, and many of the beneficial aspects of blockchain technology were disregarded. Since then, the broader economic community has gradually begun to see the potential benefits that public blockchains, in conjunction with other technologies such as smart contracts, can provide to businesses and individuals. Today, the underlying blockchain technology is not merely regarded as a revolutionary force but a true disruptor with the immense potential to transform a multitude of businesses concurrently. However, the lack of scalability continues to be a significant concern for the majority of public blockchains, preventing a wide range of promising use cases from being implemented. According to recent research, scalability has emerged as the most pressing issue that must be addressed in order to gain widespread acceptance of blockchain technology. This is especially true given the increasing popularity of permissionless blockchains in recent years.

Scalability is almost certainly the primary difficulty that the majority of established public blockchains, such as Ethereum or Bitcoin, face. Indeed, scalability has been a point of contention since the inception of public blockchains. When Satoshi Nakamoto published the Bitcoin whitepaper [1] and invented public blockchains on his own in late October 2008, one of the first public reactions came from James A. Donald on November 2, who stated: "We desperately need such a system, but your proposal does not appear to scale to the required size" [2]. Of course, these concerns about scalability were different, but even now, more than a decade later, the public blockchain's lack of scalability endures.

The root cause of this issue stems from the underlying network protocol, which requires every transaction to be processed by every node within the network. Both Bitcoin and Ethereum now employ a proof-of-work-based distributed consensus method, which drastically slows down block production. This means that miners are competing on computationally complex problems, or more accurately, on the challenge of finding a nonce that fulfills a certain target difficulty, which is a time- and energy-intensive task. As a result of this consensus mechanism, each node in the network is required to verify the miners' efforts and maintain a copy of the blockchain's current state. In Ethereum, new blocks are created every 10 to 20 seconds, but in Bitcoin, new blocks are added to the network every ten minutes. This significantly reduces both of these public blockchains' transactional throughput. When the number of transactions within a block on the Ethereum blockchain is broken down, this results in an average of about 12–25 transactions per second [3, 4].

Attribute-based Encryption (ABE): Foundations and Applications within Blockchain and Cloud Environments, First Edition.
Qi Xia, Jianbin Gao, Isaac Amankona Obiri, Kwame Omono Asamoah, and Daniel Adu Worae.
© 2024 The Institute of Electrical and Electronics Engineers, Inc. Published 2024 by John Wiley & Sons, Inc.

8.1.1 Scalability Trilemma

Scalability trilemma is a trade-off between three desirable characteristics of a public blockchain architecture: decentralization, security, and scalability as shown in Figure 8.1. According to the trilemma, it is impossible to optimize all three of these attributes equally. Satisfying two of them will always mean ignoring the third. It is referred to as the scalability trilemma due to the fact that established public blockchains frequently struggle to scale enough. The Ethereum blockchain offers a compelling perspective through which the trilemma becomes unmistakably evident. While this particular blockchain is extremely secure and completely decentralized, its scalability suffers significantly. As said previously, scalability is a necessary component of public blockchains in order to attain mass acceptance and lure mainstream applications to the blockchain. On the other hand, security is an unavoidable and necessary component of any operating system or network. As a result, decentralization may appear to be the lesser of the three.

However, a decentralized architecture comprising thousands of nodes is the fundamental component of a public blockchain and is directly responsible for all of the benefits. Naturally, none of these properties are binary in nature and can be aligned to fulfill a particular use case. Indeed, this trilemma results in the proliferation of blockchains with a variety of applications, as participants choose to focus on their own demands. For instance, Enterprise Operating System (EOS) is one of the aforementioned newer public blockchains that scales extremely well while being secure. However, EOS's drawback is its lack of decentralization, particularly in comparison to Ethereum. This trilemma can be pushed to its logical conclusion when applied to a centralized (non-blockchain) architecture. VisaNet, which we utilized as a scalability benchmark in Section 8.1.7, is totally centralized and hence scales virtually infinitely while being secure. Vitalik Buterin, the Ethereum blockchain's founder, asserted that the holy grail of creating a blockchain platform that maximizes all three characteristics is almost unachievable. As a result, my strategy is to concentrate on Ethereum, a well-established public blockchain that currently excels at both of these characteristics, and to assess alternatives that could result in a considerable increase in scalability without jeopardizing security or decentralization [4–7].

In many domains, a lack of scalability is a fundamental impediment to widespread use of blockchain technology. Sharding can aid blockchains in achieving greater scalability and efficiency, making them more competitive against established centralized alternatives.

At the moment, each node in a blockchain network is responsible for processing or handling all of the transaction volumes within the network. All of the data in a decentralized network is maintained and stored by the nodes in a blockchain, which are independent and responsible for this responsibility. As a result, each node must be able to store crucial information, such as account balances and transaction histories, locally. Blockchain networks are created in such a way that every node on the network is responsible for processing all of the operations, data, and transactions on the network at the same time.

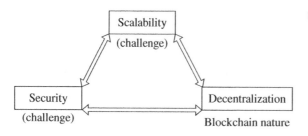

Figure 8.1 Scalability trilemma.

While it increases the security of a blockchain by keeping every transaction in all of the nodes, this architecture causes transaction processing to be significantly slowed. It is not encouraging to think about a future in which blockchain will be accountable for millions of transactions if transaction processing rates are slow today. Sharding is one of the solutions to the scalability challenge that blockchains are experiencing. A key component of this strategy is splitting the database into so-called "shards," with each shard processing a piece of the data flowing via the network. This greatly minimizes the amount of time required for processing.

Sharding was first proposed by Wu [8] and is now widely utilized in distributed databases and cloud architecture, among other applications. According to the pioneering proposals integrating sharding with permissioned and permissionless blockchain, respectively, the sharding technology is thought to be capable of partitioning the network into different groups (shards), so that the compulsory duplication of three resources (i.e. the communication, data storage, and computation overhead) can be avoided for each participating node, whereas these overheads must be incurred by all full nodes in traditional non-sharded networks. Due to the restrictions imposed by the three resources controlled by a single node, it is necessary to partition the system in order for it to fully exploit a scalable consensus process. As shown in Figure 8.2, sharding is currently one of the most viable options for achieving a scale-out system in which processing, storage, and computation can all be done in parallel. This makes it feasible to have capacity and throughput that are proportional to the number of participating nodes or the number of shards, while still maintaining decentralization and security.

The fundamental idea is as follows: Consider a proof-of-stake chain with a large number of validators (e.g. 10,000) and a large number of blocks to verify (e.g. 100). Prior to the arrival of the next batch of blocks, no single machine will be able to validate all of these blocks. Consequently, we distribute the verification tasks at random. The validator list is randomly shuffled, and the first 100 validators are assigned to verify the first block, the next 100 validators are assigned to verify the second block, etc. A committee is a group of randomly selected validators entrusted with verifying a block (or executing some other activity). When a validator verifies a block, they publish a signature to attest to their activity. In lieu of verifying 100 complete blocks, everyone else must now only verify 10,000 signatures, which requires far less effort. Instead of sending each block over the same P2P network, each block is sent over its own sub-network, and nodes only need to join the sub-networks for the blocks they are responsible for or interested in for other reasons. Consider the effects of doubling the computational power of each node. Because each node can now safely

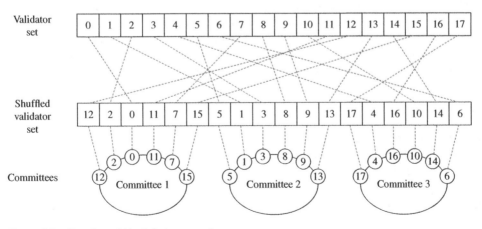

Figure 8.2 Sharding of blockchain network.

validate twofold more signatures, the minimum staking deposit amount can be dropped to accommodate twofold more validators, enabling the formation of 200 committees as opposed to 100. As a result, you can now verify 200 blocks per slot instead of 100. Additionally, the size of each individual block may be doubled. As a result, you have 2x more blocks of 2x the size, or a total of 4x greater chain capacity.

By purposefully partitioning the network into n shards, we can significantly enhance throughput in $O(n)$, where rational miners choose to disperse their mining power across several shards (at most n shards) to maximize their rewards. This, however, reduces the security of PoW in each shard by $O(1/n)$. Due to the smaller shard size in comparison to the total network size, the system may be more susceptible to double-spend attacks by malicious miners P who just need to control the total amount of mining power among the network $\mathbb{P}$, i.e. $P > \mathbb{P}/n \times 50\%$. This issue worsens as n increases in order to achieve a higher throughput, and thus becomes the most important impediment to implementing PoW for the intra-consensus protocol of a sharding mechanism.

However, to solve the security concern, byzantine fault tolerance (BFT)-based consensus techniques are being proposed in instead of PoW. However, the BFT-based consensus introduces a varied set of vulnerabilities, including those related to intra-consensus safety and cross-shard atomicity. The following enhancement can be used to address sharding-related issues.

8.1.2 Nakamoto-Based – Monoxide – Chu-ko-nu Mining

Monoxide is the first sharding solution that eliminates the need for randomness generation and does it by utilizing the Nakamoto consensus algorithm for intra-consensus. It begins with one-to-one bootstrapping, in which each node (miners and non-miners alike) is divided into different shards based on their unique identifier addresses. Monoxide can construct a large-scale network with a large number of shards and a variable shard size by utilizing the proposed Chu-ko-nu mining algorithm. It makes use of a Merkle Patricia Tree (MPT) root, which distributes all proposed blocks among many shards, allowing P/n to be raised by a factor of k. (k denotes the amount of shards mined by a particular miner). As a result, dispersed mining power can be combined to defeat the 1% attack, i.e. $\mathbb{P}k/n \simeq P$ as $k \to n$.

Monoxide requires the majority of miners to execute Chu-ko-nu mining over as many shards as feasible in order to achieve the condition of $\mathbb{P}k/n \simeq P$, i.e. $k = n$ in the best scenario. However, if miners only mine on k out of n shards, i.e. $\mathbb{P}k/n$, where $k \ll n$, the factor required to amplify the effective mining power will be enough to secure the mining process, resulting in a lower attack cost. On the other hand, rational miners would mine on all n shards in order to maximize profit, which may lead to power centralization due to the high cost of bandwidth, disk storage, and computer processors, which only professional mining operators can afford.

8.1.3 Elastico

Elastico [4] is a protocol for decentralized agreement on permissionless blockchains. Elastico tries to address the scalability issue by combining two paradigms: sharding and fault-tolerant Byzantine transactions. It is the first secure sharding technique designed specifically for Byzantine environments. Elastico partitions incoming transactions into shards. Each shard is independently verified by separate node committees.

Elastico is divided into epochs, each of which consists of five steps:

1. **Establishment of identity and committee formation**: Nodes cannot be permitted to select a committee to join, as this would enable opponents to take control of some shards. To join the network, a node must first solve a Proof-Of-Work challenge, following which their identity is established. Each node must generate a nonce, similar to how Bitcoin miners operate. The following hash function is used to generate the ID : $ID = H$(EpochRandomness, IP, Public key, Nonce) $< D$, where D is the difficulty, EpochRandomness is a random number created by the consensus committee every epoch, the IP and public key are node inputs, and the nonce is the puzzle that the node must solve. Elastico then distributes identifications (IDs) equitably to committees by utilizing the last k bits of each identity.

2. **Committee overlay configuration**: Elastico use a hierarchical architecture and directory committees in step 2 to broadcast all identities. The first C identities function as directory servers, with C denoting the number of committees and being hardcoded in a global configuration file. Each committee must consist of a minimum of C members. The remaining nodes communicate their identities to directories, which broadcast the list of IDs. This method, the number of messages is reduced from $O(N^2)$ to $O(NC)$.

3. **Intra-committee consensus**: After establishing the committees, a pre-existing BFT protocol, such as PBFT, is utilized to achieve consensus within each committee (i.e. intra-shard consensus). Each transaction requires the signatures of at least half of the committee members and is then forwarded to the final consensus committee.

4. **Broadcast of final consensus**: A final committee is created in stage 4. The final committee's members validate each transaction using a Byzantine consensus process.

5. **Epoch randomness creation**: In this step, the final committee generates EpochRandomness for the next epoch using a distributed commit-and-xor mechanism. Elastico's disadvantages include the inability of PBFT to scale as an intra-shard consensus protocol and the vulnerability of the commit-and-xor strategy for generating EpochRandomness, both of which are addressed in OmniLedger and RapidChain.

8.1.4 OmniLedger

OmniLedger seeks to be a permissionless distributed ledger with the scalability and performance of centralized payment systems like Visa. OmniLedger is composed of multiple shards that make use of a variety of techniques such as RandHound, cryptographic sortition, ByzCoinX (OmniLedger's enhanced version of ByzCoin), and Atomix (OmniLedger's novel two-step atomic commit protocol) to ensure security and correctness within and across shards while ensuring high performance and scalability.

Validators are nodes that ensure no transaction in a block is spent twice. OmniLedger secures shard validators by utilizing a global identifying blockchain and distributed randomness generation technology. As with Elastico epochs, validators desiring to join OmniLedger must first register with the identity blockchain. On the gossip network, their identities and supporting documentation are made public. As with Elastico, validators are unable to choose which shard to join. When validators are randomly assigned, malicious nodes are likely to be evenly distributed throughout all shards. OmniLedger derives its randomization from RandHound and cryptographic sortition. At the start of each epoch, OmniLedger uses RandHound to assign new validators and reassign existing validators to new shards and groups within shards. The number of groups in each shard is specified in a shard policy file. RandHound is a large-scale distributed protocol that "provides publicly verifiable, unexpected, and unbiasable randomness against Byzantine attackers." Because RandHound requires a leader, OmniLedger uses cryptographic sortition based on verifiable random functions VRFs to choose a random leader at the start of each epoch. If the block is valid (i.e. it is endorsed by at least two-thirds of validators), the leader requires a collective signature and adds it to the identity blockchain.

Internally, each shard uses ByzCoinX to reach consensus. ByzCoinX is a version of the ByzCoin protocol that has been enhanced [9]. ByzCoin uses a tree-based communication architecture to distribute blocks and incorporates a slow lane for fault tolerance. OmniLedger introduces a revolutionary communication mechanism that prioritizes robustness above scalability. OmniLedger modifies the message transmission protocol and assigns a leader to each group. Each group leader is responsible for communicating with the protocol leader and the members of his or her group. During the configuration described above, validators are randomly assigned to not only each shard, but also to each group inside the shards. Parallel processing is available for non-conflicting transactions with no unspent transaction output (UTXO) dependencies. OmniLedger processes transactions atomically across shards using the Byzantine Shard Atomic Commit protocol Atomix. The initialize step creates and propagates a cross-shard transaction over the network, eventually reaching all input shards. In the second step (Lock), each input shard validates the transaction to ensure it has not been spent. In the third phase (Unlock), the client unlocks-to-commit the transaction if all shards accept it, or unlocks-to-abort the transaction if not all shards accept it.

In comparison to Elastico, OmniLedger provides a more secure mechanism for shard assignment, an atomic protocol for inter-shard communication, and significant communication overhead savings. OmniLedger, on the other hand, has not resolved a number of difficulties. To create an initial configuration for seeding VRF, OmniLedger requires a trusted configuration. Clients must engage actively in cross-shard transactions, and malicious clients can block the lock and unlock stages indefinitely.

8.1.5 Rapid Chain

RapidChain is the first permissionless blockchain technology based on full sharding that is Byzantine fault resistant and does not require any trusted setup. Utilizing a unique intra-committee consensus algorithm, it achieves great throughput and scalability. RapidChain is divided into three distinct phases: bootstrapping, consensus, and reconfiguration. At the start, the bootstrap phase is run only once. RapidChain then progresses through epochs, each of which include a Consensus phase and a Reconfiguration phase. RapidChain bootstraps by selecting a root group with $O(n)$ nodes, where n denotes the total number of nodes. This group generates and distributes a random bit sequence that is used to form an O-dimensional reference committee ($\log n$). The reference committee then produces k random committees (shards) with $m = c\log n$ members each, where n is the number of nodes and c is a security parameter that is commonly set to 20. Each epoch, nodes wishing to join or remain, must solve a Proof-Of-Work puzzle that is randomly generated. The referenced committee validates their solutions, generates a reference block containing a list of all active nodes and their committees, and distributes it to all other committees. RapidChain leverages the Cuckoo rule [10], a technique for selective random shuffling, to ensure reconfiguration is safe and protected against a slowly adapting Byzantine opponent. This makes it more difficult for adversaries to zero in on a particular committee. Once committees are constituted (or reformed), an intra-committee consensus mechanism is utilized to reach consensus inside each committee.

The protocol is composed of two components: a gossiping protocol for propagating messages (e.g. transactions and blocks) among committee members, and a synchronous consensus procedure for agreeing on the block's header and hash. The gossiping protocol is based on the Information Dispersal Algorithm (IDA) and erasure coding. A huge message is segmented into chunks, each of which contains one parity chunk. A Merkle-tree is constructed, with the chunks serving as leaves. Each neighbor is supplied with a distinct subset of chunks and their Merkle-proofs. The IDA-Gossip protocol is more efficient and faster than reliable broadcast protocols at reducing communication overhead. However, it is unreliable and requires the root to conduct a consensus process to achieve consistency.

Crossshard verification is required for transactions with inputs and outputs from distinct committees. The transaction's input committees contain the transaction's inputs, while the transaction's output committees are determined by the hash of the transaction id. RapidChain's inter-shard communication is based on the Kademlia routing algorithm. Each node keeps track of the members of their committee and logs log n nodes in each of their log n nearest committees. When a message comes, it is distributed to all nodes in the sender committee. Each receiver uses the IDA-gossip protocol to distribute the message to the members of their committee. RapidChain, in comparison to Elastico and OmniLedger, does not require a trusted setup and significantly improves performance. However, it continues to rely on synchronization for survival, and there is no mechanism in place to reward active nodes.

8.1.6 Learnings

With the sharding protocols, BFT protocols for permissionless blockchains such as Proof-Of-Work and Proof-Of-Stake are extensively used to establish identities and allow nodes to join/rejoin the network. Preventing shard takeovers is critical for the security of a sharded blockchain system. A node must be permitted to select which shard to join; otherwise, malevolent nodes can seize control of a shard and alter the associated data. As a result, protocols that generate randomness, such as RandHound, are used to distribute nodes randomly. As a result, each shard has a nearly equal proportion of malicious nodes. After establishing shards, BFT algorithms are utilized to achieve consensus and validate transactions both within and across shards.

Cross-shard transactions contribute significantly to the overhead of data transmission across shards, reducing system throughput and increasing confirmation time. When it comes to cross-shard transactions, sharded blockchains take one of two techniques.

The first option is to establish a full-mesh connection between nodes (see, for example, OmniLedger and RapidChain). Verifying a transaction that spans several shards needs communication between validators located in separate shards. OmniLedger introduces the Atomix protocol, which delegated responsibility for transacting across shards to clients. Clients must obtain proofs of acceptance from all input shards in order to lock input transactions and transfer them along with their proofs to the output shards. RapidChain enhances the Atomix protocol by the addition of a three-way confirmation mechanism. To facilitate communication between shards, each committee in each shard keeps a routing table of log2 n committees. While this strategy distributes storage and eliminates a bottleneck in the main chain, it may introduce communication cost and security concerns. It generally requires nodes to reorganize into new shards on a periodic basis and download the ledger of the new shard to which they are being reshuffled. Due to the fact that transactions are divided into distinct chains, if an attacker gains control of a shard, other shards will be unable to validate transactions that are dependent on the attacked shard.

Another option is to keep a global root chain, like Elastico and Ethereum 2.0. After nodes in each shard finalize and gain consensus on local transactions, some nodes forward them to the final committee, and the final block is stored in a global ledger. In Ethereum 2.0, the global chain – the beacon chain – ensures that all shards' transactions are in sync and discards any transaction that has been double-spent. Parallelism is increased through the use of shards, while the root chain handles cross-shard transactions. In comparison to the first approach, this approach minimizes data migration cost while managing cross-shard transactions and ensures that the system remains valid even when one shard is controlled by an adversary. Additionally, nodes can join shards without rearrangement.

8.1.7 General Improvements

This section covers some of the primary challenges and potential solutions associated with each of the sharding processes examined thus far. As illustrated Figure 8.3 such modifications can be used generally to address the new challenges introduced by the researched sharding strategies. They include transaction latency, inter-shard communication protocol, sharded ledger pruning, decentralized bootstrapping, securing epoch reconfiguration, securing sharded smart contracts, and replay attacks and defenses against cross-shard transactions.

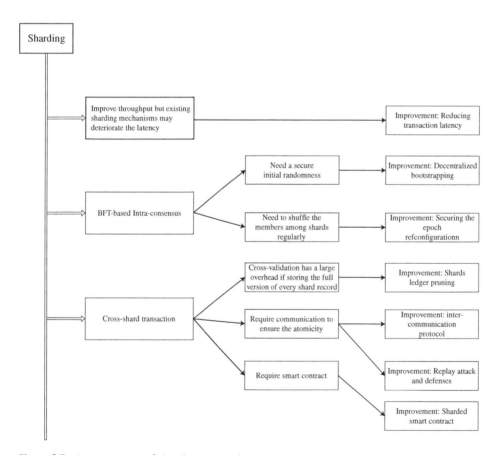

Figure 8.3 Improvements of sharding mechanism.

8.1.7.1 Reducing Transaction Latency

With the exception of throughput, transaction latency, which is the time required to algorithmically confirm and finalize a transaction, is probably more sensitive to individual users. It has been established that the BFT-based 1% attack can be mitigated either by implementing a scalable BFT consensus, such as OmniLedger or Ethereum 2.0, or by increasing the FT inside a single shard, such as RapidChain. However, as noted below, transaction latency remains a concern.

- The transaction latency worsens when a scalable BFT consensus employs a large-scale shard size to combat the 1 percent attack. The trust-but-verify transaction validation system, which runs within each shard to offer real-time transaction confirmation time, is thus introduced in Omniledger, and can be applied in any suitable sharding scheme, such as Ethereum 2.0, to achieve real-time transaction confirmation time. The validation process is broken down into two stages: an optimistic validation and a core validation. The transaction can be accepted once the optimistic validation is passed by those users who are more concerned with latency than with security.

  Thus, real-time transaction latency can be obtained at the expense of security, as the additional 1% attack is still possible in optimistic groups. As with IoTA, this real-time transaction latency can be employed in only a limited number of cases with low security needs.

- The transaction latency increases as the communication overhead associated with a non-scalable 50% BFT consensus increases. As a result, the 50% consensus agreement is limited to a digest of the block. RapidChain leverages the information dispersal algorithm (IDA)-based gossip protocol to more efficiently transport huge payloads. To put it another way, the sender breaks the original message into n equal-sized chunks and then uses a (m, n) erasure code scheme to compress the n chunks into m chunks. As a result, each node can recreate the original message by obtaining valid n chunks from its neighbors using certain proofs, for example, the MPT proofs, considerably reducing the latency.

8.1.7.2 Inter-Communication Protocol

In contrast to the protocol used to establish cross-shard atomicity, the inter-communication protocol concentrates on the overhead associated with data transmission across shards. The two major types of solution are as follows.

- A global root chain is constructed to operate as a message distributor, and each validator (or miner in the context of Monoxide) is responsible for storing this chain. Ethereum 2.0, Monoxide with identical PoW targets, and Elastico all utilize this type of sharding technique. However, because the structure is single-chained rather than sharded, the bottleneck is moved to the global root chain. This is a temporary, not a permanent, solution.
- OmniLedger and Chainspace adopt the most straightforward method, which is a full-mesh connection. This condition is frequently met in latency-sensitive systems, which imposes a significant overhead.

To circumvent the full-mesh connection, RapidChain adopts a novel intercommunication protocol based on a routing table maintained by each validator; see Figure 4.3 on the top. It is inspired by the Kademlia-based routing protocol, in which each validator keeps a routing table comprising all members of its shard as well as $\log_2\log_2 n$ validators from other $\log_2 n$ shards that are distance 2^i for $0 \leq i \leq 2n - 1$ away. All validators in the sender shard communicate with all validators on the receiver side via messages. The communication overhead can be greatly decreased by utilizing a peer-to-peer network.

8.1.7.3 Shards Ledger Pruning

The majority of existing Blockchain systems with a single-chained topology store the entire version of their chain in order to reduce censorship and audition communication and processing overhead. Validators must maintain the history of each shard in order to facilitate cross-shard transactions and re-allocation (bootstrapping) during each epoch, so storing a full version of the ledger for each shard incurs an unreasonable overhead of disk storage for validators. OmniLedger offers the creation of state blocks as a solution (SB).

SBs of a shard contain the state of the shard as well as any transactions related with each epoch. SBs are modeled after stable checkpoints in PBFT, fast-sync mode in Ethereum, and stable checkpoints of Node HashChains in Chainspace. According to [11], such pruning incurs an overhead of $O(m + logT)$ for partial audits and $O(T)$ for full audits, where m denotes the shard size and T denotes the number of transactions. The partial audit enables any user to acquire an evidence of the existence of any transaction in any shard; the full audit enables a complete verification by replaying a shard's whole history. However, the design of SB poses two issues: the overhead of transaction proofs may constitute a bottleneck; however, this can be alleviated by using Simple Payment Verification (SPV), numerous multi-hop backpointers, or Proofs of Proof of Work (PoPoW)). State blocks suffer the same issue as the Atomix Protocol in OmniLedger and the light-client protocol in Ethereum 1.0 (if utilized in Ethereum 2.0), namely delegating the most critical responsibility to the client.

8.1.7.4 Decentralized Bootstrapping

With regard to sharding mechanisms that employ a randomness generator that is responsible for a PoW-based entry ticket in the context of a BFT-based intra-consensus protocol, it is critical to choose the initial set with an honest majority, such as the final committee in Elastico and the reference committee in RapidChain2. To achieve this decentralization, RapidChain proposes a samplergraph election network, which requires only a hardcoded seed and some network configurations to be used in its bootstrapping. The participants in such an election network are uniformly distributed into a few groups, within which a PoW-based result is computed by each member using the randomness supplied by the verifiable secret sharing (VSS)-based deterministic random bit generator (DRG) protocol (Section 4.2.5) and the identification ID of the election network participant. Each group can be subdivided based on the outcome of the analysis. The iteration of this procedure results in the creation of a unique root group (which selects members of the reference committee at random) that can be obtained with a 50 percent honest majority (a high probability). This results in a reduction in the communication cost, which is reduced from $\Omega(n2)$ to $O(\sqrt{n})$, where n is the total number of validators who are participating in a given validation session.

8.1.7.5 Securing the Epoch Reconfiguration

To prevent attacks from slowly adaptive adversaries, validators must be swapped out and re-allocated in other shards every epoch in order to prevent attacks from corrupt or Distributed Denial of Service (DDoS)-attack validators. Such attacks can be carried out in a limited amount of time, but they are not as effective as they could be if they were carried out immediately. As a result, the epoch length should be carefully calculated to be less than the restricted time interval.

Remember that Elastico and Chainspace do not provide such a solution, but Ethereum 2.0 solves the intra-consensus problem with a global validator pool by updating the member participating in the intra-consensus protocol for each shard on a consistent basis. For each of them, validators must be used to track the status of each shard in order to expedite the reconfiguration phase. OmniLedger uses a random permutation strategy to swap out the validators, ensuring that the total number of validators switched at any given time is bounded by $k = logn/m$, where n denotes the total number of participating validators and m denotes the total number of shards. It is also at this point that new validators who need to register their ID on a global identity Blockchain are assigned to randomly selected shards of the network. As a result, the number of honest validators left can be sufficient to reach consensus while certain validators are swapped out, allowing the idle phase to be reduced and the throughput to be increased. But because of the substantial delay and moderate scaling of this approach, it causes a 1-day-long epoch, which is not suitable for highly adaptive adversaries who can adjust quickly (when the bounded time becomes smaller).

As an alternative to this, RapidChain suggests using the Cuckoo rule to implement a light-weighted reconfiguration protocol, with a constant amount of validators allowed to shift between committees in each epoch. For example, by the end of epoch I the reference committee (Cr) will have announced a PoW puzzle based on the randomness generated in epoch I1 (Ri) by the DRG protocol, and validators who wish to participate in epoch I + 1, including those who have participated in epoch I 1 and I can solve the puzzle and inform Cr. As part of the process of creating the active and inactive lists of validators for epoch I + 1, Cr swaps out a constant number of validators from one committee to another based on the Ri+1 generated in epoch 1 during the second iteration of the process. Finally, Cr agrees on a reference block that is recorded in Cr's local ledger and broadcasts it to the entire network as a result of their agreement. If you compare this architecture to that of OmniLedger, you will notice that it incurs less expense and enables for more frequent epoch reconfiguration to accommodate more highly adaptive adversaries [5, 11].

8.1.7.6 Sharded Smart Contract

Except for Chainspace, which introduces smart-contract oriented sharding functionality for the first time by utilizing a novel transaction structure based on new atoms, none of the other explored sharding mechanisms have accomplished smart-contract oriented sharding to date. Objects indicated by the letter o. As part of its definition, objects include a slew of new parameters such as input objects (x), output objects (y), reference objects (r), contracts (c) (which are treated as special objects), procedures (proc), and checkers (v). The atomicity of smart contracts in Chainspace can be ensured by following a strict set of procedures and actions.

It is possible to safely shard a smart contract with strong atomicity by altering the transaction structure and incorporating the concept of additional atoms and objects; however, this comes at the expense of significant complexity and, as a result, limited throughput.

8.1.7.7 Replay Attacks and Defenses Against Cross-Shard Protocols

As highlighted for the first time by Low [5], replay attacks and countermeasures against BFT-based cross-shard protocols have gained growing attention (i.e. Monoxide is based on Nakamoto and uses a lock-free cross-shard protocol, making it immune to this type of replay attack). By leveraging the virtue of unanimous voting, the replay assaults method can compromise cross-shard atomicity and launch a low-cost double-spending attack. To be more precise, each shard participating in a cross-shard transaction must communicate its own choice (i.e. accepting/abandoning the transaction) to the other participants in order to lock/unlock the internal objects and so ensure cross-shard atomicity. However, the following approach can simply be used to launch an effective replay attack. Consider an attacker and a trustworthy client preparing to send a cross-shard transaction $T(x1, x2)! (y1, y2, y3)$, where xi denotes the input objects that shard-i manages and yi denotes the output objects that shard-i manages.

- **Extraction and invalidation of shard-1's decision-message**: By sending a T0 (x2,) to shard-2, the attacker races the client and locks the involved objects in shard-23. T is then submitted to shard-1 and shard-2 by the attacker. When T reaches shard-1, an accept(T) is sent out, which the attacker can record in advance. In shard-2, on the other hand, T will be nullified. Due to the locked items on shard-2, an abort(T) will be sent out and captured by the attacker.

- **Compromising the consistency**: At any point when shard-1 is due to send the decisions, the attacker can race shard-1 by broadcasting and repeating a pre-recorded message that is constantly in opposition to shard-1. As a result, shard-1's input objects remain active while new output items are created in shard-2 and shard-3, compromising the system's consistency.

The authors of [5] also discussed the reasons for the replay attacks' feasibility.

- To begin, there is no mechanism for the input shards to determine the relationship between a received protocol message (i.e. accept(T) or abort(T)) and a specific transaction T.
- Second (2), there is no way for output shards to determine the context of a particular transaction because they are omitted from intermediate processing.

To solve these constraints, we offer Byzcuit [5], a modified version of Chainspace with two new features. To address 1, a sequence number scheme is applied to each transaction to verify correspondence, while a dummy object representing each output shard is added to the transaction's input field (i.e. forcing the output shards to participate in intermediary processing) to address 2.

Attacks and defenses against BFT-based cross-shard protocols that have been presented are noteworthy and should be given more attention. In contrast, the sequence number scheme continues to have a synchronization problem, and the dummy object continues to have poor scalability. Both of these issues are being worked on, and both are striving for better performance.

We conclude that RapidChain and Ethereum 2.0 include optimizations that alleviate the limits imposed by Elastico and OmniLedger, resulting in RapidChain and Ethereum 2.0 being the most advanced BFT-based sharding techniques in terms of throughput and cost, respectively. However, Monoxide raises the throughput upper-bound to the Mega-level and provides up a new route for the Nakamoto-based sharding mechanisms to explore. For sharded-smart contracts, Chainspace has a lot of potential for development in terms of performance.

8.2 Off-Chain Solution: Layer 2 Solutions

Layer 2 solutions, sometimes referred to as off-chain solutions, are developed on top of the base layer and are not implemented on the primary blockchain. They plan to relocate transaction calculation off-chain, which will shift strain away from the blockchain. Bobn though the transactions are no longer completed on-chain, the Ethereum blockchain serves as an arbiter in this scenario, providing clarity and security. This concept opens the door to a wide range of cryptoeconomic systems that can improve the efficiency and throughput of underlying blockchains. However, it remains critical that these multi-layer designs do not compromise decentralization or security [12].

8.2.1 State Channels

State channels are essentially two-way channels of communication between two parties. These state channels can be built via multisignature transactions or smart contracts, in which users agree on the channel's terms and deposit monies. Due to the fact that these peer-to-peer exchanges would otherwise take place on the main blockchain, state channels can be extremely useful for providing a very low-cost and rapid method of sending and receiving micropayments. The primary advantage of state channels over standard blockchain transactions is their immediate finality and low transaction fees. Once the sequence of interactions between the parties is complete, the final state is published and put to the blockchain.

The Raiden network is a well-known state channel strategy. Raiden is a lot like the Bitcoin lightning network, which enables micropayment channels within the Bitcoin ecosystem. Unlike the lightning network, Raiden is optimized for the Ethereum blockchain by permitting more complicated channel interactions between members, including the usage of smart contracts. Additionally, Raiden functions as a payment channel network, allowing many parties to communicate directly through bidirectional token payment channels. This facilitates the establishment of multi-party channels involving more than two people. One significant disadvantage of state channels in general is that users must be online at all times in order to sign and approve to state modifications. Additionally, they must put funds directly into the channel for an extended length of time, which will remain unavailable until the channel is reopened [4, 13–16].

Bob and Alice are rapidly "countersigning" updated game states, as seen in Figure 8.4, in a cryptographic acknowledgement that says "Yes, this is indeed the current state." Using the most recent "state," a winning move can now be claimed by players.

There are situations when the most recent state update "trumps" the prior one. A record of these past states is kept by each side. Alice may provide the most recent end state and show that Bob cheated if he lost and presented an outdated, "state" state. It is now up to Bob to face the

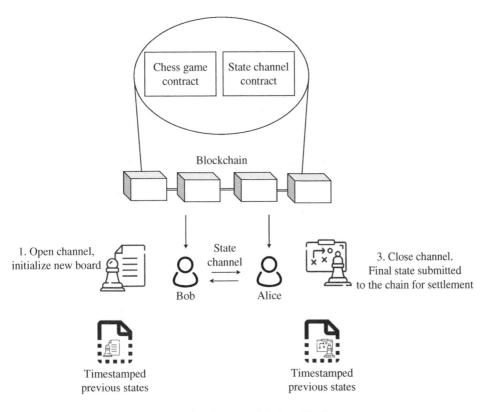

Figure 8.4 State channel.

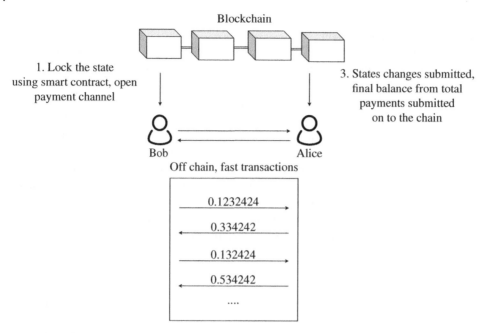

Figure 8.5 Payment channel.

consequences that were agreed upon. Figure 8.5 illustrates payment channels, a state channel type that deals specifically with payment transfers, at a high level. State channels, on the other hand, enable for any form of action that updates the state of programs running on the blockchain (e.g. Lightning Network on Bitcoin). Additionally, state channels are a wider variety of payment channels, which can be used for a wide range of purposes, from simple transactions to more complicated ones.

Transactions in a state channel could take place on the blockchain; however, they are carried out off the blockchain in order to increase scalability. Only settlement and verification take place on the main blockchain.

For the sake of clarity, the on-chain contract is not being referred to as part of any transactions here. For example, Etherscan uses this form of interaction to "see" the blockchain without making any changes, which is why it is free.

8.2.2 Side Chains of the Plasma

Sidechains are sub-blockchains that are connected to a larger public blockchain. They are designed to move transactions away from the mainchain and onto faster, more efficient, and less busy sidechains. Historically, using a sidechain has required trusting a third party, which is obviously not the optimal way to scale an originally trustless blockchain. As a result, in 2017 [9], Poon and Buterin introduced the concept of plasma. This framework was designed to reduce the amount of trust required of operators, allowing sidechains to become a viable layer 2 scaling option. As a result, when plasma was first released, it was regarded as a very promising option for resolving Ethereum's scalability issues and enabling Visa-like transaction throughputs.

Poon and Buterin established the concept of fraud proofs with the goal of limiting a sidechain operator's authority. In theory, if fraudulent behaviors such as double spending occur within or between separate sidechains, fraud proofs can be filed and published to the Ethereum blockchain, and all fraudulent transactions will be reversed. Again, the main Ethereum blockchain functions as an arbitrator, resolving disagreements and thereby ensuring the network's shared security.

Individual plasma chains are linked to the main Ethereum blockchain via a smart contract, and the operators will commit completed transactions to the main layer on a regular basis. Indeed, just the block headers will be published to the mainchain, while the transaction data would remain on the sidechain. This rooting configuration enables plasma networks to borrow securities from the parent Ethereum blockchain without establishing their own consensus. Additionally, when implemented properly, it theoretically allows for exponential scalability improvements [4, 9, 13, 14, 17].

However, a significant disadvantage of plasma is its inability to store data on-chain, colloquially referred to as the data availability problem, which I shall discuss in Section 8.2.3. This exposes plasma chains to dishonest operators and renders the fraud proofing notion ineffective in practice.

8.2.3 Problems with Data Accessibility

As previously stated, plasma was introduced with the intent of enabling trustless sidechains. However, completely off-chain storage of transaction data introduces a unique issue, particularly when users wish to depart the sidechain and rejoin the Ethereum blockchain. This is referred to as the data availability problem, and it presents a significant barrier to numerous layer 2 technologies, including plasma.

To be more exact, transactions that are not directly published to the Ethereum mainnet are not reconcilable by other Ethereum users. As a result, there is always a risk that some information will be lost in the process of returning from the sidechain to the main blockchain – either accidently or deliberately. For example, the operator's selective censoring of participant submissions may result in fraudulent transactions occurring without the participants' knowledge. Due to the fact that this operator only broadcasts the block header and not the underlying transaction data to the mainchain, nobody can check the sidechain's correctness.

Due to such dishonest operators, many users would like to depart and take their funds from such a fraudulent sidechain back to the Ethereum network. However, a successful escape is only possible when a one-week challenge period has passed. During this time frame, all legitimate users would be required to publish proof corroborating the sidechain operator's fraudulent conduct. These fraud proofs entail uploading the sidechain's whole legitimate state to the mainnet, which results in the Ethereum blockchain settling the disagreement and punishing the offending party. This is arguably impossible in practice, as plasma chains can grow infinitely vast and could never be realistically published on the Ethereum mainnet. Additionally, each user would have to be a full node capable of maintaining the entire sidechain's transaction history in order to give such fraud evidences. This is referred to as the mass exit problem in the conventional sense [4, 9, 13, 17–19].

8.3 Rollups

Rollups became popular in 2018 when a user going by the name Barry Whitehat uploaded a GitHub repository titled roll up [20]. Shortly afterwards, Vitalik Buterin, the founder of Ethereum, published an enhanced version of this initial concept, dubbed zk-rollups [21]. The primary goal of a rollup is to keep all transaction data on-chain while offloading transaction computation to achieve efficiency improvements. As a result, I view rollups as a semi-layer 2 solution rather than a true layer 2 solution. Rollups are connected to plasma but claim to be trustless due to the fact that they solve the data availability problem by publishing only the data necessary on-chain. They combine many transactions into a single transaction bundle in order to reduce transaction size and cost, hence enhancing overall efficiency. Rollups are able to greatly strengthen the security assurances for individual transactions because they keep transaction data on-chain.

These compressed (off-chain) transactions are not approved by Ethereum's consensus algorithm, but rather by a variety of techniques designed to assure transaction validity. We are either talking to zero-knowledge rollups in Section 8.4 or optimistic rollups in Section 8.5. As both names imply, zero-knowledge rollups are legitimate when based on zero-knowledge proofs, whereas optimistic rollups utilize an optimistic model based on fraud proofs. I thoroughly describe the methodologies and components of both rollup systems in Section 8.3 before evaluating their unique merits and downsides in Section 8.6. In some circumstances, it is fair to avoid discussing the various components, benefits, and drawbacks of a single rollup solution in isolation until we can evaluate and compare both techniques in Section 8.4.

8.3.1 Rollups Based on Zero Knowledge

When the concept of zero-knowledge rollups first surfaced in 2018, plasma was a hot topic and was considered to be Ethereum's future scaling answer. Consider the plasma concept, which relies on fraud proofs to maintain security on a sidechain where all transaction data is kept and processed, resulting in the data availability issue.

In summary, while the fundamental concept of zero-knowledge rollups is plasma-related, the construction is quite unique and difficult. Rather than relying on fraud proofs, as plasma does, zk-rollups rely on zero-knowledge proofs to provide security. These so-called zk-SNARKs have the advantage of validating big transaction bundles and so representing anything that occurs off-chain. By utilizing such zero-knowledge proofs, the rollup chain's transaction data becomes publicly accessible on the Ethereum blockchain. As a result, rollups can effectively address the aforementioned data availability issue [8]. Now, we will discuss the concept of zero-knowledge proofs, as they are the primary component and distinguishing aspect of zero-knowledge rollups. Following that, I will present an in-depth introduction to the design and implementation of zk-rollups, highlighting some of their advantages and disadvantages along the way. However, a thorough assessment of all the benefits and drawbacks will be available only in Section 8.6, when we will compare zk-rollups to optimistic rollups.

8.3.2 Proofs of Zero-Knowledge

Although zero-knowledge proofs are a popular topic at the moment, particularly in the context of public blockchains, they date all the way back to the early 1980s, when Goldwasser et al. [22] published their initial proposal. Simply described, a zero-knowledge proof is a circumstance in which an honest prover may demonstrate his knowledge of a piece of information to a skeptical verifier without providing the verifier with any relevant information. This may appear to be a contradiction at first glance, but consider an example that demonstrates the fundamental notion extremely intuitively.

The following example is somewhat called "Strange Cave of Ali Baba" [23]. The zk-basic cave's setup is depicted in Figure 8.6. Allow Bob to act as an unbiased prover and Alice to act as a skeptical verifier. There is only one entrance to the zk-cave, which abruptly splits into two corridors, A and B. These two passageways are linked by a secret tunnel secured by a door. This door is only accessible via a special key that Bob claims to possess. Alice is aware that a door exists but is unsure how to unlock it. Additionally, Alice enters the zk-cave after Bob has already entered the hidden tunnel;

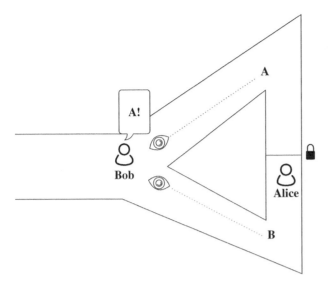

Figure 8.6 the zk-cave.

thus, she is unaware of which passageway he used to get there. Alice has now invited Bob to either site A or B.

Assume she selects location A. Bob unlocks the door and enters the desired spot A. Alice, however, should not be convinced just yet, as there is a 50% probability that Bob has already been on that side of the secret tunnel. Alice and Bob will need to repeat this method multiple times (n) in order to achieve a sufficiently significant probability ($1/2n$) that convinces Alice that Bob truly does know how to open the door. For example, after 20 rounds, the counter probability of arriving at the correct end of the secret tunnel is already absurdly low (9.54107). As a result, Bob has probabilistically demonstrated to Alice that he does indeed know how to open the door in the secret tunnel, without disclosing how he does it.

The zk-cave experiment described above illustrates an interactive zero-knowledge proof, in which the verifier and prover interact and repeat the process until the verifier is convinced. To be called secure, an interactive zero-knowledge proof must satisfy the following three properties.

1. **Completeness**: This property holds true if both the verifier and the prover are trustworthy. As a result, Alice can attest that Bob consistently traveled to his designated spot without cheating or conspiring with anyone.
2. **Soundness**: This means that a dishonest prover cannot persuade an honest verifier. In our binary scenario, this assumption of soundness can be satisfied only if Alice and Bob repeat this process numerous times, until the counter probability becomes small. This repeat is necessary because proofs of zero-knowledge are probabilistic, not deterministic.
3. **Zero-knowledge**: This characteristic distinguishes zero-knowledge proofs from other types of proofs. Alice learns just that Bob is aware of a piece of information from the experiment above, but not anything about the information itself. Additionally, a third party eavesdropping on them has no way of determining whether or not this experiment was genuine or staged.

Now, we will offer two very typical zero-knowledge protocols to demonstrate how such zero-knowledge proofs can be constructed using quite easy mathematics. Consider once more that Bob is the prover of a piece of knowledge, in this case a secret number, and Alice is the verifier [16, 22–24].

8.3.3 Protocol Schnorr

Claus-Peter Schnorr devised a protocol [25] in 1991 that provides interactive zero-knowledge proofs in three steps. Not the original zero-knowledge protocol, the Schnorr protocol is the most widely used today. As is the case with many other cryptographic protocols, the Schnorr protocol is predicated on the Rivest–Shamir–Adleman (RSA) problem's difficulty, which implies that given c and n, it is impossible to effectively compute the coefficients g and x in the equation $c = g^x \bmod n$. We will describe the protocol's fundamental theoretical ideas in this section, as well as provide a simple overview with a numerical example.

A simple numerical example of the Schnorr protocol is illustrated in Figure 8.7. Here, c denotes a committed value and g denotes the associated generator, both of which are publicly accessible. Bob is the only one who knows the secret number x. Bob can prove her knowledge of a value x that corresponds to the committed value c using the Schnorr protocol without disclosing any information about x. Bob can demonstrate this by completing the following three steps:

- Bob chooses a variable r at random. This enables her to calculate $t = g^r (\bmod n)$ and communicate the result to Alice.
- Alice now selects a variable e at random and transmits it to Bob.
- Then Bob calculates $u = r + ex$ and transmits it to Alice. Alice can now compare Bob's $g^u \bmod n$ result to his *tce* result $\bmod n$. If Bob and Alice arrive at the same conclusion, Bob has successfully demonstrated her knowledge of x without divulging any information about it. Notably, x may alternatively be referred to as a private key, with c serving as its counterpart public key. The mathematical argument that follows in equation (8.1) demonstrates how this zero-knowledge protocol works and why Alice may trust it. It computes $g^u (\bmod n) = g^{r+e+x} (\bmod n) = g^r g^{e+x} (\bmod n) = g^r (g^x)^e (\bmod n) = t \cdot c^e (\bmod n)$, demonstrating that $g^u (\bmod n)$ equals $t \cdot c^e \bmod n$).

Bob	Alice
$n = 6 \rightarrow \quad \bmod 6$	$n = 6 \rightarrow \quad \bmod 6$
$c = g^x = 9^4 = 6561$	$c = 6561$
$g = 9$	$g = 9$
$x = 4$ secret number	
$r = 3$	
$t = g^r \quad \bmod n = 9^3 \quad \bmod 6 = 3 \quad \xrightarrow{\quad t \quad}$	
$\xleftarrow{\quad e \quad}$	$e = 2$
$u = r + e \cdot x = 3 + 2 \cdot 4 = 11 \quad \xrightarrow{\quad u \quad}$	
$g^u \quad \bmod n = 9^{11} \quad \bmod 6 = 3 \quad \boxed{f = 3} \dashrightarrow$	$g^a \quad \bmod n = f$
	$9^{11} \quad \bmod 6 = 3$
	$t \cdot c^e \quad \bmod n = f$
	$3 \cdot 6561^2 \quad \bmod 6 = 3$

Figure 8.7 A numerical example of the Schnorr protocol.

$$g^u \mod n = g^{r+e+x} \mod n \tag{8.1}$$
$$= g^r \cdot g^{e+x} \mod n \tag{8.2}$$
$$= g^r \cdot (g^x)^e \mod n \tag{8.3}$$
$$= t \cdot c^e \mod n, \tag{8.4}$$

which proves that $g^u \mod n == t \cdot c^e \mod n$.

8.3.4   Protocol Pedersen

Torben Pryds Pedersen introduced the second zero-knowledge protocol, which I will discuss in further detail, in 1991 [26]. The Pedersen protocol is nearly as important as the Schnorr protocol, and is arguably best known for its use in the Zerocoin protocol, a Bitcoin variant that employs zero-knowledge proofs to further enhance participant anonymity. Pedersen protocol's security is also based on the discrete logarithm issue, although it is slightly more complicated than the Schnorr protocol, despite the fact that it requires only three exchanges.

Figure 8.8 illustrates the Pedersen technique numerically. This time, the protocol's security is strengthened slightly by extending the initial discrete logarithm issue to the following form: $c = g^x \cdot h^r (\mod n)$. At first glance, the individual variables are identical to those in the Schnorr protocol, with one exception. A new variable h is derived in the following manner from the public generator g and a random variable $h = g^a (\mod n)$. Bob wishes to demonstrate her knowledge about x without divulging any information:

Bob	Alice
$n = 6 \rightarrow \mod 6$	$n = 6 \rightarrow \mod 6$
$c = g^x \cdot h^r = 9^4 \cdot 3^3 = 177147$	$c = 177147$
$g = 9$	$g = 9$
$h = g^a \mod n = 9^2 \mod 6 = 3$	$h = 3$
$x = 4$ secret number	
$r = 3$	
$a = 2$	
$p = 2$	
$q = 3$	

$d = g^p \cdot h^q \mod n = 9^2 \cdot 3^2 \mod 6 = 3$ ──────── d ───────→

←──────── e ──────── $e = 2$

$u = p + e \cdot x = 2 + 2 \cdot 4 = 10$

$v = q + e \cdot r = 3 + 2 \cdot 3 = 9$ ──────── u,v ───────→

$g^u \cdot h^v \mod n = 9^{10} \cdot 3^9 \mod 6 = 3$ ⟶ $\boxed{f = 3}$ ⟶ $g^u \cdot h^v \mod n = f$

$9^{10} \cdot 3^9 \mod 6 = 3$

Figure 8.8   A numerical example of the Pedersen protocol.

- Bob chooses the variables p and q at random. This enables her to compute $d = g^p \cdot h^q \mod n$ and communicate the result to Alice via the variable d.
- Alice now selects a variable e at random and transmits it to Bob.
- Bob then calculates $u = p + ex$ and $v = q + er$ and transmits these variables to Alice.
- Alice can now compare Bob's $g^u \cdot h^v \mod n$ result to his $d \cdot c^e$ result $\mod n$. As previously demonstrated, if both obtain the same result, Bob has successfully established her knowledge of x.

8.3.5 zk-SNARKs

Interactive zk-proofs are excellent for developing an intuitive understanding of how zero knowledge proofs work and the possible applications. However, such back and forth interactions are ineffective in practice, even more so in a public blockchain setting. As a result, a concept known as non-interactive zero-knowledge proofs is far more appropriate for such an architecture. Non-interactive proofs of zero-knowledge require only a single iteration to establish knowledge. Due to the fact that these non-interactive proofs may later be confirmed by anybody, they can simply be made public and deemed a digital signature.

A non-interactive proof structure is referred to as zk-SNARK, an acronym for zero-knowledge. ARgument of Knowledge in a Succinct and Non-Interactive Form [27]. The term concise inside the acronym alludes to the fact that the length of the proof and the time required to verify it are determined solely by a security parameter, not by the magnitude of the assertion to be proven. Naturally, this is comparable to a hash function, where the hash value of the SHA-256 method, for example, will always have the same length (256 bits) regardless of the security parameter (256 bits). As a result, a single zk-SNARK proof is only a few hundred bits long and verifiable in milliseconds. This enables a single prover to persuade a large number of distinct verifiers simultaneously with a single message.

Yuan [16] proposes an interesting analogy between a zk-SNARK and a hash method. Converting arbitrary calculations to zkSNARKs is analogous to converting arbitrary data to hash values. Additionally, because Ethereum's main functionality is to verify arbitrary computations, zk-SNARKs are well-suited to a public blockchain architecture. They could, among other things, ensure that any operator is unable to submit invalid or malicious transactions, thereby guaranteeing the authenticity of a sidechain. Despite the numerous exciting possibilities associated with zero-knowledge proofs and zk-SNARKs, there remains a critical disadvantage to zkSNARKs. Producing such proofs is computationally demanding and thus time consuming. This might be a serious issue for a public blockchain like Ethereum, which updates its ledger every 15 seconds [16, 27–31].

8.4 Summary

The primary benefit of any layer 2 solution is that it has no impact on the Ethereum core protocol or consensus mechanism. They are compatible with practically every on-chain solution because they are essentially add-on solutions on top of the foundation layer. Indeed, they could coexist and even complement some future layer 1 solutions. As a result, they are far easier to execute, as they avoid the risk of altering an operating system and eliminate the need for meticulously upgrading the underlying blockchain's fundamental characteristics via hard forks. However, both state channels and sidechains face the data availability issue and its associated trust issue. This issue has made it more difficult for both of these systems to live up to the initial promises made by their inventors.

As a result, there has been a shift toward a more recent generation of level-2 scaling solutions that are geared on resolving this data availability issue – rollups.

At first appearance, zk-rollups appear to be a good approach for Ethereum scalability. The general concept of using zero-knowledge proofs to address the problem of data availability is amazing. There is no implication of life. Exiting a zk-rollup contract is quick and painless because it does not require a lengthy exit procedure. Bobn in worst-case scenarios, the scalability improvements are considerable. Indeed, implementation is not simple, but it is certainly solvable. Technically, the added latency may be ignored, as a transaction is nearly safe as soon as the relayer posts his commitment to a set of transactions. On the other side, there are several disadvantages to zk-rollup construction. At the moment, zk-SNARK constructs rely on a trusted initial setup between a prover and a verifier. This implies that a set of public parameters must be encoded within the protocol, introducing an initial level of centralization due to the fact that they are developed by a small group of developers.

References

1 Nakamoto, S. (2008). Bitcoin: a peer-to-peer electronic cash system.

2 Oparin, I. (2018). The First Thread - depicting the moment of divergence in perception of Bitcoin evolution.

3 Croman, K., Decker, C., Eyal, I. et al. (2016). On scaling decentralized blockchains. In: *Financial Cryptography and Data Security, Lecture Notes in Computer Science*, vol. 9604 (ed. J. Clark, S. Meiklejohn, P. Ryan et al.), 106–125. Berlin, Heidelberg: Springer.

4 Wu, X.B., Zou, Z., and Song, D. (2019). *Learn Ethereum*. Packt Publishing.

5 Low, R. (2020). What is the scalability trilemma?

6 Qin, K. and Gervais, A. (2018). *An Overview of Blockchain Scalability, Interoperability and Sustainability*. Hochschule Luzern Imperial College London Liquidity Network.

7 Viswanathan, S. and Shah, A. (2018). The scalability trilemma in blockchain.

8 Wu, K. (2019). ZK Rollup and Optimistic Rollup (En).

9 Poon, J. and Buterin, V. (2017). Plasma: scalable autonomous smart contracts.

10 Floersch, K. (2020). EthCC 2020 talk: optimistic virtual machine: full Ethereum smart contracts with optimistic rollup.

11 Adler, J. (2020). Optimistic rollups for the rest of us.

12 Fouda, M. (2020). The State of Ethereum L2.

13 Adler, J. and Quintyne-Collins, M. (2019). Building scalable decentralized payment systems.

14 Mosse, P. (2018). Ethereum's layer 2 scaling solutions.

15 Wallace, P. (2020). Layer 1 vs layer 2: what you need to know about different Blockchain Layer solutions.

16 Yuan, M. (2019). *Building Blockchain Apps*. Addison Wesley, Place of publication not identified.

17 Ramachandran, A. and Qureshi, H. (2020). The Life and Death of Plasma.

18 Al-Bassam, M., Sonnino, A., and Buterin, V. (2018). Fraud and data availability proofs: maximising light client security and scaling blockchains with dishonest majorities.

19 Payvin, A. (2019). The data availability problem.

20 Whitehat, B. (2018). Roll-up.

21 Buterin, V. (2018). On-chain scaling to potentially 500 tx/sec through mass tx validation.

22 Goldwasser, S., Micali, S., and Rackoff, C. (1985). The knowledge complexity of interactive proof-systems. *Proceedings of the 17th Annual ACM Symposium on Theory of Computing - STOC 85*. ACM Press.

23 Quisquater, J.J., Quisquater, M., Quisquater, M. et al. (1989). How to explain zero-knowledge protocols to your children. In: *Conference on the Theory and Application of Cryptology, Lecture Notes in Computer Science*, vol. 435 (ed. G. Brassard), 628–631. New York: Springer.

24 Bangerter, E., Barzan, S., Krenn, S. et al. (2013). Bringing zero-knowledge proofs of knowledge to practice. In: *Security Protocols XVII, Lecture Notes in Computer Science*, vol. 7028 (ed. B. Christianson, J.A. Malcolm, V. Matyáš, and M. Roe), 51–62. Berlin, Heidelberg: Springer-Verlag.

25 Schnorr, C.-P. (1991). Efficient signature generation by smart cards. *Journal of Cryptology* 4 (3): 161–174.

26 Pedersen, T.P. (1991). Non-interactive and information-theoretic secure verifiable secret sharing. In: *Advances in Cryptology - CRYPTO'91* (ed. J. Feigenbaum), 129–140. Berlin, Heidelberg: Springer-Verlag.

27 Ben-Sasson, E., Chiesa, A., Genkin, D. et al. (2013). SNARKs for C: verifying program executions succinctly and in zero knowledge. In: *Advances in Cryptology - CRYPTO 2013, Lecture Notes in Computer Science*, vol. 8043 (ed. R. Canetti and J.A. Garay), 90–108. Berlin, Heidelberg: Springer-Verlag.

28 Franco, P. (2014). *Understanding Bitcoin: Cryptography, Engineering and Economics*. Wiley.

29 Nitulescu, A. (2020). zk-SNARKs: A Gentle Introduction.

30 Schaffner, T. (2021). Scaling Public Blockchains, A comprehensive analysis of optimistic and zero-knowledge rollups. Master's thesis. University of Basel.

31 Zcash (2020). What are zk-SNARKs?

Part III

Applying Blockchain with Real-Time Technologies

9

Blockchain Technology for Supply Management

9.1 Introduction

The supply chain serves as a vital link between a corporation and its suppliers, facilitating the development and distribution of specific products or services. This intricate network encompasses a series of interconnected processes that work cohesively to deliver the end product or benefit to the client. Customers are ultimately served by the entire supply chain system. A vendor provides raw materials, a producer creates the product, a distributor distributes the product to the store, and the retailer displays the product to the customer. Supply chains regulate value chains since consumers cannot be served with their desired items without them. The supply chain motivates producers to produce the best products for customers; manufacturers compete fervently to improve the quality of their products and correct flaws, which is highly beneficial to customers because the environment of producer competition will bring the highest quality goods to the consumers [1].

A supply chain is made up of various stages that involve multiple organizations. Planning, development, manufacture, and delivery are examples of these phases. The initial step in the supply chain operations is planning, which aims to meet consumer requests. The product's development plan, which includes marketing and pricing, is the subject of the second stage. Design, production, testing, and packaging are all part of the manufacturing process. An enterprise resource planning system is usually in charge of the first two steps. Several production lifecycle management information systems cover the third stage. The fourth stage is concerned with product delivery. It begins with a pre-shipment process in which the provider prepares the product for shipment, followed by a transportation step generally administered by a carrier.

A supply chain comprises three basic phases: information flow, material flow, and capital flow. The digital thread that documents the product's transit is known as information flow. The order details and shipment information are also included in this digital thread. The physical product is transported by a carrier from the supplier to the customer during the material phase. The payment and transfer of asset ownership are the foundations of capital flow.

The accurate and real-time dissemination of information to all collaborators is referred to as supply chain visibility. Reduced business and supply chain risks, improved lead times and performance, and early detection of shortages and product quality issues are all advantages of enhancing supply chain visibility. Lack of transparency can lead to inaccurate forecasts and unanticipated delays, resulting in higher product costs. The supply chain scenario is shown in Figure 9.1. In business, collaborative processes entail two or more parties (individuals or corporations) cooperating to accomplish or obtain a product for a specific purpose. There is a requirement for cooperation and confidence in such a process in order to deliver a service on time. To facilitate comprehension of the business process, a collaborative process in connection to business settings is mapped onto

Attribute-based Encryption (ABE): Foundations and Applications within Blockchain and Cloud Environments, First Edition.
Qi Xia, Jianbin Gao, Isaac Amankona Obiri, Kwame Omono Asamoah, and Daniel Adu Worae.
© 2024 The Institute of Electrical and Electronics Engineers, Inc. Published 2024 by John Wiley & Sons, Inc.

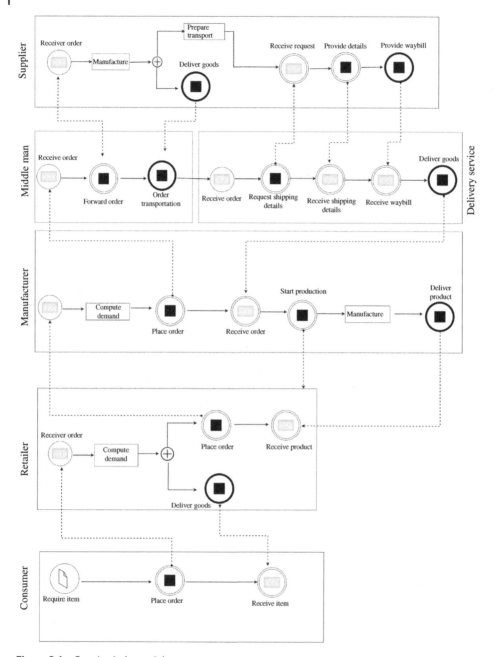

Figure 9.1 Supply chain model.

a simple supply chain scenario. The supply chain scenario is depicted in Figure 9.1. The procedure begins with a customer requirement. The retailer receives an order from the consumer. The merchant determines demand based on the order and makes provisions for delivering the item while it is in stock at the shop or sets an order with the manufacturer to create the item when it is sold out. The manufacturer ascertains the request, performs demand estimates, and submits a request for an order of the materials necessary to manufacture the items via a middleman. The middleman then forward the requested order to a supplier and arranges for the materials to be delivered via a delivery service. After fabricating the materials, the supplier either sends them to the intermediary, who then makes them available to the delivery service, or waits for the delivery service to collect them. The delivery service delivers the things to the manufacturer, indicating that the needed items have been completed. When the things are completed, they are delivered to the retailer, who then delivers them to the consumer. The entire process is a series of stages performed by two or more entities at any moment in time, with no single entity having complete control over the process's transactions. The supply chain scenario described above presents significant difficulties since the six parties involved would blame one another for delays and faults in ordering and delivering items. Assuming the store receives the ordered items several days later than the agreed upon delivery date or with a shortage of the agreed upon quantity of goods to be delivered, or both, both parties will claim that the service given was exactly what was ordered. This scenario is not dissimilar to disagreements between the manufacturer and the middleman, or between the supplier and the delivery provider. This type of situation results in each party assigning blame for their failures to other players responsible for any stage of the process. When participants refuse to accept delivery as a result of the aforementioned delays and faults, the situation becomes difficult. Payments are not completed, and individual parties will be liable to pay companies with whom they had direct contact at the time of the error. This is a significant issue in any supply chain system.

Lack of transparency is one of the most glaring issues confronting businesses with complex supply chains. Frequently, with several suppliers spread across multiple geographic locations and organizational domains, it is exceedingly difficult to keep track of all the activities involved. Current supply chain management systems are constantly looking for ways to reduce costs and improve transparency and efficiency across all of their activities. While centralized, board-level systems have been established to handle the flow of commodities and data, one persistent issue remains. Because data can be manipulated in ways that circumvent present detection systems, parties within the supply chain allege that the process is not completely visible to all relevant stakeholders.This may open the way for fraudulent activity or the perception of fraudulent activity as a means of undermining trust in procedures and supporting systems.

The fundamental pillars of trust in joint endeavors [2] such as supply chains are equity, integrity, and accountability. Whether in collaborations between corporate partners or rival entities, these defining characteristics permeate all transactions. Moreover, they are essential for advancing noble objectives. The reason being, regardless of one's personal preferences, no individual or entity relishes becoming a victim of their absence [2, 3]. Thus, business processes and their supporting systems have worked to develop trust-based products, services, and environments over time. However, commercial and economic institutions are inextricably linked to human needs and relationships for survival [4]. As a result, these systems are vulnerable to malicious user intervention and, in some situations, interference [4]. Indeed, one can anticipate one or more parties to a transaction acting counter to the agreed terms. In this industry, the importance of credible arbiters cannot be overstated [5]. This difficulty has led to the current state of affairs, where trusted parties, fully aware of the immense power inherent in their positions, have acted in direct opposition to the very interests for which they were originally established.

The aforementioned are not the only challenges that hinder supply chain companies' commercial transactions. To solve the difficulties of the establishment and maintenance of trust [6] effectively, regardless of the theater of action, identification, authentication, authorization, and some sort of accountability must be invoked [7]. To a large extent, identification continues to be determined by trusted authorities such as governments and token-issuing companies. That is why passports and drivers' licenses remain important as the principal means of identification across a variety of geographic and organizational settings. Authentication and permission are considerably more difficult to get right [8], as they are heavily reliant on identification and are still mostly delegated to tokens (passwords, USB key tokens, etc.). It's worth noting that these issues have dogged the digital world from the start, owing to the fact that the transactional entities have remained essentially same. They appear to have been amplified in recent years, owing to the massive volume of trade that digital platforms must handle, the worldwide character of business, the requirement to disclose transactions with all interested parties, and the presence of bad actors, some of whom stay covert. A mechanism for establishing trust, maintaining it, and evaluating how it affects digital transactions is increasingly critical. The blockchain, the underlying technology that enables Bitcoin, is a contender solution to the trust problem in the digital realm [8].

The blockchain is a decentralized public ledger (DPL) of transactions [9] that all nodes in the Bitcoin blockchain network can verify. Due to the distributed nature of the ledger, all transactions are transparent and accessible to all participating nodes. Following their completion, transactions are validated and grouped into "blocks." Newly validated blocks are subsequently added to the list of previously verified blocks, forming the blockchain, with each block cryptographically connected to the previous one [10]. The blockchain's design assures that tampering with or revising transactions is computationally infeasible. This aspect of the blockchain makes it the ideal technology for securing and protecting transactions between mutually suspect parties [9], as it is capable of addressing circumstances that require a credible, algorithmic audit of transaction data.

The financial sector was the first to capitalize on the benefits presented by blockchain technology for securing transactions, and many other industries have subsequently followed suit [9]. Every business, from military to real estate, insurance, and precious metals, is experimenting with and fine-tuning the blockchain in order to facilitate and improve their operations. The Supply Chain Industry is one such industry that is in desperate need of innovation, both to improve its operations and to overcome a fundamental lack of trust among its actors [11].

In an ideal world, the Supply Chain Industry's operations and associated activities would be defined by economic demands. One actor asks services, and another responds by providing them, typically via a mediator or other appropriate intermediary [12]. However, the nature of business today necessitates collaboration between numerous actors [13] who may be unfamiliar with one another and the likelihood of at least one collaborator operating outside of established bounds (sometimes the accidental result of too many parts of the long supply chain process). As is frequently the case, this leads in substandard products and services being delivered to the original requester of the services, necessitating restitution and expensive arbitration [14] between the transacting parties, not to mention the effect of temporarily suspending production. Finally, commercial entities, manufacturers and producers, middlemen and clearing houses, all of whom believe in their institutions' alleged infallibility, refuse to accept responsibility for the mishap [15, 16], leaving the process of conducting business with less trust than it had previously.

To be more specific, the requirement for teamwork in business, combined with the competition for individual advantage and consequent profit, frequently serves to reduce or eliminate trust in the supply chain. The blockchain, with its strong emphasis on cryptographically linked transactions [9] and underlying peer-to-peer architecture, is well suited to developing solutions to the supply chain industry's trust dilemma.

Given that blockchain technology has been lauded for its potential to significantly increase Supply Chain transparency [17], it's unsurprising that 80% of respondents to the Chain Business Insights survey indicated they are more likely to use blockchain to track product movement throughout the supply chain. Additionally, blockchain technology might be used to share information with suppliers, track payment information such as payment orders, and verify and monitor suppliers.

Satoshi Nakamoto industrialized blockchain technology through the creation of a digital token called Bitcoin, and many people confuse the two names. However, Blockchain and Bitcoin are two entirely different concepts. Bitcoin was the first application to leverage blockchain technology, and Bitcoin in particular demonstrates its strength.

9.1.1 System Design

The system makes use of a private, permissioned blockchain, which is defined as a blockchain in which direct access to blockchain data, transaction submission, and processing is restricted to a specified list of known entities. The following requirements must be met by the system:

1. It should be user-friendly in the first place.
2. The incorporation of blockchain technology and smart contracts is significant.
3. Transactions involving distinct parties, such as sellers, Purchasers, retailers, and so forth should all be recorded on the blockchain.
4. **Traceability**: The parties can keep track of their transactions using the system.
5. Dispute-resolution mechanisms should be ensured.
6. Fine-grained access control should be ensured for the supplied chain to guarantee data security.

9.1.2 System Architecture

The system is composed of four components, three of which are critical in achieving the system's objectives. The Application Layer, the User Layer, the Smart Contract Network, and the Blockchain Network all comprise these components. The application layer includes components such as web applications, Internet of Things applications, and legacy enterprise resource planning (ERP) systems.

Users are made up of nodes representing participating producers, suppliers, buyers, and others who make requests for goods and services. Each of these users runs a network node that participates in the generation, transmission, receiving, and forwarding of service/goods requests. The process of providing a service begins when one party contacts the other with a particular request for that service. This group often consists of merchants, manufacturers, distributors, and suppliers. Additionally, we include logistical service providers, consulting firms, financial institutions, government and regulatory organizations, manufacturers and suppliers of machinery and equipment, as well as indirect materials suppliers. These are frequently in pairs and are responsible for initiating and carrying out systemic activities.

The blockchain system is made up of two components: a smart contract [18] hub and a blockchain network. After transacting parties have agreed on service provider requirements, they collaborate to construct smart contracts. Additionally, they ensure that transaction quantities and dates are transparent to all parties required to monitor the transaction.

The smart contracts center validates received requests (contracts) for the qualities required to proceed with the service request. It verifies the accuracy of signatures on requests and verifies quantities, delivery conditions, and fines for non-compliance. Additional checks may be necessary as determined by the transacting parties and system requirements. When a service request is completed, it is timestamped and a hash is generated and sent to the blockchain network. Once this occurs, the transaction is copied to all active nodes. We provide two concurrent transactions between any pair of users: an "opening" and a "closing" transaction. While many transactions and communications are permitted between parties, we demand only opening and closing transactions to keep network traffic light and performance optimal. Intervening messages may be freely sent between the parties via purpose-built off-blockchain channels. Given that the system is built on the blockchain and that it carries implications (legal punishments and financial penalties) for all parties involved, starting and terminating transactions should be straightforward.

9.1.3 Entities of the System

The system distinguishes three distinct entity types. The Users (contracting parties), the Smart Contract Network, and the Blockchain Network are all examples of these. Each Supply Chain party operates nodes that, once configured, engage in the system's protocol, verifying submitted contracts and notifying them of infractions as necessary.

9.1.3.1 Users

The User Layer is a meta-layer that abstracts all system users. This layer refers to all of the entities and processes that comprise the supply chain's network. The layer is made up of pairs of users who interact in order to initiate network transactions. We examine relationships between manufacturers and middlemen, middlemen and retailers, and retailers and consumers in the current work. Additionally, we evaluate how all of the above-mentioned parties collaborate with Delivery Companies to transport things between locations.

It is crucial to remember that each pair of system users has unique security, visibility, and transparency requirements. This necessitates the development of customized security policies that permit network interactions in a manner that is favorable to transacting parties. The policy may make reference to the known identities or identifiers of transacting parties, the terms under which commerce is conducted, and other criteria that are specific to the parties. All of these transactions must occur across secure communication channels. Certain requirements, on the other hand, are universally applicable to network participants. For instance, all systems require tamper-resistant features for their records, which is why the blockchain's timestamped records are required.

As illustrated in Figure 9.2, we assume that all participants to the transaction are connected to the blockchain network and are communicating over the network's broadcast channel. To simulate secure communication, messages between parties are encrypted using their respective public encryption keys. That is, because the information shared between participants is so sensitive (including the monetary values), a secure covert communication-based solution must be implemented into the blockchain network. We used the work of [19] to do this. It should be noted that the literature on building secure communication channels is currently sparse. The proposed solution is based on inserting a single bit within each block's transaction section. Taking into account that the consumer generates many public–private key pairs. He generates a number of relevant payment addresses as a result of this. The buyer then transfers the payments to the blockchain in the correct order for the seller to see the payments associated with a certain message (it may be any type of interaction or negotiation between them), as illustrated in Figure 9.3. While different types of users can follow and review the history of transactions kept. While different types of users can follow and review the history of transactions kept on the blockchain, the system prevents them from performing actions outside their agreed-upon role. To use our system, the user must first become a member, at which point the user will register. A user who wishes to join the group is issued the key. Users are not permitted to join the group without the membership granting key. The membership issuing key provides access to the Membership Verification Key, as well as the parameters required to generate the user's transaction key pair.

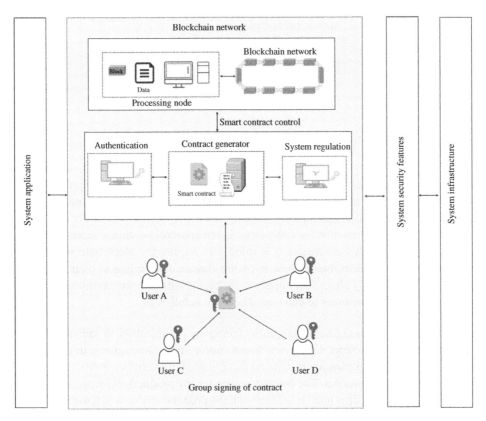

Figure 9.2 System.

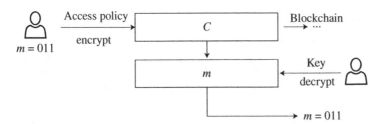

Figure 9.3 A simplified overview of the suggested secure covert communication.

As shown in Figure 9.4, the authentication center receives the credentials initially. For the proposed system, the credentials may include the customer's full name, social security number, or an email address, which are supplied by users throughout the user's layer registration process. At the authentication center, the registrar processes this information and generates a unique ID for the associated user. The unique ID is the identification that is used to uniquely identify each user on the system.

Transacting parties should be able to conduct transactions securely following authentication. The ciphertext-policy attribute-based encryption (CP-ABE) scheme is used for the data encryption. Only parties with sufficient attributes meeting the access policy encoded in the ciphertext should be able to decrypt the ciphertext using their attribute key. Due to the large number of stockholders in the system, CP-ABE can provide a mechanism for the encryptor to modify the access structure so

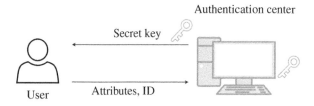

Figure 9.4 Membership issuing key.

that the encrypted message is only accessible to the organizations with which the encryptor wishes to share it. As secrecy is the weapon that enables a firm to survive and earn a big profit, those entities that lack an adequate access policy are unable to read the ciphertext. For future reference, the data created by business transactions is safely saved in the appropriate storage infrastructures.

The system is developed with the consumers in mind who require the blockchain solution to deliver or get anything of value in mind. These users are classified according to their roles and responsibilities inside the supply chain. The supply chain begins with the service/initiators product's and concludes with the consumer or end user. These are as follows:

1. **Consumer**: The consumer is defined as any entity (company, organization, or individual) that makes use of a service or product. Consumer-driven supply chains have grown in popularity over the last few years, when consumers demand compliance with certain conditions in order to continue consuming the product. The primary reason for the product's existence is the consumer. As a result, their concerns must be addressed if the product/service is to remain relevant and lucrative.
2. **Retailer**: The retailer is the supply chain entity that has direct contact with the consumer. The retailer acquires the goods or service from the producer, distributor, or wholesaler and sells it to the consumer at a predetermined price. The merchant requires precise conditions for the product before passing it on to the consumer and hence values the supply chain's transparency.
3. **Manufacturer**: Manufacturing is the process of creating goods for use or sale by utilizing all available production variables such as labor, machinery, and tools in order to meet an established need. Manufacturers are obligated to follow industry standards in order to ensure continued patronage of their items after production. Transparency in operations enables compliance with industry laws, thereby assisting the company in maintaining its position as a critical component of the supply chain.
4. **Middleman**: The middleman acts as a conduit between merchants and manufacturers. They may receive the products directly from the producer in some instances and sell them direct to the consumer. Again, industry standards require this actor to maintain compliance in proportion to the goods being offered. As a result, it is critical for all supply chain participants to be transparent, allowing for effective service delivery.
5. **Delivery companies**: These are tasked with the responsibility of transporting items from the manufacturer's warehouse to various distribution points, acting as the supply chain's physical connection agent. However, various items require distinct transit circumstances. Refrigeration at specified temperatures is required for perishable items. Delivery businesses may occasionally fail to comply with this for a variety of reasons. To be trusted, the supply chain must account for all such events from the time the product leaves the manufacturer until it reaches the end customer.

9.1.4 Smart Contract Control

The Smart Contract Control is a critical component of the system because it is responsible for producing, executing, and verifying contracts. It is made up of the following constituents:

1. **Contract generator**: As the name implies, the contract generator's role is to generate smart contracts that adhere to the system's regulations.
2. **System regulation**: Transactions between system users generate enormous amounts of data that can leak, posing network security concerns. As is the case with several existing methods of system assault, network traffic analysis identified trends that attackers may exploit to carry out their exploits. As a result, the System Regulation component is intended to enable network participants to develop, monitor, and/or change policies governing the appropriate use of their data. This component relies on communication with other system components to establish safe intra-component interactions. It contains the rules upon which a smart contract is based. These rules will be treated as contract terms at the time the contract is produced. Both parties to the conversation should agree to these terms upon registration and authentication.
3. **Authentication**: This entity is in charge of authenticating the created contracts through the use of a set of cryptographic keys embedded in them. These keys will be used to encrypt reports linked with contract activation.

Generally, the contract document submitted is subjected to a set of rules. After that, the center generates a hash of the document and a timestamp and sends them to the blockchain network. Once the contract is uploaded to the blockchain network, all connected nodes receive a copy of the hash and timestamp. The hash identifies the fact that the parties engaged in a transaction. The only legitimate hash to append to the preceding one (the contract's hash in the blockchain) is the hash of the concluding transaction, which contains information about the order's fulfillment under the specified conditions.

9.1.5 Blockchain Network

9.1.5.1 Processing Nodes

These nodes receive requests from requestors and, in collaboration with the Smart Contracts Centre, verify permissions associated with relevant data, perform necessary transaction processing, and eventually generate blocks from the requests. They are assigned with the responsibility of processing and verifying the legitimacy of transaction details and then creating blocks. They then distribute these blocks through the blockchain. Additionally, their processing jobs designate these processing nodes as the nodes responsible for detecting requests made to the system via blocks that violate network consensus norms. Additionally, they detect permission infractions and so identify and report systemic abnormalities. To accomplish this, we propose a blockchain network based on Practical Byzantine Fault Tolerance (PBFT), which is preferred to PoW (Proof of Work) or PoS (Proof of Stake) for a system with fewer interacting nodes [20]. Byzantine Fault Tolerance (BFT) evolved largely from the Byzantine Generals' Problem. It is a common term in the field of computer science to refer to a circumstance in which all parties must agree on a single strategy in order to avoid complete failure. However, it presupposes that some of the parties involved are corrupt or otherwise untrustworthy. This makes it applicable to a straightforward adaptation to blockchain-based systems, which require the establishment of trust in a dispersed network of suspicious nodes. Without PBFT, a peer can transmit and upload fake transactions, effectively undermining the blockchain's integrity.

9.1.5.2 System Application Layer

This layer comprised a Distributed Application (DApp). This latter is an application that makes use of smart contracts while also offering a friendly user experience for them. A decentralized application structure is composed of two interfaces: a front-end and a back-end. The back-end interface facilitates communication between the application and smart control layers.

9.1.5.3 Storage Infrastructure

Each layer has been associated with a different storage infrastructure. Internal storage within the smart contracts control center is required to store various regulations and contracts. Additionally, a decentralized cloud storage system is required for storing blockchain data in a form that nodes can access and read it. There are already several blockchain storage infrastructures (services) available on the market, including the InterPlanetary File System (IPFS).

9.1.6 System Decryption

The system is designed to ease transactions between mutually suspicious parties by assuring operational transparency, the accuracy of requested quantities, and processes for detecting and penalizing system attacks without the use of trusted third parties. After receiving a request to register a user in the network, the issuer generates a set of membership issuing and membership verification keys. This is accomplished by including a unique id string in the user request. The string can be the customer's full name, social security number, or email address, for example. The complete scheme(s), method(s), and channel(s) for production, administration, and transmission of cryptographic keys to network actors and entities/nodes may be any of the secure and efficient ones already devised. Likewise, the identification and authentication processes are identical. A user wishing to join the system submits an application to the Issuer. The Issuer is responsible for authenticating the user and granting or denying him/her/it access to the group.

To initiate the procedure, the system requires the presence of two participants, A and B. Party A makes a request for a service or products, and party B fulfills the request by providing the requested goods or services. In a contract, party A sends party B a request (including information about the quantity, place, time, and date of delivery, among other things). After receiving the request, party B reviews it together with its terms and conditions and provides an acknowledgment to party B if the request's content is acceptable. Party B is free to change elements of the contract or its conditions and request approval from party B before to proceeding, or to reject the intended transaction entirely. At the initial stage, such messages may be passed back and forth between the transacting parties using CP-ABE until an agreement is reached. By signing the contract using their private keys, both parties agree to participate in the transaction. The final party to sign the contract submits it to the Smart Deal Network for verification of the contract's terms. The submitted contract document is subjected to a set of rules at the Smart Contracts Center. After that, the center generates a hash of the document and a timestamp and sends them to the blockchain network. Once the contract is uploaded to the blockchain network, all connected nodes receive a copy of the hash and timestamp. The hash identifies the fact that the parties engaged in a transaction. The only legitimate hash to append to the preceding one (the contract's hash in the blockchain) is the hash of the concluding transaction, which contains information about the order's fulfillment under the specified conditions.

A block containing all of the transaction's timestamps and properties is broadcast into the blockchain. The block is now a component of a chain system and contributes to the block's height in the blockchain system. When additional blocks are generated after this block, the hash of the

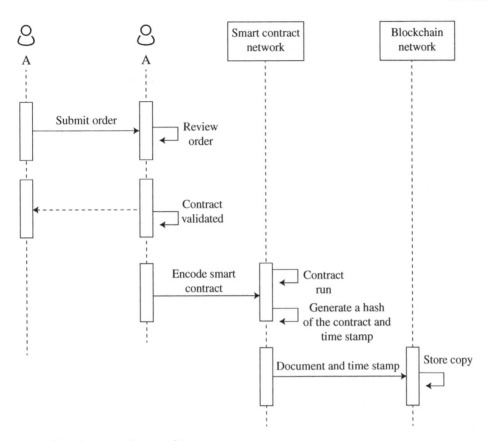

Figure 9.5 Sequence diagram of the system.

last block in the network is attached to the header of the newer block, which has not yet been chained into the network's linked blocks.

The components of an individual block that provide sufficient security for data exchangeability, as well as auditing and data forensics, primarily comprised recordings of the preceding block's hash and Merkle root's hash in each block. Each occurrence in the system may be traced back to its genesis block via a current block. This step ensures an adequate level of protection against malicious nodes. Figure 9.5 depicts the system's sequence diagram, in which party A sends a request for ordering products to party B, who, after analyzing the order details, sends feedback to party A. After obtaining comments from party B, party A should sign the agreement and return it to party B for signature.

Once both parties have signed, the contract conditions will be submitted to the smart contract center, where they will be executed according to the set of instructions established in our smart contract for the formation of smart contracts. Following the creation of the smart contract, the system will generate its time stamp and hash and then send it to the blockchain network, which will store a copy of the contract for the benefit of both parties' transparency and security.

9.1.7 Blocks

Transactions are recorded in the system as events that occur between two parties. Each party maintains its own nodes that maintain its blocks and side-blocks. Given that the blocks represent the same transactions from the perspective of various system entities, reconciling events should be straightforward. Side-blocks keep track of subsequent transactions between the same parties. According to the paper's illustration, the red portion indicates the shared perspective of the transacting parties, which contributes to greater transparency and event coordination.

9.1.7.1 Block Design

The system's block structure is derived from the conventional bitcoin blockchain and modified to meet the requirements of this study. A block has a format that identifies it uniquely within the network. This is followed by the block size, which refers to the block's size. The block headers are the following structure.

As with Bitcoin headers, the block header is hashed using SHA-256. The block header is critical to the blockchain network's immutability. To modify the records in a block, an attacker must modify its header and be able to modify all subsequent block headers starting with the genesis block, a feat that currently demands enormous computer power that is judged unavailable to any single entity. This protects the network's security and also ensures the provenance of data. In the case of malicious activity, a block mismatch alerts the system to an ongoing suspicious event, which starts data forensics. The block header contains the data version, which specifies the validation criteria that should be followed for a certain data type. The data version provides information about the attributes and type of data accessed. The header is also constructed from the preceding block's hash, which is a SHA-256 hash whose purpose is to ensure that no prior block's header may be modified without also altering the header of this block.

The Merkle root hash is included in the header and is obtained by hashing pairs of transactions and then hashing the resulting hashes until only one hash remains. The output of this operation is appended to the current block. The header contains a date indicating when the block was formed, as well as a target difficulty value indicating how the processing and consensus nodes gain processing.

This is a system-specific feature that makes processing tough for malicious nodes but efficient and solvable for verified nodes. Finally, there is a nonce, which is an arbitrary number generated by the processing nodes to modify the header hash in order to produce a hash that is less difficult to compute than the goal difficulty. The block header has six elements: the Version Number, the Previous Block Hash, the Merkle Root, the TimeStamp, the Target Difficulty, and the Nonce.

The block has a transaction counter whose function is to record the total number of transactions in the entire block. The transaction is a composite of the Base transactions and the Patient transactions. The Base transactions are categorized into two parts that are, the timestamps and the data.

The block structure used in the system is adapted from the traditional bitcoin blockchain and adapted to fit the requirement of this work. The transactions portion contains fields that facilitate components of secure collaboration between transacting parties. As shown in Figure 9.6, there are nine fields in the transaction. The details of each field are explained below:

1. **Timestamp (TS)**: The TS indicates when a business transaction's block was initiated and created.
2. **Customer ID (C.ID)**: The C.ID identifies the individual requesting a service.
3. **Service provider ID (SP.ID)**: The SP.ID identifies service providers.
4. **Sequences number (SN)**: The SN denotes a set of transaction sequences used to determine the order of a single business process that has been divided down into many processes to produce transactions.

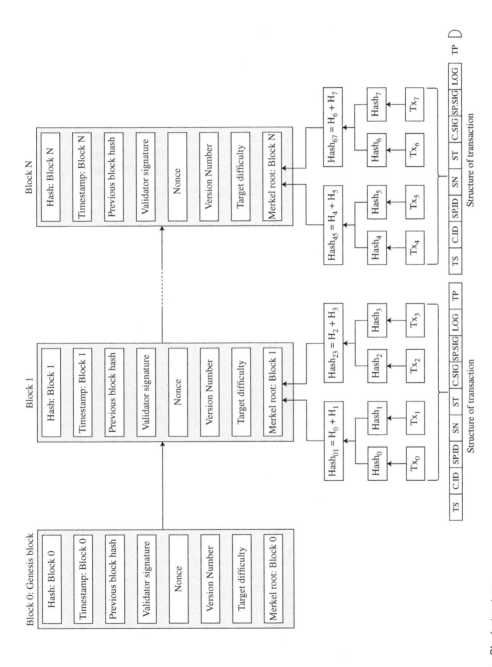

Figure 9.6 Block structure.

5. **Service time (ST)**: The ST represents the conclusion of a transaction as indicated by a service time. This can be used to determine the overall amount of time required to complete a transaction.
6. **Customer signature (Csig)**: The Csig indicates the signature derived from the public key of the customer.
7. **Service provider (Spsig)**: The Spsig represents the signature of the service provider.
8. **LOG**: Contains every event which happens in the network.
9. **Total processing (TP)**: When the last transaction in the block has been entered, this is the timestamp added to the list of transactions in the block. It encrypts the block and causes the hash to be calculated for inclusion in the superblock. The whole block structure employed in the system is depicted in the diagram below.

Figure 9.7 depicts the blockchain structure in which our system's transactions are stored. Every transaction is recorded separately for both parties so that we can simply monitor the records and hazards associated with each transaction. The parent blocks are Genesis and its horizontal blocks, while the blocks in the vertical position are the leave blocks, which are used to record the series of transactions in our system step by step.

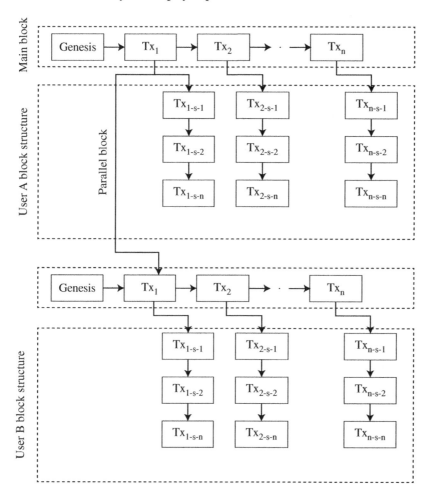

Figure 9.7 Block structure for a transaction pertaining to different transacting parties.

9.2 System Flow

A centralized database method is often more than suitable for supply networks with known and trustworthy players. This isn't to say that all of these supply chains are truly end-to-end; in fact, many of them rely on segregated databases that hold data with poor traceability. As a result, many of these supply chains do not require blockchain technology to address these concerns because they may use existing technologies that are better suited to their high-volume transactions, either alone or in collaboration with others.

Blockchain technology, on the other hand, can offer trust, transparency, and traceability to supply chains when actors are unknown or untrustworthy. These supply chains are almost by definition complex, multi-tiered, and multi-party, and they operate in a regulated environment that requires a higher level of traceability.

Furthermore, the supply-chain industry is unlikely to adopt open access since its users do not want to divulge private facts at all stages of the value chain to unknown actors, such as demand, capacity, orders, pricing, and margins. As a result, supply-chain blockchains would need to be permissioned, with access controlled centrally and limited to known parties having access to certain data segments. For the sake of simplicity, we consider a transaction involving two parties: users A and B, who have gained attribute and signature keys for decoding ciphertext and signing transactions, respectively. To ensure that neither party defaults, the security money deposit must be sufficiently deterrent to avoid fraud. The activity diagram in Figure 9.8 depicts the steps involved in placing an online order and receiving the item.

9.2.1 System Advantages

1. **Transaction traceability**: From the time a transaction is initiated until it is completed, it is tracked in the system. Each of the transacting parties can see the transaction details and monitor subsequent occurrences all the way back to the start of the transaction. This opens up the possibility of preventing the spread of errors in transactions and the high expenses associated with arbitration when parties have difficulty accepting the results.
2. **Immutability**: New blocks are chained to previous ones using cryptographic protocols and procedures, producing a record of transactions. An attacker must edit all blocks preceding the current block in order to successfully modify or destroy transactions. This necessitates massive computational capacity that no single organization has access to, ensuring that data (and consequently transactions) cannot be updated after they have been placed on the blockchain.
3. **Secure audit**: The blockchain system's timestamping and secure hashing techniques are employed to ensure provenance and secure audit. Transaction timestamps are used to create a precise chronological order of events, making cause-and-effect deductions for auditing processes and applications more easier. The combined effect improves the system's traceability and thus transparency.
4. **User untraceability**: In each session, a user's transaction identification must be anonymous and changeable. This is because an adversary should be unable to link the various login and authentication of each session before a transaction begins.
5. **Anonymity**: During the authentication process, the identities of transacting participants in the system must not be divulged to entities other than the authenticator. Adversaries would be defined as entities other than the authenticator. Knowing the identity of a transacting party, an adversary may attempt to obtain information from the system (by logging in as the identified user) and authenticating transactional messages and other relevant information and procedures.

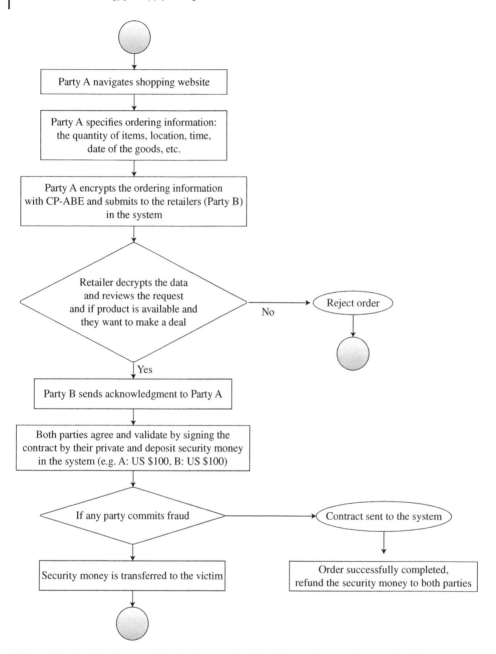

Figure 9.8 Activity diagram of a simple scenario of two interacting parties based within our system.

9.2.2 Conclusion

This chapter outlines a blockchain-based supply chain system that can be used to create a transparent and beneficial process between suppliers and customers. The blockchain technology offers a safe way to buy stuff online from untrustworthy sources. Members of the network profit from the proposed system in various ways. As the supply chain sector grows, it has numerous challenges in managing the system and its infrastructure, resulting in high management costs and time-consuming deployments. To make matters worse, if the supply chain system experiences certain problems in sending and receiving requests, the products may be delayed, resulting in significant financial penalties. Several other industries may suffer as a result of this.

As a result, it's critical to eradicate incorrect data; otherwise, orders may be delayed, resulting in greater shortages. Because smart contracts are a fundamental component of the systems, this work focuses on Blockchain Technology, which is useful for supply chain management. Because of its numerous benefits, blockchain was chosen as the foundational structure.

No modified data is allowed in the blockchain system. Any fraudulent behavior will be clearly evident on the blockchain, which is the system's most prominent feature; therefore, this study focuses on the system's most significant attributes. In the supply chain flow, this completely removes the concept of product counterfeiting.

Because trust is the single most important aspect that can make or destroy a business, this chapter establishes faith in the system and encourages corporations and international organizations to choose the blockchain system for their future benefit. Trust is at the heart of blockchain technology, which encourages parties to do business in a straightforward, transparent, and open manner. With all of the data flying around, such as invoices, contracts, and other secret facts and figures, the blockchain assists businesses in protecting their data using the most advanced cryptographic techniques available. Visibility and efficiency are aided by the supply chain. It has the potential to be one of the most efficient and well-organized processes in the industry. Producers and consumers can save a lot of time by using it.

This handout emphasizes one of the benefits of smart contracts: all of the agreement's provisions are visible to all parties involved. Certain expectations have been established for fair commercial interactions, and contracts can be fulfilled once the signatories agree to the requirements. Smart contracts guard against unintended changes in data. Payments, goods, or anything of value can be exchanged more easily with virtual agreements. The self-executing nature of such contracts opens up a lot of possibilities for use in any industry where data is used to drive transactions.

Smart contracts can save money and time by automating processes that rely on blockchain-verified data. The greatest method to improve supply chain management is to implement smart contracts. We can simply track deliveries at numerous geographic areas and track shipments depending on the fulfillment of smart contract terms with the help of smart contract services. Smart contracts are self-contained and run by themselves. Therefore, the smart contracts and blockchain can pave way for a smarter, faster, and more secure supply chain from manufacturers to consumers.

References

1 Seppälä, J. (2016). The role of trust in understanding the effects of blockchain on business models. Master's thesis. Aalto University Learning Centre.

2 Fawcett, S.E., Jones, S.L., and Fawcett, A.M. (2012). Supply chain trust: the catalyst for collaborative innovation. *Business Horizons* 55 (2): 163–178.

3 Wilson, M.M., MacDonald, I.A., and Monnane, M.M. (2015). Governance of procurement relationships in the wine industry: the importance of trust and the legal system. *International Journal of Wine Business Research* 27 (4): 299–311.

4 Chen, J. and Zhu, Q. (2022). A cross-layer design approach to strategic cyber defense and robust switching control of cyber-physical wind energy systems. *IEEE Transactions on Automation Science and Engineering* 20 (1): 624–635.

5 Marvuglia, A., Bayram, A., Baustert, P. et al. (2022). Agent-based modelling to simulate farmers' sustainable decisions: farmers' interaction and resulting green consciousness evolution. *Journal of Cleaner Production* 332: 129847.

6 Cisneros-Cabrera, S., Pishchulov, G., Sampaio, P. et al. (2021). An approach and decision support tool for forming Industry 4.0 supply chain collaborations. *Computers in Industry* 125: 103391.

7 Anumukonda, N.S.K., Yadav, R.K., and NS, R. (2021). A painstaking analysis of attacks on hypervisors in cloud environment. *2021 6th International Conference on Machine Learning Technologies*, pp. 150–157.

8 Akhter Md Hasib, K.T., Chowdhury, I., Sakib, S. et al. (2022). Electronic health record monitoring system and data security using blockchain technology. *Security and Communication Networks* 2022: 2366632.

9 Hilary, G. (2022). Blockchain and other Distributed Ledger Technologies, an advanced primer. In: *Innovative Technology at the Interface of Finance and Operations, Springer Series in Supply Chain Management*, vol. 11 (ed. V. Babich, J.R. Birge, and G. Hilary), 1–21. Cham: Springer.

10 Maffei, M., Casciello, R., and Meucci, F. (2021). Blockchain technology: uninvestigated issues emerging from an integrated view within accounting and auditing practices. *Journal of Organizational Change Management* 34 (2): 462–476.

11 Sarkar, S., Dharavath, R., and Jadav, B.H. (2022). Ethereum MongoDB: integrating blockchain with non-relational databases. In: *Proceedings of International Conference on Computational Intelligence and Data Engineering, Lecture Notes on Data Engineering and Communications Technologies*, vol. 99 (ed. N. Chaki, N. Devarakonda, A. Cortesi, and H. Seetha), 17–28. Singapore: Springer.

12 Kramarz, M. and Kmiecik, M. (2022). Quality of forecasts as the factor determining the coordination of logistics processes by logistic operator. *Sustainability* 14 (2): 1013.

13 Xia, X. (2022). SCM PMA supply chain models—a case study of Tesla motors. *International Journal of Frontiers in Engineering Technology* 4 (4): 33–40.

14 Campajola, C., D'Errico, M., and Tessone, C.J. (2022). MicroVelocity: rethinking the Velocity of Money for digital currencies. *arXiv preprint arXiv:2201.13416.*

15 Dasaklis, T.K., Voutsinas, T.G., Tsoulfas, G.T., and Casino, F. (2022). A systematic literature review of blockchain-enabled supply chain traceability implementations. *Sustainability* 14 (4): 2439.

16 Cetindamar, D., Shdifat, B., and Erfani, E. (2022). Understanding big data analytics capability and sustainable supply chains. *Information Systems Management* 39 (1): 19–33.

17 Wamba, S.F. and Queiroz, M.M. (2022). Industry 4.0 and the supply chain digitalisation: a blockchain diffusion perspective. *Production Planning & Control* 33 (2–3): 193–210.

18 Giancaspro, M. (2017). Is a 'smart contract' really a smart idea? Insights from a legal perspective. *Computer Law & Security Review* 33 (6): 825–835.

19 Mohanta, B.K., Panda, S.S., and Jena, D. (2018). An overview of smart contract and use cases in blockchain technology. *2018 9th International Conference on Computing, Communication and Networking Technologies (ICCCNT)*, 1–4. IEEE.

20 Zou, W., Lo, D., Kochhar, P.S. et al. (2019). Smart contract development: challenges and opportunities. *IEEE Transactions on Software Engineering* 47 (10): 2084–2106.

10

Satellite Communication

10.1 Introduction

In 2018, 5G communications have begun the commercial process in various regions of the country. From multiple perspectives, including technology, economics, society, and the environment, 5G communications are bound to be game-changers around the world. In the future, the service that needs to be met by 5G communications mainly include: enhanced mobile broadband services with about 2 billion users worldwide, as well as high-reliability and low-latency services for applications in some vertical industries [1].

5G communications have a key performance metric that requires "ensuring that anyone, anywhere, has access to a wider range of applications and services at a lower cost." The most basic device support for a terrestrial broadband network is a terrestrial base station. However, due to economic costs, technology, and other natural environmental factors, ground base stations only cover about 20% of the global total area. Building base stations in sparsely populated areas does not meet economic benefits. Geographical locations in deserts, polar regions, oceans, and some where it is impossible or difficult to establish base stations are even more out of line with reality. At the same time, in the face of various force majeure effects on the ground, such as earthquakes, tsunamis, storms or fires, and other extremely destructive special scenarios, the ground base station is easily destroyed, and cannot be quickly repaired in the short term, cannot provide communication capabilities in time, thus affecting emergency rescue and other work.

Due to the large coverage area of satellite communication network and flexible networking, satellite communication network can well cope with and solve the problems of signal coverage of ground base stations or easy destruction of equipment [2–6]. Moreover, as explained in the literature [4], satellite communication networks can also bring more benefits to 5G, such as: can provide elastic support when the traffic of the terrestrial network is severely overloaded or users move out of the base station coverage; at the same time, satellites can be used to cache hotspot data, thus providing users with faster request response; in the future, a large number of IoT devices will be connected to 5G Communication networks, for complex IoT applications, such as monitoring equipment deployed around the world, the use of satellite communication networks can also make it easier to access the network and reduce consumption. Even, there is the chief network architect of the BT Group, Neil McRae, who believes that 6G will be an organic combination of 5G and satellite communications [7]. It can be seen that satellite communication networks occupy a pivotal position in the global communication system in the future.

At the same time, the era of the Internet of Everything has arrived, the number of devices located at the edge of the information network and the data generated by them are growing rapidly, and the traditional "central cloud model" can no longer efficiently process network edge data, and cannot

Attribute-based Encryption (ABE): Foundations and Applications within Blockchain and Cloud Environments, First Edition.
Qi Xia, Jianbin Gao, Isaac Amankona Obiri, Kwame Omono Asamoah, and Daniel Adu Worae.
© 2024 The Institute of Electrical and Electronics Engineers, Inc. Published 2024 by John Wiley & Sons, Inc.

meet the performance requirements of business applications in terms of real-time, bandwidth, energy consumption, and security. In order to solve the above problems, the "edge computing mode" of using edge computing [8–13] resources to complete the massive data computing generated by edge devices came into being. The core idea is that the computation should be closer to the data source and closer to the user terminal. "Edge" refers to an intermediate node on the path from the data source head to the cloud computing center on the back end of the network, such as a mobile base station or WiFi gateway. Edge computing is not the antithesis of the back-end cloud computing center, but its expansion and extension. Compared with the traditional back-end cloud computing center, the edge computing model has three obvious advantages:

1. processing a large amount of raw data at the edge of the network, no longer uploading all to the cloud, which greatly reduces the pressure on network bandwidth and power consumption of the back-end cloud computing center;
2. doing data processing near the data source, without the need to transmit it back to the back-end center cloud processing through the network. Effectively reduce the latency of computing task services;
3. no longer upload end user data, but store and process on edge devices, reduce the risk of data leakage, and protect user data security and privacy. At present, the development of edge computing technology is in the early stage, and the industry is conducting in-depth theoretical research and extensive application practice in the fields of Internet of Things, telecom broadband network, and industrial Internet.

Therefore, the introduction of edge computing into satellite communication networks can provide more perfect communication services for terminal equipment anywhere in the world. According to the different orbital altitudes of the satellites, the satellite communication network can be divided into three categories: high-orbit satellites (geosynchronous equatorial orbit [GEO]) with an orbital altitude of 36,000 km from the ground, medium-orbit satellites (MEOs) with an orbital altitude ranging from 2,000 to 35,786 km, and low-orbit satellite (LEO) with an orbital altitude ranging from 160 to 2,000 km. For different satellite communication networks, low-orbit constellation communication networks have the following advantages over other types of satellite networks:

1. Since the orbital altitude of the low-orbit constellation communication network is the lowest in the three types of satellite communication networks, its communication propagation delay is also the lowest, and the round-trip delay (RTT) of the low-orbit constellation communication network is generally less than 100 ms of RTT, while the RTT of the GEO satellite network will even reach about 600 ms [14].
2. Due to the relatively short propagation distance of the low-orbit constellation communication network, the propagation attenuation of the signal will be smaller, which helps to limit the energy consumption of the terminal equipment to a certain range, so that the volume of most satellite terminal equipment can be designed to be smaller, which is more conducive to the realization of the handheld of the terminal of the device.
3. The low-orbit constellation communication network can better communicate with the ground terminal equipment. The low-orbit constellation communication network will not cause communication obstacles due to the terrain of the environment in which the terminal equipment is located, and even if obstacles are placed near the terminal equipment, the LEO can smoothly communicate with the ground terminal.
4. Compared with other satellite communication networks, the single satellite in the low-orbit constellation communication network has less coverage of the ground, and in order to achieve

global coverage, this requires the use of more satellites to form a constellation network to have this capability, which usually requires dozens or even hundreds of satellites. At the same time, this means that in the orbit of LEOs, there will be more satellites, so that more hardware resources can exist to form a resource pool and provide users with good services.

Therefore, compared with other satellite communication networks, combining low-orbit constellation communication networks with edge computing will bring a better communication experience to end users and devices anywhere in the world.

Due to the large spatio-temporal scale, high dynamic time-varying topology, and strong resource heterogeneity of low-orbit constellation communication networks, which are significantly different from traditional ground-based networks, the application and deployment of edge computing technology needs are also very strong. The specific reasons are as follows: (i) The satellite-ground and interstellar links are longer than the typical ground-based network links, and the data transmitted by the terminal to the back-end cloud computing center needs to pass through multiple satellite-ground and interstellar links to introduce longer communication delays. Therefore, the edge computing technology can more significantly reduce the mission service delay of low-orbit constellation communication network applications, thereby improving network performance; (ii) the satellite communication link bandwidth is smaller and more expensive than the ground-based optical fiber link, and the edge computing technology is used to preprocess the original data close to the user, which can effectively reduce the amount of backhaul data and save expensive satellite network bandwidth; (iii) The low-orbit constellation communication network is a wide-area wireless network, and the transmission of data in non-guided broadcast media is easily intercepted, resulting in potential information security problems, and the use of edge computing mode can protect user data security and privacy.

10.1.1 Low-Orbit Constellation Communication Networks

Low-Earth-Orbit (LEO) satellites are closer to the ground than other types of satellites, so their coverage area is relatively small. To achieve global coverage, multiple LEOs must be combined into satellite constellations and work together. This requires a good understanding of the design of low-orbit constellation communication networks.

At present, LEO constellations are divided into oblique orbital constellations and polar orbit constellations according to the degree of orbital inclination. Among them: the inclination angle of the orbital surface of the oblique orbit constellation is generally around 50°, and the spatial distribution of the satellites of this constellation is relatively uniform, and the number of satellites in each orbital plane is the same, but it is not suitable for inter-satellite link connection. In polar orbital constellations, because satellites in adjacent orbits operate in the same direction, it is more conducive to establishing and maintaining inter-satellite links, thereby forming an air network, and global communication can be achieved without the need for relays of ground equipment. Most constellations of satellites that use interstellar links use polar orbits. The chapter will use polar orbital constellations for follow-up research.

1. **LEO constellation topology**: Take, for example, the constellation network topology of the classic Iridium system. The system has a total of 6 orbital surfaces, each with 11 satellites evenly distributed, for a total of 66 satellites, with an orbital altitude of 778 km from the ground. Each satellite in the system can establish interstellar links and communicate with two north–south satellites in the same orbit and two satellites in adjacent east–west orbits by establishing interstellar links. Among them, the inter-satellite link of two satellites in the same orbit

is called the inter-orbit inter-satellite link, and the inter-satellite link of adjacent inter-orbit satellites is called the inter-orbit inter-satellite link. As the gap between the two orbiting satellites in the polar region gradually shrinks, in order to avoid interference, the inter-orbital interstellar link will be temporarily disconnected when it is close to the high latitude of 75°, and the inter-orbit satellite link will remain connected. The specific constellation topology is shown in Figure 10.1.

2. **Satellite coverage model**: A schematic of the coverage of a single satellite relative to the Earth's surface is shown in Figure 10.2, where O is the center of the Earth, Re represents the radius of the Earth, h is the orbital altitude of the satellite relative to the ground, and R represents the satellite relative to the Earth's surface.

The coverage radius of the surface, B, known as the substellar cover point, is the intersection of the satellite to the center of the Earth's sphere at the Earth's surface α is the minimum elevation angle, and the γ is half of the lower angle of the satellite covering the star. In general, the orbital height and minimum elevation angle of the satellite relative to the ground are determined according to the satellite constellation, that is, it is known. According to geometric knowledge, the correspondence between the parameters can be expressed according to the following equation:

$$\frac{\sin\left(\alpha + \frac{\pi}{2}\right)}{h + Re} = \frac{\sin \gamma}{Re} \tag{10.1}$$

Figure 10.1 Schematic diagram of satellite constellation topology.

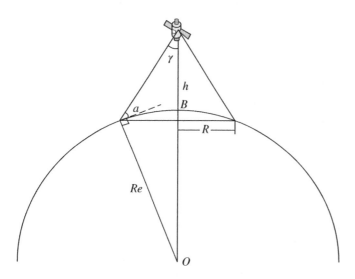

Figure 10.2 Satellite coverage diagram.

Thus, the formula for calculating γ can be obtained as:

$$\gamma = sin^{-1} \left[\frac{sin(\alpha + \pi/2)}{h + Re} \cdot Re \right] \tag{10.2}$$

where $\gamma \in [0°, 90°]$. In turn, the radius of the satellite's coverage of the ground can be calculated:

$$R = Re \cdot sin \left(\frac{\pi}{2} - \alpha - \gamma \right) \tag{10.3}$$

10.1.2 Interstellar Link Length

Since the distance between two satellites in a satellite constellation is far apart in space, the length of the inter-satellite link will lead to a non-negligible propagation delay compared to the traditional ground-based wireless link, which will affect the total delay of the entire communication process. Therefore, this section will further analyze the length calculation of inter-satellite links.

For in-orbit interstellar links, because the chapter mainly considers the polar orbit satellite constellation, the azimuth of satellites in the same orbit is unchanged, and these satellites are evenly distributed on the orbital surface, then the length of the inter-orbit interstellar link is mainly related to the number of satellites in orbit and the radius of satellite orbits. You can get its length calculation formula:

$$l_{ita} = (h + Re)\sqrt{2 - 2cos(2\pi/N)} \tag{10.4}$$

where N is the number of satellites in an orbit. For inter-orbit interstellar links, the length of the link is inversely proportional to the latitude at which the satellite node is located. When a satellite is at a low latitude, its inter-orbital inter-satellite link is the longest, and when a satellite is in a high-dimensional region, its inter-orbit inter-satellite link is the shortest.

First, calculate the length of the inter-orbital interstellar link with a satellite orbital phase factor of 0. At this time, the inter-orbital interstellar link is parallel to the equatorial plane of the Earth, and its length is mainly related to the number of orbits, the radius of the satellite's orbit, and the latitude at which the satellite is located, and the calculation formula is as follows:

$$l_{ita} = \sqrt{2(h + Re)\sqrt{1 - cos\frac{\pi}{x}} \cdot cos(late)} \tag{10.5}$$

where X represents the number of orbits of the satellite constellation, and *late* is the latitude at which the satellite is located at this time. Then, calculate the length of the inter-rail interstellar link when the phase factor is not 0. At this point, the inter-orbital interstellar link will exhibit an angle to the equatorial plane of the Earth, and its length is calculated as follows:

$$l_{ite} = \sqrt{\left[\sqrt{2(h + Re)}\sqrt{1 - cos\frac{2\pi F}{XN}} \right]^2 + l_{ite}^2} \tag{10.6}$$

10.1.3 Model of Satellite Motion

According to Kepler's law, the expression for satellite movement speed vs can be derived:

$$v_s = \sqrt{\frac{u}{Re + h}} \tag{10.7}$$

and the calculation expression for the satellite motion period T_s:

$$T_s = 2\pi \sqrt{\frac{(Re + h)^3}{u}} \tag{10.8}$$

where u is the Kepler constant, $u = 3.98601508 \times 10^{14} \, \text{m}^3/\text{s}^2$.

To further understand the motion of a satellite around the Earth, we can use Eqs. (10.7) and (10.8) which relate the speed and period of a satellite to its altitude. Equation (10.7) shows that the speed of a satellite is equal to half of the product of the gravitational constant of the Earth and the sum of the radius of the Earth and the altitude of the satellite. This means that the higher the satellite's altitude, the slower its speed will be. Equation (10.8) gives the calculation for the period of a satellite, which is the time it takes to complete one orbit around the Earth. It is directly proportional to the cube of the sum of the radius of the Earth and the altitude of the satellite, meaning that the higher the satellite's altitude, the longer its period will be. The schematic diagram of Figure 10.3 illustrates how a satellite's altitude affects its speed and period as it moves in an elliptical orbit around the Earth.

10.1.4 Edge Computing Technologies

The emergence of edge computing is mainly to solve the problem of high latency and high bandwidth consumption of offload requests back to the back-end cloud computing center. It brings the computing and storage capabilities of the cloud computing center to the edge of the network, so that tasks can be processed close to the user, so as to achieve the purpose of reducing hourly latency and bandwidth consumption.

1. **Edge computing logic platform**: The edge computing platform consists of three main parts: the infrastructure layer, the platform management layer, and the application layer [15], the logical structure of which is shown in Figure 10.4. Among them, the infrastructure layer includes hardware resources such as computing, storage, and networking of the edge computing host, as well as the virtualization layer on it. Through the virtualization layer, the hardware resources of the host are abstracted to form virtualization.

   Resource pooling, which is thus provided to the upper layer of the platform management layer for use. The platform management layer consists of two parts, namely resource management and platform services. Among them, resource management supports the management

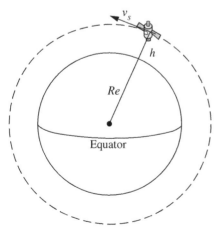

Figure 10.3 Schematic diagram of satellite motion.

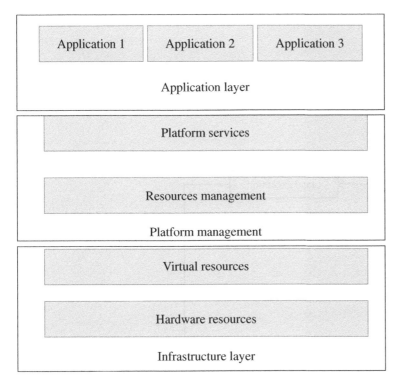

Figure 10.4 Edge computing platform logical structure.

of efficient multi-tenant isolated environments, while platform services provide low-level support for service registration and discovery and mutual invocation between Application Service Programs. The application layer forms logical functional entities through network function virtualization technology, combines the basic services provided by the platform management layer to form virtual machine applications, and then provides users with application services.

2. **Calculate the uninstallation-related process**: At present, the complexity of applications on mobile devices is increasing, followed by the increase in computing resources and energy consumption, but due to the resource limitations of mobile devices themselves, a large part of the tasks cannot be completed on mobile devices, so it is necessary to send these computing tasks to the computing nodes with stronger computing power and lower resource constraints in a requested manner for processing, including edge computing nodes and cloud computing center nodes, and then return the results to users after the processing of the computing nodes. Referring to the study [16], there is an offload flow as shown in Figure 10.5. For a computing task of the user application, the user program will first determine whether it needs to be evaluated and unloaded. The main purpose of the compute offload decision is to decide whether this compute task chooses to execute itself locally or to send the task to the compute node for remote execution. The advantage of local execution is that there is no need to transfer the task to the network, there is no transmission energy consumption and transmission delay, but it aggravates the computing energy consumption of the user device itself. Conversely, the benefit of remote execution is that the user device does not need to bear the computing energy consumption, but adds the energy consumption and delay of network transmission. However, because the computing power of the computing node is generally stronger than that of the terminal device and

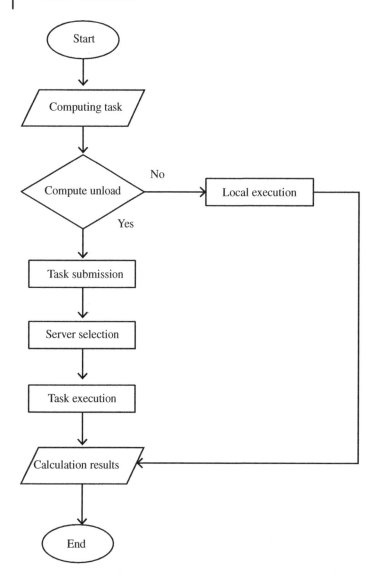

Figure 10.5 Calculation offload execution flowchart.

the processing speed is faster, the computation time consumed when executing at the remote end will be reduced, but the transmission delay will be increased. Therefore, the basis for judging the uninstall decision includes: which calculation method can reduce the runtime delay of the application, which calculation method can reduce the energy consumption of its own terminal equipment. Once a compromise is made between the two, it is possible to determine whether computational unloading is required. If the user program decides to offload the computing task, the end device transmits the task over the network to the compute service node. The specific computing service node to be transferred to can be confirmed by the compute node selection algorithm, and then the task is transferred to the service node, and the computing result is returned to the user after the computing node is processed.

10.2 Analysis of Edge Computing Requirements of Low-Orbit Constellation Communication Networks

With the continuous development of emerging applications such as the Internet of Things, streaming data analysis, autonomous driving, and telemedicine, the latency and bandwidth requirements for communication networks have become more demanding. At the same time, being able to connect all users on Earth to the network to test Internet applications is the vision of future low-orbit constellation communication networks.

However, traditional satellite communication networks cannot be processed to meet these requirements. It is to transmit data to the back-end cloud computing center, and then pass it on to the user after the back-end cloud computing center processes it. Obviously, this processing mode will generate a large response delay and occupy the bandwidth of the entire satellite communication network, affecting the quality of user experience and network performance. This requires that LEO communication networks innovate in the overall architecture. It can learn from the relevant research of edge computing in terrestrial broadband networks and apply edge computing to low-orbit constellation communication networks to achieve this purpose.

However, the purpose of edge computing is not to eliminate the back-end cloud computing center; on the contrary, edge computing is an extension of the processing power of the back-end cloud computing center, and the combination of the two can better improve the performance and business processing power of the low-orbit constellation communication network.

The transformation of LEOs into edge computing nodes provides data storage and computing capabilities on edge computing nodes, which can avoid the frequent transmission of hotspot data and reduce the bandwidth consumption of low-orbit constellation communication networks; at the same time, the computing tasks of time-sensitive services can be planned to be completed on edge computing nodes, thereby reducing the delay consumption of data backhaul and reducing the data transmission pressure of satellite backbone networks. It can be seen that the introduction of edge computing can effectively improve the real-time performance of low-orbit constellation communication networks and save network bandwidth.

In addition, satellites in the low-orbit constellation communication network use inter-satellite links to communicate, and data transmission between satellites is realized through routing exchange on the satellite, which significantly improves the performance of satellite communication systems and reduces communication losses. However, because the satellite nodes in the network have been in a state of high-speed motion, the inter-satellite link changes with the change of the relative position between the satellites, and the satellite needs to establish a new link to maintain the communication capabilities of itself and the entire network after the original inter-satellite link is disconnected, so the network topology of the LEO has always been there. Due to the changing state, the satellite link may be interrupted, at which point the satellite cannot establish a communication connection with the back-end cloud computing center. Therefore, when designing the edge computing architecture of the low-orbit constellation communication network, we need to design an autonomous working ability for each satellite edge computing node to ensure that it can provide continuous services to end users.

10.2.1 Design of Edge Computing Architecture for Low-Orbit Constellation Communication Networks

The architecture of the edge computing in the low-orbit constellation communication network, as proposed in the study, is depicted in Figure 10.3.

In the scenario, in order to simplify the model, only one satellite orbit is considered, and the number of LEO edge computing satellites in orbit is recorded as N as the access layer of the satellite network. The height of the LEO satellite orbit from the ground is represented by the variable h in kilometers denoted as hKm. Dotted lines extending from the LEO edge computing satellites to the ground represent the signal coverage of a single satellite. It should be noted that in the actual low-orbit constellation communication network, there is a certain range of overlap in the signal coverage area between two adjacent LEOs. As the backbone of the satellite network, including Y GEO satellites, it is used to transmit the data collected by the access layer to the ground customs station, connecting to the back-end cloud computing center. GEO satellites have no processing power and are only used as data forwarding transmission devices.

10.2.2 Satellite

1. **Virtual resource design**: Because of the unique environment in which the satellite edge computing node is located, it is a resource-constrained device, and the various resources on it are precious, so it is particularly important to improve the resource utilization of satellite edge computing nodes, which requires the use of virtualization technology. At the same time, virtualization technology can also unify the hardware resources of the cloud computing center and the edge computing platform, making the combination of the two more compact from the underlying hardware.

   Virtualization technology mainly implements virtual resources at the infrastructure layer. It will virtualize the computing, storage, and network resources of the physical host, abstraction into a virtualized resource pool, when the application service needs, can be configured to complete the matching of application services and hardware resources, is to achieve the transition from the physical host to the virtual host technical means.

2. **Platform management design**: The platform management layer efficiently manages virtual resources while providing underlying communication services and invocation support. The platform management layer includes two parts: the control layer and the implementation layer. Among them, the control layer corresponds to the control center of the entire platform management layer of the edge computing platform, which is the brain of the edge computing architecture of the entire low-orbit constellation communication network, providing support for the management of efficient multi-tenant isolated environments; the implementation layer is used to implement platform services, which provide intermediate application services and infrastructure services for applications, including transparent support for service discovery and mutual invocation between applications.

   In order to be able to cope with the scene of the link interruption between the satellite edge computing node and the back-end cloud computing center, the satellite edge computing system architecture needs to be specially designed, so that the satellite edge computing node can ensure the continuous operation of application services and process the user's application request under the "offline" situation, thereby steadily improving the quality of experience of satellite end users. Specifically, we designed an edge controller for the edge computing node component. This edge controller is a proxy for a control layer entity on the edge compute node, ensuring that the application service instance continues to run on the edge compute node.

   The model design of the platform management layer in the software architecture is shown in Figure 10.6, which is logically divided into a control layer and an implementation layer. At the same time, the model diagram also illustrates the correspondence between functional entities and satellite equipment.

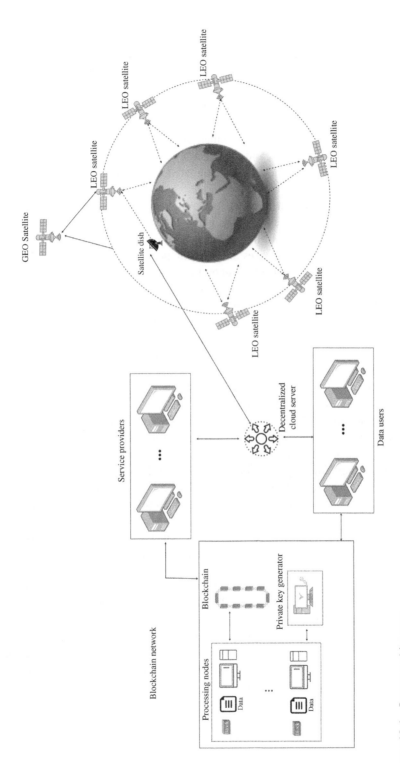

Figure 10.6 System architecture.

a. **Control layer components**: The control layer is the brain of the entire satellite network edge computing model and is the general command center. Its main internal components consist of two parts: the orchestrator and the resource manager. Among them, the orchestrator is mainly responsible for the binding of the application service program and the target edge computing node, and the resource manager is mainly responsible for the management and maintenance of the entire edge computing satellite system and the application service program. The orchestrator is the core of the satellite network edge computing model, which understands the resource usage of the entire satellite network through the resource manager. At the same time, combined with the requirements of application services for resources, such as CPU resources, storage services, and the maximum location from users, according to the specified scheduling algorithm, the establishment of new application services is bound to the target edge computing service satellite.

The Resource Manager is responsible for monitoring and managing the real-time status of satellite hosts and application services throughout the satellite network system. It collects resource usage for all edge computing satellites and provides information to orchestrators to complete the deployment of services. Because the pool of virtualized resources for each edge computing satellite may be insufficient or unavailable, it is important to monitor them. At the same time, the resource manager is also responsible for the monitoring function of the application service in the entire satellite network, it will periodically detect the current state of each application in the entire edge computing platform, ensure the integrity and authenticity of the application, ensure that the application meets the expected specified state, so as to ensure the continuous operation of the application service on the satellite platform to provide users with stable services, if it detects that an application service is inconsistent with the expected state, it will request the edge computing platform to carry out the corresponding addition, deletion and modification operation.

b. **Platform management implementation components**: The implementation layer (satellite host) is the performer of the entire edge computing platform action, which contains the basic components such as the edge controller, satellite platform, and virtualized infrastructure. Among them, the edge controller will synchronize the information of the control layer under normal circumstances of the network to control the generation or deletion of application services on the satellite host; the virtualization infrastructure provides virtual resources such as computing, storage, and networking according to the application needs, and the virtualization infrastructure will execute the forwarding rules received by the satellite platform, and route traffic between the application and dependent services to provide network functions.

In particular, the edge controller is the agent of the control layer components on the edge computing satellite. In the case of a normal link between the satellite host and the control layer, it will be managed and controlled by the control layer. In the case of link interruption, responsible for the "proxy" control layer, complete the autonomous control, so that the application service can continue to run on the satellite host, even if the satellite host restarts, can ensure that the application service can effectively provide stable services for end users. At the same time, the edge controller periodically reports its resource usage and the status of the App Service program to the resource manager. Its communication with the virtualization infrastructure is mainly used to manage the virtualized resources of the satellite host and to manage the application images provided for instantiation requirements.

It further improves and maintains the reliability of application services running on satellite hosts.

A satellite platform is a collection of basic functions that are necessary to run the corresponding application services on the satellite host and enable those application services to discover, broadcast, provide, and use the services on which they depend on each other. The service on which it depends may be provided by a satellite or a designated application service, and the application service may in turn use the services provided by the satellite. The basic function of a satellite platform is to control network traffic between application services and services. The satellite platform can receive traffic forwarding rules from the edge controller and application services, and provide forwarding instructions to the underlying kernel based on these rules and certain policies. In addition, the satellite platform supports the configuration of a local domain name system (DNS) proxy/server that can be used to direct user traffic to the desired application. Satellite platforms can communicate with other satellite platforms through infrastructure, so that several satellite platforms can be combined to forward service requests to neighboring satellites when their own computing or storage resources are insufficient, or, depending on the strategy.

Application Services operate as containers on a virtualized infrastructure provided by satellite hosts. These application services can interact with the satellite platform to use the basic services provided by the satellite platform. In turn, application services can also provide services to satellite platforms, which can further provide themselves to other application services in the system for use. App Services may explicitly request the hardware resources or services they require, and they can also make explicit requests or restrictions on their use of resources. These requirements can be verified at the control layer of the satellite edge computing platform, and the selection of the target satellite host is performed according to the strategy.

c. **The process of creating an App Service program**: This section takes the creation of an application service program as an example, as shown in Figure 10.5, which describes the process of forwarding control layer data between modules in a satellite network edge computing architecture.

First, the creation request for the App Service program, along with its requirements for resources, is sent to Resource Manager and stored. Among them, resource requirements can include requests for CPU resources, storage resources, network bandwidth and ports, or requests for application creation on a specific satellite platform. The orchestrator then listens to the resource manager's application service changes, and selects the most suitable satellite platform among all possible satellite platforms to be selected according to the resource requirements of this application service, and binds the target satellite platform to the Application Service program. The resource manager will then issue a build command to the target satellite platform's edge controller. After receiving the command, the edge controller of the target satellite platform will first generate an application service instance through the virtualization infrastructure, and configure the traffic forwarding rules for this application service instance through the satellite platform. This step allows other App Service instances to discover each other and make app requests to each other. After the App Service instance and the traffic forwarding rules have been generated, the notifying edge controller is complete. Eventually, the application service creation request is mapped to an application service instance that is ultimately generated using the virtualization infrastructure on the target satellite platform.

10.2.3 System Entities

The system entities are as follows:

1. **Processing nodes**: The processing nodes are the heart of the blockchain. They validate user attributes and identity before they can participate in system proceedings.
2. **Private key generator (PKG)**: This entity is authorized to generate attribute private keys for the system users after the blockchain network has verified the users.
3. **Service providers**: This entity is in charge of generating tokens that will enable data users to access satellite information.
4. **Decentralized cloud server**: This repository is primarily immune to a single point of failure and provides a storage point for the information received from the satellite, which is worthwhile for data users.
5. **LEO satellites**: These satellites are empowered with the most recent technology to serve as proxy servers by computing data provided by GEO satellites. This approach cuts down the time of using earthly satellites for data processing.
6. **GEO satellites**: These satellites are primary concerns with generating information about space and sending the information back to the LEO satellites. After the results are returned from LEO satellites to GEO satellites, the GEO satellites use that acquired information to further process information in space. The communication continues back and forth until the processing part-task is done and the result is returned to the decentralized cloud server for storage.

10.2.4 System Process Flow

The process flow involved with the secure data sharing on the proposed system architecture is as follows:

- **Setup**: The PKG first runs the setup algorithm to private, public parameters that will be essential for the generation of the system user's private keys and encryption of messages. Figure 10.7 provides a generalized over of the setup algorithm's procedural execution to obtain a master secret key and public parameters.
- **Registration**: The system entities such as data users, service providers, GEO, MEO and LEO satellites register onto the blockchain network to get their identity and attribute private keys. Here the digital signature is required based on the system user's identity to perform transactions on the blockchain network. Upon reception of the identities and attributes of the system users on the blockchain network, the authenticity of the identities and attributes is verified. After services verification, a token is present to the requested users, which will enable them to request the private key with PKG on the blockchain network. Eventually, the processing nodes on the blockchain network mine block to capture the log of the registration of the system users on the blockchain.
- **Private key generation**: The system entities such as data users, service providers, GEO, MEO, and LEO satellites bring their tokens when registering their credentials with the blockchain network. After the PKG has successfully validated the credentials from the blockchain network, the KeyGen algorithm is executed to attribute a private key to the system users for the decryption of ciphertext. Additionally, private keys are generated for the system users based on their identity, basically for signing transactions on the blockchain network. The procedure is presented in Figure 10.8.

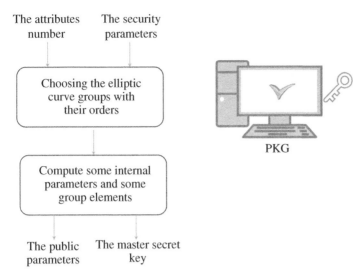

Figure 10.7   System setup.

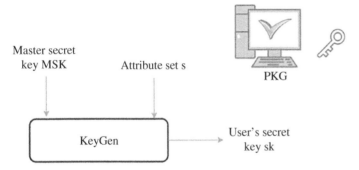

Figure 10.8   KeyGen.

- **Data encryption**: The data is mainly generated by the satellites in the system. As the GEO satellites might not have enough computational power, the data is processed at the LEO satellites, which serve as edge computers to reduce further the latency of data being transmitted to earth servers for processing. Note that the process for GEO and LEO satellites can continue back and forth until, eventually, the final output of the data is achieved. Eventually, the end data is encrypted by the LEO satellites using a symmetric encryption key obtained from the service provided. With all the communication among satellites and Service providers, the digital signature is used to prevent the involvement of malicious entities. Eventually, the generated ciphertext is saved on the Decentralized cloud server. Afterwards, the Service provider uses attribute-based encryption (ABE) to encrypt the symmetric key used by the LEO service for data encryption. The process of the data encryption using attribute-based is presented in Figure 10.9.
- **Data decryption**: The process of data decryption is not complicated. First, data users used an attribute-based decryption algorithm to obtain the symmetric private keys (Figure 10.10). Afterwards, the resultant symmetric private key is used to decipher the ciphertext created by the LEO satellites. Data users can access ciphertext if their attribute qualifies the constraints embedded into the ciphertext.

Service provider

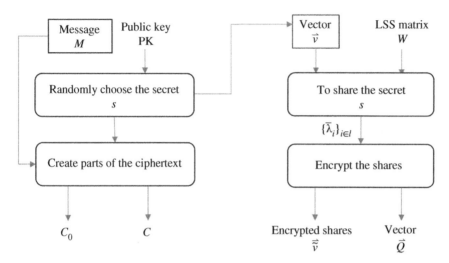

Figure 10.9 Data encryption.

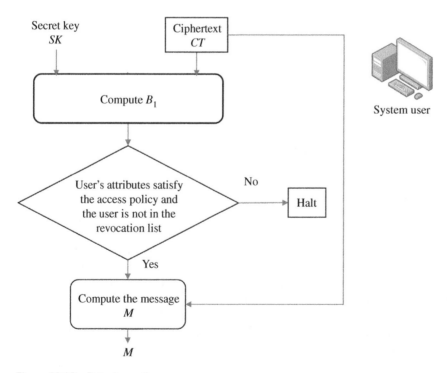

Figure 10.10 Data decryption.

10.2.5 Security Properties

As satellite data generated in the system contains sensitive information, the best approach for the satellite is encryption. The application of ABE and symmetric encryption in the system ensures that no unauthorized party can access the information they have not been authorized with a private key. This requirement reflects the confidentiality of a message encrypted on the system to prevent leakages of data to the adversary. The digital signature is required in the system to ensure that users communicate with the people they claim to be. The prime purpose is to avoid man-in-the-middle attacks and any impersonation.

10.3 Summary

In order to improve satellite communication and computing in space, this chapter examines ABE techniques and blockchain technology. The recently launched, highly computationally capable lower-orbit satellite is used as an edge computer. This method cuts down on the explicit amount of time a signal must travel to the edge server on Earth for processing before the output is delivered back to the satellite in orbit. By ensuring that all parties involved in communication and computation are permitted, the usage of blockchain primarily aims to ensure identity security. The main goal of confirming the identity of system users is to stop the malicious device from accessing the system and causing havoc. It is beneficial to utilize ABE to provide fine-grained data security, and only authorized users with a specific scope of access privileges can view the plaintext of the encrypted data. This is because data may contain sensitive information.

References

1 Afolabi, I., Taleb, T., Samdanis, K. et al. (2018). Network slicing and softwarization: a survey on principles, enabling technologies, and solutions. *IEEE Communications Surveys & Tutorials* 20 (3): 2429–2453.

2 3GPP TR 38.913 (2017). Study on scenarios and requirements for next generation access technologies.

3 Giambene, G., Kota, S., and Pillai, P. (2018). Satellite-5G integration: a network perspective. *IEEE Network* 32 (5): 25–31.

4 Yan, L., Cao, S., Gong, Y. et al. (2019). SatEC: a 5G satellite edge computing framework based on microservice architecture. *Sensors* 19 (4): 831.

5 Di, B., Zhang, H., Song, L. et al. (2018). Ultra-dense LEO: integrating terrestrial-satellite networks into 5G and beyond for data offloading. *IEEE Transactions on Wireless Communications* 18 (1): 47–62.

6 Choi, J.P. and Joo, C. (2015). Challenges for efficient and seamless space-terrestrial heterogeneous networks. *IEEE Communications Magazine* 53 (5): 156–162.

7 Yan, X. and Teng, H. (2021). Study on security of study on security of 5G and G and satellite converged communication network. *ZTE Communications* 19 (4): 79–89.

8 Luan, T.H., Gao, L., Li, Z. et al. (2015). Fog computing: focusing on mobile users at the edge. *arXiv preprint arXiv:1502.01815*.

9 Mach, P. and Becvar, Z. (2017). Mobile edge computing: a survey on architecture and computation offloading. *IEEE Communications Surveys & Tutorials* 19 (3): 1628–1656.

10 Hu, Y.C., Patel, M., Sabella, D. et al. (2015). Mobile edge computing-a key technology towards 5G. *ETSI White Paper* 11 (11): 1–16.

11 Feng, Y., Wang, W., Liu, S. et al. (2017). Research on cooperative caching strategy in 5G-satellite backhaul network. In: *Space Information Networks. SINC 2017. International Conference on Space Information Network, Communications in Computer and Information Science*, vol. 803 (ed. Q. Yu), 236–248. Singapore: Springer.

12 Hsieh, H.C., Lee, C.S., and Chen, J.L. (2018). Mobile edge computing platform with container-based virtualization technology for IoT applications. *Wireless Personal Communications* 102 (1): 527–542.

13 Shi, W., Cao, J., Zhang, Q. et al. (2016). Edge computing: vision and challenges. *IEEE Internet of Things Journal* 3 (5): 637–646.

14 De Sanctis, M., Cianca, E., Araniti, G. et al. (2015). Satellite communications supporting internet of remote things. *IEEE Internet of Things Journal* 3 (1): 113–123.

15 ETSI, M. (2014). Mobile edge computing-introductory technical white paper. etsi2014mobile.

16 Wang, B., Feng, T., and Huang, D. (2020). A joint computation offloading and resource allocation strategy for LEO satellite edge computing system. *2020 IEEE 20th International Conference on Communication Technology (ICCT)*, 649–655. IEEE.

11

Foundation of Information-Centric Communication

11.1 Introduction

Looking at today's data traffic patterns, it may appear that the Internet is developing toward a "content-centric" approach. That is partially correct. The information that the majority of people desire to read, however, is not created under a broadcast model. Instead, people are actively producing and donating massive amounts of content through a few channels like Twitter, Facebook, and YouTube. So, while content creation is spread (and has nothing to do with network architecture), content distribution is becoming increasingly concentrated in the hands of a few companies.

What we're seeing is a result of how content is disseminated these days. People are no longer as reliant on direct person-to-person connections as they were on connection-oriented networks like the telephone. They now create and publish information that can be accessed by others at any time and from any location. It's an asynchronous content model, with consequences for content creation and consumption, data traffic, and network architecture.

We transfer a packet to a specific destination address in a host-centric architecture, and communication is from one host to another host. On the other hand, in information-centric architecture, we fetch the data identified by a given name. We are just interested in contents, and we are unconcerned about the information that is presented to us.

Information-centric networking (ICN) is a modern network architecture that tries to address the shortcomings of Internet protocol (IP)-based network architecture, which places a greater emphasis on content such as data and how it moves through the network. After being published, content is no longer under the control of the owner (publisher), and copied content can be cached in several locations. As a result, the effectiveness of policy control over copy content becomes critical.

11.2 Information-Centric Communication

In contrast to a host-centric networking architecture, the term ICN is commonly used to refer to the complete class of Internet architectures that focus on content/data as the central entity. Content-centric networking (CCN) is a subset of ICN; in 2007, it began as a research project.

Unlike standard IP, ICN treats content as a first-class entity across the whole network. Whenever an end user requires information from a content source, it sends an interest packet to the network, which includes the name of the desired material. The packet is sent to the node that carries the requested data based on this name. The content of the data packet is returned to the requester by the node that has it. When a customer sends interest packets to obtain data based on their unique names, the interest packet does not include source or destination addresses. Routers in the network

Attribute-based Encryption (ABE): Foundations and Applications within Blockchain and Cloud Environments, First Edition.
Qi Xia, Jianbin Gao, Isaac Amankona Obiri, Kwame Omono Asamoah, and Daniel Adu Worae.

must forward them based on the content's names. It means that everything in ICN is linked to content names, and that every single action revolves around the content. As a result, rather than the host-centric approach used in transmission control protocol (TCP)/IP, ICN offers content-centric communication [1].

Previously to the development of the Internet of Things (IoT) [1], research groups were attempting to tackle challenges imposed by the existing TCP/IP communication paradigm. The current Internet architecture was designed in the 1960s, when the goal of communication was different and confined to communication between a few connected resources spread across a geographically scattered user base. However, Internet consumer habits have shifted dramatically, with more bandwidth-intensive applications now being used. This implies a transition to the new Internet paradigm known as information-centric networks. Internet users are more concerned with the content than with the source of the content. Rather than specifying explicit IP addresses, the entire communication of interest and data packet is based on the name of requested content. This makes ICN a location-independent data-centric networking network, because it can be reached solely by its name, regardless of where the requested content is located.

Unlike the existing Internet architecture, which assigns an IP address to each node in the network, the ICN assigns a unique name to material that is unrelated to its location. Requests for data are redirected to content nodes based on content names rather than IP addresses. This makes

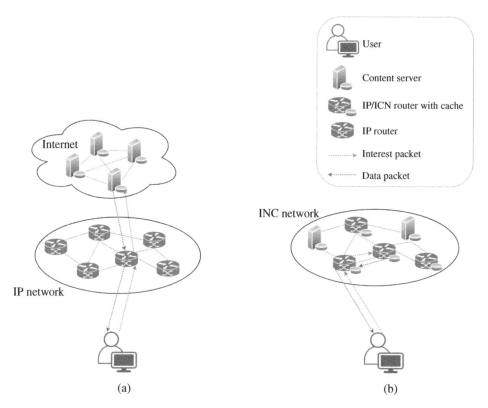

(a)   (b)

Figure 11.1 Content delivery overlay. In panel (a), content is delivered using an Internet Protocol (IP) address with an internet-based application. This method has the drawback of redundancy and wastage of bandwidth. Panel (b) depicts the use of an Information Centric Network, which is superior to the IP network because content is routed based on its name, rather than the IP address. Additionally, the content is cached on the server, enabling immediate delivery of the content.

using a CCN to provide in-network caching more appealing [2]. As shown in Figure 11.1 in-network caching indicates that each intermediary router in the network saves a copy of the data it has just sent. When a router with a copy of the content encounters an interest packet for the same content, it delivers the content from its cache instead of forwarding the interest packet to the data producer. This significantly reduces data delivery latency and network traffic strain. It also improves data accessibility. After submitting the request to the network, it minimizes the time it takes to retrieve the needed content. Furthermore, separate nodes in the network that have cached the same item can serve numerous requests. It also decreases the workload on a single data producer which must respond to all queries relating to the same content.

Before commencing a data transfer, the communication paradigm needs to be on active state. The receiver must be awakened (not in sleep mode), in order to complete the transmission. Otherwise, all data packets received will be dropped, although, as wireless nodes evolved, this issue was overcome by allowing base stations to cache data packets while the requester node is in sleep mode [3].

11.3 Name-Based Routing of Content

ICN is defined as the separation of "content's address" and "what content is." As a result, routing under this approach involves the creation of pathways to various name prefixes related with content rather than address prefixes. When routers forward interest messages in ICN, state information is built in order to transmit data packets back to the user. It creates a backward path using the state information kept by the router [4]. Based on the state information held in the router, the router can explore several pathways for particular name prefixes. ICN has made it easier to retrieve content quickly and timely in a congested network by facilitating such multipath forwarding features in the network system. Furthermore, in TCP/IP-based networks, such as the current version of the Internet, routing is based on IP addresses. Routing in ICN, on the other hand, is based on name prefixes in interest packets.

Since any action in ICN is based on the content name, it is crucial to choose a naming system for data that is unique, permanent, and independent of its location. Different naming strategies based on flat and hierarchical namespaces (like uniform resource locators [URLs]) have been proposed, each with its own set of advantages and disadvantages. The end user looks for content based on its name. Thus, having a unique name linked with each content piece existing in the network is absolutely essential [5].

Another requirement of ICN is object authentication using naming schemes. Whereas the contents are not provided by the original producer, they are provided by any of the nodes that have the content. As a consequence, incorporating security provisioning into naming allows the architecture to leverage third-party security protocols in the same way as it is done in TCP/IP allows.

11.4 Benefits of Using ICN

The name of the content is used by an ICN node to find it, and the node does not need to know where the content is located. To identify the required content, it employs a management package known as "interest." This request is routed throughout the whole network, as shown in Figure 11.2. Any intermediary router that has the requested material creates a data packet and transfers it back to the requester. The client is served by the source or producer of the data if no intermediate router stores the data. There are the two primary advantages of ICN over a host-oriented approach: a

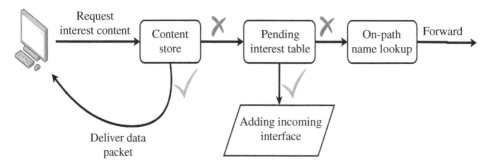

Figure 11.2   Name-based routing at a router.

reduction in network load/traffic, as well as a reduction in the time spent waiting. As ICN allows content caching at intermediate nodes in the network, for the several clients' requesting for the same content, it can be provided by different nodes in the network that have already cached the content, or by the content source itself. These actions minimize network traffic by diverting it to a variety of network nodes rather than a single content source. Because of the caching feature, content retrieval takes less time because there is no or a small queue of awaiting interests at a single content source. The provision for content caching in the network also decreases content retrieval delay and assures high content availability.

There are several advantages of ICN-based architecture as compared to that of TCP/IP-based network architecture [6]. A few of these advantages are listed below:

- **Content identity and location separation**: The existing Internet is based on the identification of participating nodes by being recognized by their IP address, which is dependent on their geographical location or subnet. Therefore, when a data source is relocated from one geographical location to another, the data source is altered. As a result, the data source must be registered again, or mobility-related protocols must be employed.
- **Energy-efficient interaction**: Before starting the data transfer, the communication paradigm needs active status. In case the receiver is in sleep mode, it must be switched to active, in order to accomplish the communication. Otherwise, all data packets received will be dropped, although, as wireless nodes evolved, this issue was overcome by allowing base stations to cache data packets while the requester node was in sleep mode [3]. With the advancement of ICN and in-network data caching, the aforementioned problem can be resolved to a large extent. In this scenario, every intermediate router capable of caching will operate as a wireless network base station in terms of caching. Hence, the energy of sleeping nodes in the network can be conserved while no data is lost.
- **Traffic across client–server**: Client–server traffic accounts for a significant portion of today's Internet traffic. The following is an example of a distributed service model: One user is attempting to access YouTube, which is not a single system [7]. In actuality, it is a form of distributed service that consists of numerous systems placed in multiple locations. For speedier responses, end customers are directed to the nearest service offering servers. However, because of the related location with a server, all users in the locality will be allocated in the same server so the distributed idea will not be employed in practice. However, if content is delivered based on content identification, the same data can be served from multiple locations, resulting in dispersed content or service delivery.
- **Privacy and authenticity**: With today's Internet technology, privacy and authenticity are two big concerns. Auxiliary protocols are used to provide it to data communications. Many scholars

have presented major and well-known ways to address such problems, but the problem has not been fully overcome. The forthcoming ICN technology has developed self-authentication content solutions [8]. It will undoubtedly address the two difficulties mentioned above. This novel technique eliminates the requirement for third-party protocols for security provisioning. Furthermore, privacy and non-repudiation can be addressed effectively according to the employment of public and private key encryption.

- **Internet asymmetric and symmetric protocols**: The majority of protocols in the current Internet architecture are symmetric [9]. It's designed for end systems that have similar setups. In fact, the Internet connects a wide range of devices, from handheld or palm devices to wireless sensors. The end systems are constrained in terms of resources in such cases. Thus, it is fair to allow the usage of asymmetric protocols in future Internet generations. As a result, ICN should support such advanced asymmetric protocols.

- **Requirements for isolation**: In a shared scenario, the end users demand application isolation. This is especially true in applications that are mission-critical, such as different monitoring and military applications. Isolation means that the performance of one application should not be impacted by the performance of other apps that use the same resources. It is tough to achieve in practice [1]. Still, allocating specialized resources to these types of applications is an option. Virtual private networks (VPNs) are a potential solution. In addition, the future Internet based on ICN will provide programmable combinations of sharing services for applications and subsequent isolation to end users.

- **Quality of Service (QoS)**: The Quality of Service (QoS) is defined as the degree to which a customer is pleased with a service. It is related to a service that is directly or indirectly associated with data that impacts the given services, as the name implies. The goal of any communication domain is to provide satisfactory services to end users via wired or wireless architectures [3]. Therefore, during an ongoing session between any pair of source destination is assured throughput and packet latency are the primary considerations. In conventional IP-based networks, QoS is difficult to implement. In contrast, the future Internet architecture will allow assured QoS criteria to be set before sessions are established.

11.5 Cost-Efficient and Scalable Distribution of Content Design Principles

The data is administratively distributed on separate caches in content-centric distribution networks. Thus, the content delivery network (CDN) strategy is transparent to end users, as it redirects resource requests to caches. However, there are still some drawbacks with both systems in the network overhead. As a result, there is a growing demand for content distribution that is both efficient and scalable. Instead of putting the full load on servers, peer-to-peer scalability is achieved by proposing self-organized, fault-tolerant, and adaptive distribution across different peers.

ICN must be designed as a long-term sustainable network with built-in support for energy-efficient solutions. It must also be flexible enough to evolve over time. Similarly, ICN must be developed and expanded in response to changing societal needs, adaptable, available (it must retain its usable operation rate), and reliable (i.e. it should recover from faults if at all faults are there).

The process of distributing billions of things to billions of interconnected devices is a major challenge in ICN. In order to avoid naming conflicts, synchronization between contents is required; the challenge is to verify that the contents have globally unique names. As an outcome, naming the contents will be done using efficient methods that are distributed and self-managing and can handle a large number of dynamically formed content objects. Another design basis is that network management should be easy and efficient, with the goal of self-configuring and self-optimized networking.

Despite the network's huge scale, the ICN is expected to be loosely connected, with few interdependencies between components. Users of the Internet are more interested in having access to the desired data than the location of the data (i.e. where the data is stored), the URL, or the IP address of the server that hosts the data; therefore, the focus should always be on data or content. In the ICN, content discovery, advertisement, and retrieval should be easier to implement. A content-centric routing protocol will make it easier to get a specific content to a user by forming the most convenient location for the user.

In ICN, achieving QoS is a difficult task. Due to the lack of end-to-end flow concept in ICN, QoS must be expressed in terms of objects or contents. Since the contents are pervasive, replicated, cached, and dispersed, creating a QoS-aware ICN becomes complex. Furthermore, the information might be acquired or even originated from a variety of sources. Consequently, the content can be delivered in different of paths, which might pose a difficult problem when considering QoS.

11.6 ICN Design Challenges

Users' access patterns for bandwidth-sensitive Internet activity will be altered by the ICN. Researchers have been proposing effective protocols and procedures for a variety of difficulties such as naming, routing, and security measures which aim to tackle this new paradigm. The creation of such protocols and procedures is not straightforward because of the many technical needs in these protocols and procedures. Some of the obstacles in designing ICN are listed in this section, along with brief descriptions. Everything in any ICN revolves around data or content; however, there are a few tasks related with these data or content that can be thought of as building blocks to establish an ICN. These include content naming, content storage, routing, caching, content forwarding, and network security.

11.6.1 Content Naming

The naming of items in ICN is a major aspect that improves data availability and reduces retrieval time. Consider a scenario in which a user requests content based on its name via an interest packet (Figure 11.3). This interest packet is delivered to the content source, and the content source responds with the exact data as well as the content name. Depending on the in-network caching method, the communicated data may get cached at all intermediate locations along the reverse path from content provider to requester. So, in future, if same or another node requests the same content, it will be fulfilled by the nearest intermediate node in the middle. However, the difficulty is to provide every single piece of available on the Internet. This creates a unique circumstance that necessitates extra caution while implementing ICN [4, 10]. For example, the names given to the contents must be globally unique. For ease of discovering and validating the producer, the name must also identify the content's producer. The routing information table in the router should be named in such a way that the size of the table is manageable and follows a hierarchical structure.

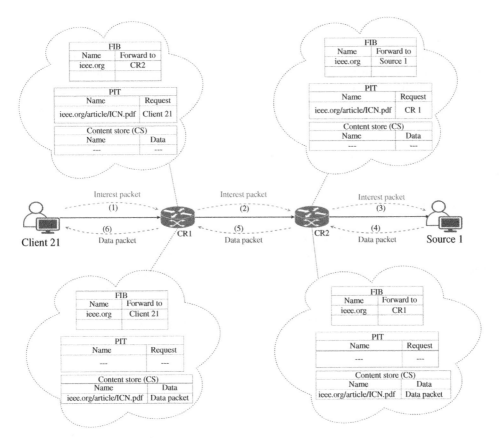

Figure 11.3 Name-based routing mechanism.

11.6.2 Caching of Content

In ICN, caching content at intermediate nodes improves performance, but the difficulty is figuring out how to do it properly. There is always the option of caching all chunks of data or a subset of them also, data can be cached in all intermediate routers or in a subset of them.

All of these solutions have advantages and disadvantages, and the cache size provision for nodes in network caching is another consideration. The recent emergence of video portals in Internet traffic results in massive amounts of data creation, and storage space in a router is always a problem in such cases. All of this should be taken into account while implementing the ICN [11, 12]. To propose an effective caching method for ICN architecture that can manage all of these challenges and deliver an optimal solution is the major challenge. It is critical to conduct a series of rigorous tests on ICN that are tested under a variety of input situations. The following are some of the issues that ICN users face when it comes to content caching:

Placement of cache: Determining the cache's location to store content is a challenging task. Caching can take place in the network or at the edge; however, both have restrictions, and selecting the best location for cache storage a difficult task. If the method is edge caching, then content retrieval requires the redirection of requested packets over a lengthy distance to the requester. In such caches, the location should be determined by specific algorithms, resulting in minimal delay due to request redirection to fetch cached data. On the other hand, while an in-network caching technique is simple to implement, the decision about which nodes should be equipped with a fixed-size cache poses a problem because it is dependent on a number of other topology and traffic-related limitations. In order to execute the cache memory at line speed, the cost is also a crucial consideration during its implementation. There is a demand for faster memory, which raises the cost of implementation indirectly. Other criteria, such as node centrality, expensive interdomain communication lines, traffic patterns, and domain size. It may be considered by an Internet service provider (ISP) when deciding cache placement strategy based on a determined capital expenditure.

Content distribution: The pattern in which a particular piece of content is stored in the network or at the edge is known as content distribution. This type of content distribution has an impact on a number of system factors, including request packet redirection and cache hit gain. The easiest method for placement is to cache all content in each node along the path; this reduces communication delay and message overhead, but it may lead to caches being totally filled. Due to the large content, the cache content will need to be replaced compared to storage capacity. With the increase in copies for a certain content within the system, there is also a requirement to efficiently manage network resources, which is a problem [2]. Furthermore, copying each item of data in each network node results in redundant data replication, which is undesirable. There is some coordination among network elements needed before they take decision regarding caching content. So, eliminating redundancy in cache content is also a challenge.

11.6.3 Data Integrity

In the existing Internet architecture, naming a data object is just as important as assigning location-dependent IP addresses. The validity of data cannot be assumed because these data objects can be cached at any location. The term "data-name binding verification" refers to the process of establishing verifiability between an object's name and the object itself. Data integrity refers to the ability of an intermediate sender other than the producer to ensure that the data received in the recent past is the same identified data object that was originally requested. The authentication of content's origin is a distinctive security method that is related to content naming. This means that a designated data object is only published by the authorized respective publisher to validate the information in reality. This can be identified by the related name prefix; nevertheless, in order for ICN to work properly, it must be guaranteed [13]. If this fails, neither users nor the network entity will trust with data object's authenticity. The lack of trust may lead to several attacks, such as denial of service (DoS) attacks.

11.6.4 Resolution System's Scalability and Name-Based Routing

The term "routing" in ICN refers to the process of determining routes to nodes that contain named data objects based on the content name provided by the sender. Resolution of name, route discovery, and content delivery are the three processes that make up the routing process. In first phase, requested object name is converted into the corresponding locator. In the second phase, data objects are routed based on their names. In last phase, the data object is routed back to the requester (the client). The routing methods in ICN is classified as lookup by name routing (LBNR), route by name routing (RBNR), and hybrid routing (HR). The challenges of the previous three categories are described next.

- **LBNR**: The first phase of name resolution is used in this routing approach to translate the requested data object name into a location (IP addresses). The second phase (discovery phase) is based on the existing IP paradigm which route discovery is dependent on the locator. The third phase of content delivery can be implemented similarly to IP-based routing. The sender's address is included in the request packet, and the requested content is returned to the sender based on the locator. The challenges in LBNR are as follows. During lookup and update, there are challenges in constructing the scalable resolution system. The lookup process maps data objects to their relevant locators and duplicates them. In such scenario, designing an optimal solution is a significant challenge. Additionally, data object locations may vary frequently, and multiple data objects may change positions at the same time. It's difficult to respond to such changes, and creating a network replica during routing is another challenge. To avoid frequent cache misses and to use efficiently the router storage, caching and cache replacement must be performed optimally.

- **RBNR**: This routing approach ignores the first phase of name resolution and routes a request to the content based on the data object's name. Hence, a routing table should contain routing information for each individual data object. However, due to the large number of data objects, the size of a routing table is an issue unless a technique for aggregating is implemented. This routing method reduces the overall delay and makes the routing process simpler than the exclusion of name resolution phase. For the third phase, this method requires other ID of any location or host to send the requested content back to the sender. Otherwise, a new routing technique will have to be implemented. Aggregation of names for data items is challenging and requires special attention in order to reduce the number of entries in the routing table. Another difficult issue in RBNR is determining the name that is framed for the aggregation by the content provider.

- **HR**: This routing method combines the advantages of the preceding two strategies. By considering an ISP in the single-network domain, where scalability difficulties can be addressed by network planning. The RBNR can be used to skip the name resolution process, reducing total time. LBNR will be used to route packets between different domains that each have their own locators. The following are some of the challenges that are specifically tied to HR:
  - Framing a scalable mapping system by giving the named data object and subsequent return of locator are complicated tasks to perform. As solution, the destination domain should request encapsulation of the content;
  - Assuring secure mapping of information to prevent any malicious node to seize the request packet;
  - In case of content name modification, verifying origin of data and certify data Integrity are problematic.

References

1 Nagle, J. (1984). RFC0896: congestion control in IP/TCP internetworks.

2 Chai, W.K., Katsaros, K.V., Strobbe, M. et al. (2015). Enabling smart grid applications with ICN. *Proceedings of the 2nd ACM Conference on Information-Centric Networking*, pp. 207–208.

3 Rexford, J. and Dovrolis, C. (2010). Future internet architecture: clean-slate versus evolutionary research. *Communications of the ACM* 53 (9): 36–40.

4 Varvello, M., Schurgot, M., Esteban, J. et al. (2013). SCALE: a content-centric Manet. *2013 IEEE Conference on Computer Communications Workshops (INFOCOM WKSHPS)*, pp. 29–30. IEEE.

5 Amadeo, M. and Molinaro, A. (2011). CHANET: a content-centric architecture for IEEE 802.11 MANETs. *2011 International Conference on the Network of the Future*, pp. 122–127. IEEE.

6 Ahmed, S.H., Bouk, S.H., and Kim, D. (2016). Contentcentric networks: an overview, applications and research challenges.

7 Stuckmann, P. and Zimmermann, R. (2009). European research on future internet design. *IEEE Wireless Communications* 16 (5): 14–22.

8 Jacobson, V., Smetters, D.K., Thornton, J.D. et al. (2009). Networking named content. *Proceedings of the 5th International Conference on Emerging Networking Experiments and Technologies*, pp. 1–12.

9 Wikipedia (2022). Named data networking - Wikipedia, the free encyclopedia. http://en .wikipedia.org/w/index.php?title=Named%20data%20networkingoldid=1076845884 (accessed 14 June 2022).

10 Ren, Z., Hail, M.A., and Hellbrück, H. (2013). CCN-WSN-A lightweight, flexible content-centric networking protocol for wireless sensor networks. *2013 IEEE 8th International Conference on Intelligent Sensors, Sensor Networks and Information Processing*, pp. 123–128. IEEE.

11 Yu, K., Arifuzzaman, M., Wen, Z. et al. (2015). A key management scheme for secure communications of information centric advanced metering infrastructure in smart grid. *IEEE Transactions on Instrumentation and Measurement* 64 (8): 2072–2085.

12 Yu, K., Zhu, L., Wen, Z. et al. (2014). CCN-AMI: performance evaluation of content-centric networking approach for advanced metering infrastructure in smart grid. *2014 IEEE International Workshop on Applied Measurements for Power Systems Proceedings (AMPS)*, pp. 1–6. IEEE.

13 Katsaros, K.V., Chai, W.K., Wang, N. et al. (2014). Information-centric networking for machine-to-machine data delivery: a case study in smart grid applications. *IEEE Network* 28 (3): 58–64.

12

Security Overall in Information-Centric Networks

12.1 Introduction

We need ways to use data effectively while preventing data breaches, ensuring data privacy, data protection, and access control. The world is producing data at astounding rates, in part because Internet of Things (IoT) applications are collecting a constant stream of data from various sensors and devices.

A viable approach for redesigning content delivery on the Future Internet is the information-centric network (ICN) concept. Despite its potential (to reduce data traffic in the network backbone, for instance, and to make content distribution efficient and scalable), there are still a number of issues that need to be resolved. Access control is one of the most significant and essential measures for ICN's effectiveness. Security measures must be in place to guarantee that only authorized users can access protected contents as they are retrieved from distributed in-network caches.

Due to its scalability and ability to give data security and privacy to a vast pool of data, blockchain technology can be a potential method for overcoming ICN constraints and addressing many ICN security challenges. All of the performed transactions that represent the actions of the ICN node are committed to the global blockchain and checked for any illegal access or action using the blockchain paradigm. Every blockchain object maintains a copy of the data. As a result, once a transaction has been approved by the blockchain, it cannot be denied or rejected by any ICN node.

The ABE feature of flexibility increases the length of ciphertexts and private keys and adds additional computational overheads to encryption and decryption. Public-key encryption has always been an all-or-nothing issue since its conception many years ago. If you had the right key to unlock any particular encrypted dataset, or ciphertext, you had access to the complete dataset. None of it was accessible if you lacked the proper key.

12.2 Content-Centric Network (CCN) Architecture

Content-centric network (CCN) is being investigated further by a project called named data networking (NDN), which has specific ideas on protocols and algorithms as well as a fully operational model. In contrast to a host-centric Internet protocol (IP)-based network, the CCN [1] considers content as primitive and accesses it by name instead of their location. It distinguishes data or content's location address from its identity, security, and accessibility. The architecture's essential components were established by CCN's original work, which included stability and security. However, the design decisions keep transmission control protocol (TCP)/IP facile, resilient, and are scalable. Users always launch the communication, which employs two types of packets: interest

Attribute-based Encryption (ABE): Foundations and Applications within Blockchain and Cloud Environments, First Edition.
Qi Xia, Jianbin Gao, Isaac Amankona Obiri, Kwame Omono Asamoah, and Daniel Adu Worae.

and data. The client, who wants to request a data, creates an interest packet by stating the content's name. The interest packet is subsequently distributed over all of the system's accessible links. CCN, on the other hand, applies hierarchical name prefixes in its naming system. Whether it has the required data, each node that receives the interest responds by providing it to the client. If the node somehow doesn't hold the content, the interest packet is forwarded over all networks. All the nodes wishing to engage in the same material can share the same copy since resource is identified by name instead of location.

As shown in Figure 12.1, the content store (CST), forwarding information base (FIB), and pending interest table (PIT) are three data elements stored by each forwarding node in CCN. The FIB is applied to transmit interest packets to the source(s) of requested data; it provides a list of departing interface(s) to transmit requested data, and the CS stores data packets for possible use. Instead of forwarding to the legitimate source, any interest packet containing CS content is provided from that node. If the cache becomes full when new data arrives, the least frequently used (LFU) or least recently used (LRU) replacement method is applied to make space for the incoming data. It distinguishes from IP queuing in that IP utilizes a replacement mechanism called most recently used (MRU). Self-authenticating, self-identifying, and Idempotent are some CCN packets features. As a result, each packet has the capability to be helpful to a large number of users, increasing the likelihood of data packets being shared for as long as feasible. The CCN suggests that the content packet be sent in the reverse way as the interest packets. It allows transporting nodes to use the CS to cache data. It employs a data structure known as PIT for this function. The PIT keeps a record of packets that have been transferred but have not yet arrived at the destination nodes. The PIT entries are cleared as the packet arrives. Entries that do not discover a connection are subsequently timed out and deleted [2].

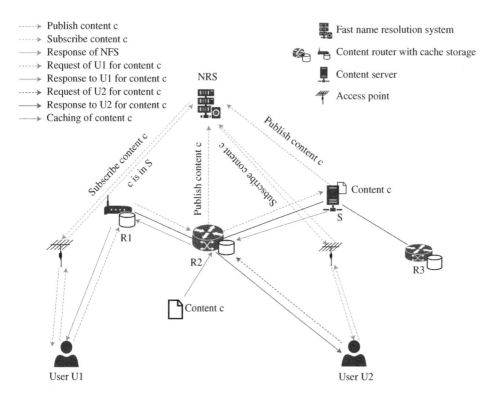

Figure 12.1 CCN architecture.

12.3   Naming System Design

An accurate and unique naming scheme is required to locate resources in ICN. This incorporates the identification of all network components, as well as the data. Routing is applied based on the content data name. As a result, routing efficiency is also influenced by how effectively the naming scheme is implemented and how long it takes to identify provided names. Every name has to be a unique identification for each particular network asset, as well as location agnostic. The goal of an information-centric network will be to center on "what" rather than "where." Every network node and connection on the present Internet is assigned an IP address [3]. ICN, on the other hand, assigns data a unique name. In practice, giving all content chunk in the network a unique, functional name is a difficult task. Furthermore, the naming strategy must be self-contained in the face of any network threats. It should also be low power in terms of operation, such that ICN-based IoT platform can use it. To give data a name, some prominent ICN projects have implemented a number of existing naming techniques.

The established name scheme in ICN is developed on the basis of Internet's domain name system (DNS) operation. However, because to its inherent constraints, the DNS procedures cannot be directly applied to the ICN. The present DNS handles the workload which has accumulated as the number of total client nodes grows. If numerous Internet nodes become too numerous, a resolution mechanism that is simple to operate in terms of distribution, administration, and scalability is required. Each domain name and hostname are mapped to an IP address using this resolution process. Users only have to provide human-readable names to retrieve the content from remote nodes or gain connection to remote nodes, making the procedure smoother. Because the DNS system has no knowledge about the client's location, it is unable to respond to a question about the location of the closest current sources.

Naming a data element, like naming a host on the existing Network, is a critical and crucial aspect of an ICN. ICN requires unique IDs for each named data element since it is used to identify data elements regardless of their media access control (MAC) address. For the efficient application of naming designs in information-centric networks, a number of difficulties must be solved.

- Because ICN's core assumptions contravene, methods for modifying and updating named data items might be difficult. If a named data can be replicated and kept in in-network caches for upcoming retrieval, the identifiers must be long-lasting and the binding between name and data must not change, altering the data without creating a new identification is not possible. Version control may be a viable approach, but it requires a suitable naming scheme. It also requires a method for users/content seekers to understand how to connect earlier and newer versions.
- Data hashes could be used as part of data identification to name fixed contents, allowing data providers to generate the hash value across requestors and existing content. By recalculating the hash value and matching it to the identifier component, each ICN node can validate the identifier-data association.
- It's also difficult to keep track of accessibility. The basic assumption in an ICN is to provide ubiquitous access to named collected data, although there are related-use cases when access to content should be restricted, such as to a specific user. There are several approaches to this, including object encryption (which necessitates the distribution of keys and linked mechanisms) and the concept of scopes, where it requires relying on identifiers that may only be resolved/used under particular circumstances.
- The requestor's privacy is also a challenge that needs to be dealt with. If the network can view the request and the transferred packets, it can also keep query packet histories/logs for certain

network segments or users. This is not a good strategy because identifiers are meant to persist a long period. That is, even though the identification does not provide significant detail, it is anticipated that the identification could be used in the future to retrieve the linked content items.

12.4 Secure Naming Scheme for Information-Centric Networks

The naming scheme proposed in [4] provides a safe naming approach for identifying and locating various resources within ICN. The main goal is to enable secure data collection from various dubious or unknown sources within the network. The suggested technique is adaptable since it is backward compatible with the current URL-based naming method. By separating the address recognition principles and a source within URI/URL authority parts, it also allows independent data identification regardless of transferring, routing, or storage processes. We can securely collect contents from any of the sources within a network using the proposed naming scheme. It also has full backward compatibility with the old naming technique, as well as data transportation and data analysis for the original/actual source. The proposed method requires two key aspects for deployment: a content manager and a name resolution. Name resolution can be installed as a browser plug-in to enable data collection from multiple sources. To validate the authority for each given URL, the plug-in initially verifies whether it has the certificates in its trustworthy store of a key. Otherwise, the plug-in launches a name resolution technique to retrieve the certificate of authorization including the data identification, performs authentication, and stores the certification in the keychain's local store. The name resolution then transmits a request toward the domain name system to convert the authoritative name to metadata and the webserver's network address. The header structure used in data chunk collection is shown in Figure 12.2. The message type is determined by the field type. The setting of the required material or the data provider's ID is specified in the second field. The third column is the data's cryptographic fingerprint, which is used to prevent unwanted data alterations. The length of the data included in the fifth field is stored in the fourth field.

12.5 Data Transmission – Content Delivery

The requestor of data emits an interest packet, which initiates data transmission in the ICN. The distinct name of the content sought is included in the interest package. Whenever an interest packet is received by a content distributor or a node with valid queried material, a data packet is transferred to the content requestor. The content's specific name is also included in the data packet. "Producer" refers to the node that provides or produces the data, while "provider" refers to the node which transfers a copy stored in its store [5]. In this chapter, these two concepts are applied to identify data-caching routers and the genuine producer. The routing schemes in ICN are engaged with network topology design and techniques that deal with long-term network changes. They're also in charge of creating and maintaining the forwarding table. The underlying routing mechanisms

Type	Context/ID of authority	Data Hash	Data Length	Data

Figure 12.2 Data header format.

operate along with ICN's forwarding function to determine which network interfaces are available for data transmission. In contrast to IP, the ICN distinguishes between routing and forwarding. Routing in ICN informs users about the accessibility of a pathway (or route) to the data, while forwarding provides the best pathway to the content's address depending on performance. Despite IP-based routing protocols such as open shortest path first (OSPF), link-state, and others being reliable, they cannot be deployed with ICN directly. These algorithms are oriented on the host, whereas ICN is oriented on the content. However, with a few tweaks, they're excellent enough to employ in ICN [6].

The FIB, PIT, and CS are all managed by a content router. Interest packets are transmitted to the data source through the FIB, which contains route metadata for content names. The PIT of a content router captures the interface through which interest packets come to the content router, allowing the delivered data packets to be forwarded to their rightful requester effectively. It's worth mentioning that if a content router receives request for the same content chunk from several interfaces, it should keep track of all of them in its PIT. Some previously received content chunks are cached using the CS. Once an ICN content router collects the interest packet for a content chunk with a unique content name, it provides with the correct data packet if the copy is cached in its CS; otherwise, it searches its PIT. The interface where the interest packet arrived to the content router is recorded if the content router identifies an entry for such content name among its PIT. If the content router's PIT does not contain an entry for the content name, it consults its FIB before forwarding the interest packet toward the content source. Whenever a content router receives a data packet, the data packet is first cached in its CS. It then consults its PIT and sends the data packet toward the next hop by sending it to the interface established in the PIT entry for the content name in query. Following then, the content router discards the content name entry from its PIT.

12.6 Traffic Load in Network Caching

When an in-network caching is transparent and ubiquitous it can increase content availability and as a result, it reduces end-to-end latency as well as traffic load in an ICN. It also considerably reduces the workload on network capacity caused by fast growth in the traffic. Although caching has shown to be an effective strategy for reducing network load in the existing web and P2P networks, similar methods are not ideal for ICN for a variety of reasons. There is indeed a shortage of unique identification items on the web or existing Internet, which leads to the same object being identified under multiple names.

Because the content of the ICN is more important than the generator (or producer, to be more specific), content caching is a crucial concern. The more content is cached in the network, the higher the chance of having a low network load and low end-to-end delay. As a result, effective caching management is a major concern in ICN. In ICN, caching management is divided into two categories: cache replacement policies and cache permission policies. Cache permission policies, as well known as caching strategies, decide whether or not content should be cached and, if so, where the content should be stored. In contrast, if somehow the cache storage is saturated, cache replacement policy indicates which data should be erased from the cache to make room for new data.

The primary goal of caching data in a system is to improve content availability to end users by allowing content queries to be fulfilled via an intermediate cache rather than having to access the content source every time the content is required. Content retrieval delays can be considerably reduced by storing data in intermediary router caches. In the ICN architecture, caching has been implemented as an extra functionality. This feature can improve end-user Quality of Service (QoS),

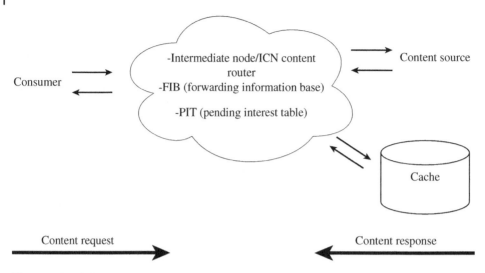

Figure 12.3 Traffic load in data caching.

drastically reduce network congestion, prevent Denial of Service (DoS) attacks, and increase data availability.

Figure 12.3 depicts the role of the cache when an end user queries a content. Whenever the instant content router gets an interest packet, it first stores the receiving requested information into the PIT table. Then it looks inside its own cache, which is shown in Figure 12.3 on the right-hand side, to verify if it has already cached the same packet. If it has, the query will be addressed by that cache to the receiver. The router will be able to determine the feedback path by consulting its PIT table. In the same way, all of ICN's intermediate content routers that possess cache. If any node request for the same material is made to that router in the future, it can now provide the relevant data to the end user without having to contact the content source. The duration of data retrieval is significantly reduced as a result of this activity. A content router is depicted in Figure 12.3, along with its numerous data structures.

12.6.1 Store Unique Naming of Content in Caches

ICN's primary requirement is content identification by name. To do this, each component of data must be given a unique name; otherwise, the same component may be cached under many names, resulting in content duplication. As a result, one of the most important problems in the efficacy of ICN caching is naming data uniquely. Due to the utilization of names instant of numbers, such as IP addresses, unique naming is incredibly challenging. Several proposals may be found in the literature, naming system is still not mature yet for a better ICN caching, an effective and appropriate content naming convention is still required. Apart from naming data, we also need to name several caches that exist within the network. Caches are named by referring to the name and type of the content router which includes in it. Cache naming must be unique in order to keep track of caches that contain the specific data that was requested by the end user. This information can be used to route future related data requests to that cache; for example, a content-based routing mechanism in ICN might be using the same name for the content router and the cache it holds. As a result, an accurate naming method for content is essential, and unique naming for each cache in ICN is also essential.

12.6.2 Storage Limitation in Caching Space Devices

It is self-evident that the Internet contains an endless amount of materials that users are expected to access. The ICN underlines the importance of naming each of these contents separately. On the other side, caching advises caching data in network nodes to enhance content access efficiency. To decrease data retrieval latency, the most common contents could be stored within in-network caches. Even if only the most common contents cached, the volume of this content is big and cannot be handled in network node caches. As a result, maintaining cache storage in ICN network nodes is another difficulty. Furthermore, because different forms of traffic seek for the same amount of storage space, cache management becomes extremely important. Many recent research papers have been published in the field of cache management, although more progress is still needed in this subject. The research presented here [7, 8] presents a perception into the problem as well as some potential alternatives. They claim that innovative and adaptive techniques can significantly boost the performance.

12.7 Content's Freshness Detection

Most of the time, the contents disposable on the Internet usually are dynamic in nature. However, this content dynamism is only represented in the data's source or provider. As a result, cached content may not be in the most recent condition or updated as it is in the original producer at the time of the request; hence, it is essential to identify or manage the staleness of a content in an ICN environment. Another difficult job in ICN caching is detecting the staleness of cached content, due to named content copies being widely distributed in in-network caches. For improved synchronization of data producers and in-network caching nodes, the ICN architecture should be capable of providing a staleness checking method. So far, the literatures have identified two significant techniques to resolving the staleness issue: direct and indirect methods to staleness verification or freshness determination. The direct method is ideal for some named contents, as it implies that each replica of the cached data includes a timestamp indicating when it was cached. This timestamp directly indicates the freshness of the cached content, depending on the dynamism of the data in the recent history, the cached data may be used or deleted as expired. The indirect method, on the other side, does not offer any basic information about its freshness, the data must be checked for staleness before being sent to a client. It occurs when it is difficult to establish the expiration period of a material in advance.

12.8 ICN Security

Video traffic is becoming more common on the Internet, the amount of video traffic is currently growing as a result of the development of mobile devices and the IoT. Any device in the IoT ecosystem can act as a provider, resulting in a many-to-many communication network. This expands the volume capacity of routing tables, perhaps resulting in inefficient data distribution. The ICN model originated from research on reliable content delivery and scalable Internet [9]. ICN stresses on a content-centric model in which identified content objects are separated from the hosts on which they exist [10]. Under the current host-centric architecture all hosts are specified by IP addresses and the queries for data are sent to the host where the data are stored. Content with a unique name can be hosted anywhere on the network.

ICN reduces transport latency while also posing a number of security concerns. DoS attacks, as well as many vulnerabilities in the scope of ICN, such as content poisoning, cache pollution, name assaults, and so on, are all security breaches in ICN. Various security threats may increase the effectiveness of retransmissions, resulting in a reduction in network throughput.

Different copies of the same material may be dispersed over the network in the ICN networking model. This requires a distinction between the security protocols applicable to standard host-centric networking and those applicable to ICN. In contrast with the standard host-centric networking, security in ICN cannot be limited just to the end points or storage source. It is necessary to develop new security measures that may be deployed to the content directly. Furthermore, security measures must be embedded into the architecture itself, rather than being applied as an afterthought.

Security measures for ICN diverge from those for typical host-centric networks. In ICN, content security is more important, while route security is less important than in the host-based networking architecture. Existing security risks, including as DoS, snooping, and impersonation attacks, are still present in ICN. As a result, solutions to these threats are both required and necessary to comprehend.

In this section several security challenges in ICN have been discussed. Several types of cyber-attacks that have been viewed: Secure Routing, Cache Pollution, Secure Naming, Secure Forwarding, Content Poisoning, Application Security, DoS attacks.

12.9   Attacks in ICN Architectures

Routing-related attacks, naming-related attacks, content provisioning attacks, and caching-related attacks are some of attacks that harm ICN architectures. Various cyberattacks are focused on disrupting ICN services. At this point, attackers establish illegal access, and the attacks eventually result in insufficient or inaccurate data delivery. These are some of the security issues that ICN architectures confront.

Key security concerns: ICN is differentiated from previous technologies in at least five ways. These qualities are listed below:
1. In ICN, security must be built into the architecture directly. In many host-centric systems, a distinct security layer is used as an overlay.
2. Any user has the ability to publish/subscribe any data. As a result, attackers can create erroneous publications and subscriptions.
3. In ICN structure the system is ubiquitous in the idea that any user is allowed to access any accessible copy from any place. Authorizing user access becomes more complicated as a result of this process.
4. There is no host identification in the ICN architecture. As a result, limiting user queries becomes challenging.
5. The requests are seen by many nodes in the network. As a result, there is a threat of losing privacy.

Key privacy concerns: In ICN, privacy threats are tied to routers, cached data, content names, content signatures, and users. These privacy risks are present in all ICN designs. Timing attacks, communication monitoring attacks, censorship and anonymity assaults, protocol attacks, and naming-signature privacy attacks are all examples of privacy attacks. An attacker uses a timing and communication monitoring technique to probe a router's cached material over time.

The attacker evaluates the cache's popularity by looking at the content, and the attacker also monitors the behavior of the requestor when it comes to content access. The importance of anonymous communication in ICN cannot be overstated. User's data and requested data can always be revealed if anonymity is not protected. This can be used to provide restriction in the future. Another type of privacy attack is a protocol assault, in which the attacker exploits design loopholes in the protocol level, and attackers also may take advantage of pitfalls in design features. The data's name and the signature are attached to a specific producer in ICN (publisher). The producer's privacy is jeopardized as a result of this fact.

ICN has a number of security problems that need to be solved. In ICN, there are a few attacks that are new in present-day. Such attacks had never happened before. Furthermore, these attacks had no apparent influence on existing network architectures. Furthermore, several threats that are common in other systems may also exist in ICN situations [11–15]. Following ICN attacks [16], taxonomy divides both new and existing attacks into four groups. These four types of attacks are as follows: routing, caching, naming, and other unrelated assaults. This ranking is based on the primary target of the attacker.

Although each attack is classified into only one area, it is significant to remember that an attack may have an impact on other classifications as well. For example, there are two types of attacks: unpopular request and flooding attacks, which both harm ICN routing and caching. The primary purpose of a flooding attack is to overburden and exhaust routing capabilities. As a result, the caching system is also affected by this attack.

Similarly, in an uncommon requests attack, the attacker's primary goal is to breach cache relevance, but the attack's impacts also harm the routing system. Next, we briefly discussed some of these cyberattacks:

1. **Naming-related attacks**: The data requests in ICN are broadcast to the network, and this fact elevates the risk of privacy violation. As user queries for certain content become more transparent, attackers' influence over data flow grows, and they can more easily block particular information exchange. In this type of attack, the attacker can block the circulation of a certain piece of content. This is accomplished by preventing the content to be transmitted [17, 18].
2. **Routing-related attacks**: Content distribution in the ICN is mainly reliant on asynchronous publication and subscription. The goal is to maintain data consistency across remote data versions. Jamming and timing are two routing-related attacks that try to disrupt information consistency. This may eventually result in undesired traffic flows, DoS could also be an outcome from these attacks. There are two other types of attacks: infrastructure and flooding. These attacks attempt to limit network hosts' resources, such as memory and processing power.
3. **Caching-related attacks**: Caching is one of the most key parts in ICN because it is responsible for transferring the nearest accessible copy of a requested data to a user. Receiver–sender caching is essential to the overall performance of the ICN network. The attacker may try to corrupt or poison the caching system in this type of attack [19–21].
4. **Content poisoning attacks**: As previously said, the whole focus of ICN is on data. In this kind of attack, the attacker attempts to load router caches with corrupt data. To carry out this attack, the attacker must have access control of one or more intervening routers; after establishing the connection the attacker can inject his or her own content into the network [22].
5. **Miscellaneous attacks**: The attackers in this category are attempting to downgrade some ICN services as well as gain unauthorized access. Such attacks eventually lead to limited and/or incorrect data distributions in the ICN [23].

12.10 ICN Attributes to Ensure Security Threats

There are several aspects that contribute for potential security violation in ICN. In-network caching, ubiquitous publication/subscription, location-independent naming, and state decorrelation are some of the factors that contribute to ICN vulnerabilities. These characteristics of ICN make it easier for attackers to undertake more difficult-to-detect attacks in networks. Because of these characteristics, attacks in the ICN might have a significant impact. The following points highlight the attributes of ICN that pose security threats.

- **Location-independent naming**: The contents of ICN are allocated among multiple nodes, some of which are not always reliable. This allows content to be retrieved from any place, even if it is an unknown or untrustworthy node. As a result, ICN requires a secure naming scheme to name contents regardless of their address or form.
- **Ubiquitous publication/subscription**: Any member, from any place, can connect to an ICN network. Furthermore, users can serve as content producers or consumers. As a result, some people may submit disagreeable content or even requests. Such actions may cause the networks overall disintegrate performance.
- **In-network caching**: Caching is very essential and noticeable in ICN. The features of ICN layouts benefit the consumers, while on the other hand, they present some obstacles. In ICN network nodes have the ability to cache any information that flows through it. Furthermore, in order to satisfy user requests, the data can be transferred from the nearest cache that contain the desired data, which is in the user's proximity. The requestor doesn't need to look for the data on the hosting server.
- **State decorrelation**: Two asynchronous phases predominate in ICN: request routing and content delivery. Between these two stages, there must be a stability in ICN. If the configuration consistency fails, it could result in a DoS or unexpected traffic congestion.

12.11 Traffic Analysis and Prediction

Network traffic prediction enhances the stability of a high-quality communication network in advance. Traffic prediction is beneficial in a variety of ways, including effective data management in network routers, power conservation and QoS provisioning in wireless sensor networks (WSN). Due to the high computational demands to handle high traffic, the Internet routers adopt traffic prediction to conserve electricity. The more data flows, the more processors are demanded and the more complex the system becomes. As a consequence of these factors in the routers, more power is consumed. High power consumption necessitates a costly cooling system, which raises operational costs. In order to save power, appropriately forecasted network traffic allows these core routers to turn down superfluous extra processors during low traffic times. Traffic prediction also aids in the optimum utilization of network resources. Accurately estimated network traffic at access points aids in the provision of high-quality services to end users through resource allocation. WSN may take advantage from traffic prediction as well, as it consumes less energy. In low-traffic or no-activity intervals, the nodes turn into a sleep mode, it can extend WSN lifetime dramatically. Unusual traffic patterns caused by intruder or hacker can also be detected using machine learning (ML) algorithms. It primarily aids intrusion detection systems (IDS) or intrusion prevention systems (IPS) by detecting DoS or Distributed Denial of Service (DDoS) attacks before they cause any serious damage on the system. Furthermore, any typical congestion caused by a surge in user requests might affect the system management. To deal with such unpredictable network traffic behavior, the ML algorithm aids network administrators to a large extent. Such machine learning algorithms ensure proactive prediction with good precision, allowing the system to anticipate for a traffic jam. As a result, there is less network congestion and retransmission, lowering network overburden. In the deficiency of effective forecasting, it would only be noticed after a crisis had occurred, resulting in significant transmission errors and latency. Routing is an elementary function in the network operations, and significant study has been done on a wide range of topics, spanning the network's area, wireless networks, Internet service provider (ISP) networks, data centers, and interdomain routing via Border Gateway Protocol (BGP). Route optimization, in generally, addresses an unknown element regarding the upcoming traffic patterns from one of the following methods: Optimization of route setups based on previously analyzed traffic patterns, as well as optimization based on potential traffic patterns. However, in the most of cases, optimizing routing configurations for a certain traffic pattern fails to provide a satisfactory result. Machine learning suggests that knowledge about previous traffic patterns be used to generate effective routing designs in the future. Although the precise future traffic requirements are unknown for a decision maker, it is a reasonable assumption that previous traffic requirements contain information about the future, such as traffic skewness and changes in traffic patterns over time. As a result, a machine learning technique monitors traffic flows on a frequent basis and adapts routing strategies based on future projections.

12.12 Some Key Problem Statements

In terms of security and data integrity, the ICN paradigm is still dealing with several challenges. One of these challenges is the possibility of information being altered when a publisher registers their material in ICN nodes. Additionally, the network will experience additional lag when a malicious ICN node refuses to forward data to other ICN nodes or users.

Although the ICN model is a promising approach that addresses a variety of current Internet problems, it is still ineffective in terms of security. Although the ICN paradigm lays a high priority on security, it nevertheless has a number of problems that compromise both its performance and security resilience, including the following:

- The majority of ICN models employ public-key cryptography-based self-certifying naming. This kind of naming method suggests several problems, such as key compromise, and it requires a third party to handle it through public key management;
- ICN might have many users publishing the identical data content, which would compromise processing, mining (verification), and storage resources on ICN nodes. Replicated material from many sources will likewise compromise ownership integrity and obscure the true owner;
- When malicious users clog the cache with unpopular content, the real request will take longer to process which is called cache pollution. Moreover, cache pollution will have an influence on the cache performance in ICN nodes since replicated data will reserve numerous unused spaces in the cache;
- Access control and how to safely govern the process of publishers joining ICN should also be considered.

Due to some characteristics like decentralization, immutability, consensus-based, and timestamp-based, blockchain technology has the potential to be a useful tool for overcoming ICN limits and addressing these ICN security challenges.

12.13   Blockchain-Based ICN Scheme Improvement

ICN begins the design process by taking security into consideration. Its security model, known as intrinsic security, is connected to the data and naming scheme [24]. A significant piece of technology in realizing the design of ICN is public key cryptosystems. The public key infrastructures (PKIs) [25] were the most widely used method of managing and distributing public keys in the original design. The evolution of ICN architecture and naming design has drawn attention to this approach's inadaptability. ICN is a massively distributed system; hence, the centralized PKI model severely restricts its ability to grow and maintain security [26]. Furthermore, academicians have given identity-based cryptography (IBC) and recommendation networks more consideration.

The following are some key improvements broadcast (BC) might make to the ICN structure:

- A decentralized and safe alternative to public key authentication in ICN is to employ a secure identification method that binds users' genuine identities based on blockchain without disclosing their privacy to partially trusted nodes;
- Publishers and subscribers build a trust connection based on public key cryptography in order to accomplish dependable asynchronous data transmission in an untrusted network environment.
- A public key management schemes to ensure network security.

ICN achieves high speed and low latency data distribution by separating content identifiers from network addresses.

Through the employment of an identity-based signature (IBS), the authentication of the data source is combined with a distributed system. The recommended process can only be used in small group settings and implies a certain level of confidence between group members. As a result, IBSs cannot be applied as an authentication method in scenarios involving large-scale network applications. Another method to improve this escrow problem and share the key with a large group scenario is implementing attribute-based encryption (ABE). This way allows us to expand our network application.

12.13.1   Protection Against DDos

DDos yields web resources inaccessible by sending a large number of fake packages to overload the traffic flow, making it one of the most popular techniques used by hackers to shut down servers, routes, and networks. By employing blockchain technology, this security risk can be mitigated because there is no single point of verification and several nodes are participating in the process of validation.

The amount of attacks and the number of nodes an attacker can break in a brief period of time are only two examples of the many elements that need be taken into consideration in order to be protected against DDos. Numerous nodes work together to verify information. Because blockchain is decentralized, it is difficult to hack and compromise several distinct nodes in a short period of time; doing so requires a synchronized attack and strong computational skills.

12.14   A Secured Information-Centric Network Based on Blockchain

A vital challenge in ICN is how to guarantee reliable content transmission and transparency. Users must certify that the data they received originated from a legitimate source rather than a spoofing attacker. To develop a technique of identification that connects the data packet to its producer, public key cryptography was proposed. PKIs, IBSs, and recommendation networks are the most prominent approaches for ensuring the authenticity and accessibility keys in the current prototypes.

The decentralized public key infrastructure (DPKI) is a potential solution to the security and scalability challenges that centralized PKI schemes have. Developing a DPKI-based distributed authentication scheme with ICN that incorporates CCN and blockchain can provide effective, trustworthy, and robust support for the adoption of a distributed public key authentication method for the ICN infrastructure.

With blockchain's distributed ledger technologies and smart contract, the system enables a distributed management and key validation; furthermore, users can use the reliable information to validate their identity. In this method, the blockchain consensus nodes automatically verify the users' exact identification when they apply for a trustworthy registration process.

12.14.1 Blockchain-Based ICN Structure

The purpose of merging CCN and blockchain is to establish a decentralized key exchange protocol (DPKI) on an ICN that allows other peers to access and verify the authenticity and attributes over an encrypted data exchange. The deployment of certificates, as well as data compilation and processing, as well as the modification, permission, and installation of new and old device certificate libraries are all operations of DPKI processes. Blockchain is employed as the core framework to transmit data distributed consistency to the network.

A Blockchain-based ICN network consists of several elements: subscribers, publishers, fast name resolution system (NRS), content router with cache storage (R), and content servers (CSs) nodes, as shown in Figure 12.4. They all work together to support confidence in Blockchain-based ICN architecture, which has the functionalities of reliable name mapping and detectable content delivery.

To transfer data content, the publisher who intends to deliver its content to the subscriber should first generate a unique naming for the content. If there is a new user and wants to participate in the network, sharing contents, the user first must upload the unique name to the blockchain to be able to conduct a transaction. After the name is verified, the NRS will be open to the publisher for registration. The query and transfer messages also carry with unique name or content, depending on the demands of the publisher's and subscriber purpose. As Figure 12.4 shows, the publisher sends the register message to the nearest nodes (NRS/user node/R/CS) and the nearest node propagates the message to another nodes.

All of the conducted transactions that contain the behaviors of the ICN node are submitted to the blockchain network and evaluated against any illegal behavior. A replica of the data is stored by each blockchain node. As a result, any ICN node that has been validated by the blockchain cannot reject or refuse transactions that have been approved by majority of blockchain nodes. When a transaction is found to be contradictory, it will be removed immediately. The secure provision of data in ICN is ensured by blockchain features like non-repudiation and non-tampering.

12.14.1.1 Data Integrity

The non-tampering and verifiable data structure of the blockchain is support by all nodes. S. Nakamoto recommended that Bitcoin be run on the fully decentralized Internet [27]. Blocks are produced in time sequence by default, and each block contains transactions that record asset transfers.

Because data can be altered, tempered, or even destroyed, traditional ICN systems can suffer from a shortage of data protection. Because information (transactions) is verified and validated by

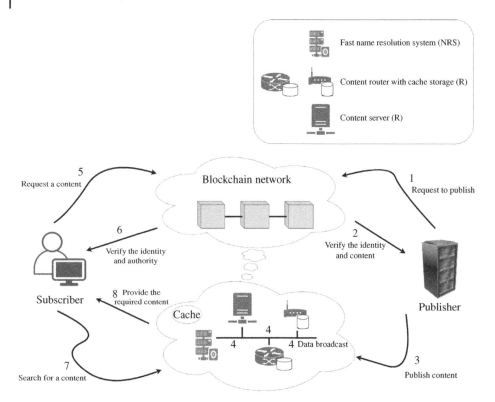

Figure 12.4 ICN based on blockchain architecture.

all the majority nodes in blockchain, data in blockchain are difficult to be altered or removed. This procedure is based on the fact that each transaction in the blockchain has a hash value, it is linked to a block with a hash number, and each block is linked to the last block's hash number as we see in Figure 12.5. Consequently, any alteration in the content will affect the block hash to differ from the previously confirmed block hash, as well as the other hashes from another blocks. As a result, any modifications made by the miners are easily noticed.

When a user requests data, the publisher adds their material to the ICN via transactions, which is then confirmed and archived in the block. Each transaction represents a publisher that wants to add new content into the system. After the transaction been verified the BC system uses a secure Hash Algorithm to sign the transaction into a block (mining the block) and distribute it to nodes in the system.

12.15 Attribute-Based Encryption Scheme for the Information-Centric Network

The growth of the ICN denotes a shift in the way that content is shared and information is exchanged. Additionally, ICN's requirements for data security differ from those of traditional IoT [28, 29]. It is necessary to safeguard the confidentiality of the shared content in an ICN network [30–32]. Data access control is a useful tool for promoting safe data sharing. The security of the conventional access control mechanism is entirely dependent on the administrator and requires a delegation administrator to manage access privilege. But the widely dispersed and pervasive

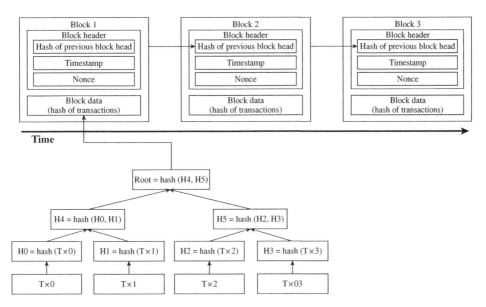

Figure 12.5 Block structure.

ICN environment forces the need for a more scalable and adaptable access control method [33]. Fortunately, ABE can offer precise ciphertext access control for ICN as a security cryptosystem. ABE offers a one-to-many encryption scheme, in contrast to other types of cryptography including symmetric and asymmetric cryptography. This suggests that a set of multiple secret keys can be used to decrypt an ABE ciphertext, increasing ABE's scalability and versatility.

ABE's flexible and expressive access policy, which is used to represent fine-grained data access privilege, is by far its most appealing feature. Furthermore, a scalable method of managing the access policy is possible [34]. The intricate policy, however, also results in significant ciphertext redundancy.

In this section, we approach a compact ABE for ICN scheme to compact the policy scale and reduce ciphertext redundancy.

The main contributions that ABE can bring to ICN are:

- Share the access policy and public attribute ciphertext units with public parties to reduce the redundancy of the ciphertext;
- Offer a sizable pool of data several levels of data protection and privacy;
- **Collusion-resistance**: A key-holding adversary should only be permitted access to data if at least one specific key authorizes it;
- Find a solution to the one-to-many encryption's secrecy issue.

12.15.1 Applying Ciphertext-Policy ABE (CP-ABE) Scheme in ICN

Collusion-resistance is an essential security attribute of ABE. It assures that a dishonest user, who collaborates with other users, can only obtain information that this dishonest user can decrypt with their own private key. The secret data are protected with an access policy; meanwhile, user keys are assigned with a set of attributes and the encryption function establishes a shared secret key for data access policy. A user key assigned with a set of attributes involves one or several key elements for each attribute. If a user's private key matches the access policy's parameters, the shared secret data can be generated by integrating the required key and ciphertext components for the attributes associated. Consequently, to decrypt various data with one user private key, different key attributes will be used to assign it. In order to perform ABE on the peer's data, the following sequence of operations is performed:

- **Setup** $(1^\lambda) \rightarrow (msk, pp)$: It takes a security parameter 1^λ and returns a master secret key msk and public parameters pp.
- **Enc** $(m, pp, \mathbb{A}) \rightarrow ct$: It takes message m, public parameters pp, and an access structure $\mathbb{A}$. It outputs the ciphertext ct.
- **KeyGen** $(pp, msk, S) \rightarrow sk_\mathbb{A}$: It takes public parameters pp, master secret key msk, and a set of attributes S. It output a secret key sk_S.
- **Dec** $(pp, ct, \mathbf{sk})$: It takes public parameters pp, ciphertext ct, and secret key sk and returns a message m or $\perp$.

$$\left[m = m^* \left| \begin{array}{l} pp, msk \leftarrow \textbf{Setup}(1^\lambda) \\ ct \leftarrow \textbf{Enc}(pp, m, \mathbb{A}) \\ sk \leftarrow \textbf{KeyGen}(pp, msk, S) \\ m^* \leftarrow \textbf{Dec}(pp, ct, sk) \end{array} \right. \right]$$

12.15.2 System Design of CP-ABE Scheme in ICN

Whenever a user wants to interact with an ICN Application (a software program that allows users to share content using the ICN framework) to construct a group, a confidential content sharing is launched. The generation of a member identification (a private key) and the transfer of this key to the users are both steps included in the adding user's stage. It is vital to provide a secure way for transfer the keys.

The workflow of resilient content sharing groups is represented in Figure 12.6 (architecture general), with the group's setup and enrollment administration highlighted. Its reliable content access control in ICN is based on the idea that each user can operate as both a provider and a purchaser of content, and it tries to keep cost to a minimal.

Group creation: The admin starts the procedure by connecting with the ICN application, as mentioned before (phase 1 in Figure 12.6). This procedure generates a pairing of public and master keys to the group, which is accomplished with the service of the CP-ABE module. After this the public key is broadcast in the network as an asset with the group name as an id (phase 2). The administrator must keep the master key confidential. Each group has its own set of attributes that are applied to classify the representants.

Adding users to the group: The administrator launches this operation by providing the additional member's attributes across the ICN interface (phase 4). This method is split into three processes:
1. Generating the user's private key inside the group;
2. Sharing the key in the subnet, so the new add user could receive and decrypt the data;
3. Acquiring the key through the network is the first step.

The private key is established in the first phase with the help of the CP-ABE component. The administrator must designate an attribute set for the user to achieve this. The master group key is also necessary for the establishment of the private key. The second step phase involves publishing the private key (together with the added properties) on the network so that the intended user can access it. Since having a private key materializes group membership, the delivery must take place in private. In other words, the private key is used to access protected content shared among group

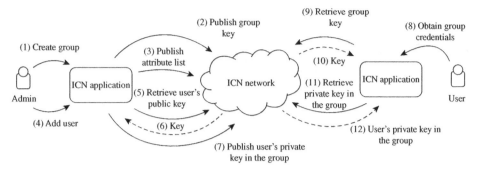

Figure 12.6 CP-ABE in ICN design.

members. The administrator must obtain the user's public key from the network and utilize a PKI mechanism to verify it in order to carry out this delivery (phases 5 and 6). The user's public key is used to encrypt the private key, resulting in the encrypted key, which is then broadcast as a network object (phase 7).

The target user must get the group's public key and the group's private key from the network in the third step before using them to publish to or consume material from the group. The user selects the group he wants to join at the beginning of this process (phase 8). The application then receives the user's encrypted private key in the group along with the group's public key (phases 9 and 10) (phases 11 and 12). Using their own private key, the user decrypts the group's private key. From this point on, the user is able to publish and access group content.

Content publication: Figure 12.7 illustrates the dynamics of a content publishing process. The user initiates this process by interacting with the ICN application (phase 1 in Figure 12.7), by informing the content to be published. Subsequently, five steps are carried out at this time. In order to provide the user with the most recent group attribute list, the program first turns to the network (phases 2 and 3). Then, the user creates an access policy, according to the desired access restrictions (phases 4 and 5). The third step, carried out by the application, consists in encrypting the content using a symmetric key. The fourth phase entails, as was previously mentioned, building the enabling block of the content. The protected content is constructed in the final phase, encasing the encrypted content and the identifier for the enablement block. Finally, the network publishes the enabling block along with the protected content (phases 6 and 7).

Content retrieval: The retrieval process, illustrated in Figure 12.8, initiates when the user requests a content (phase 1). The application requests to the network the corresponding protected content (phases 2 and 3), which is obtained from the nearest source. When opening, the application identifies which enabler block is related to that content (through the identifier contained in the tuple).

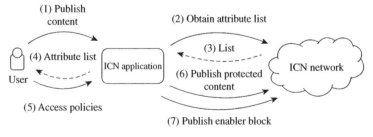

Figure 12.7 Data publication process.

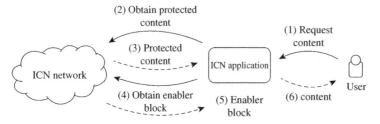

Figure 12.8 Data retrieval process.

The encrypted symmetric key is then requested by the application from the network (phases 4 and 5). The CP-ABE component receives the returned key and begins the decryption process. The user uses his or her own private key within the group to accomplish this. If the attributes used by the group administrator and the access policy used to encrypt the key are compatible, the key is decrypted (when adding the user to the group). If it is successfully decrypted, the user receives the plain content (phase 6).

References

1 Jacobson, V., Smetters, D.K., Thornton, J.D. et al. (2009). Networking named content. *Proceedings of the 5th International Conference on Emerging Networking Experiments and Technologies*, pp. 1–12.

2 Carofiglio, G., Gallo, M., and Muscariello, L. (2012). Joint hop-by-hop and receiver-driven interest control protocol for content-centric networks. *ACM SIGCOMM Computer Communication Review* 42 (4): 491–496.

3 Zhang, M., Luo, H., and Zhang, H. (2015). A survey of caching mechanisms in information-centric networking. *IEEE Communications Surveys & Tutorials* 17 (3): 1473–1499.

4 Wong, W. and Nikander, P. (2010). Secure naming in information-centric networks. *Proceedings of the Re-Architecting the Internet Workshop*, pp. 1–6.

5 Saxena, D., Raychoudhury, V., Suri, N. et al. (2016). Named data networking: a survey. *Computer Science Review* 19: 15–55.

6 Zhang, L., Estrin, D., Burke, J. et al. (2010). Named Data Networking (NDN) Project. Relatório Técnico NDN-0001, Xerox Palo Alto Research Center-PARC, 157:158.

7 Psaras, I., Chai, W.K., and Pavlou, G. (2012). Probabilistic in-network caching for information-centric networks. *Proceedings of the Second Edition of the ICN Workshop on Information-Centric Networking*, pp. 55–60.

8 Chai, W.K., He, D., Psaras, I., and Pavlou, G. (2013). Cache "less for more" in information-centric networks (extended version). *Computer Communications* 36 (7): 758–770.

9 Ghodsi, A., Shenker, S., Koponen, T. et al. (2011). Information-centric networking: seeing the forest for the trees. *Proceedings of the 10th ACM Workshop on Hot Topics in Networks*, pp. 1–16.

10 Tyson, G., Sastry, N., Rimac, I. et al. (2012). A survey of mobility in information-centric networks: challenges and research directions. *Proceedings of the 1st ACM Workshop on Emerging Name-Oriented Mobile Networking Design-Architecture, Algorithms, and Applications*, pp. 1–16.

11 La Polla, M., Martinelli, F., and Sgandurra, D. (2012). A survey on security for mobile devices. *IEEE Communications Surveys & Tutorials* 15 (1): 446–471.

12 Mpitziopoulos, A., Gavalas, D., Konstantopoulos, C., and Pantziou, G. (2009). A survey on jamming attacks and countermeasures in WSNs. *IEEE Communications Surveys & Tutorials* 11 (4): 42–56.

13 Igure, V.M. and Williams, R.D. (2008). Taxonomies of attacks and vulnerabilities in computer systems. *IEEE Communications Surveys & Tutorials* 10 (1): 6–19.

14 Xiao, Z. and Xiao, Y. (2012). Security and privacy in cloud computing. *IEEE Communications Surveys & Tutorials* 15 (2): 843–859.

15 Hansman, S. and Hunt, R. (2005). A taxonomy of network and computer attacks. *Computers & Security* 24 (1): 31–43.

16 AbdAllah, E.G., Hassanein, H.S., and Zulkernine, M. (2015). A survey of security attacks in information-centric networking. *IEEE Communications Surveys & Tutorials* 17 (3): 1441–1454.

17 Dannewitz, C., Golic, J., Ohlman, B., and Ahlgren, B. (2010). Secure naming for a network of information. *2010 INFOCOM IEEE Conference on Computer Communications Workshops*, pp. 1–6. IEEE.

18 Arianfar, S., Koponen, T., Raghavan, B., and Shenker, S. (2011). On preserving privacy in content-oriented networks. *Proceedings of the ACM SIGCOMM Workshop on Information-Centric Networking*, pp. 19–24.

19 Xie, M., Widjaja, I., and Wang, H. (2012). Enhancing cache robustness for content-centric networking. *2012 Proceedings IEEE INFOCOM*, pp. 2426–2434. IEEE.

20 Mohaisen, A., Zhang, X., Schuchard, M. et al. (2013). Protecting access privacy of cached contents in information centric networks. *Proceedings of the 8th ACM SIGSAC Symposium on Information, Computer and Communications Security*, pp. 173–178.

21 Ghali, C., Tsudik, G., and Uzun, E. (2014). Needle in a haystack: mitigating content poisoning in named-data networking. *Proceedings of NDSS Workshop on Security of Emerging Networking Technologies (SENT)*, pp. 1–10.

22 Tourani, R., Misra, S., Mick, T., and Panwar, G. (2017). Security, privacy, and access control in information-centric networking: a survey. *IEEE Communications Surveys & Tutorials* 20 (1): 566–600.

23 Fotiou, N., Marias, G.F., and Polyzos, G.C. (2012). Access control enforcement delegation for information-centric networking architectures. *Proceedings of the Second Edition of the ICN Workshop on Informationcentric Networking*, pp. 85–90.

24 Chen, Z., Meng, H.W., and Guan, Z. (2016). Research on intrinsic security in future internet architecture. *Journal of Cybersecurity* 1: 10–13.

25 Vehovar, V. (2004). *The Internet Encyclopedia*, vol. 2. Wiley.

26 Fayazbakhsh, S.K., Lin, Y., Tootoonchian, A. et al. (2013). Less pain, most of the gain: incrementally deployable ICN. *ACM SIGCOMM Computer Communication Review* 43 (4): 147–158.

27 Eyal, I., Gencer, A.E., Sirer, E.G., and Renesse, R.V. (2016). Bitcoin-NG: a scalable blockchain protocol. *13th USENIX Symposium on Networked Systems Design and Implementation (NSDI 16)*, pp. 45–59.

28 Shahzad, A., Lee, M., Lee, C. et al. (2016). The protocol design and new approach for SCADA security enhancement during sensors broadcasting system. *Multimedia Tools and Applications* 75 (22): 14641–14668.

29 Shahzad, A., Landry, R., Lee, M. et al. (2016). A new cellular architecture for information retrieval from sensor networks through embedded service and security protocols. *Sensors* 16 (6): 821.

30 Shahzad, A., Lee, M., Kim, H.D. et al. (2015). New security development and trends to secure the SCADA sensors automated transmission during critical sessions. *Symmetry* 7 (4): 1945–1980.

31 Wu, Z., Xiong, N., Huang, Y., and Gu, Q. (2014). Optimal service distribution in WSN service system subject to data security constraints. *Sensors* 14 (8): 14180–14209.

32 Xiong, N., Wu, Z., Huang, Y., and Xu, D. (2014). Analyzing comprehensive QoS with security constraints for services composition applications in wireless sensor networks. *Sensors* 14 (12): 22706–22736.

33 Anggorojati, B., Mahalle, P.N., Prasad, N.R., and Prasad, R. (2012). Capability-based access control delegation model on the federated IoT network. *The 15th International Symposium on Wireless Personal Multimedia Communications*, pp. 604–608. IEEE.

34 (a) Wang, J., Huang, C., Xiong, N.N., and Wang, J. (2018). Blocked linear secret sharing scheme for scalable attribute based encryption in manageable cloud storage system. *Information Sciences* 424: 1–26; (b) Afolabi, I., Taleb, T., Samdanis, K. et al. (2018). Network slicing and softwarization: a survey on principles, enabling technologies, and solutions. *IEEE Communications Surveys & Tutorials* 20 (3): 2429–2453.

13

Subscriber Data Management System Based on Blockchain

13.1 Introduction

In the past few years, data has become the most significant asset for Information and Communication Technology (ICT) and many other industrial sectors in the information-oriented digital world. Large volumes of data are gathered and distributed by many service providers across several technical disciplines [1, 2]. Data is a company's most important asset. The knowledge necessary to make sound judgments and take appropriate actions is dependent on useful facts. A firm may grow if its data is useful, relevant, comprehensive, and up to date. Otherwise, it is a pointless and resource-wasting product for the company. Companies who do not appreciate the value of data use will most likely fail to thrive in the present economic climate since the modern marketplace is data-driven. Business executives want data to understand market trends based on facts and numbers. They need to obtain the correct information at the right time to make the right decisions for the business's success [3].

Government legislatures have established rules and regulations on subscriber privacy and data protection in recent years, as public awareness of personal privacy protection has grown. The European Parliament's General Data Protection Regulation (GDPR) went into force in EU member states on 25 May 2018 [1]. This rule has a very broad reach, and it applies to any institution that collects, transmits, maintains, or processes personal information involving all EU Member States. The data providers (DPs) must maintain personal data in such a way that data subscribers (DSs) (which can be a data owner [DO] or a data user [DU]) own and control their personal data, including the rights to access personal data, update or delete stored data, authorize access, and query access records. A binding legislative act on processing data with regard to DPs, as an organization processing personal data on behalf of DSs. Subscriber data management (SDM) is a critical network function offered by mobile communication systems. SDM network functions and databases gather and analyze a range of data for subscriber authentication and service authorization. Telecommunication service providers are required to comply with data protection regulations since collecting, storing, and utilizing customers' personal data is required for the provision of telecommunication services [2].

Moreover, traditional SDM systems have a centralized storage design, which results in DOs having no control over the data. Large websites, for example, gather not just personal information like users' hobbies and browsing histories, but also personal privacy data, posing significant dangers to personal privacy security. As a result, the DO's control over the data must be strengthened, and it must be determined if other users have the right to access the data. Despite government legislatures, in order to meet their needs, businesses must purchase data from other businesses. However, there are several other reasons why firms fear sharing their data with others, despite the fact that

Attribute-based Encryption (ABE): Foundations and Applications within Blockchain and Cloud Environments, First Edition.
Qi Xia, Jianbin Gao, Isaac Amankona Obiri, Kwame Omono Asamoah, and Daniel Adu Worae.
© 2024 The Institute of Electrical and Electronics Engineers, Inc. Published 2024 by John Wiley & Sons, Inc.

it is a profitable strategy. These reasons are privacy, security, access control, data governance, data owners' selfish conduct, and a lack of adequate business models and rules to optimize data owners' revenue.

Many scholars have proposed various data-sharing models to address these challenges. The combination of attribute-based encryption (ABE) and blockchain is one of these suggested solutions suitable for resolving these challenges [4–8]. ABE schemes such as ciphertext policy-attribute-based encryption (CP-ABE) [9] and key policy-attribute-based encryption (KP-ABE) [10] were introduced to allow the convergence of data privacy protection with access control. The user's private key and ciphertext are both defined by a set of attributes in the ABE mechanism, and the user can successfully decrypt the plaintext only when the number of attribute intersections between the attribute set connected with the user's private key linked with the ciphertext reaches the system's threshold value. Satoshi Nakamoto introduced blockchain technology, a distributed and decentralized ledger, in 2018 [11]. It is a series of data chunks that are created and linked chronologically. Blockchain technology is a peer-to-peer (P2P) network consisting of a distributed ledger, a consensus mechanism, and smart contracts. However, several flaws and weaknesses exist in blockchain technology, with storage being one of the most significant [12].

13.1.1 Motivation

Data sharing has now become critical in practically every aspect of life. Blockchain-based data-sharing models are gaining popularity because they make data safe and trustworthy while also protecting it and specifying different degrees of access. The goal of this work is to investigate the data management strategy for a secure data sharing network systems and to create a secure SDM scheme, supporting distributed ledger technologies (DLTs) such as blockchain as the trust anchor for Authentication, Authorization, ABE smart contracts for Access control (AAA), and interplanetary file system (IPFS) (i.e. made up of distributed hash table [DHT] for data storage).

13.1.2 Problem Statement

Data sharing necessitates close interaction between a range of entities and subscriber data, which introduces a number of threats, including security, privacy, access control, decentralization (single point of failure), immutability, decentralized storage, and so on. Furthermore, past studies did not thoroughly study the particular policy management processes that are at the heart of guaranteeing confidence between the DSs and DPs.

13.1.3 Contributions

1. This chapter highlights certain authentication and authorization mechanisms based on data access and enforces policy-based data access control based on Blockchain (i.e. smart contracts) and CP-ABE. As a result, it achieves a mix of fine-grained access control and efficient data sharing.
2. We also present an IPFS data storage that stores raw data in order to prevent blockchain storage congestion problems.
3. This work also highlights a comprehensive set of SDM transactions to guarantee that all information logs and raw data is maintained in a tamper-proof distributed ledger.

13.2   Literature Review

The authors of [13] proposed a decentralized personal data management system that ensures users' control and ownership over their data, with blockchain acting as an automatic access-control manager instead of a third party. Following the implementation of GDPR, authors of [14] presented a personal data management scheme that allows data owners to regulate access and log all data activities by utilizing blockchain and smart contract technology. Similarly, a system for data collecting and safe data sharing for mobile crowd-sensing by merging blockchain with deep reinforcement learning was presented by authors of [15]. They employed blockchain technology to transfer data among mobile terminals with varying levels of security.

Moreover, authors in [16] suggested a dynamic access control approach based on blockchain technology and CP-ABE. The time attribute is used to provide dynamic data access, and only a user whose attribute fulfills the access control policy within the defined period can access the data. To eliminate a single point of failure and data manipulation, authors of [17] suggested an attribute-based access control system that employs a set of characteristics to define devices and tracks the distribution of attributes on the chain. Furthermore, this technique simplifies the access control protocol by utilizing signature technology and hash operations. While the approaches presented in these research can accomplish data access control, including fine-grained access control, there are still constraints in blockchain storage.

Therefore, to help solve this problem authors of [18] presented a blockchain-based safe data-sharing network. The suggested model utilizes IPFS to securely store the data. The suggested concept stores metadata in IPFS, which is further separated into sectors. In the proposed paradigm, users are authenticated using digital signatures. After the data has been successfully shared among the approved individuals, they are prompted to update their reviews. Users are then motivated based on the network reviews they have updated. The authors of [19] presented a data-sharing paradigm based on the IPFS, the Ethereum blockchain, and ABE technologies. The model's primary goal was to enable data privacy and fine-grained access control. Furthermore, the keyword search feature in the decentralized storage system's encrypted text was built, and the problem of the cloud server not delivering proper search results was resolved. However, the scheme did not specify how users' permissions may be revoked in order to amend access policies.

13.3   System Design Description

This section will go through the specifics of the system assumptions, system components such as DSs, DPs, IPFS distributed storage, and the blockchain platform.

13.3.1   Assumptions

All methods are based on the following assumptions:

1. All system participants are curious but honest.
2. Our system employs both symmetric and asymmetric cryptography for encryption and digital signatures, which serve as proof of identity. Key generation and distribution center (KGDC) is a trusted entity.
3. Subscribers (DOs, DUs) and DPs have finished initial authentication with the blockchain system and a pair of private and public keys $\{P_{pub}, P_{priv}\}$ has been issued. The transactional logs are recorded on the blockchain network.

4. The DPs create the control access policy using the CP-ABE method. Only when the DSs' attribute set matches the policy's requirements can the data be accessed by DSs.
5. All operations are stated without any exceptions, such as an invalid signature or authorization. When the blockchain platform or IPFS distributed network detects irregular access, it will immediately provide a message stating that access has been prohibited.

13.3.2 Ciphertext-Policy Attribute-Based Encryption (CP-ABE)

The sender uses a collection of attributes $\mathcal{A}$ to encrypt the message in the general ABE method, while the receiver uses a set of attributes $\mathcal{A}'$ to characterize the identity matching to the private key. The message recipient can decode the ciphertext only when the intersection number of $\mathcal{A}'$ and $\mathcal{A}$ reaches the system's threshold value t. This method, however, is constrained by access control mechanisms that can only support the threshold policy. Similarly, the ciphertext of CP-ABE [9] is linked to access control, and the key is linked to the attribute set. It can only be decrypted if the user's attribute set matches this access control structure. Furthermore, the message sender controls the CP-ABE access control authority. As a result, the CP-ABE encryption strategy can be used to secure the data owner's control over the data and to achieve fine-grained data access control.

13.3.3 CP-ABE Construction

1. **Setup:** The setup algorithm chooses a bilinear group of order $N = p_1 p_2 p_3$. G_{p_i} represents the subgroup of order p_i in G. The setup algorithm Setup(λ) runs $(N = p_1 p_2 p_3, G, G_T, e) \leftarrow \mathcal{G}$. Next, it chooses randomly $\{\alpha, a, \kappa\} \xleftarrow{R} Z_N$ and a random group element $g \in G_{p_1}$. For every attribute $i\mathcal{U}$, it selects a random element $h_i \in Z_N$. Finally, the setup algorithm returns the public parameters pp as:

$$pp = \{N, g, g^a, g^\kappa, \ldots, e(g,g)^\alpha, H_i = g^{h_i} \forall i\} \tag{13.1}$$

The secret master key MSK is:

$$MSK = \{g^\alpha, g_3\} \tag{13.2}$$

Note: g_3 is a generator of G_{p_3}.

2. **KeyGen**(PP, MSK, S): The algorithm computes a secret key associated with attribute set S that enables the user to decrypt encrypted message only if the key satisfies the access structure $\mathbb{A}$. The algorithm selects random elements $t, u, \in Z_N$ and $R, R', R'', \{R_i\}_{iS} \in G_{p3}$. The secret key SK_S is returned as:

$$SK_S = \begin{cases} k = g^\alpha g^{at} g^{\kappa u} R \\ k' = g^u R' \\ k'' = g^t R'', \ K_i = H_i^t R_i \forall_i \in S \end{cases} \tag{13.3}$$

3. **Enc**((A, ρ), PP, M): To encrypt a message $m \in G_T$ under access structure A an $\ell \times n$ matrix and ρ a map from each row A_j of A to an attribute $\rho(j)$, the encryption algorithm selects a random vector $v \in Z_N^n$, denoted $v = (s, v_2, \ldots, v_n)$. For every row A_j of A, it selects a random $r_j \in Z_N$. The ciphertext is (we also include (A, ρ)) in the ciphertext, here it is omitted) as:

$$C_T = \begin{cases} C_0 = me(g,g)^{\alpha s} \\ C = g^s \\ C' = (g^\kappa)^\kappa \\ C_j = (g^a)^{A_j \cdot v} H_{\rho(j)}^{-r_j} \\ D_j = g^{r_j} \forall_j \in [\ell] \end{cases} \tag{13.4}$$

(The notation $[\ell]$ denotes the set $\{1, \dots, \ell\}$.)

4. **Dec**(PP, C_T, SK_S): Given a ciphertext C_T and decryption key SK_S, first the key holder checks if $S \in (A, \rho)$. If not the output is empty. If $S \in (A, \rho)$, then the key holder computes constants $\omega_j \in Z_N$ with $\sum_{\rho(j) \in S} \omega_j A_j = (1, 0, \dots, 0)$. It the computes

$$e(C, K)e(C', K')^{-1} \Big/ \prod_{\rho(j) \in S} \left(e(C_j, K'')e(D_j, K_{\rho(j)})_j^\omega = e(g,g)^{\alpha s} \right) \tag{13.5}$$

Eventually, the message M is retrieved as $C_0/e(g,g)^{\alpha,s}$.

Correctness: We observe that $e(C, K)e(C', K')^{-1} = e(g,g)^{\alpha,s}e(g,g)^{sat}$. For every $j, e(C_j, K'')$ $e(D_j, K_{\rho(j)}) = e(g,g)^{at \, A_j \cdot v}$, So we have:

$$\prod_{\rho(j) \in S} \left(e(C_j, K'')e(D_j, K_{\rho(j)})_j^\omega \right) = e(g,g)^{at \sum_{\rho(j) \in S} \omega_j A_j \cdot v} = e(g,g)^{sat} \tag{13.6}$$

13.3.4 System Components

As illustrated in Figure 13.1, this research introduces a blockchain-based SDM method. It addresses SDM challenges through the use of decentralized technologies such as blockchain and DHT. System participants made up of DSs and DPs, the KGDC a blockchain platform, and an IPFS distributed network are the four functional components in the proposed architecture.

13.3.4.1 Data Subscribers (DSs)

Individuals or corporations that require data are referred to as DSs. They subscribe to specific kinds of data from DPs in order to meet their data needs. They are permitted to view the specific data provided by DPs after subscribing. For example, a data subscriber/requester may be a DU or Data owner, but for the sake of this research we treat them as DS. Access is possible if and only if the private key of the DS corresponds to the attribute set specified by the DP. Data-approved entities are typically connected with several DSs who have registered for a service and have direct access to the data.

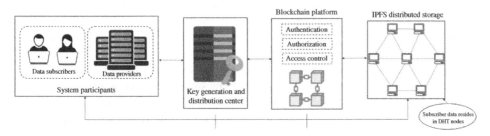

Figure 13.1 SDM scheme based on blockchain.

13.3.4.2 Data Providers (DPs)
A DP provides DSs with on-demand data access regardless of their physical location. DPs collect data from many sources (including human input) and perform all essential procedures to increase data quality (such as validation, transformation, matching, enriching, and filtering). The cleansed and formatted data sets are then sold to third parties. Data transfers between authorized agencies are permissible with the DP's authorization. Nonetheless, data sharing should not breach the DP policies. There are other participants in our system who seek data in order to give services to a larger group of people. Through a rewritten policy set, the DPs can determine specific access to the DS depending on essential concerns and considerations.

13.3.4.3 Key Generation and Distribution Center (KGDC)
A KGDC is a unit designed to mitigate the risks associated with key generation and exchange. KGDC frequently functions in systems where certain users may have authorization to utilize particular services at some times but not at others. They are used to invoke CP-ABE and advanced encryption standard (AES) algorithms in this research.

13.3.4.4 IPFS Distributed Storage
IPFS incorporates features such as the DHT, incentivized block exchange, and self-authentication namespace. Furthermore, IPFS data is scattered across several devices, and multiple backups exist to eliminate a single point of failure. Unlike the conventional web system, which accesses resources via URLs, IPFS allows for file retrieval by getting a unique hash value from the file content. As a result, when the file's content changes, the file's address changes, resulting in tamper-proof data. The amount of storage space required by the blockchain will grow inexorably over time. The ciphertext of the file is kept in the IPFS network in the suggested manner, which can mitigate the rapid increase of the blockchain caused by too much data. When a customer's request arrives at the system, it is routed to servers and processed via the DHT technique. DHT is a distributed hash table that is used to transmit a set of keys to all nodes in a distributed system [20, 21]. A hash table may immediately get the target location based on the provided key value using the hash function.

13.3.4.5 Blockchain Platform
The blockchain is a distributed and decentralized ledger that records all P2P network transactions. The ledger is shared by all network participants. The primary goal of blockchain technology is to eliminate the third party, or central authority, so that no single person can manage the entire network [22]. Blockchain is a series of blocks connected together by cryptographic hashes. Each block includes the hash of the preceding block and prevents data on the blockchain from being modified. It is the primary underlying technology of bitcoin; however, it is no longer just concerned with cryptocurrencies. A smart contract is a computer program or a blockchain transaction protocol that is activated automatically when certain parameters are satisfied. It executes trustworthy transactions and agreements in the absence of a third-party authority.

The blockchain technology used in this study serves two goals: one is to provide authentication, authorization, and access control (AAA), and the other is to record logs of all data access and policy management operations for safety and audit reasons. It is worth mentioning that the IPFS distributed network is used to store all encrypted raw subscriber data, since blockchain is not suited for directly storing original data owing to its openness and non-tamperability, which will trigger privacy issues and blockchain congestion. And the CP-ABE technique is employed to establish fine-grained data access control via smart contracts. To capitalize on the immutability of smart contracts and prevent the bottleneck problem induced by the consensus protocol, blockchain transactions in our system are defined as data access tasks and management operations on access control policies that will be saved in the distributed ledger for traceability and auditability purposes. The blockchain simply stores data hash values, IPFS content hash values, access control policies, timestamps, and other metadata information, drastically reducing storage overhead.

The blockchain platform primarily consists of the following entities:

1. **Issuer**: This entity registers the DSs and DPs on the blockchain network. It gives out membership keys to them and that serves as their identity (ID).
2. **Verifier**: It functions as an authentication unit, determines if a user who requests access is a member of the blockchain network.
3. **Transaction processing**: This is the blockchain network's core function. It is responsible for processing all transactions and storing its logs on the network.
4. **Smart contract deployment**: It's in charge of creating smart contracts from user policy sets. This procedure is required to guarantee that only authorized participants retrieve the desired data while complying to the policies established by the DP.

Figure 13.2 depicts the block structure, i.e. the block header and the block body. The block header, like the bitcoin application, holds the current block ID, the preceding block hash value, timestamp, nonce, and current block hash. The Merkle tree is used in the block body to allow for rapid verification of block data. After performing a hash operation on every transactional data in a block, the hash value produced is kept in a leaf node, as hash1 in Figure 13.2, and it represents the hash value of Transaction 1 (Tx1). The leaf node hash values are then merged into a new string of characters, and the hash value is acquired and stored in a matching intermediate node, such as hash12,

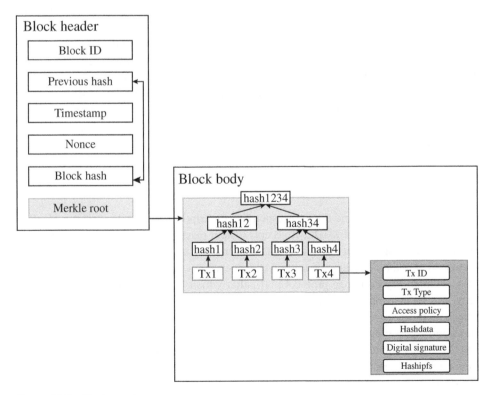

Figure 13.2 Block structure.

which is the result of combining hash1 and hash2. Repeat the previous steps until there is only one node left, which is the Merkle root. Transactions are recorded on the blockchain as blocks for later auditability. The transactional data includes the tx ID, tx type, the subscriber data pointer used to obtain the original data address, the data access policy, the digital signature used to validate the initiator's identity, the hash values of the source data (hashdata), and the hash values created by IPFS (hashipfs). The SHA256 algorithm generates hashdata, which takes up 32 bytes; hashipfs is the hash value returned after uploading the file to the IPFS network, which also takes up 32 bytes; and policy is the DPs access control strategy.

1. **Authentication**: To authenticate users and messages on a blockchain, public key cryptography and digital signatures are utilized. Before transmitting a message, the sender signs it with his private key, and the recipient validates it using the sender's public key. The transaction is executed if the signature is valid. Otherwise, the message is ignored by the recipient. The key distribution and authentication methods comprise the security aspect of our system. It is responsible for verifying the validity of system users. Verification is achieved by assigning keys to system users, which are then validated using pre-generated parameters. These keys are linked to the unique identities of users and are used to digitally sign transactions in the system. This method tries to guarantee that inquiries from suitable system members are authentic and that they are permitted to interact in the data sharing system without harmful intents or actions.

2. **Authorization**: Permissions and access control techniques are critical in a multi-user network for controlling users. An administrator can utilize access levels to allow users to access restricted resources while restricting them from utilizing sensitive resources. It facilitates efficient data processing, policy management, and user management. It also guarantees that the policies issued are in the correct data format and contains the parameters required to enforce efficient data circulation management in the system.

3. **Access control**: CP-ABE via the deployment of smart contract is used in regulating data access. These smart contracts are based on user policy sets. This procedure is required to guarantee that only eligible users retrieve the desired data while complying to authorization sets imposed by a data owner on the usage of subscribed data. Smart contracts, as part of our data system, govern the result of data inquiries by system users. The DPs creates the control access policy using the CP-ABE method. Only when the DS's attribute set matches the policy's requirements can the data be accessed.

13.3.5 Process Description

Table 13.1 presents the notations and their corresponding descriptions used in the section. The DP runs the registration algorithm via KGDC. It accepts system master key MK and DU's attributes set $\mathcal{A}$ as inputs. It generates secret key SK. The DS's secret key is encrypted with the AES algorithm and embedded in a blockchain transaction (the encryption key is the shared key generated by the Diffie–Hellman key exchange protocol [23]), after which DP sends the tx ID, smart contract address, and smart contract application binary interface (ABI) to DS via a secure channel. The blockchain platform serves as a decentralized system for smart contract-based authentication, authorization, and access management. To ensure data integrity, the hash of the data is computed using the (SHA256) hashing technique. To provide subscribers control over their own data, the data requester must first get permission from the DPs before accessing personal subscriber data. The data storage organization may only return requested data after authenticating the data requester, i.e. the DS.

Table 13.1 Notation description.

Notations	Definitions
DS	Data subscriber or data requester
DP	Data provider
S_{policy}	Access control policy
S_{reg}	DS registration transaction
$S_{DataReq}$	Data request transaction
$S_{DataStr}$	Data store transaction
PK	CP-ABE generated public key
MK	CP-ABE generated master key
SK	CP-ABE generated private key
$\mathcal{A}$	DS attribute set
XK	AES generated key
Hashdata	Data hash value
Hashipfs	Ciphertext address of the data on IPFS
Encdata	Data ciphertext
Enckey	Ciphertext encryption key
Deckey	Ciphertext decryption key
Decdata	Decrypted data
Dechash	Hash value of decrypted data

For users to subscribe to its data services, each DP has pre-defined subscription plans. Anyone can see and subscribe to the DPs' data services (subscription plans). Every DP has a distinct public key and each subscription plan has a distinct id that it corresponds to. A DS initiates a subscription request by choosing a DP and an appropriate subscription plan. When the DP gets a subscription request from a DS, it checks the ID, signature, and attribute set via the KGDC and blockchain. Following successful validation of DS, DP gives access to the data stream for a certain length of time, with the transactions log being maintained in the blockchain and the raw data being saved on the IPFS network. Otherwise, DP denies DS data request access. Subscription and payment plans are not explored in our chapter since they are developed by the DPs based on their policies and rules.

1. **Initialization stage**: The random initialization procedure is executed by the trusted KGDC. The input is the security parameter ρ, and the output contains the public key *PK* and master key *MK*:

$$Setup(\rho) = (PK, MK)$$

2. **Key creation stage**: The KGDC conducts the key creation algorithm. The inputs are the *PK* and *MK* and the user-defined attribute set $\mathcal{A}$, and the output comprises a private key *SK*:

$$KeyGen(PK, MK, \mathcal{A}) = SK$$

3. **Data encryption stage**: The DP conducts the encryption algorithm; the inputs are PK, the message m to be encrypted, and the access structure AC, and the output is the ciphertext CT:

$$Encrypt(PK, m, AC) = CT$$

4. **Data decryption stage**: The DS performs the decryption algorithm; the inputs are PK, SK, and CT, and the output is the plaintext message m:

$$Decrypt(PK, CT, SK) = m$$

13.3.5.1 Subscriber Registration

When a DS submits a registration request, he must include his preassigned public key. The DP authenticates the DS's identity via the blockchain and assigns appropriate attributes set $\mathcal{A}$ for the DS before adding his account address to the smart contract's list of authorized users. As a result, subscriber data is saved in the IPFS distributed network, and the associated access policy S_{policy} and logs of S_{reg} transactions are added to the blockchain.

13.3.5.2 Subscriber Data Storage

1. The DP initiates the $S_{DataStr}$ by picking the data to be stored and determining the file's access control policy S_{policy}. The DS can successfully access the file only if the DS's attribute set $\mathcal{A}$ matches the requirements of the access control policy S_{policy}.
2. The DP has a one-of-a-kind AES key XK. If the data owner has not already produced the key, the KGDC invokes the AES key creation procedure.
3. The KGDC then invokes the AES encryption method to encrypt the file and retrieve the encrypted file. It invokes the IPFS storage mechanism in order to store the encrypted file in the IPFS distributed network and keeps track of the hash value (hashipfs) needed to decrypt the ciphertext. To obtain the file hash value, the KGDC uses the SHA256 method to hash the file (hashdata).
4. The previously created hashdata, hashipfs, and S_{policy} are then transmitted to the blockchain network. When the blockchain network gets a data storage request, it activates the storage smart contract, which stores the hashdata, hashipfs, and S_{policy} on the blockchain.
5. The DP has a distinct public key PK and a distinct master key MK. If the DP has not already created the PK and MK, the KGDC will invoke the CP-ABE algorithm's initialization algorithm *Setup* to generate and store PK and MK, and will then deliver PK to the DP.
6. The KGDC invokes the CP-ABE algorithm's encryption algorithm *Encrypt*, takes the S_{policy} and PK as inputs, encrypts the key to obtain the ciphertext of the *Enckey*, and saves it.

13.3.5.3 Subscriber Data Request

Subscriber data comprises the subscribed and approved Quality of Service (QoS) parameters; access to subscriber data is quite widespread. A vast number of users or applications require subscriber data to ensure that the subscribed QoS-guaranteed services are supplied to individual subscribers. A data requester demands data access authorization from the blockchain platform via DP. The access control policy and digital signature are validated by the blockchain platform through the use of smart contracts. To implement fine-grained permission management, the permission scope is compatible with the subscriber data policy. If all goes well, it returns data access authorization on specified subscriber data to this data requester.

1. The DS submits a request $S_{DataReq}$ to access the data, which includes the DS's attribute set $\mathcal{A}$. The KGDC requests the hash value of the file (hashdata) and the hash value used to access the

---

Algorithm 13.1 Subscriber Data Storage

Data: [DS || DP || S_{reg}, $S_{DataStr}$, S_{policy}]
Result: Storage Successful

---

1 **if** *XK not exit* **then**

2   Generate AES key $= XK$ ▷ this is done by KGDC

3   **if** *Encdata* $==$ *AES.Enc (XK,Data)* **then**

4   Hashipfs $==$ IPFS.Store*Encdata*

5   Hashdata $==$ SHA256. Hash(data)

6        $S_{DataStr} ==$ (hashdata, Hashipfs, S_{policy}

7   **if** *PK and MK don't exist* **then**

8   *PK* and *MK* $==$ CP-ABE.Setup(r)   ▷ Invoke the CP-ABE scheme Enckey $==$
       CPABE.Encrypt(PK, *XK*, S_{policy})

---

ciphertext of the data to the IPFS network (hashipfs) from the blockchain network after receiving the request from the DS.

2. When the blockchain network receives a data access request, it initiates the smart contract to obtain the hashdata and hashipfs, and delivers them to the KGDC. The DS side uses its public key *PK* and private key *SK* in order to decrypt the file afterwards.

3. According to the data consumer's *PK*, *SK*, and attribute set $\mathcal{A}$, the KGDC conducts the CP-ABE algorithm's key generation algorithm (KeyGen) to produce the private key *SK* and *SK*. The KGDC uses the hashipfs from the chain to query the IPFS distributed storage in order to acquire the ciphertext of the data *Encdata* from the IPFS network.

4. The KGDC acquires the AES key ciphertext *Enckey* that encrypts the file locally and invokes the CP-ABE method's decryption algorithm *Decrypt* to decrypt *Enckey* and obtain the decryption key *Deckey*. The *Deckey* uses the AES decryption technique to decode *Encdata* and retrieves the decrypted file *Decdata*.

5. The KGDC uses the SHA256 method to hash *Decdata* and returns the hash value *Dechash*. The access is successful if hashfile and dechash are the same

13.3.6   Benefits of Proposed Design

In comparison to some existing system which are highly vulnerable to single point of failure and Distributed Denial of Service (DDoS) attacks, our proposed system which utilizes blockchain is very effective. One important element is that subscribers regain ownership of their personal data since the data access policy is created by them and every data access activity requires a permit granted by the blockchain platform based on the access policy. As blockchain transactions, data access activities are recorded on the immutable distributed ledger. Our design steers clear of the problems of blockchain technology. To mitigate the impact of blockchain immutability on data privacy, only logs of data addresses and access policies are stored in the blockchain as element of the blockchain transaction, while raw relevant data is saved in an off-chain distributed cloud storage, which is also encrypted to reduce data leakage. This on-chain and off-chain arrangement ensures the "right to be forgotten" by technological reasons, whereas faith in DPs is required in any data sharing networks. Furthermore, it prevents blockchain from using large amounts of storage

---

Algorithm 13.2 Subscriber Data Request

Data: [DS || DP || S_{reg}, $S_{DataReq}$, S_{policy}, PK, MK, XK]
Result: Request Successful

1 **if** *SK does not exit* **then**

2   CP-ABE.KeyGen($PK, MK, \mathcal{A}$) = SK ▷ this is done by KGDC

3   **if** *Encdata* == *IPFS.$S_{DataReq}$(data, hashipfs)* **then**

4   Enckey == Get.(DP)

5   Deckey == CPABE.Decrypt (PK, Enckey, SK)

6   Decdata == AES.Dec(Deckey, Encdata)

7   *Hashipfs* == IPFS.Store*Encdata*

8   Dechash == SHA256.Hash(Decdata) **if** *Dechash == hashdata* **then**

9   Return: Success

10   **else**

11   Return: Fail

---

on blockchain nodes, which is known as the blockchain congestion problem. There is less concern about single point of failure (SPOF) and DDoS since AAA is implemented via a smart contract implemented on the blockchain rather than depending on a single trusted third party, and the data storage is realized in a distributed fashion.

13.3.7 Security Requirements

The suggested system satisfies the requirements below:

1. **Confidentiality**: Data confidentiality is accomplished by first encrypting the data before sending it to the IPFS distributed storage. A system entity that does not know the data owner's private key cannot decode the ciphertext and get the original message.
2. **Immutability**: Before uploading data to the IPFS distributed storage, the owner signs the data, which is then cryptographically verified. The legitimacy of the data is validated by the peer nodes and the smart contract for the policies defined, before it is shared with legitimate subscribers. Furthermore, the secure hash technique used to link the transactions makes it "almost impossible" to change aggregated information (logs).
3. **Auditability**: The blockchain network provides auditability functions through transactional logs. Blocks in the network are classified as events gathered from subscriber operations and data access as logs. This functionality provides data verification, tracking, and provenance. If a user refuses an activity or access to a subscriber data, processing nodes can utilize the blocks to identify what happened.
4. **Decentralization**: The solution allows for the equitable dissemination of transaction information among system processing nodes. A failure of one or more nodes cannot result in a single point of failure.

13.4 Summary

This research focuses on a SDM framework and a data access control method based on the CP-ABE algorithm, blockchain, and IPFS technology. Decentralized authentication, permission, and access control are facilitated by the blockchain platform. To achieve privacy protection, IPFS functions as a raw data storage entity. The hash value of the data, the location information of the encrypted data, and the access control technique are all kept on the blockchain in this system.

Before immediately accessing data, the data requester sends an access permission request to the blockchain platform, and the blockchain platform grants access authorization based on the policy set. Following receipt of the access authorization, the data requester launches an access request to the IPFS, which delivers back the specific data once the permission verification answer is received. Finally, the transaction is stored in the distributed ledger for future auditability. Our approach not only assures that the data cannot be tampered with, but it also ensures that the access control strategy cannot be tampered with. The suggested technique relieves storage demand and significantly increases blockchain scalability.

References

1 Sujaritha, M., Shunmugapriya, S., Hariharan, S. et al. (2018). Decentralized crowdfunding platform using smart contracts. *2022 IEEE International Conference on Signal Processing, Informatics, Communication and Energy Systems (SPICES)*, Volume 1, pp. 302–307. IEEE.

2 Yadav, N. and Sarasvathi, V. (2020). Venturing crowdfunding using smart contracts in blockchain. *2020 3rd International Conference on Smart Systems and Inventive Technology (ICSSIT)*, pp. 192–197. IEEE.

3 Markus, M.L. and Tanis, C. (2000). The enterprise systems experience-from adoption to success. *Framing the Domains of IT Research: Glimpsing the Future Through the Past* 173: 207–173.

4 Yuan, C., Xu, M., Si, X., and Li, B. (2017). Blockchain with accountable CP-ABE: how to effectively protect the electronic documents. *2017 IEEE 23rd International Conference on Parallel and Distributed Systems (ICPADS)*, pp. 800–803. IEEE.

5 Lu, X., Fu, S., Jiang, C., and Lio, P. (2021). A fine-grained IoT data access control scheme combining attribute-based encryption and blockchain. *Security and Communication Networks* 2021: 1–13.

6 Guan, Z., Lu, X., Yang, W. et al. (2021). Achieving efficient and privacy-preserving energy trading based on blockchain and ABE in smart grid. *Journal of Parallel and Distributed Computing* 147: 34–45.

7 Pournaghi, S.M., Bayat, M., and Farjami, Y. (2020). MedSBA: a novel and secure scheme to share medical data based on blockchain technology and attribute-based encryption. *Journal of Ambient Intelligence and Humanized Computing* 11: 4613–4641.

8 Zhang, Z. and Ren, X. (2021). Data security sharing method based on CP-ABE and blockchain. *Journal of Intelligent & Fuzzy Systems* 40 (2): 2193–2203.

9 Alimoglu, A. and Özturan, C. (2017). Design of a smart contract based autonomous organization for sustainable software. *2017 IEEE 13th International Conference on e-Science (e-Science)*, pp. 471–476. IEEE.

10 Rouselakis, Y. and Waters, B. (2013). Practical constructions and new proof methods for large universe attribute-based encryption. *Proceedings of the 2013 ACM SIGSAC Conference on Computer & Communications Security*, pp. 463–474.

11 Ma, H., Huang, E.X., and Lam, K.-Y. (2018). Blockchain-based mechanism for fine-grained authorization in data crowdsourcing. *Future Generation Computer Systems* 106: 121–134.

12 Nawari, N.O. and Ravindran, S. (2019). Blockchain and the built environment: potentials and limitations. *Journal of Building Engineering* 25: 100832.

13 Zainal, M.A.G., Borda, R.F.C., Abd Algani, Y.M. et al. (2022). A decentralized autonomous personal data management system in banking sector. *Computers and Electrical Engineering* 100: 108027.

14 Liao, C.H., Guan, X.Q., Cheng, J.H., and Yuan, S.M. (2022). Blockchain-based identity management and access control framework for open banking ecosystem. *Future Generation Computer Systems* 135: 450–466.

15 Nkenyereye, L., Islam, S.R., Bilal, M. et al. (2021). Secure crowd-sensing protocol for fog-based vehicular cloud. *Future Generation Computer Systems* 120: 61–75.

16 Guo, L., Yang, X., and Yau, W.C. (2021). TABE-DAC: efficient traceable attribute-based encryption scheme with dynamic access control based on blockchain. *IEEE Access* 9: 8479–8490.

17 Zhang, G., Liu, J., and Liu, J. (2013). Protecting sensitive attributes in attribute based access control. *Service-Oriented Computing-ICSOC 2012 Workshops: ICSOC 2012, International Workshops ASC, DISA, PAASC, SCEB, SeMaPS, WESOA, and Satellite Events*, Shanghai, China (12–15 November 2012), Revised Selected Papers 10, 294–305. Berlin, Heidelberg: Springer-Verlag.

18 Hartmann, F., Grottolo, G., Wang, X., and Lunesu, M.I. (2019). Alternative fundraising: success factors for blockchain-based vs. conventional crowdfunding. *2019 IEEE International Workshop on Blockchain Oriented Software Engineering (IWBOSE)*, pp. 38–43. IEEE.

19 Zaidi, S.Y.A., Shah, M.A., Khattak, H.A. et al. (2021). An attribute-based access control for IoT using blockchain and smart contracts. *Sustainability* 13 (19): 10556.

20 Ghodsi, A. (2006). Distributed k-ary system: Algorithms for distributed hash tables. PhD dissertation. KTH.

21 Araújo, F., Rodrigues, L., Kaiser, J. et al. (2005). CHR: a distributed hash table for wireless ad hoc networks. *25th IEEE International Conference on Distributed Computing Systems Workshops*, 407–413. IEEE.

22 Niranjanamurthy, M., Nithya, B.N., and Jagannatha, S.J.C.C. (2019). Analysis of Blockchain technology: pros, cons and SWOT. *Cluster Computing* 22: 14743–14757.

23 Faz-Hernández, A., López, J., Ochoa-Jiménez, E., and Rodríguez-Henríquez, F. (2017). A faster software implementation of the supersingular isogeny Diffie–Hellman key exchange protocol. *IEEE Transactions on Computers* 67 (11): 1622–1636.

14

A Secure Data-Sharing Blockchain-Based Crowdfunding System

14.1 Introduction

Crowdfunding platforms are gaining a lot of attention recently due to their wide reach, high efficiency, and ease of presentation. This platform is largely regarded as a viable option to obtaining venture funding. Crowdfunding has been identified as one of the greatest ways to raise financing for small firms and individuals with unique ideas but limited financial resources. As an alternative to traditional financing methods, many online crowdfunding sites have emerged in recent years. A safe and dependable crowdfunding platform plays an important part in the development of smart cities and smart nations [1]. Researchers discovered that over US $34 billion was obtained through crowdfunding efforts, with a total valuation of US $90 billion added to the global economy, surpassing venture capital fundings [2].

Crowdfunding is a method of obtaining funds for new businesses and creative initiatives. It is the technique of gathering funding from a large number of individuals, known as backers or investors, usually using internet platforms like Kickstarter or Republic [2]. One of the key factors driving crowdfunding's appeal is the ease with which both fundraisers and investors or donations may operate over the internet. Crowdfunding systems facilitate ecosystem funding, particularly inasmuch as these platforms assist finance initiatives for a range of goals. As a result, a crowdfunding platform may be thought of as a community of investors, fundraisers, and entrepreneurs working toward a common goal [3]. Crowdfunding may be useful for personal purposes, real estate, loans, start-ups, and other enterprises. Crowdfunding sites such as Kickstarter, Indiegogo, Startengine, GoFundMe, Ketto and others are excellent examples. These platforms promote entrepreneurship and are most typically utilized for creative ventures ranging from music to art to film to technology. They often impose a fee of 4–5%. Sometimes the incentives take the shape of items or even participation in the design process [1, 4].

Crowdfunding is a popular method of fundraising that relies on contributions from a large number of individuals. In recent years, blockchain technology has emerged as a promising solution for enhancing the security and transparency of crowdfunding platforms. Nathan et al. [12] propose a decentralized personal data management system that empowers users to control their data, turning a blockchain into an automated access-control manager without the need for third-party trust. Truong et al. [13] present a GDPR-compliant personal data management platform leveraging blockchain and smart contracts, enabling data owners to impose usage consent and ensuring only authorized parties can process data, with all activities recorded in an immutable ledger. Liu et al. [14] address IoT challenges with blockchain-enabled data collection and secure sharing, combining Ethereum blockchain and deep reinforcement learning (DRL) for reliability and security. However, there are concerns that inadequate security measures in

Attribute-based Encryption (ABE): Foundations and Applications within Blockchain and Cloud Environments, First Edition.
Qi Xia, Jianbin Gao, Isaac Amankona Obiri, Kwame Omono Asamoah, and Daniel Adu Worae.

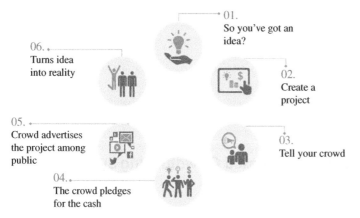

01.
So you've got an
idea?

06.
Turns idea
into reality

02.
Create a
project

05.
Crowd advertises
the project among
public

03.
Tell your crowd

04.
The crowd pledges
for the cash

Figure 14.1 Simplified crowdfunding process.

blockchain-based crowdfunding platforms can undermine the trust and confidence of users. Studies cited in references [5, 11, 15] have shown that data privacy issues and information theft are major concerns that can outweigh the benefits of using blockchain for sharing information, as highlighted in references [16–21].

The advantage of using blockchain technology is that it guarantees data integrity, while attribute-based encryption ensures fine-grained access control [5]. Therefore, implementing these security measures on a crowdfunding platform is essential, especially when sensitive data is being shared among authorized parties. In particular, attribute-based encryption can help to protect the privacy of data by only allowing authorized parties to access specific information based on their attributes, such as their role or identity

Figure 14.1 illustrates the step-by-step process of crowdfunding. It begins with the conception of an idea (step 1), followed by the creation of a project based on that idea (step 2). The third step involves informing the crowd about the project, which could potentially win their support and pledges (step 4). Step 5 entails the crowd promoting the project to the public, and finally, step 6 involves the realization of the idea into a tangible reality. Through this process, crowdfunding has enabled many innovators and entrepreneurs to turn their ideas into successful projects with the help of a supportive community.

One intriguing element of crowdfunding is that it allows non-professional investors to participate in early-stage projects. This investment category was previously designated for professional (approved) investors prior to the rise of crowdfunding. As a result, crowdfunding may be viewed as a means of democratizing the financial industry [3]. In general, when people need to collect funds to start a firm, they must first develop a strategy, statistical surveys, and models, and then offer their ideas to attract people or organizations. Banks, angel investors, and venture capital firms were among the sources of funding. It is a means of untying the huge quantity of cash held by regular investors, which may benefit the investing business. Nonetheless, authorities have enacted very stringent rules to safeguard ordinary investors. On the one hand, authorities are attempting to protect vulnerable market participants from high-risk investments, while on the other, they are limiting their access to the potentially large rewards that those investments may provide [2].

Moreover, there are certain problems with traditional crowdfunding systems such as expensive fees, sham start-ups, dangers to intellectual property, a lack of trust, no accountability, and single point of failure (SPoF). However, blockchain technology can help solve the above problems. The developing decentralized blockchain-based networks are more safe and dependable than existing centralized platforms. These services make it possible to utilize cryptocurrencies for crowdfunding. To gather cash from the community, smart contracts are being deployed, and the traditional initial public offering (IPO) is being replaced by an initial coin offering (ICO). Blockchain-based crowdfunding, as seen by the rise of ICOs and, more recently, security token offerings (STOs), has emerged as a new kind of crowdfunding.

Although blockchain-based crowdfunding is comparable to traditional crowdfunding, it has its own distinct features. As a result, the success criteria that influence traditional crowdfunding outcomes may not apply to blockchain-based crowdfunding. There is a misunderstanding about the success criteria for blockchain-based campaigns when compared to traditional crowdfunding elements. Such information is essential for understanding the key differences and similarities of the various crowdfunding models, may aid in the right design of successful blockchain-based fundraising campaigns, and allows potential investors to consider certain assessment parameters [2].

Consequently, there hasn't been much research into authorization functions of blockchain-based crowdfunding platforms. Therefore, this research qualitatively suggests a blockchain-based crowdfunding system that utilizes a ciphertext-policy attribute-based encryption (CP-ABE) [8] for fine-grained data authorization to protect sensitive data generated by business startups. CP-ABE is a useful cryptographic tool for controlling fine-grained access to shared ciphertexts. To allow for the management of data access permission in an untrusted environment. Access control rules can be created based on data type, investments/funds, and other factors. Many data management systems can utilize CP-ABE to pre-process the encryption operations and integrate an access policy into each associated ciphertext to lessen their retrieval and encryption effort. Data can be retrieved by selecting the bare minimum of attributes based on the access rules of the specific requested data. To accomplish fine-grain permission, the data-sharing system can construct the data requester's attribute private key, and the requester can only retrieve and decode the ciphertexts and get data using that key.

We alter the classic CP-ABE system to eliminate the trusted private key generator (PKG) and instead set the fundraisers/business start-ups to manage the ownership of the data and issue the private keys to investors to enable fine-grained authorization of fundraisers in data crowdfunding. Fundraisers encrypt the sensitive data to form a data ciphertext using symmetric encryption and a session key, then encrypt the session key to obtain a session-key ciphertext with the CP-ABE, and upload these ciphertexts to cloud servers. However, if fundraisers just have non-sensitive of data, they can perform data sharing without using CP-ABE.

1. In this chapter, we provide the results of a thorough literature research that we did in order to identify the success determinants for both traditional and blockchain-based crowdfunding campaigns.
2. We suggest a novel blockchain-based crowdfunding system that utilizes smart contracts and a CP-ABE for fine-grained data authorization to safeguard the sensitive data generated by business startups.

14.2 Literature Review

This section discusses some facts about existing crowdfunding platforms, types, problems, and the benefits of blockchain-based crowdfunding.

14.2.1 Present-Day Centralized Crowdfunding

Today, all crowd financing transactions are reliant on a variety of crowdfunding platforms, which require large sums of money from both investors and contributors in order to complete their requests, which are occasionally inadequate. Many platforms act as gatekeepers, with rigorous rules and restrictions that make it difficult for both investors and contributors to have a say in the project's success. Having a brilliant concept on a crowd fundraising platform is not a guarantee of success. Users will demand techniques to increase the visibility of their crowdfunding page on search engines and attract new consumers to that project, which will necessitate large spending in advertising alone [2].

The modern crowdfunding concept is based on three types of on-screen characters: the task initiator who presents the idea or venture to be financed, individuals or investors who invest in the idea, and a platform that connects these two characters to ensure the venture's success. Despite the fact that the basic structure of crowdfunding mainly comprises these three key stakeholders, there are multiple connections between them. The availability of crowdfunding platforms enables firms/startups to offer ideas to the general public and seek funds. Crowdfunding platforms publicize ideas, so creating an investment opportunity for backer/investors (i.e. regular individuals who would not be able to invest in any other manner). Investors evaluate new concepts and fund those they like and believe in. Furthermore, because investors enjoy and believe in the financed concept or project, and want it to succeed, they tend to (if such a chance exists) offer recommendations from their expertise for the business start-ups. Business startups give backers something in exchange for their money, i.e. a reward, gifts, shares, percentage of profits, or something similar. When an idea or project is successfully crowdfunded, businesses startups are frequently committed to paying a fee (typically a proportion of the amount collected, about 5–10%) to the platform.

Crowdfunding is utilized to fund a wide range of start-ups and new concepts, such as inventive activities, medical advancements, travel, and social commercial enterprise projects. Several crowd financing systems do not guarantee that the commitments made to contributors will be delivered, and this can be unfair to contributors, causing them to be hesitant to engage in the business and causing project management challenges. Sometimes project managers have watched their entire business fail before they ever had a chance to begin production because when an idea becomes highly popular on crowdfunding portals, many different business people are inspired and try to produce comparable items, increasing competition.

Kickstarter, Indiegogo, and GoFundMe are prominent centralized crowdfunding platforms. All of these platforms allow users to see a list of active projects and, if they want to raise funds, they may submit the necessary details about their project. If any investor is interested in supporting the project, they will contribute the appropriate amount. If the fundraising request is approved, the funds will be deposited to the fund raiser account. When the project is completed, the investors will receive their benefits.

Figure 14.2 illustrates the crowdfunding process, encompassing steps A–F. In this process, project initiators and project startups are represented by two distinct colors, dark gray and light gray respectively. Step A involves the conception of the project idea by the initiators. Subsequently, in step B, they utilize a crowding platform, denoted by the light-yellow rectangle, to present their idea to potential investors, aiming to attract their interest and secure investments. Moving forward to steps C and D, investors not only provide funds but also offer valuable advice to the project initiators. This collaboration enables the transformation of the idea into a tangible reality. The decision to invest

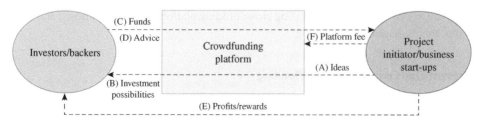

Figure 14.2 Traditional crowdfunding process.

and contribute to the project hinges upon the investors' assessment of its potential for success. Once the project is executed, step F entails the project initiators making a payment to the platform as a fee for utilizing its services. Finally, as an expression of gratitude and recognition for the investors' support, the project initiators distribute the rewards of the project, thus acknowledging their efforts and involvement.

14.2.2 Crowdfunding Models

Figure 14.3 illustrates the hierarchical structure of crowdfunding models, delineating the various levels of the framework. At the highest level, we have crowdfunding, which serves as the overarching category. Below this, we encounter two branches: investment models and non-investment models. The investment model, positioned one level down, branches out into two distinct paths or terminal nodes. The first path leads to debt/lending-based crowdfunding, which involves raising funds by issuing debt instruments or facilitating lending activities. The second path leads to equity-based crowdfunding, where individuals invest in a venture in exchange for equity ownership or a share of the profits. On the other hand, the non-investment models branch from the same level as investment models. This category also features two terminal nodes: reward-based crowdfunding and donation-based crowdfunding. In reward-based crowdfunding, individuals contribute funds with the expectation of receiving a non-financial reward or product/service in return. In donation-based crowdfunding, contributors make financial contributions without any expectation of receiving tangible rewards.

The sort of crowdfunding to be employed is typically determined by the type of business or activity that is being established. The kind is also influenced by the company's aims and ambitions.

1. **Debt/lending-based crowdfunding**: This type of crowdfunding ensures that investors or donors are paid back their money plus interest. It is often known as "peer to peer" lending and does not generally include standard banking techniques. Thus, investors grant loans in return for a repayment.
2. **Equity-based crowdfunding**: The investors become shareholders of the company initiative using this strategy. They are also entitled to profits. This is somewhat of a bet since, if the project is successful, the share value will rise; otherwise, it will fall.
3. **Donations-based crowdfunding**: In this type of crowdfunding, investors are not looking for cash rewards. They put their faith in the endeavor, which is generally for a good reason. However, benefits might be offered to express thanks to the donors. Charities, disaster assistance, and other non-profit organizations are examples of such endeavors.

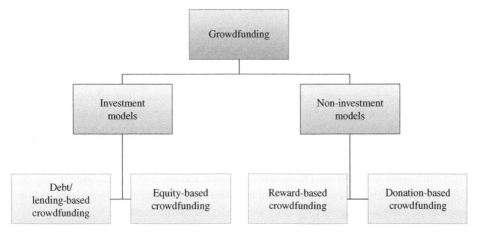

Figure 14.3 Crowdfunding models.

4. **Rewards-based crowdfunding**: Individuals participate in this type of crowdfunding in exchange for rewards and benefits, which might be profit or a product. These days, there are several sites that employ this type of crowdfunding.

14.2.3 Problems of Traditional Crowdfunding

The primary issue with the centralized solution is a lack of trust because most of these platforms stipulates that returns are not guaranteed to investors and that they are not liable for the loss of money. There is no guarantee that the investors' money will be returned if the project is successfully funded. Some of the limitations of traditional crowdfunding are discussed below.

1. **Expensive fees**: Typically, traditional crowdfunding sites charge a fee for each project that is featured. It is sometimes a precise amount, and other times a percentage of the contribution provided by the donors. This is a disadvantage for the availability of capital since start-ups actually need every penny to assist themselves.
2. **Scam start-ups**: In certain circumstances, start-ups turn out to be scams, leaving investors with little choice but to lose their money [6].
3. **Risks to intellectual property**: Some start-ups fail to safeguard their intellectual property, exposing them to more experienced investors who can steal their idea and join the market with the resources they can organize [6].
4. **Transparency issues**: After a project is successfully funded, the investors have no clue how the fund raiser would use their money. There is no accurate information supplied regarding the project's investors. Some people started projects without a clear understanding of their purpose. Because any user may establish a project without due verification, many fraudsters produce false information about projects, resulting in the loss of investment funds [1].
5. **Inadequate security**: There is no assurance that users' information will not be leaked or altered with, and there is no protection for their funds. In February 2014, the prominent crowdfunding portal Kickstarter was hacked, resulting in the disclosure of consumer data; as a result of such instances, faith in centralized systems was severely decreased. There have also been claims that crowdfunding sites are being exploited as money laundering platforms, and that as a result of these concerns, no genuine trust is being formed with the users [1].

14.2.4 Blockchain-Based Crowdfunding

We are a generation that expects to see the effects of our contributions right away. The next generation of investors does not want to be only passive donors. Stakeholders want to know how the business is doing, whether it is meeting its objectives, and how it may be improved. This necessitates complete transparency and accurate financial information on the linked project activities. This problem can be solved with blockchain.

Blockchain is essentially an autonomous and transparent platform that lowers uncertainty between parties trading values. Despite the fact that it is a novel technology, it may be employed in real-world applications such as crowdfunding. It is a peer-to-peer network that collectively follows a protocol for inter-node communication and new block validation, so no one can edit any block without the consent of more than half of the nodes in the blockchain, making it secure and safe. Ethereum [7] is a public blockchain with a decentralized structure that is entirely independent and not controlled by anybody. A smart contract is a computer protocol that enables us to facilitate and verify contract fulfillment. These transactions can be tracked and are irrevocable. Smart contracts outline an agreement's terms and consequences in the same manner that traditional contracts do. The solidity programming language is used to create these smart contracts.

Blockchain technology enables decentralization in crowdfunding, meaning that no single platform or group of platforms controls the smart contracts. This makes them transparent to everyone on the blockchain [2]. With blockchain, anyone can launch a project on the platform, and anyone with internet access can contribute to it. Unlike in traditional crowdfunding, contributors do not have to worry about empty promises. All transactions are managed by smart contracts, which store the funds instead of sending them to a third party. Blockchain also provides greater flexibility to project managers and contributors, allowing for fractional contributions to be made. Cryptocurrencies can be utilized for crowdfunding through the deployment of smart contracts on platforms such as Ethereum, replacing the traditional IPO with an ICO [8].

14.2.5 Advantages of Blockchain-Based Crowdfunding

1. **Tokenization**: While crowdfunding necessitates the creation of actual goods, blockchain often depends on asset tokenization to give investors with equity or comparable notions, particularly ICO [6]. Investors would be able to witness the success that is related to the company's subsequent progress in this manner. This essentially implies that it has the ability to capitalize on the world's numerous investment possibilities. With funds being a primary consideration for start-ups, this might assist them in saving money on employee recruitment by offering them remuneration equal to the ownership of the firm, so transforming it into an employee-owned corporation. In this situation, asset tokens function as their own currency, enabling organizations to hire additional specialists, notably in marketing and advertising.

2. **Fraud elimination**: Individuals who engage in crowdfunding utilizing blockchain technology benefit in the sense that "fraud" is eliminated because investors acquire ownership or a portion of the venture instantly.

3. **Decentralization**: The benefit of this strategy is that start-ups will not rely on the services of any platform(s) to acquire money. They are no longer required to follow any rules or restrictions imposed by various platforms. As a result, any initiative with the potential for exposure might get funds and so avoid the need to pay fees to the platforms. As a result, crowdfunding becomes more inexpensive to investors and contributors.

4. **Transparency**: Blockchain is essentially a digital ledger that maintains track of all ongoing transactions. The investors will be able to see how the fund raiser is using their money. The platform allows users to learn about the investors and the projects to which they have contributed. If a user is seeking funds, it indicates that he or she will share information about the project, their prior work, and the benefits for the investors when the project is completed. This gives investors with a high level of openness while examining the project.

5. **Accountability**: There are several ways in which smart contracts enabled by blockchain technology might increase accountability in crowd fundraising. First and foremost, smart contracts would erect barriers that would prevent cash from being disbursed without reference to a project or any other lawful activity. As a result, large quantities of money would be prevented from being embezzled by people with malicious purpose or those who are ineligible to conduct the campaign in the first place. It is self-executing and, if all criteria are satisfied, automatically transfers the amount of funds for future growth.

6. **Immutability and traceability**: Blockchain transactions cannot be tampered with and the smart contract handles logical situations in code, consumers may be certain that the platform is not controlled by a centralized system. The amount of cash and projects raised by a certain user may also be tracked so that a bond and trust may be formed between investors and fund raisers.

14.3   Proposed System

In this section, we first propose a novel blockchain-based crowdfunding scheme for data-sharing authorization in untrusted platforms. We build a system framework based on this paradigm. Following that, we will go through the execution procedure in further detail.

14.3.1   System Model

Figure 14.4 illustrates the system model depicting various entities involved in the process. The system consists of the following components: cloud, investors/backers, crowdfunding platform, blockchain network, and business start-ups. These entities interact and function together within the system. The process begins with business start-ups conceiving their ideas, which may be sensitive and require protection from unauthorized access. To ensure confidentiality, the data is encrypted offline, resulting in ciphertext. This ciphertext is then transmitted to the cloud server, which serves as a secure repository for data storage.

Next, the project data is sent to the crowdfunding platform. However, only the necessary information required to retrieve the actual data from the cloud server is shared with the platform.

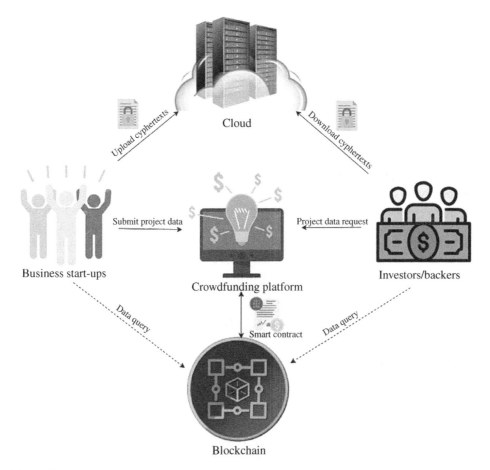

Figure 14.4   System model.

This approach leverages the advantages of cloud computing while safeguarding sensitive data. It is important to note that the cloud is susceptible to attacks, which is why data encryption is crucial for protecting sensitive information.

The investors/backers can access the project data and request further details. They retrieve the encrypted data from the cloud server and utilize their private key to decrypt the ciphertext, converting it back to plaintext. The blockchain network plays a vital role by providing a trusted authority with smart contract capabilities. It serves as a mechanism to enforce adherence to the contract between business start-ups and investors/backers. Through punitive measures such as the allocation of funds associated with defaulting on the contract, the blockchain simulates real-world consequences for non-compliance. We employ blockchain and smart contract techniques as a data sharing platform in this system since there is no trustworthy central authority. Certain blockchains can use a Turing-complete programming language to build smart contracts in Virtual Machines (VM) to guarantee cryptographically tamper-proof trustworthy execution and enforcement. Second, the VM's environment guarantees that programs run without interruption. Business start-ups can use the CP-ABE primitive to pre-encrypt data while achieving securely fine-grained ciphertext sharing. We utilize blockchain technology to make data sharing more transparent and equitable. Investors can access data on demand using smart contracts and associated attributes unless the business start-ups' data content meets the investors' data request and the investors' attribute set matches the business start-ups access policy. When the business start-ups and the investors establish an agreement, the business start-ups can acquire fine-grained permission for the investors based on the investor's attributes.

We employ blockchain and smart contract techniques as a data-sharing platform in this system since there is no trustworthy central authority. Certain blockchains can use a Turing-complete programming language to build smart contracts in virtual machines (VM) to guarantee cryptographically tamper-proof trustworthy execution and enforcement. Second, the VM's environment guarantees that programs run without interruption. Business start-ups can use the CP-ABE primitive to pre-encrypt data while achieving securely fine-grained ciphertext sharing. We utilize blockchain technology to make data sharing more transparent and equitable. Investors can access data on demand using smart contracts and associated attributes unless the business start-ups data content meets the investors data request and the investors attribute set matches the business start-ups access policy. When the business start-ups and the investors establish an agreement, the business start-ups can acquire fine-grained permission for the investors based on the investor's attributes.

14.3.1.1 Key Components

1. **Investors**: These entities evaluate new concepts or ideas and fund those they like and believe in. They are denoted by a series of $\{N = (N_1, N_2, \ldots, N_m)\}$ publish data requests by sending data descriptions into smart contracts. Each investor N_i is identifiable by his or her identity and attribute set $(pk_{Ni}, sk_{Ni}, \alpha_{Ni}, A_{Ni} = (A_1, A_2, \ldots, A_K))$, where $pk_{Ni}, sk_{Ni}, \alpha_{Ni}$ signify his or her public key, private key, and address, respectively, and A_{Ni} is a set of attributes.

2. **Business start-ups**: This is the task initiator who presents the idea or venture to be financed. They are denoted by a collection of $B = (B_1, B_2, \ldots, B_m)$ that hold the intellectual property of valuable data and can designate various access control rules for distinct sensitive data. Every business start-up B_j is identified by the identification and attribute information $\{(pk_{Bj}, sk_{Bj}, \alpha_{Bj}, A_{Bj} = (A_1, A_2, \ldots, A_K))\}$, where $pk_{Bj}, sk_{Bj}, \alpha_{Bj}$ signify his/her public key, private key, and address, respectively, and A_{Bj} is $\hat{d} = (\hat{d}_1, \hat{d}_2, \ldots, \hat{d}_n)$ for $P = 1, 2, 3, \ldots, n$ and that every data piece $\hat{d}_P$ is subject to an access policy $A(\hat{A}, \sigma)_P$. To lessen the cost of retrieval and encryption

of project data, the business start-up B_j preprocesses his/her sensitive data using CP-ABE and symmetric encryption.

3. **Application layer**: This is the crowdfunding platform. It enables firms/startups to offer ideas to the general public and seek funds. Crowdfunding platforms publicize ideas, so creating an investment opportunity for backer/investors (i.e. regular individuals who would not be able to invest in any other manner). It may be operated on the user's local computer, and is regarded as a crucial interface for semi-trusted business start-ups and investors. Business start-ups and investors can use the platform to register and verify their identities and attributes, and the platform can generate smart contracts for them.

4. **Cloud storage**: To alleviate the cost of storing data locally, the business start-ups B_j uploads the ciphertexts to cloud servers. The business that operates cloud servers to store encrypted data for the system is referred to as a cloud storage provider (CSP). CSP may return the ciphertext's location Loc_{CT} to the B_j and send the ciphertext to the N_i based on the ciphertext's location Loc_{CT}. B_j uploads and publishes a project data description $D = (D_1, D_2, \ldots, D_m)$, where $D_P = S_{id}, H(\hat{d}_P)$, $Sign(H(F_P), sk_{Bj}), pk_{Bj}, \hat{k}_P, A(\hat{A}, \sigma)_P, H(\hat{d}_P)$ is the hash value of data $\hat{d}_P$, $\hat{k}_P$ is the data keyword set, $Sign(H(F_P), sk_{Bj})$ is the signature of B_j and $A(\hat{A}, \sigma)_P$ is the data access policy.

14.3.2 System Framework Overview

Figure 14.5 illustrates the application layer, the blockchain layer, and the cloud storage layer comprising our system framework.

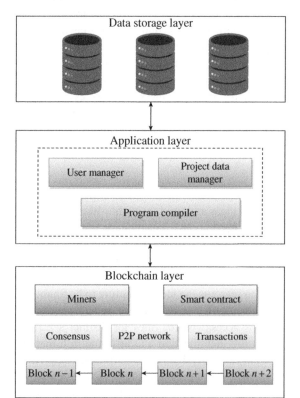

Figure 14.5 System framework.

The application layer, the blockchain layer, and the cloud storage layer comprise our system framework. The application layer consists primarily of a user manager, a project data manager, and a program compiler. Each business start-up can publish project data descriptions, which are accessed by investors at the application layer, i.e. crowdfunding platform. The blockchain layer uses the state changes of data sharing as inputs to establish agreements. We only put the description information of project data (such as business-startup's signature, data size, hash value, cipher-text location) onto the blockchain layer, and store encrypted data on the cloud storage tier, due to the blockchain's limited ability to hold data. Investors may use the blockchain layer to verify the authenticity and integrity of data without relying on the data storage layer. We assume the blockchain layer contains a software compiler and enables smart contract execution. The user interface in crowdfunding platform is used to communicate with smart contracts and blockchain by the business start-ups and investors.

14.3.2.1 Application Layer

The application layer provides a user interface for crowdfunding. It comprises mostly of the crowd-funding platform and three modules: user manager, project data manager, and program compiler. The user manager module is in charge of managing the user's registration information. Users must first register their key pairs (a public key and a secret key) by giving their identities and attributes before they may build smart contracts. The smart contracts check their identities and attributes, and the results of the verification are stored in blockchain. Project data managers handle data description information and data sharing. The program compiler module is used to convert the new smart contract into blockchain executable language. If the smart contract is put into the blockchain, the user has successfully registered. The user can then submit or request project data description information from the project data manager. Our framework is represented by smart contracts that operate on the blockchain, such as publishing sensitive project data descriptions, request data descriptions, finding project data information, and fine-grained authorization.

14.3.2.2 Blockchain Layer

The blockchain layer should facilitate smart contract execution and establish consensus on data-sharing state changes. Furthermore, the blockchain must facilitate cryptocurrency payment services like e-wallets and money transfers (but that it outside the scope of this research). The blockchain should be callable in order to restore machine state, accept new transaction inputs, and trigger state modifications of data transactions based on legitimate application layer input. Smart contracts should be able to be stored as an input from the application layer in blockchains such as Ethereum. To regulate the logic of a secure data sharing, we deploy smart contracts. We specifically want to extract metadata (such as the owner signature, data hash, access policy, keyword set, and ciphertext location) from encrypted data storage and utilize it as an input into the blockchain while the encrypted data is stored off-chain on cloud servers. This storage method can considerably increase the blockchain's data storage capacity and help to network synchronization.

14.3.2.3 Data Storage Layer

The data storage layer is mostly used to store encrypted data as well as private/sensitive information on cloud storage servers. Sensitive project data is stored on cloud servers, and only authorized individuals have access to it. The private key of the business start-ups is used to sign the data hash. The data hash value and signature on the blockchain layer can be used by users to verify data integrity and authenticity. To enable fine-grained permission of ciphertext sharing, we encrypt the data with

CP-ABE and symmetric encryption technology, allowing the business start-ups to integrate multiple access control policies into separate ciphertexts. As a result, data owners can preprocess an part of the data's encryption task prior to data sharing, and investors can utilize their attributes to acquire data on demand. In data sharing, CP-ABE can significantly lower the business start-up's retrieval and encryption effort when compared to typical symmetric encryption approaches. To alleviate the cost of ciphertext storage locally, the business start-ups can upload the ciphertexts to cloud servers.

14.3.3 System Assumptions and Threat Model

1. The blockchain platform is safe and secure.
2. Business start-ups and investors must take precautions to keep their passwords and secret keys safe.
3. A malicious user may attempt to acquire information about encrypted data values from the query output of a particular ciphertext.

14.3.4 Process Description

1. **Stage 1**: Business start-ups and investors must first register in the system. The crowdfunding platform uses the user's identification and attributes as input to generate smart contracts for the user registration. Third-party entities utilize the platform to verify their identities and attributes, and smart contracts are used to enter the results of the verification onto the blockchain. Each registered user has an identity, set of attributes, and a public–secret key pair that may be used to establish a secure channel between two users.
2. **Stage 2**: Every registered business start-up goes through the CP-ABE setup algorithm to receive his or her system public parameters and master secret key $Setup(\rho) = (pk, msk)$. Assuming that the business start-up has a piece of data $\hat{d} = (\hat{d}_1, \hat{d}_2, \ldots, \hat{d}_n)$ for $P = 1, 2, 3, \ldots, n$ and that each piece of data $\hat{d}_P$ is subject to an access policy $A(\hat{A}, \sigma)_P$. The business start-up encrypts his/her sensitive project data using CP-ABE and symmetric encryption, uploads the ciphertexts to cloud servers, and obtains the location Loc_{CT} of the ciphertexts given by CSP.
3. **Stage 3**: Each registered business start-up retrieves metadata about the raw data $\hat{d}_P$ such as data hash value $H(\hat{d}_P)$, business start-up's signature $Sign(H(F_P), sk_{Bj})$, ciphertext location Loc_{CT}, keyword set $\hat{k}_P$ and access policy $A(\hat{A}, \sigma)_P$.
4. **Stage 4**: In the analysis of smart contracts, each registered investor obtains the project data information and identifies the relevant business start-ups only if the investor's information can meet the necessary condition functions. The investor can determine his/her minimal attribute set $\mathcal{A}_{Ni}$ that will satisfy all access restrictions $A(\hat{A}, \sigma)_P$ of the requested data and send it to the business start-ups. They reach an agreement after the business start-ups validates the attributes.
5. **Stage 5**: After obtaining the investor's $\mathcal{A}_{Ni}$ attribute set, the business start-up uses the CP-ABE key generation scheme to construct the investor's attribute private key Nk. The business start-up employs an asymmetric encryption technique $Enc(pk_{N_i}, Nk)$ to get the attribute-key ciphertext CT_{Nk}, which is then included in the data access smart contract.
6. **Stage 6**: The investor examines the blockchain ciphertext CT_{Nk} and generates the attribute private key $NK = Dec(sk_{Ni}, CT_{Nk})$. Then he/she scans the blockchain information and gets the ciphertext $CT = [(CT_{KP}, CT_P)_P = 1, 2, 3, \ldots, n]$ from the cloud server based on the location Loc_{CT}. The investor uses the CP-ABE decryption technique to obtain the session key K_P and calculates the data $\hat{d}_P = Dec(K_P, CT_P)$. The investor then obtains his or her requested project data set $[\hat{d}_P]$.

14.3.5 Smart Contract Interactions

This section discusses the various smart contract interactions in our system.

14.3.5.1 User Registration Contract (URC)

Every business start-up or investor gives his or her genuine identity and attributes during registration and is issued a key pair (public key, secret key). After the certification of the identities and attributes of users, the user registration contract (URC) gets input from the user registration program and creates transactions to register the user on the blockchain. It produces the user's address by hashing his or her public key and contains user identifying information, attributes set, data description, his or her public key, and a digital signature. The investor's attribute set is a critical parameter that decides whether the he/she may proceed with the data access procedure. A keyword set $\hat{k}_p$, an access policy $A(\hat{A}, \sigma)_P$, size, kind, and viable period concerning the project data are the fundamental components of data description.

14.3.5.2 User Verification Contract (UVC)

The user verification contract (UVC) maintains the user profile, attribute set, data description. The profile primarily comprises user identifying information, a digital signature, and the identities of users may be validated using their public keys. The attribute set $\mathcal{A}_{Ni}$ and keyword set $\hat{k}_p$ of the investor will be two critical elements that will decide whether the investor can access the data. A keyword set, an access policy $A(\hat{A}, \sigma)_P$, a signature, data size, and data type regarding the business start-up are the basic components of data description. Investors can identify the data sources they need by querying business start-up's UVC and verifying the signature using business start-up's public key. UVC additionally provides a data address list that can refer to business start-ups' past project data access contract (PDAC) data.

14.3.5.3 Project Data Access Contract (PDAC)

The PDAC enforces and administers data access agreement between business start-ups and investors, which comprises the procedures of data sharing. It can be produced once the business start-up B_j submits and publishes a data description information $D = (D_1, D_2, \ldots, D_M)$,where $D_P = S_{id}$, $H(\hat{d}_P)$, $Sign(H(F_P), sk_{Bj})$, pk_{Bj}, $\hat{k}_p$, $A(\hat{A}, \sigma)_P$, $H(\hat{d}_P)$ is the hash value of data $\hat{d}_P$, $\hat{k}_p$ is the data keyword set, $Sign(H(F_P), sk_{Bj})$ is the signature of B_j and $A(\hat{A}, \sigma)_P$ is the data access policy. The investor N_i obtains the list of data descriptions in URC and verifies the needed data description D_P using the business start-up's public key. After the UVC produces the needed data description set $[D_P]$, the PDAC contract may be established, and it will accept as inputs the member blockchain addresses, UVC's contract addresses, data hash values, and the ciphertext's location. Each business start-up defines a pool N_{pool} to contain the addresses of permitted investors. If the approved investors need to be included to the pool N_{pool}, the business start-up modifies the PDAC contract by broadcasting it to the blockchain network, allowing them to engage the data-sharing process successfully.

14.3.6 Concrete Implementation

In this part, we discuss a blockchain-based framework for fine-grained data access authorization. It is made up of five algorithms: User Registration, Data Encrypt, Data Access, Fine-grained Data Access Authorization, Data Decrypt and Transaction Confirmation. The crowdfunding platform allows users (business start-ups and investors) to communicate with the blockchain.

14.3.6.1 User Register

The business start-up B_j or investor N_i can register to get his identity and attribute information via a URC contract, i.e. $B_j = (pk_{Bj}, sk_{Bj}, \alpha_{Bj} A_{Bj})$ and $N_i = (pk_{Bj}, sk_{Ni}, \alpha_{Ni} A_{Ni})$.

14.3.6.2 Data Encrypt

Let G and G_T be two multiplicative cyclic groups that have a prime order p and g be a generator of G. Define $e : G \times G \rightarrow G_T$ as a symmetric bilinear map, δ be a security parameter, the universal attribute $U = Z_p$. Every business start-up selects the elements $g, h, u, y, f \in G$ at random, and $\alpha \in Z_p$ and publishes their system public parameters $\rho = (g, h, u, y, f, e(g,g)^\alpha)$, master secret key $msk = \alpha$. The business start-up must keep msk confidential and can post ρ on a public website available to all investors. We suppose that the business start-ups allocate each piece of data $\hat{d}_p$ to a matching access policy $A(\hat{A}, \sigma)_P \in (Z_p^{l \times b}, \sigma([l]) \rightarrow Z_p$, where the definition of this policy $A(\hat{A}, \sigma)_P$ is the same as the description of the access structure in [9]. The matrix denoted by $\hat{A}$ is referred to be the share-generation matrix for the linear secret-sharing system similar to [10]. Every piece of data $\hat{d}_p$ can be assigned to a matching access policy $A(\hat{A}, \sigma)_P$, which includes things such as scope of data-sharing scope, project data value, and user attributes. For each piece of information $\hat{d}_p$ $(P = 1, 2, 3, \ldots, n)$,

The business start-up selects a session key K_P at random and uses the symmetric encryption procedure to construct the data ciphertext $CT_P = Enc(K_P, \hat{d}_p)$. Following that, the business start-up selects a random vector $q = (s, q_2, q_3, \ldots, q_b) \in Z_p^b$, where s is the randomly generated shared secret, and computes the share's vector $\beta = (\beta, \beta_2, \beta_3, \ldots, \beta_l) = \hat{A}q$. The business start-up randomly selects $v_1, v_2, \ldots, v_l \in Z_p$, and calculates $C = K_P \times e(g,g)^{\alpha s}$, $C_0 = g^s$, and for every $x = 1$ to l, calculate $C_{x,1} = y^{\beta x} f^{vx}$, $C_{x,2} = (h^{\sigma(x)} u)^{-vx}$, $C_{x,3} = g^{vx}$, and creates the ciphertext session-key $(CT_{KP} = A(\hat{A}, \sigma)_P, C, C_0, [C_{x,1}, C_{x,2}, C_{x,3}]_{x \in [l]}$. Next, the business start-up transmits the ciphertext $CT = (CT_{KP}, CT_P)_{P=1,2,3,\ldots,n}$ to the cloud servers and saves the Loc_{CT} obtained from the CSP. Finally, using a UVC contract, the business start-up calculates the file's hash values $H(\hat{d}_p)$ and integrates the values $H(\hat{d}_p)$ and Loc_{CT} into the ciphertext transaction. Then the business start-up can utilize the UVC contract to undertake the following data access actions after transaction is registered on the blockchain.

14.3.6.3 Data Search

The investor N_i collects project information from business start-up's UVC contracts and can access numerous suitable project data only if he/she can fulfill the relevant condition functions set by the access policy $A(\hat{A}, \sigma)_P$. If N_i wishes to access the project data of a specific business start-up, he or she can identify his or her minimal attribute set A_{Ni} that can meet all access policy conditions $A(\hat{A}, \sigma)_P$ of the needed data and present it to the system.

14.3.6.4 Fine-Grained Access Authorization

After authenticating the investor's attribute set $A_{Ni} = (a_1, a_2, \ldots, a_k)$, the business start-up B_j uses the CP-ABE key-generation method [9] to generate the attribute private key for the investor N_i. B_j selects $k+1$ values $r, r_1, r_2, \ldots, r_k \in Z_p$, calculates $K_0 = g^\alpha y^r$, $K_1 = g^r$, and for $x = 1$ to k, calculates $K_{x,2} = g^{rx}$, $K_{x,3} = (h^{ax} u)^{rx} f^{-r}$, and generates the attribute private key $Nk = (A, K_0, K_1, [K_{x,2}, K_{x,3}]_{x \in [k]})$. The business start-up then calculates and integrates the attribute private key ciphertext $CT_N k = Enc(pk_{Ni}, Nk)$ into the PDAC contract. Whenever the address of PDAC is stored on the blockchain's transaction index $Tx_d k$. The business start-up uses the investor's public key to encrypt the transaction index $Tx_d k$ and the PDAC contract address, application binary interface (ABI), source code, and transmits the ciphertext $CT_N k$ to the investor.

14.3.6.5 Data Decrypt

The approved investor first examines the data CT_{Nk} in the blockchain transaction T_{xb} and calculates his or her attribute private key $NK = Dec(sk_{Ni}, CT_{Nk})$. He/she scans the information on the blockchain data D and downloads the ciphertext $CT = [(CT_{K_p}, CT_P)_P = 1, 2, 3, \ldots, n]$ from the cloud server based on the location Loc_{CT}. Since the approved investor's attributes fulfill the access policies $A(\hat{A}, \sigma)_P$ of his/her project data, the investor determines the set of rows in $\hat{A}$ that can give a share to attributes in $\mathcal{A}_\rangle$, i.e. $W = [x : \sigma(x) \in \mathcal{A}]$. Afterwards, the constants $[c_x \in Z_p]$ are computed such that $\sum_{x \in W} c_x A_x = (1, 0, \ldots, 0)$, where $\hat{A}_x$ is the matrix's xth row. The investor decrypts the key ciphertext CT_{KP} using the attribute private key $Nk = (A, K_0, K_1, [K_{x,2}, K_{x,3}]_{x \in [k]})$ and calculates

$$K_P = \frac{C \times \prod_{x \in W}(e(C_{x,1}, K_1)e(C_{x,2}, K_{i,2})e(C_{x,3}, K_{i,3}))^{C_x}}{e(C_0, K_0)}$$

Lastly, the investor decrypts the data ciphertext CT_P with the session key K_P and computes $\hat{d}_P' = Dec(K_P, CT_P)$. If $H(\hat{d}_P') = H(\hat{d}_P)$, the investor accepts the project data file $\hat{d}_P$ as being genuine and not tampered with. Otherwise, the data access via the PDAC contract will be terminated by the investor. In the end, the investor acquires the purchase data set $[\hat{d}_P]$.

14.3.6.6 Transaction Confirmation

The process of developing or amending a smart contract is considered a transaction that must be recorded on the blockchain. We describe the state change process as a pair of (Blk_i, Blk_{i+1}), where Blk_{i+1} is the current block and Blk_i is its prior one, to emulate transaction confirmation and constructing blocks. $Blk_{i+1} = blk_{id}, timestamp, H(Blk_i), add_n d+, L_{Tx} = (tx_0, tx_1, \ldots, tx_k)$, where $add\ _n d+$ is the location of a blockchain node and L_{Tx} is a list of smart contracts that must be verified by a majority of blockchain network nodes. Only if the block is on-chain are all contracts in L_{Tx} immutably recorded on the blockchain.

14.3.7 Security Requirements

In this section, we examine the vulnerabilities that our suggested solution prevents.

14.3.7.1 Fine-Grained Access Control

The deployment of the CP-ABE system with smart contracts results in effective user access management. The business start-up determines the attribute set, and hence there must be a match between the attribute set and the private key set in order to access data. Furthermore, depending on the level of confidence between the business start-ups and the investors, decryption of all or part of the data can be given to the user selectively.

14.3.7.2 Key Counterfeiting

Our system is protected from the usage of fake keys. Attacks that include gaining access to the keys or counterfeiting public keys in a system are thwarted. This frequently results in the decryption of sensitive project data. The blockchain serves as the certificate authority (CA) in our system. The users' public keys are placed in published blocks, and the data is distributed throughout the participating nodes with connections to both the previous and subsequent blocks. This makes the public key immutable and makes it more difficult for attackers to publish bogus keys. Furthermore, because of the decentralized nature, there is no SPoF.

14.3.7.3 Data Integrity

Data tampering occurs when hackers penetrate a system and insert their own copies of data into it. If the hash can be hacked and modified, there is no definitive method to ensure that the data has not been tampered with. In contrast, our blockchain-based solution allows each user to publish a hash linked with a specific piece of data that must be secured against manipulation. While an attacker can breach the storage location and tamper with the data, he cannot modify the hash published on the blockchain. This will alert everyone that the data has been tampered with.

14.4 Summary

We propose a novel idea of a blockchain-based approach for fine-grained permission in the crowdfunding process in this research. In the introduced crowdfunding concept, we highlight some weaknesses of conventional crowdfunding systems and discuss some benefits of a decentralized blockchain-based crowdfunding platform. Furthermore, to obtain fine-grained data access permission, business start-ups can use CP-ABE to pre-process the complicated encryption workload and create the attribute private key for data query. Based on plausible assumptions, we demonstrate that our system can effectively resist harmful internal and external user attacks.

References

1 Voigt, P. and Von dem Bussche, A. (2017). The EU general data protection regulation (GDPR). In: *A Practical Guide*, vol. 10, 1e, 10–5555. Cham: Springer International Publishing.

2 Yan, X., An, X., Ye, W. et al. (2021). A blockchain-based subscriber data management scheme for 6G mobile communication system. *2021 IEEE Globecom Workshops (GC Wkshps)*, pp. 1–6. IEEE.

3 Al-Zahrani, F.A. (2020). Subscription-based data-sharing model using blockchain and data as a service. *IEEE Access* 8: 115966–115981.

4 Goyal, V., Pandey, O., Sahai, A., and Waters, B. (2006). Attribute-based encryption for fine-grained access control of encrypted data. *Proceedings of the 13th ACM Conference on Computer and Communications Security*, pp. 89–98.

5 Xia, Q., Sifah, E.B., Agyekum, K.O.-B.O. et al. (2019). Secured fine-grained selective access to outsourced cloud data in IoT environments. *IEEE Internet of Things Journal* 6 (6): 10749–10762.

6 (a) Agyekum, K.O.-B.O., Xia, Q., Sifah, E.B. et al. (2019). A secured proxy-based data sharing module in IoT environments using blockchain. *Sensors* 19 (5): 1235; (b) Sifah, E.B., Xia, Q., Xia, H. et al. (2021). Selective sharing of outsourced encrypted data in cloud environments. *IEEE Internet of Things Journal* 8 (18): 14141–14155.

7 Wang, H. and Song, Y. (2018). Secure cloud-based ehr system using attribute-based cryptosystem and blockchain. *Journal of Medical Systems* 42 (8): 1–9.

8 Bethencourt, J., Sahai, A., and Waters, B. (2007). Ciphertext-policy attribute-based encryption. *2007 IEEE Symposium on Security and Privacy (SP'07)*, pp. 321–334. IEEE.

9 Park, N., Kwak, J., Kim, S. et al. (2006). WIPI mobile platform with secure service for mobile RFID network environment. In: *Advanced Web and Network Technologies, and Applications. Asia-Pacific Web Conference, Lecture Notes in Computer Science*, vol. 3842 (ed. H.T. Shen, J. Li, M. Li et al.), 741–748. Berlin, Heidelberg: Springer-Verlag.

10 Nakamoto, S. and Bitcoin, A. (2008). Bitcoin: a peer-to-peer electronic cash system, vol. 4. https://bitcoin. org/bitcoin.pdf (accessed 7 April 2023).

11 Guochao, Z. and Ruijin, W. (2019). Blockchain shard storage model based on threshold secret sharing. *Journal of Computer Applications* 39 (9): 2617.

12 Nathan, O., Pentland, A., and Zyskind, G. (2015). Decentralising privacy: using blockchain to protect personal data. *IEEE Security and Privacy Workshops*.

13 Truong, N.B., Sun, K., Lee, G.M., and Guo, Y. (2019). GDPR-compliant personal data management: a blockchain-based solution. arXiv e-prints, pp. arXiv–a1904.

14 Liu, C.H., Lin, Q., and Wen, S. (2018). Blockchain-enabled data collection and sharing for industrial IoT with deep reinforcement learning. *IEEE Transactions on Industrial Informatics* 15 (6): 3516–3526.

15 Jemel, M. and Serhrouchni, A. (2017). Decentralized access control mechanism with temporal dimension based on blockchain. *2017 IEEE 14th International Conference on E-Business Engineering (ICEBE)*, pp. 177–182. IEEE.

16 Ding, S., Cao, J., Li, C. et al. (2019). A novel attribute-based access control scheme using blockchain for IoT. *IEEE Access* 7: 38431–38441.

17 Naz, M., Al-zahrani, F.A., Khalid, R. et al. (2019). A secure data sharing platform using blockchain and interplanetary file system. *Sustainability* 11 (24): 7054.

18 Wang, S., Zhang, Y., and Zhang, Y. (2018). A blockchain-based framework for data sharing with fine-grained access control in decentralized storage systems. *IEEE Access* 6: 38437–38450.

19 Stoica, C., Morris, R., Liben-Nowell, D. et al. (2003). Chord: a scalable peer-to-peer lookup protocol for internet applications. *IEEE/ACM Transactions on Networking* 11 (1): 17–32.

20 Sifah, E.B., Xia, Q., Agyekum, K.O.-B.O. et al. (2021). A blockchain approach to ensuring provenance to outsourced cloud data in a sharing ecosystem. *IEEE Systems Journal* 16 (1): 1673–1684.

21 Bresson, E., Chevassut, O., and Pointcheval, D. (2002). Dynamic group Diffie-Hellman key exchange under standard assumptions. In: *EUROCRYPT 2002. International Conference on the Theory and Applications of Cryptographic Techniques, LNCS 2332* (ed. L.R. Knudsen), 321–336. Berlin, Heidelberg: Springer-Verlag.

Index

Attribute-based Encryption (ABE): Foundations and Applications within Blockchain and Cloud Environments, First Edition.
Qi Xia, Jianbin Gao, Isaac Amankona Obiri, Kwame Omono Asamoah, and Daniel Adu Worae.
© 2024 The Institute of Electrical and Electronics Engineers, Inc. Published 2024 by John Wiley & Sons, Inc.

Printed and bound by CPI Group (UK) Ltd, Croydon, CR0 4YY

16/04/2025

14658604-0004